Colonial and Postcolonial Literature

Migrant Metaphors

Second Edition

Elleke Boehmer

OXFORD

UNIVERSITY PRESS

OXFORD

UNIVERSITY PRESS

Great Clarendon Street, Oxford OX2 6DP

Oxford University Press is a department of the University of Oxford.
It furthers the University's objective of excellence in research, scholarship,
and education by publishing worldwide in

Oxford New York

Auckland Cape Town Dar es Salaam Hong Kong Karachi
Kuala Lumpur Madrid Melbourne Mexico City Nairobi
New Delhi Shanghai Taipei Toronto

With o ces in

Argentina Austria Brazil Chile Czech Republic France Greece
Guatemala Hungary Italy Japan Poland Portugal Singapore
South Korea Switzerland Thailand Turkey Ukraine Vietnam

Oxford is a registered trade mark of Oxford University Press
in the UK and in certain other countries

Published in the United States
by Oxford University Press Inc., New York

© Elleke Boehmer 2005

The moral rights of the author have been asserted

Database right Oxford University Press (maker)

First published 1995
Second edition published 2005

British Library Cataloguing in Publication Data
Data available

Library of Congress Cataloging in Publication Data
Data available

Typeset by RefineCatch Limited, Bungay, Suffolk
Printed in Great Britain
on acid-free paper by
Ashford Colour Press Ltd, Gosport, Hampshire

ISBN 0–19–925371–4 (Pbk.) 978–0–19–925371–5 (Pbk.)

Acknowledgements to the 2005 edition

THE process of returning to a book in order to produce a revised edition is, as many people warned me, a daunting prospect. To update, finesse, or elaborate one section immediately means that others, too, demand a counterbalancing attention, till eventually the whole structure, like a precarious house of cards, appears to require rebuilding from the ground up, or top-to-toe lamination, to prevent further interference. The concern to avoid undue interference was especially intense in the case of *Colonial and Postcolonial Literature: Migrant Metaphors*, as the book has been generously received across its ten years of shelf life, and has, in its small way, become incorporated into the broad landscape of postcolonial reading and teaching.

With this in mind, I have generally avoided excessive tampering with the text. I have, however, tried to elaborate, finesse, and refresh the critical observations of the book throughout to reflect on and respond to some of the new critical interventions and historical investigations in the vigorously expanding field of postcolonial literary and cultural studies. Throughout I have substantially added to and updated—and I hope sharpened and enriched—its illustrative examples, to the extent indeed that a number of new names and titles has crowded into the text. I have nowhere unduly subtracted material. The overall shape and content of the book remains as it was.

Key additions are as follows. The new Afterword, 'Belated Reading', looks at new developments and current preoccupations in postcolonialism, particularly as concerns the impact, or not, of global forces on postcolonial writing and studies. The Chronology has been updated to 2004, but also extended outwards or backwards in time in order to include, for example, more 'postcolonial' and/or anti-colonial texts published pre-1950. The first edition's Further Reading section has been elaborated in several ways. A fully annotated and updated Bibliography provides interested readers and students with multiple pointers and new directions to support and stimulate their further exploration in the field. Each chapter also ends with a Further Reading section specific to the period and writing discussed. In the case of each chapter, too, the references have been extended, updated, and elaborated. The objective of the OPUS series in which this book originally appeared was to avoid excessive referencing. That has now been revised, although to a reasonable extent. All references are once again intended to assist and to encourage readers new to the postcolonial field. (Place of publication for a university press (UP) may be assumed to be the town for which the university is named; where no place is cited, London is understood.)

I am deeply indebted to a number of people whose support was invaluable in the pressured months of working on this second edition. My gratitude is to Ranka Primorac for her excellent help with the Annotated Bibliography, and for her morale-boosting words. Without Alison Donnell's writerly fellowship, sharp critical eye, and mutual mania-checks I might have given up before the summer was out. I am grateful to Fiona Kinnear and Andrew McNeillie at OUP for their patience and commitment to this book, and to Shirley Chew and Rajeswari Sunder Rajan for their sustaining friendship and sound advice. John McLeod, Stuart Murray, and Sarah Nuttall gave helpful pointers in the latter stages of revision. Lisa Hill's painting, *Bushfire 10*, I am privileged to have on the cover. And to Steven, Thomas, and Sam, thanks again, and always, for bringing balloons into the back room.

Acknowledgements to the 1995 edition

FIRST to Steven Matthews, without whose companionship, dense coffee, and Midas flair the last months of completing this book would not have been the unexpected exhilaration that they were— inadequate words, thanks.

To the School of English at the University of Leeds I also owe many thanks, in particular for support to do research in India. Rebecca Stott, Jill Le Bihan, Shirley Chew, Alison Donnell, Andrew Hadfield, Jonathan Hope, Lynette Hunter, David Richards, Helen Richman, Sue Spearey, John Whale, and Keith Williams at the School gave much-appreciated guidance or help with references. I am also indebted to Laura Chrisman and Kenneth Parker, my co-editors on another book. Our conversations over the years have often helpfully resurfaced in the process of writing of postcolonial literature. During my early tentative days in this field, Peter Quartermaine at the University of Exeter, too, was wonderfully encouraging and always open to questions and requests for help. I should also like to remember the advice and support I have been privileged to receive over the past few OPUS-dominated years, in various different ways, from Terence Cave, Richard Drayton, Leo Flynn, Meenakshi Mukherjee, Carol Phipson, Mark Pottle, Rob Nixon, Sarah Nuttall, Jon Stallworthy, and Rajeswari Sunder Rajan. To Satish Keshav and Anna Donald, thanks for help with time lines. Catherine Clarke, Simon Mason, and Christopher Butler at Oxford University Press in Walton Street, and Rukun Advani at OUP, New Delhi, were generous with insightful comments and with their time.

To Mary Blundell—how to say thanks for the house at no. 17, which has made so much possible?

And finally, I owe gratitude to Michael Anderson, for fresh insights, irises, the printer, and unflagging interest.

For
Mary Blundell
Steven Matthews

When I next saw the picture of Columbus sitting there all locked up in his chains, I wrote under it the words 'The Great Man Can No Longer Just Get Up and Go'. I had written this out with my fountain pen, and in Old English lettering—a script I had recently mastered. As I sat there looking at the picture, I traced the words with my pen over and over, so that the letters grew big and you could read what I had written from not very far away.

Jamaica Kincaid, 'Columbus in Chains', *Annie John*, 1985

Gone the ascetic pastimes, the Persian
scholarship, the wild boar run to ground,
the watercolours of the sun and wind.
Names rise like outcrops on the rich terrain,

like carapaces of the Mughal tombs
lop-sided in the rice-fields, boarded-up
near railway-crossings and small aerodromes.

'India's a peacock-shrine next to a shop
selling mangola, sitars, lucky charms,
heavenly Buddhas smiling in their sleep.'

Geoffrey Hill, *A Short History of British
India* (III)

Contents

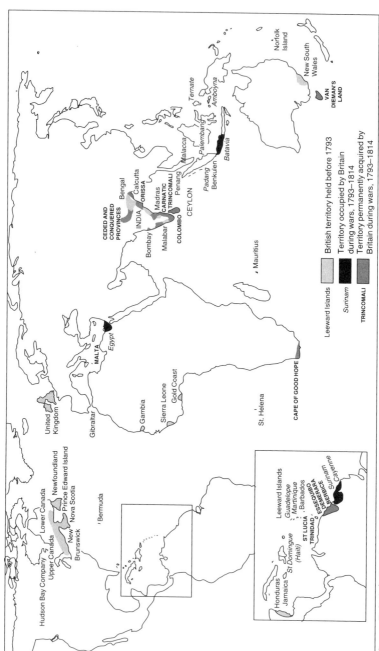

Map 1. Britain's Empire in 1815

Reproduced by kind permission of Routledge from Martin Gilbert's *British History Atlas*

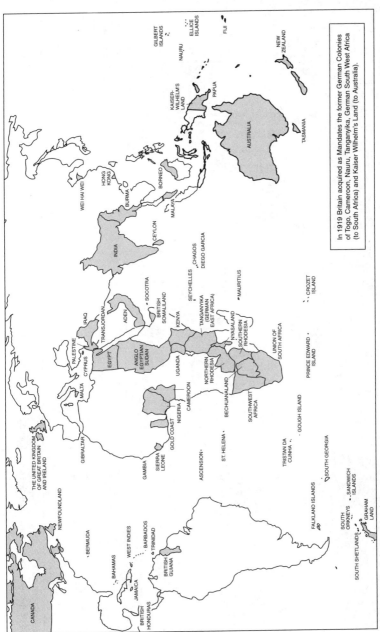

In 1919 Britain acquired as Mandates the former German Colonies of Togo, Cameroon, Nauru, Tanganyika, German South West Africa (to South Africa) and Kaiser Wilhelm's Land (to Australia).

Map 2. Britain's Empire in 1920
Reproduced by kind permission of Macmillan Press Ltd.

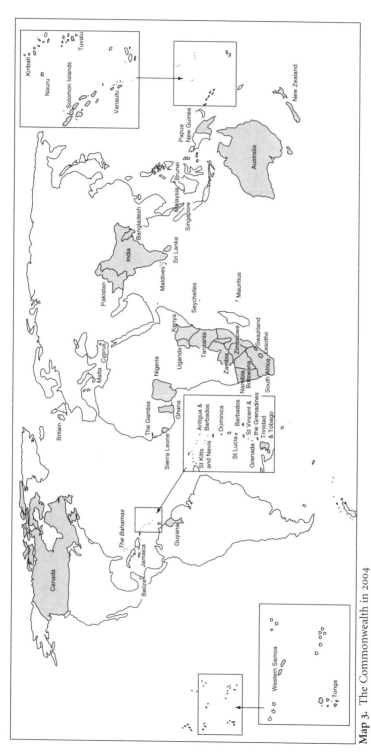

Map 3. The Commonwealth in 2004

Reproduced by kind permission of the Commonwealth Secretariat from the *Commonwealth Day Handbook*

Introduction

This is a book about the writing of empire, and about writing in opposition to empire. It looks at a historical series of imaginative acts involved with colonization and its aftermath. The subject is peculiarly large. And the project of critical overview is itself, ironically, almost imperialistic in scope. It appears to demand from the critic a 'grand narrative' of literature in English from the 1700s to the present. Indeed what could be more global, or more vast, than the writing of and against empire, unless it is the attempt to generalize about that writing?

The book's subject, 'colonial and postcolonial literature', would on a superficial reading seem to embrace the majority of the world's modern literatures. If it is agreed that the history of the world for the past few centuries has been profoundly shaped by colonial interests, then there is a sense in which much of the literature produced during that time can be said to be colonial or postcolonial, even if only tangentially so. Geographically anyway, the terrain potentially covered by the title reaches across the time zones of the globe. Historically, it extends back five hundred years or so to the days of European mercantile expansion, Columbus's landing in America, and the exploration of the coast of Africa past the Cape of Good Hope. But some might feel that even this wide definition of the colonial is too constricting. Marlow at the beginning of Joseph Conrad's 'Heart of Darkness', for example, draws attention to the similarities between the British colonization of Africa and the conquering of Britain by imperial Rome many centuries before. According to this view, *Beowulf* and Chaucer's *Canterbury Tales* could be read as postcolonial texts.

So I shall begin by drawing limits. This study is chiefly concerned with literature written in English, which even if only to an extent narrows the field. It is on the British Empire that my attention will be focused—though I might equally have looked at Spanish, Portuguese,

French, or Dutch colonialism. The last two hundred years have witnessed both the moment of greatest expansion of that Empire, and its demise. In the late Victorian age the projection of British authority abroad was particularly powerful and far-reaching. The period also saw unprecedented dominance of world trade and communications systems by European powers. It is this period which outlines the boundaries of discussion: the century of British colonialism on a grand scale, or high imperialism, and the decades of anti- and/ or postcolonial activity which followed.

It is difficult to proceed much further without indicating more clearly, if in a preliminary way, what words like *colonial, imperial,* and *postcolonial* mean. In this book, imperialism can be taken to refer to the authority assumed by a state over another territory—authority expressed in pageantry and symbolism, as well as in military and economic power. It is a term associated in particular with the expansion of the European nation-state in the nineteenth century. Colonialism involves the consolidation of imperial power, and is manifested in the settlement of territory, the exploitation or development of resources, and the attempt to govern the indigenous inhabitants of occupied lands, often by force.

Colonial literature, which is assumed to be literature reflecting a colonial ethos, usually lacks more precise definition, partly because it is now not much canonized, and partly because it is so heterogeneous. In general, texts described as colonial or colonialist are taken to be those, like *King Solomon's Mines* or Rudyard Kipling's poems, which exhibit a tinge of local colonial colour, or feature colonial motifs—for example, the quest beyond the frontiers of civilization.

To be more explicit about what is being discussed, I make a distinction in this book between the terms *colonial* and *colonialist* when applied to literature. Colonial literature, which is the more general term, will be taken to mean writing concerned with colonial perceptions and experience, written mainly by metropolitans, but also by creoles and indigenes, during colonial times. Controversially, perhaps, colonial literature therefore includes literature written in Britain as well as in the rest of the Empire during the colonial period. Even if it did not make direct reference to colonial matters, metropolitan writing—Dickens's novels, for example, or Trollope's travelogues—participated in organizing and reinforcing perceptions of Britain as a dominant world power. Writers contributed to the

complex of attitudes that made imperialism seem part of
of things.

As we shall see, colonialist literature in contrast was that
specifically concerned with colonial expansion. On the whole it was
literature written by and for colonizing Europeans about non-
European lands dominated by them. It embodied the imperialists'
point of view. When we speak of the writing of empire it is this
literature in particular that occupies attention. Colonialist literature
was informed by theories concerning the superiority of European
culture and the rightness of empire. Its distinctive stereotyped language was geared to mediating the white man's relationship with
colonized peoples.

Rather than simply being the writing which 'came after' empire,
postcolonial literature is generally defined as that which critically or
subversively scrutinizes the colonial relationship. It is writing that sets
out in one way or another to resist colonialist perspectives. As well as
a change in power, decolonization demanded—and still demands—
symbolic overhaul, a reshaping of dominant meanings. Postcolonial
literature forms part of that process of overhaul. To give expression
to colonized experience, postcolonial writers sought to undercut
thematically and formally the discourses which supported colonization—the myths of power, the race classifications, the imagery of
subordination. Postcolonial writing, therefore, is deeply marked by
experiences of cultural exclusion and division under empire. Especially in its early stages it is also often a nationalist writing. Building
on this, *postcoloniality* can be defined as that condition in which
colonized peoples seek to take their place, forcibly or otherwise, as
historical agents in an increasingly globalized world. Following recent
usage, the postcolonial must be distinguished from the more conventional hyphenated term *post-colonial*, which in this book will be
taken as a period term designating the post-Second World War era.
Of course, neither term need apply only to the English-speaking
world, nor only to literature.

Postcolonial writing in English also goes by the names of new writing in English, world fiction, international or transcultural writing,
and (the somewhat dated if still durable) Commonwealth literature,
the Commonwealth being a loose cultural and political amalgam of
nations which before 1947 formed part of the British Empire. Dis-
tancing himself from the implications of 'coming after' embedded in

'postcolonial', the writer Ben Okri has also offered the description 'literature of the newly ascendant spirit'.[1] However, while it may remain for the foreseeable future a subject for debate, *postcolonial* continues to draw support for its usefulness as an umbrella term, underpinned by a now considerable archive of critical and theoretical discourse. It is a way of bracketing together the literatures written in those countries which were once colonies of Britain, as well as, increasingly, some branches of British writing, most notably black British literature. The United States is excluded because it won independence long before other colonial places, and its literature has therefore followed a very different trajectory. Ireland too is believed to represent a different case because its history has been so closely linked to that of Britain. Moreover, relative to postcolonial studies, Irish studies has had the long-term benefit of organized metropolitan support networks and institutional backing. Yet, as the Irish resistance struggle was in certain other colonies taken as talismanic by nationalist movements, references to Ireland will be made across the course of this study. In spite of these restrictions, at times the sheer spread and flattening effect of what we name postcolonial can be a problem, such as when, say, the contemporary novel in Canada and calypso in Trinidad are both described in this way. In anglophone postcolonial criticism, admittedly, the tendency is sometimes to stress the similarity of texts written in the former colonies of the British Empire, at the expense of recognizing their differences.

Another problem is that definitions of the postcolonial can tend to assume that this category of writing is diametrically opposed to colonial literature. We are said to have on the one hand postcolonial subversion and plenitude, on the other, the single-voiced authority of colonial writing. The main difficulty with a warring dichotomy such as this is the limitations it imposes, creating definitions which, no matter how focused on plurality, produce their own kind of orthodoxy. Thus the postcolonial tends automatically to be thought of as multivocal, mongrelized, and disruptive, even though this is not always the case. Similarly, on the other side of the binary, the colonial need not always signify texts rigidly associated with the colonial power. Colonial, or even colonialist writing was never as invasively confident or as pompously dismissive of indigenous cultures as its oppositional pairing with postcolonial writing might suggest. It is worth recalling also that initiatives towards self-affirmation that we now call postcolonial first began to emerge *before* the time of formal independence, and therefore strictly speaking formed part—albeit a special part—of colonial literature.

This book is committed to looking at literature in the broad context of imperial and post-imperial history. But it does not take the mimetic view that literature simply reflected political and social developments. On the contrary, empire is approached as on many levels a textual undertaking—as are aspects of the movements that emerged in opposition to empire. Throughout, my focus is on the modes of literary interpretation which distinguished colonial and anti-colonial experience. An enormous range of different colonial and postcolonial writings might legitimately have been included in the study. But because of the interest in the figural—in efforts to imagine empire and resistance to empire—the analysis generally concentrates on that writing which is consciously *formed* or wrought, often in service to identity, community, the nation, and in which the transforming powers of invention and fantasy are predominant. The focus therefore is on literature in the sense of novels and poems, and also, though to a lesser extent, letters, plays, essays, and travelogues.

As may be obvious, one of the starting assumptions of this book, shared with Edward Said's *Orientalism* (1978) and *Culture and Imperialism* (1993), is that cultural representations were central first to the process of colonizing other lands, and then again to the process of obtaining independence from the colonizer. To assume control over a territory or a nation was not only to exert political or economic power; it was also to have imaginative command. The belief here is that colonialist and postcolonial literatures did not simply articulate colonial or nationalist preoccupations; they also contributed to the making, definition, and clarification of those same preoccupations. Symbols from well-known stories, for example, were enlisted by Europeans in their attempt to make sense of strange and complex worlds beyond the seas. The myriad writings of empire, not poems and novels only, but more functional texts such as law reports, journalistic articles, and anthropological journals, were often ornately figural and full of literary allusion. Nor was the colonial system alone in its collaboration with imaginative writing. In the post-colonial period, too, as Chinua Achebe has said, stories 'direct us'.[2] Nationalist movements have relied on literature, on novelists, singers, and playwrights, to hone rallying symbols of the past and the self through which dignity might be reasserted. The well-known image of the oppressed speaking out of silence has meant a willed intervention by colonized people in the fictions and myths that presumed to describe them.

The approach taken in this book is roughly chronological, and, if I can put it this way, at once emblematic, thematic, and analytical. The aim is to look at symptomatic patterns of perception in which writers participated, and to which they may also have contributed in their work. To survey the broad field, but also to give a sense of its immense diversity, discussion tends to oscillate between the general and the particular. An effort has been made in each case to focus on those aspects of the literature which are illustrative of wider developments. Throughout, compromises have had to be made between the listing method, which broadly reflects diversity and number, but gives relatively little sense of particularity or detail, and closer readings of key texts, which offer the detail but can otherwise miss the general shape of things.

As probably goes without saying, the commentary offered is supported, here and there sceptically so, by postcolonial critical theory. Terms and issues highlighted in the criticism—colonial alienation, mimicry, hybridity, and so on—are related to relevant texts and groups of texts in what is hoped will be an illuminating way. But the book also diverges at certain points from a particularly dominant, or standardized, approach in postcolonial studies. Influenced in part by post-structuralism, in part by political developments in the western academy, postcolonial critical discourse has developed over the past quarter-century or so, following the publication of *Orientalism*, into a still-proliferating set of reading practices directed at analysing aspects of colonial and postcolonial writing. However, because of an overriding preoccupation with *textual* resistance, these practices often produce a densely discursive, even (possibly strategically) recondite commentary that, although insightful, can be highly abstract and generalizing in its effect. Such commentary contrasts to an extent with the group of more context-based, synoptic readings which has also emerged—among them, Leela Gandhi's *Postcolonial Theory* (1998), Ania Loomba's *Colonialism/Postcolonialism* (1998), Dennis Walder's *Post-Colonial Literatures in English* (1998), John McLeod's *Beginning Postcolonialism* (2000), and the 1995 incarnation of the present book, amongst others. Owing to the emphasis on textual resistance specifically, there is also a tendency in the more generalizing or homogenizing postcolonial critical discourses for material and political contexts to be overlooked or assumed. It is a paradoxical development given that both colonial and postcolonial literatures find their defining parameters in history, and, moreover, that the postcolonial draws its energy from radical critique and efforts to intervene in situations of social injustice.

In this book, an attempt is made first to elaborate and complicate accepted definitions of the colonial and the postcolonial by exemplifying in detail, with reference to a geographically and historically wide range of texts and contexts. The second aim is to consider broader developments than are usually covered in postcolonial analysis. Attention will be directed to movements across time, to transformations and disjunctures as well as to connections and interrelations between different writings. Invoking a concept of diachrony or historical change, this kind of approach goes somewhat against the grain of current interests in difference, singularity, locale, and specific moments. However, based on the idea that there were links between writings in different parts of the Empire, and at different times in the colonized or ex-colonized world, the account is intended to be more expository and intertextual, while also contextual, than are many critical studies in the field.

My object, in sum, is to expand some of the discrete observations of postcolonial theory into a longer *durée*: a narrative about the writing that accompanied empire, and the writing that came to supplant it. By implication, therefore, what follows is also in part a story—one story amongst others—about the making of the globalized culture of the late twentieth and early twenty-first centuries; about the entry of once-colonized others into the West and the West's otherness. I will look at how imperialism disseminated European influences across the world and at native responses to these; at how vastly different cultures were brought into intensely modern and troubled proximity. In the pages of postcolonial literature we shall observe how these different cultures have continued flamboyantly to mix and mingle with one another, a development which has permanently transformed the English literary canon, and which has blown the English language, as it once was, to the four winds.

So far I have fixed limits and definitions in an effort to bring some order into what is a veritable universe of writings. But a disclaimer is still necessary. The literatures of empire and of the making of postcolonial nations are subjects which could sustain hundreds of individual studies. This book cannot claim to present an adequate summary account. There can be no unified field theory when it comes to colonial or postcolonial writing. The study singles out symptoms, tendencies, and representative concerns; it tries to do justice to the complexity of issues involved; but its lists, whether of key metaphors or of representative texts, are not exhaustive. Empire in Australia was different from empire in Africa, which was again different in India. Strategies of postcolonial self-definition in New Zealand did not correspond to those in Kenya or in the Caribbean. As Nicholas Thomas emphasizes, while colonialism needs to be analysed because its 'enduring ramifications are all too evident', at the same time these ramifications can only be 'traced through [their] plural and particularized expressions'.[3] As later chapters will make clear, the national and postcolonial interests of what were the white settler colonies are by no means the same as those of the former non-white Empire.

It is important to give some acknowledgement, too, to the period-bound limits of the book itself, in particular as concerns its selection of post-imperial themes. Any piece of writing is a product of its time, and this study is no exception. Preoccupied with writers' interpretations of identity—of the need to achieve an independent sense of being in the world—and concerned to highlight this question of decolonization over others, this book is characteristic of its twenty-first-century moment. It concentrates on identity or subjectivity as a rallying space where postcolonial peoples or cultures strive to obtain certain interests, economic, religious, military, and so on. Yet in years to come these other interests—including also questions of translation, exile, travel, public and private space—may be more intensively pursued by readers and scholars. For the present it will suffice to say that identity was not by any means the single problem which occupied the minds of those who sought to dismantle empire. But it is one that still draws particular attention.

A few more words on terminology. In the early parts of this book, *native* should be taken as a collective term referring to the indigenous inhabitants of colonized lands. Once a derogatory label for colonized people, the word has more recently been reclaimed by postcolonial critics to designate those who 'belong to a particular place by birth'. It has thus been transposed, as Trinh Minh-ha has put it, from the point of view of 'them' to that of 'us'.[4] I here identify with this particular reading of the term. Similarly, the collective term *Third World* is deployed, as it was by the Non-Aligned movement at the Bandung Conference in 1955, to signify (an often idealistically constructed) distance from the West. Initially used in French by analogy with 'third estate', meaning dispossessed, Third World came to designate those states distinct from the West, the First World, and the Second World, the Soviet bloc, in the context of the Cold War. Although the phrase at times appears to be a crude generalization, it has been taken by decolonized and/or new national governments to refer to their singular economic and political status, some might say deformation, in a globalized world. In short, the term can be held to designate embattled new sovereignty in a context of continuing imperialistic domination.

Native is related to, though should not be confused with, the appellation *nativist* which, as Chapter 3 will show, refers specifically to an early form of nationalist writing. By *creole* is meant those who are descendants of settlers yet who are indigenous to their land of settlement in the sense of being native-born. (A creole is also of course a mixed language that has formed as a result of cultural contact.) Especially in the first half of the book, the pronoun 'he', used with reference to the colonizer, is intended to be male-gendered, and is not generic. This usage is justified, as will be seen, by the ubiquity of male-dominance at many levels of colonial activity. The majority of narratives of empire involved masculine heroes and assumed a predominantly male audience.

Finally, confusion is sometimes created by the overlap between the terms postcolonial and *neo-colonial*, both of which refer to the post-independence period. A term from economic theory, current since the 1960s, neo-colonialism signifies the continuing economic control by the West of the once-colonized world under the guise of political independence, and the betrayal therefore of the ideals of postcolonial liberation.[5] Although theorists may differ in ascribing causes, they broadly agree that the decline of one sort of colonialism in the 1950s and 1960s led to the rise of another, less overt, some might say more insidious, form—what has also been called a super or new imperialism. Neo-colonial formations grew particularly pronounced from the 1970s as recession and the burgeoning of Third World debt tightened the grip of rich Northern countries on the South. With the collapse of the Soviet bloc in the late 1980s, and the triumphal development of a single world economic system, even if by default in many regions, the 'rise' of the new imperialism, a further manifestation of capitalist modernity, has in the new twenty-first century become hegemonic, certainly global. The concept of neo-colonialism is therefore a useful reminder of the optimism of all we refer to when we speak of the postcolonial, while it simultaneously emphasizes the importance, even so, of relentless pressure and resistance within and against oppressive circumstances. Despite anti-imperial developments, despite the apparently subversive energies of postcolonial writing, in a world order powered by multinational companies, colonialism is not a thing of the past.

Following the roughly chronological scheme mentioned earlier, the first two chapters of this book concentrate on colonialist writing—the literature produced in and about the British Empire. The chapters can be read as companion pieces: where the first considers in a general way what will be called the textuality of the Empire, the second focuses on the defining preoccupations and motifs of late nineteenth-century colonialist literature. In Chapter 3 the emphasis changes. The period in question is the beginning of the twentieth century, when signs of the shift from colonial to postcolonial writing can first be detected. This chapter looks at early attempts by colonized writers to find an expressive voice, and then considers some of the possible effects of colonial contact on metropolitan modernism; the accent, in other words, is on reciprocal, intertextual relations. Chapter 4 explores in greater depth what is involved in terms of language, knowledge, and self-perception when one world of expression crumbles, to give way to another. The discussion juxtaposes late colonialist writing, and the attempts by the colonized/native to claim the words to describe their own cultural realities. Again, Chapters 3 and 4 can be read as companion pieces, in that the latter considers some of the theoretical implications of writing against empire which are described in the former.

Chapter 5 deals extensively with the nationalist literature written in rejection of empire which emerged after the Second World War, the time of decolonization. Chapter 6 reviews subsequent trends and developments in postcolonial writing, so expanding on the preoccupations of the previous chapter. It looks in particular at the writing which emerged from those marginalized by the political pressures of early decolonization, those working in the interstices of the canonical histories of that time, and examines the increasingly dominant definition of the postcolonial as *migrant*. It also considers the influential co-operation that has developed since the 1980s between postcolonial and post-structuralist discourses. The new Afterword offers critical reflections on the continuing oppositionality and hence viability of postcolonial practices in an often oppressively transnational world, in the context of what is designated the new 'Empire'. Does the postcolonial continue to be a workable description of international writing in English today? Will it remain productively in question as a critical term or will it eventually be discarded as fatally universalist and indeterminate?

As far as referencing is concerned, each chapter ends with a list of suggested further reading, including historical studies, which builds on the information given in the notes. The densely annotated Bibliography gives a comprehensive list of critical studies in the field. The expanded Chronology, up to 2004, shows publication dates for almost all the literary texts cited, interlinked with important historical dates, and also includes colonial and postcolonial publications which lie beyond the compass of this relatively short study, but which are worthy of mention.

Further Reading

Kwame Anthony Appiah, *In my Father's House: Africa in the Philosophy of Culture* (Methuen, 1992).

Bill Ashcroft, Gareth Griffiths, and Helen Tiffin, *Key Concepts in Post-colonial Studies* (Routledge, 1998).

Leela Gandhi, *Postcolonial Theory: A Critical Introduction* (Edinburgh UP, 1998).

Ania Loomba, *Colonialism/Postcolonialism* (Routledge, 1998).

Anne McClintock, 'The Angel of Progress: Pitfalls of the term "Postcolonialism"', in *Colonial Discourse/Postcolonial Theory*, ed. Francis Barker, Peter Hulme, and Margaret Iverson (Manchester UP, 1994), 253–66.

John McLeod, *Beginning Postcolonialism* (Manchester UP, 2000).

Vijay Mishra and Bob Hodge, 'What is Post(-)colonialism?', *Textual Practice*, 5/3 (winter 1991), 399–414.

Anna Rutherford (ed.), *From Commonwealth to Postcolonial* (Aarhus: Dangaroo, 1992).

Ella Shohat, 'Notes on the "Post-Colonial" ', *Social Text*, 31/32 (1992), 99–113.

Dennis Walder, *Post-Colonial Literatures in English: History, Language, Theory* (Oxford: Blackwell, 1998).

Robert Young, *Postcolonialism: A Very Short Introduction* (Oxford UP, 2003).

1

Imperialism and Textuality

the world expects stories of its adventurers.

J. M. Coetzee, *Foe*, 1988

Empire is itself the strangest of all political anomalies. That a handful of adventurers from an island in the Atlantic should have subjugated a vast country divided from the place of their birth by half the globe; a country which at no very distant period was merely the subject of fable to the nations of Europe . . . these are prodigies to which the world has seen nothing similar. Reason is confounded. We interrogate the past in vain.

Thomas Babington Macaulay, *Government of India*, 1833

There is a destiny now possible to us—the highest ever set before a nation to be accepted or refused. We are still undegenerate in race; a race mingled of the best of Northern bloods. . . . There is indeed a course of beneficent glory open to us, such as never was yet offered to any poor group of mortal souls. But it must be—it *is* with us, now, 'Reign or Die'.

John Ruskin, Inaugural Lecture, 1870

Writing in Empire

At its height the British Empire was a vast communications network, a global sprawl of hubris, the world map flushed pink. It was pictured as a machine and yet also as a muddle; it was the Royal Navy and

Queen Victoria, and the One Race and One Flag. But it was also represented by texts. Present-day readers, anyway, experience Empire textually, through the medium of nineteenth- and twentieth-century novels and periodicals, travel writings, scraps of doggerel. Yet empire was itself, at least in part, a textual exercise. The colonial officer filing a report on affairs in his district, British readers of newspapers and advertisements of the day, administrators who consulted Islamic and Hindu sacred texts to establish a legal system for British India: they too understood colonization by way of text. The Empire in its heyday was conceived and maintained in an array of writings—political treatises, diaries, acts and edicts, administrative records and gazetteers, missionaries' reports, notebooks, memoirs, popular verse, government briefs, letters 'home' and letters back to settlers. The tripledecker novel and the best-selling adventure tale, both definitive Victorian genres, were infused with imperial ideas of race pride and national prowess.

Colonial settlement too was expressed textually. Writing in the form of treaties was used to claim territory. The text, a vehicle of imperial authority, symbolized and in some cases indeed—as at Waitangi in New Zealand in 1840—performed the act of taking possession. In diary descriptions of new lands, or by carving their initials on trees and stone tablets, colonists declared their intention to make a home, to begin a new history. Often the effect of their descriptions was to erase, either wholly or in part, the signs of other lives which had unfolded in that particular space. As we see, for example, in late eighteenth-century British India, in the transcription of the Islamic *sharia* and the Hindu Shastras, writing served also as an instrument of rule, as a means of collecting information and exercising power. The blending of ancient religious laws and what was seen as modern, scientific knowledge was taken to be the most effective way of administering India.

An assumption that stands at the head of the present study is this: with the onset of European migration and colonization, people experienced an intense need to create new worlds out of old stories. On few other occasions in human history did so many encounter such diversity of geography and culture in so short a time span. It was necessary to give that diversity conceptual shape: to use known rhetorical figures to translate the inarticulate. As this book will show, the business of colonization meant gamble and experimentation, with lives, with funds, above all with meanings. To decipher unfamiliar spaces—what were to all intents and purposes airy nothings—travellers and colonizers relied on and scattered about them the stock descriptions and authoritative symbols that lay to hand. They transferred familiar metaphors, which are themselves already bridging devices, which *carry meaning across*, to unfamiliar and unlikely contexts. Strangeness was made comprehensible by using everyday names, dependable textual conventions, both rhetorical and syntactic.

From the early days of colonization, therefore, not only texts in general, but literature, broadly defined, underpinned efforts to interpret other lands—offering home audiences a way of thinking about exploration, Western conquest, national valour, new colonial acquisitions. Travellers, traders, administrators, settlers, 'read' the strange and new by drawing on familiar books such as the Bible or *Pilgrim's Progress*.[1] Empires were of course as powerfully shaped by military conflict, the unprecedented displacement of peoples, and the quest for profits. Yet it is also true that Spanish, Portuguese, and later Dutch, British, and French hegemony was affirmed, underwritten, and justified in myriad forms of cultural pageantry and symbolic display. As well as oral communication (word of mouth, tall tale, and rumour), literature created channels for the exchange of colonial images and ideals. In writings as various as romances, memoirs, adventure tales, or the later poetry of Tennyson, the view of the world as directed from the colonial metropolis was consolidated and confirmed. So it also followed almost automatically that resistance to imperial domination—especially on the part of those who lacked guns or money—frequently assumed textual form. As later chapters will show, in the written word, in histories and epic re-creations of the past, early nationalists found a compelling medium to counter colonialism's self-representations, to write a self-defining story.

The focus of this chapter is the nineteenth-century era of full-blown empire: territorial expansion, occupation, and symbolic investment on a massive scale. However, it is important to note that European exploration as a metaphoric practice was already well established some three or four hundred years before this time. Indeed, interpretation of other peoples on the basis of a known symbolic system is something that is common to all cultures when they come into contact with one another.[2] As European merchant venturers set out to reconnoitre the edges of the known world, they bore with them more than a substantial freight of cultural self-confidence and a nose for profit. Most possessed a lively curiosity, stimulated by rumours of riches and marvel drawn from the fantastical tales of earlier travellers. In different ways, therefore, so-called blank unfamiliarity was not blank at all. For the questing European imagination as for the West's entrepreneurs, Africa and India, the 'Exhaustless' East, and the New World of America were filled with wonders. Travel meant imaginative anticipation, and the actual treasures and curiosities encountered on distant shores—gold and ivory, cinnamon and ginger, parrots, exotic beasts, human beings of very different cultures—could only embellish expectation.

The sources for these early colonizers' interpretations of the beyond were as extensive as were their knowledge and their experience of stories. They borrowed conceptual schemes, not necessarily consciously, from oral narrative, popular fantasy, and ancient sacred books, including those of colonized peoples. They had recourse to early travellers' tales of the distant and the barbarian: descriptions of savagery in Herodotus, or the fourteenth- and fifteenth-century accounts of Marco Polo, Mandeville, or Hakluyt. Later, they drew on the travel writings of Mungo Park (1790s) or Richard Burton (1840s–1860s), or the fictional eastern travels of Byron's *Childe Harold's Pilgrimage* (1812–18) and *Don Juan* (1819–24). Perhaps most influential of all was the monumental archive *Description de l'Égypte* (1809–28), which was produced after the Napoleonic invasion of Egypt, and set scholarly and textual trends for the scrutiny of the East for decades to come. Spreading themselves abroad by way of writing, assimilating new material in writing, travelling Europeans sketched imaginative and spatial contours in what was, from their point of view, largely a broad, flat unknown.

So, in essence, colonial expeditions, inspired by reading, became themselves exercises in reading, or interpretational. Mythic and narrative patterns, such as the quest for promised lands or biblical rivers, gave to uncertain journeys a direction and a path. Amidst the unpredictable novelty of things, metaphoric connections or the syntax of a journal plotted lines of orientation in so-called 'recordless' space. Of his first sighting of the Victoria Falls, David Livingstone wrote this plain statement: 'The entire falls are simply a crack made in a hard basaltic rock from the right to the left bank.' Then, to construct a helpful comparison for his readers, he proceeded to 'fancy' at length how the Thames might appear if forced through a similar chasm (*Missionary Travels and Researches in Africa*, 1857).

As this example suggests, within a familiar framework of grammatical and symbolic structures a traveller's imagination was able to work associatively. In explorer literature, and also in colonial fiction and poetry, even ordinary declarative sentences—'His landmark is a kopje-crest', 'At the foot of the "kopje" lay the homestead'—had the power to organize a new landscape, to plot sight-lines and give perspective, and in so doing conjured up places to believe in (Thomas Hardy, 'Drummer Hodge', 1899; Olive Schreiner, *The Story of an African Farm*, 1883). Most of what we are able to say about writing and empire keeps returning to this central principle of colonialist interpretation. The fascination with difference competed with a reliance on sameness and familiarity.

Peter Carey's *Oscar and Lucinda* (1988), a novel about nineteenth-century Australia, offers a helpful emblem of such reliance. In the latter part of the novel, Oscar Hopkins, a failed Victorian clergyman, undertakes to transport a glass church through the Australian bush. The fragility and preposterous incongruity of this object reflect the ambition, artifice, and invasive profligacy of the colonial mission of which Oscar composes a small part. But even though it shatters on arrival at its destination, the church also signifies a symbolic investment, however wayward, in the new territory. What emerges from the botched encounter between glass, a dreamer, and the vast continental mass of Australia is a new history of the land, a tale which Oscar's descendants will use to explain their belonging to it. As the spatial historian Paul Carter observes, almost any act of colonial description, any effort to carry over meanings from the old country, worked to ascribe intention and dimensionality to unknown space. Symbolic gestures of the simplest, most day-to-day kind brought a new geography into being, created a humanly viable landscape for the traveller.[3]

From the European point of view, therefore, colonialism was a metaphoric and cartographic—as well as a legalistic—undertaking. A country was 'mapped' or spatially conceived using figures which harked back to home ground. Travellers' rough, rudimentary descriptions charted unknown lands in the same tentative and provisional way as did early maps. Classifications and codes imported from Europe were matched to peoples, cultures, and topographies that were entirely un-European. And having once done the work of interpretation, the imported symbols, even if entirely arbitrary, often stuck. Colonial maps grew dense with old toponyms applied to new contexts—names like New York, Windsor, Perth, East London, Margate, or the many Newcastles the world over. New places, named after regions and towns left behind, re-created in some part the symbolic experience of the old world. But at the same time they marked out a new region, where a new life could begin to unfold. Naming set up a synchronous time frame for the colonies: though not Europe, they were declared to be contiguous to Europe, and subject and secondary to it.

In Daniel Defoe's *Robinson Crusoe* (1719), an early paradigmatic text of European colonial experience, the practice of interpretation as replication is memorably demonstrated. The lone shipwrecked settler Crusoe wards off starvation and the anxiety of the unknown by building himself a small estate. He lays claim to land by investing it with his labour, developing it according to true Protestant tradition and protecting it with high walls. He works strictly to conventions and rules retrieved from memory, using tools he saves from the wrecked ship. In the absence of society, writing a journal becomes his way of objectifying and confirming the surrounding reality. He also trains his parrot to speak to him his own name. Thus the signifiers of his past life are repeated back to him.

Yet of course neither bird nor homestead authentically recreates the experience of home. The protecting walls declare his vulnerability. That which voices his name is not something familiar but a talking bird, and an exotic one at that. As colonial writing confirmed time and again, significations transferred from England or Scotland were doomed to take on a different cast in a new context. No matter how much Crusoe, like the archetypal colonist he is, strives to assert his own reality and establish his rights to the island 'kingdom', the unknown remains a constant anxiety, represented by his horror of cannibalism. This explains Crusoe's concern to make of the cannibal survivor, Friday, an image of himself, an opposite who will confirm the reality of his own being. He is 'my man Friday', dressed like Crusoe, named for the day Crusoe saves him.

Colonial readings of the beyond were reproduced and so multiplied across different texts, as will be seen throughout this chapter. The figures of speech through which travellers and colonizers pictured the exotic, taken from Shakespeare's *The Tempest*, or Homer, the

Arabian Nights, or other travellers' tales, developed, through a process of reiteration and re-borrowing, into conventions of comprehending other lands. Searching for words to describe West Africa's vegetation and moonlit immensity, Mary Kingsley, the late Victorian travel writer and anthropologist, drew on Rudyard Kipling's images of the expanses of British India (*Travels in West Africa*, 1897). In a continuing process of historical sedimentation, travellers wrote memoirs preserving the fascinations which had tempted them out in the first place. In their turn these interpretative symbols fed the anticipations of future explorers, map-makers, scientists—and the colonizers, those who took over lands or stayed to rule. Nineteenth-century writers of empire, therefore, were heirs to long-established traditions of symbolic interpretation. They, too, sought to interpret the obscure by using symbols exotic in signification and yet manageable, domesticable. It was not unlike viewing the unnerving monotony of the bush through the fixed frame of Oscar's preposterous glass church. Manipulating their inheritance, building on the genealogy of the past, the Victorians became probably the most active and impassioned disseminators of imperial dreams witnessed in modern history.

However, interpreting the beyond, even where they dismissed local cultures as primitive, Europeans did not necessarily cancel the scripts and artefacts made by colonized peoples. On the contrary, during the early days of administration in areas such as India, South-East Asia, and the Middle East, colonizers often searched diligently for the non-European texts that would help them govern. In many cases, too, textual borrowings took place with the co-operation of colonized subjects. Famously, eighteenth-century orientalist scholars in Bengal developed Indian know-how by consulting with a range of local specialists—linguists, scribes, spiritual leaders, pundits, and interpreters. The aim was to legitimize colonial rule in an indigenous idiom. Through the medium of translation, so gaining command over a variety of texts, British administrators hoped to undermine the native monopoly on legal knowledge, and to gather the information needed to impose their own authority. To name a foreign land, to make of that land and its ways a textual artefact, was to exercise mastery.[4]

Contrary to what is sometimes supposed, the British attempt at textual take-over, whether in India or closer to home, emphasizes that out in the colonies the imperialist was never simply a lone, Prospero-like bearer of book and stylus. In Asia in particular, European scholars and colonial officials alike pored over and assiduously absorbed indigenous religious texts, laws, and legends: the Koran, the Veda, *al-Hidaya*, the *Arabian Nights*. The 'classical' and vernacular Indian languages were transformed into textual archives—grammars, dictionaries, and guidebooks. The polymath, linguist, and jurist William Jones, who took it as his life's ambition to 'know India better than any other European ever knew it', studied in depth the languages of Asia, and published the *Mahomedan Law of Inheritance* (1792) and the *Institutes of Hindu Law* (1796). As well as helping to produce a system of rule, appropriated writings were valued also for their fixing function. No matter how ancient or incomplete, texts represented stability in what were seen as highly volatile, fluid societies. Then, too, translations and evocations of local custom provided introductory readings to the colonies for those in Britain. Though often dated and unwieldy, they were regarded as more reliable guides to the enduring ways of foreign lands than any account which people on the ground might provide.

But if the ambition of the colonizer was to know, to appropriate, and to rule, the reality for colonized, enslaved, and indentured peoples, even where they were consulted about the colonial process, was very different—very far removed from the colonizers' lawcourts, city halls, and libraries. As historians and sociologists tell us, for many peoples imperialism represented, if not the destruction of their communities and populations, then a harsh existence of dispossession and privation. It was certainly no exercise in symbolism, idealism, or patriotic sentiment.[5] Unfortunately discussions of text and image often mask this reality of empire: the numbers who died in colonial wars and in labour gangs, or as a result of disease, starvation, and transportation. Colonial obedience, in the opinion of John Nicholson, commander of India's North-West Frontier, required the brutal humiliation of conquered peoples. 'War against savages', said Sir Harry Smith, hero of battles across the Empire and once Governor of the Cape Colony, 'cannot be carried out according to acknowledged rule but to common sense.' And common sense more often than not meant contempt for native life, carelessness, and violence.[6]

Notoriously, following the Spanish Conquest in the early 1500s, the 'great dying' of native American peoples began, caused by smallpox and measles epidemics. Future encounters between Europe and other lands would again and again be characterized by scenes of carnage, devastation, and the mass displacement of populations. The 5 million inhabitants of Lower and Upper Peru at the time of Conquest had declined to 300,000 at the end of the eighteenth century. Where there were 70,000 native Americans in British Columbia in 1835, 20,000 remained in 1897. The Aborigines of Australia met with a similar fate. And during the 200-year period of the European slave trade (1650–1850), as the populations of Europe and Asia more than doubled, the total population of Africa remained static.

If nothing else, by offering us insight into the imperial imagination, the texts of empire give some purchase on the occlusions of human loss that operated in colonial representation. The effects of empire on colonized peoples, and colonized responses to invasion, usually appear as mere traces in the writing of the time. Readings of imperial texts suggest, therefore, how it was possible for a world system which presided over the lives of millions to legitimate itself by way of myth and metaphor while at the same time masking suffering. Colonial writing is important for revealing the ways in which that world system could represent the degradation of other human beings as natural, an innate part of their degenerate or barbarian state. Overdetermined by stereotype, the characterization of indigenous peoples tended to screen out their agency, diversity, resistance, thinking, voices.

It is on this basis that postcolonial theorists refer to the colonized as the *subaltern* (meaning 'of inferior or subordinated rank'), the *colonial other*, or simply the *other*.[7] The concept of the other, which is built on the thought of, *inter alia*, Hegel, Sartre, and Said, signifies that which is unfamiliar and extraneous to a dominant subjectivity, the opposite or negative against which an authority is defined. The West thus conceived of its superiority relative to the perceived lack of power, self-consciousness, or ability to think and rule, of colonized peoples. Psychoanalysis, too, in particular as refracted by Lacan, has postulated that self-identity is constituted within the gaze of another.

Yet despite the occlusions, we should remain aware that the elusive presence of the other or subaltern *does* make itself felt in imperial writings. What has been called 'the space of the adversarial'—the power of extreme difference to disturb, distort, or overwhelm dominant representations—is expressed even within the most conventional of colonialist texts.[8] In the opening scene of the Anglo-Indian Alice Perrin's *The Stronger Claim* (1903), for instance, the 'sightless' punkah-wallah, stupefied by the tedium of his labour, needlessly fans a white man who has died. The narrative represents his activity as unthinking drudgery. Yet, read another way, his attitude might equally signify an indifference not only to the well-being but to the very presence of the European, an indifference unsettling because so implacable. In *Confessions of a Thug* (1839), Philip Meadows Taylor's early novel of the Raj, the thug describes his past experiences as irremediably savage. Though he seeks British justice, the sheer excess of murderous detail in his story, relentlessly listed, betrays the author's apprehension that the difference of India is daunting and possibly uncontrollable.

Again, in Kipling's 'The Judgement of Dungara' (*The Week's News*, 1888; collected in *The Man who would be King*, 1987), the Priest of Dungara donates pure white shirts woven of nettles to a Christian mission. As is his intention, the gift of itch-inducing garments has the effect of sabotaging the efforts of the 'civilizers' as well as the Christian symbolism they hold dear. In 'The Bridge-Builders' (*The Day's Work*, 1898), the civil engineer Findlayson experiences an opium-induced dream which announces the coming of new gods of 'fire-carriages'. But the prescience of the dream underscores the continuing power of the uncanny in India. Kipling at times showed a keen awareness of the insecurities which dogged colonial rule. Revealingly, in the story 'On the City Wall' (*In Black and White*, 1888; *The Man who would be King*, 1987), the same English narrator who announces that India 'will never stand alone', unwittingly helps an anti-imperial revolutionary to escape.

As has been seen, to evoke their encounter with worlds that were difficult to describe and to rule, Europeans relied on (often stereotyped) images of threat or allure. Their dependence on the unthinking security offered by stereotype again underlines an important point regarding colonial interpretation: that it was far from being merely a one-way process of imposing symbolic readings. Colonialist attitudes were formed *in response to* the culture and also the struggles of the colonized. Anglo-Indian imagery of the unbridgeable divide separating East from West, for example, grew out of the terror of the 1857 Mutiny. From the early years of the Raj, the British had adopted the Hindu idea of the present time as an era of decline (the *Kaliyuga*) and inscribed it into their own histories. Instead of European power being all-determining, or the white man being the chief arbiter of representations, as is sometimes assumed, colonization in many cases involved a transaction between cultures. Edwin Arnold, the Victorian colonial headmaster, poet, and later diplomat, presents a case in point. While promoting Empire in his leaders for the *Daily Telegraph*, Arnold was also the author of a verse biography of Buddha, *The Light of Asia* (1879), which T. S. Eliot read, and the translator of the *Bhagavad-gita* into English, in which form Mohandas Gandhi encountered the poem. Also, as Bernard Cohen and Terence Ranger have shown, colonial ceremonies of state and administrative procedures, such as Indian durbars and the investiture of African chiefs, incorporated what the colonizer believed were indigenous customs.[9] Colonial interpretation thus represented a constant jostling this way and that among parties to the colonial relationship. Symbolic imposition there was, but it was not always a blanket imposition. As Subaltern School historians in India have far-sightedly suggested since the 1980s—and as Chapter 2, too, will demonstrate—native cultures did not simply give way to colonialist metaphor.

Dealing in cashmere and turtles: the Victorian novel

Like Crusoe, the British Empire at its height required mobilizing symbols—images of treasure and 'wide, open spaces', of bearing the torch, of national valour, of building modern cities where all before had been confusion. In its attempt to comprehend other lands, and also in its need to propagate itself and, importantly, legitimize its presence, colonial authority depended on imaginative backing, what have usefully been called *energizing myths*—of the New World, of the Empire on which the sun would never set.[10] As I have pointed out, imperialism was a thing of mind and representation, as well as a matter of military and political power and the extraction of profit. The following overview of colonial imagery in nineteenth-century narrative is intended to make clearer the pervasive influence of imperial ideas in imaginative writing, and the support which such writing implicitly gave to empire. Even a cursory examination of the Victorian novel suggests how curiously invisible and yet ubiquitous were the imperial representations that contributed to the national culture's understanding of itself.

At the time of high imperialism in the late nineteenth century, most British imperialists cherished an unambiguously heroic image of themselves as conquerors and civilizers of the world. Such self-projections were of course not unique to Europe. They were pretty much standard practice for any regime with territorial ambitions, such as might be found among Arabic, Indic, and Chinese peoples also. What distinguished the colonialist mission of nineteenth-century Europe, and of Britain in particular, was first the industrial and military power that underpinned it; and secondly the often explicit ideologies of moral, cultural, and racial supremacy which backed its interpretative ventures.[11]

In the view of the British imperial nation, its history made up a tale of firsts, bests, and absolute beginnings. Where the British established a cross, a city, or a colony, they proclaimed the start of a new history. Other histories, by definition, were declared of lesser significance or, in certain situations, non-existent. A world-vision of this nature clearly required substantial cultural and discursive reinforcement. As will be seen, it was here, in giving support to the imperial vision, that the novel of domestic realism played a part. British writers of this time willy-nilly formed part of an imperial society; they shared in the imperial antipathies and controversies of the day. Their work was imbued with, if not animated by, an awareness that a vast portion of the earth's surface was subject to Britain.

Some nineteenth-century writers and thinkers—Carlyle, John Stuart Mill, Trollope, and Dickens among them—directly responded to imperial developments in essays and journalism as well as in longer work. But for most it would be true to say that their writing participated in the representation of British global power mainly by taking it for granted. The integrity, superiority, and strength of the West, the expanded new geography of the Empire—these were Victorian givens. An apparent indifference about Empire in a work of art indicated not so much a remoteness from imperial involvements as acceptance: the assumption that with Britain at the helm all was right with the world. As Edward Said has put it, mainstream realist novels, therefore, could be *of* imperial domination even if they were not *about* it.[12] Where the rest of the world was ignored in a novel, it was because that rest, the non-West, was assumed to be marginal and secondary to the metropolis.

But it is all very well to say that the nineteenth-century novel contributed to the imagination of empire mainly by reflecting the status quo. How, more precisely, did the contribution work? Not surprisingly, important signifiers for imperial values were laid down in the novel's representation of space—the focus on certain areas and not others, the attention given to the capital in relation to its outlying areas. Social hierarchy, in other words, was symbolized geographically. Status usually hinged on proximity to the imperial centre, though the significance of space as property complicated and often reinforced the hierarchy. As is dramatized in Jane Austen's *Mansfield Park* (1814), in the nineteenth-century novel as in broader society, social status and moral standing, in a word *propriety*, were contingent upon the possession of property. From the late 1700s, much of this property—in the form of estates, plantations, venture capital, slaves—was concentrated in the colonies. In Austen's novel, the West Indies figures as little more than a remote place of business, for the 'arrangement of . . . affairs'. Yet it is clear that the Mansfield Park estate is sustained by Sir Thomas Bertram's sugar plantations in Antigua—an island where slavery was practised till the 1830s.[13]

Even when appearing in the form of wealth, therefore, colonial matters tended still to be kept in the background of a novel. Indeed, the riskier or dirtier the investment involved—and reports on slavery suggest that colonial 'affairs' were often both risky and dirty—the greater the preferred distance between the penal colonies and slave plantations, and the metropolitan centre. As the historian Eric Williams has shown, in the latter half of the eighteenth century, despite massive importations of slaves from Africa, slave populations in the West Indies were in a state of consistent decline, so hard was this labour worked, so poor were their conditions. In Barbados, in the period 1764 to 1771, where '35,397 slaves had been imported; 31,897 had disappeared'.[14] The Victorian novel turned its face from these unpalatable colonial details. Characteristic of this attitude, this time with respect to the penal colony of Australia, is the distance measured between Pip and the source of his fortunes in Dickens's *Great Expectations* (1860–1). When that far from respectable source is revealed in the person of the ex-convict Magwitch, Pip responds, quite predictably, with abhorrence. For a moment he considers enlisting for India as a private soldier. Significantly, the solution to his 'colonial' troubles is to disappear into the Empire: its vast distances offer a consoling anonymity.

So, while the Empire could signify far realms of possibility, fantasy, and wish-fulfilment where identities and fortunes might be transformed, the colonies were also places of banishment, unlawful practice, oppression, and social disgrace, dark lands where worthy citizens might not wish to stray. In this sense, given that Victorian society was bent on progress and moral probity, colonial territories took on the aspect of its unconscious or hidden self. As Rudyard Kipling, that canny interpreter of the British imperial imagination, observed: it was 'East of Suez', where 'the direct control of Providence [ceased]', and where the 'mark of the beast' expressed itself (*Life's Handicap*, 1891).

In more concrete terms, the Empire enters the nineteenth-century novel chiefly as commodity, in images of riches and trade. Where Britain was assumed to be the commercial and cultural hub of the world, the centre to which wealth flowed, it followed that lands beyond the seas would manifest themselves in the form of products. In novels these products usually comprise food, clothes, and adornment, and in many cases connote luxury and the exotic: the gift of the Indian shawl in Mrs Gaskell's *North and South* (1855), the cashmere scarves, turquoise bracelets, ivory chess-men, and hot pickles liberally scattered about the Indian-born Thackeray's *Vanity Fair* (1847–8), the turtles, limes, and ginger Walter promises to send home from Barbados in Dickens's *Dombey and Son* (1846–8). In this last novel, the eponymous trading firm tellingly represents to itself the whole world solely in terms of the 'system [of trade] of which they were the centre'. To 'Dombey and Son', 'rivers and seas were formed to float their ships'. In *Vanity Fair*, the Empire is more openly represented as the source of profit-extraction. Miss Swartz, the wealthy 'mulatto from St Kitts', is targeted by the fortune-hunting Mr Osborne as a wife for his son. To the father, her stocks and plantations, which far exceed what most young English heiresses can offer, override the race aversions that trouble the son. Class considerations in this case cancel those of race.

Yet even if their occurrence was purely incidental or ornamental, exotic objects in circulation in novels—and also characters with colonial connections—carried associations of either the fascination or the fear of the forbidden. The other could signify anything from irresistible delight to social unacceptability and instability, moral pollution, nightmare, and syphilis. Bertha Mason, Rochester's first wife in *Jane Eyre* (1847), comes from the West Indies. As Jean Rhys knowingly interpreted the situation in *Wide Sargasso Sea* (1966), Bertha's madness stems from the tormented sexuality of her Caribbean past. Joseph Sedley's position as nabob and collector in the 'jungly district' of Boggley Wollah in *Vanity Fair* amplifies all that is in him of the greedy and the debauched. In *Bleak House* (1852–3), Mrs Jellyby's rank neglect of home and family is attributed to her interest in the Borrioboola-Gha project—for 'cultivating coffee and educating the natives ... on the left bank of the Niger'. For Dickens, domestic concerns outweighed philanthropy abroad.

As will be apparent from these descriptions, the Victorians' relationship to the strangeness of colonial experience showed distinct contradictions, which too were reflected in the novel. As a consequence of metaphoric projection, the colonies, certainly those in the more temperate regions, though unfamiliar, warmer, lusher, antipodean, were also depicted as being 'just like home'. The imperialist commentator Benjamin Kidd accurately observed that Britain had 'put forth vigorous reproductions of herself in the white man's lands of the world' (*The Control of the Tropics*, 1898). The mirror worlds of the white colonies proffered the possibility of beginning life on a new footing, but in a place not vastly different from England or Scotland, where success might be rated in British terms.

This combined remoteness and predictability of events on the imperial periphery created convenient strategies of narrative closure for Victorian novelists. Now complicating, now resolving action, the colonial factor could operate in the manner of a *deus ex machina*. Where all else failed there remained the exit-route to the Empire. In distant lands, as well as punishment and trials, remunerative prospects were to be had, and a hoped-for restitution of fortunes. Australia, Mr Micawber of *David Copperfield* (1849–50) believes, is 'a Spring of no common magnitude'; 'something of an extraordinary nature will turn up on that shore'. It was true that colonial characters and developments had the power to threaten the security of society at home. Yet it was equally the case that out on the periphery social problems could be solved or conveniently elided, as in certain of Captain Frederick Marryat's stories, or again, most famously, in *David Copperfield*. Mr Peggotty takes fallen Em'ly to Australia to begin a new life for 'No one can't reproach my darling' there. Transportation or migration might work like death or marriage to relieve a plot of characters who had become superfluous, such as the Micawbers, or

Hetty Sorrel in George Eliot's *Adam Bede* (1859). Hetty, like Emily, is sent to the Antipodes following social disgrace. As in Dickens, Australia acts to relieve social and sexual embarrassment. While fallen women redeem themselves and Micawber can become magistrate, gender and class proprieties are preserved in Britain.

In *The Settlers in Canada* (1844), a popular boys' story by Captain Marryat, the Campbell family lose inherited property because of a marriage mysteriously contracted in India. But later on, as a lucky compensation, they unexpectedly inherit a fortune because a family member is assumed dead in the East Indies. The interconnected Empire is potentially a place of riches and of freedom, inviting settlement: 'Land is to be bought [in Canada] at a dollar an acre, and you may pick and choose'. *The Settlers in Canada* thus encapsulates the polar opposites between which textual representations of the colonies oscillated. On the one hand, there were the sweet pastoral havens full of prizes, pleasure, and stories, contrasting with or sup-porting and reinforcing action in the 'real' world of Europe. Virginia Woolf came into her famous legacy of £500 a year following her aunt's 'fall from her horse when she was riding out to take the air in Bombay' (*A Room of One's Own*, 1929). On the other hand, how-ever, the Empire as blank space or mystery offered strategies of silence and sudden metamorphosis, which helped to end a plot, or resolved problems by erasing them.

The imperial century

As noted, Europe's attempt to cast its reflection upon lands and oceans goes back several centuries. However, it was in the nineteenth century that the economic supremacy and political authority of Europe, and in particular of Britain, became global. For the British, the post-1815 period, or more specifically the time of Queen Victoria's reign (1837–1901), represented their great age of colonization. By 1815 the nation had established itself as a dominant power in the world, a pacemaker of European industrialization and expansion. From the vantage point of 1897, the year of Queen Victoria's Diamond Jubilee, the entire course of the British nineteenth century—the expansion into new territories, the dissemination of imperialist ideas, the ramification of colonial communications networks across the globe—appeared to have unfolded in accordance with a uniquely ordained pattern. Britain, it was believed, had a destiny and a duty to rule the world, or at least that one-quarter of the earth's surface over which the Empire now extended.

Beginning to look more closely at the relationship of imaginative writing to empire, it is worth taking the time to establish first of all what it is we refer to when we speak of the colonial expansion of Britain, and what, very generally, imperialism involved. The definition of the term 'imperialism' itself changed over time. As Richard Koebner and Helmut Dan Schmidt explain, though the word first entered English to describe the French Second Empire (1852–70), in the 1860s its meaning shifted to signify the expansion of, and British responsibility for, the 'white' colonies. It was later that imperialism came to describe British colonial involvement more generally.[15]

Historians have also tended to find different period demarcations for the Age of Empire and its different phases. Eric Hobsbawm gives the dates 1875–1914 to formal Empire, describing it as the final phase in European capitalist domination.[16] The historian of India C. A. Bayly takes a different line. He argues that a 'constructive authoritarian' British imperialism came of age as early as 1783–1820. Some one hundred years before the Partition of Africa, colonial policy in Asia was aggressive, ideological, and imbued with a sense of national and Christian mission; in other words it prefigured formal imperialism.[17] In thus adjusting the parameters of empire, Bayly enters a debate which began in the 1960s with Robinson and Gallagher's contention that there was little to distinguish late from mid-Victorian imperialism. Throughout the nineteenth century, they argued, the 'official mind of imperialism' was reactive and defensive, not formally expansive. It responded more to strategic interests, proto-nationalisms, and local crises on the colonial periphery than to economic interests at the centre.[18] As the Robinson and Gallagher controversy highlighted, differences also exist among historians over the Empire's motivating forces, about the primacy of economic over strategic or political factors, for example, or the relative importance of ideologies of racial superiority when compared, say, to the motivating force of Great Power competition.

This book takes the view that, certainly in terms of public involvement and sheer global spread, for Britain the second half of the nineteenth century represented its period of high (also called formal or new) imperialism. But the foundations for this power had been laid during the decades of the late 1700s and early 1800s with the opening of the South Pacific, the annexation of territory in southern Africa, the consolidation and then dismantling of the slave trade, and, most important economically, the expansion of dominion in India. In 1784 Bengal had been placed under the dual control of the East India Company and the Crown. By 1833, as Macaulay said, the British were firmly established as the political power—the 'great potentate'—in India. Between 1790 and 1820 approximately 150 million people in lands as far apart as southern Africa, Australia, and the Indian subcontinent were declared under British control. Already imposingly imperial in aspect, Britain was now set for the phenomenal growth of the Empire under Victoria. Over the next decades, New Zealand, Natal, territories on the West African coast and in South-East Asia, Australia, and Canada were occupied or annexed. With the so-called Scramble for Africa between 1870 and 1900, British colonial possessions again increased dramatically, this time by 4.5 million square miles and 66 million inhabitants.

In brief, Victorian high imperialism was distinguished by the following: geographic magnitude; the mass organization and institutionalization of colonial power, often expressed in forms of aggressive nationalism; and, as the century matured, the formalization of imperialist ideologies, especially those pertaining to race, encouraged by the spread of Social Darwinist thought.[19] In 1876 Queen Victoria was named Empress of India, 'Kaizer-i-Hind'. In 1897 *The Times* trumpeted that this was the 'mightiest and most beneficial Empire ever known in the annals of mankind'. In the intervening years, as Britain secured vast gains in the helter-skelter race for the last unclaimed continent, the new Empire invited from its propagandists and poets comparison with Imperial Rome.[20]

In response, the British national imagination too grew extravagantly imperial in its idiom and scope. Spurred on by music-hall and the popular press, the final decades of the century saw an intense public expression of British imperial sentiment, channelled, for example, into the worship of colonial heroes. Apparently eager to participate even if vicariously in the excitements of British power abroad, the public at home developed a voracious appetite for missionary and explorer travelogues and adventure romances. Books by and about David Livingstone became best-sellers: his own *Missionary Travels* and Henry Morton Stanley's *How I Found Livingstone* (1872) and *In Darkest Africa* (1890). *In Darkest Africa*, for example, sold 150,000 copies in English. In the 1890s, G. A. Henty's militaristic boys' adventure tales were being consumed in their tens of thousands a year.

Along with the imperialist ethos inculcated in public schools, explorer and adventure tales performed the necessary service of informing Britons about what it was like to be abroad in the colonies. As the opening section suggested, not only railways, canals, and the Maxim gun were necessary to bring the Empire to its climax of self-regard. Energizing ideas and propaganda too were required. By the 1890s, the writer Jan Morris points out, imperialism had come to depend mightily on aesthetic display.[21] Empire both stimulated and satisfied the wildest imaginings. It was a style and a boast; an eye-catching assemblage of hero cults, exhibitionism, rituals of self-glorification, and a general eagerness to 'Play up! Play up! and play the game!'[22] Hence the public appetite for stories; hence, too, the widespread enthusiasm for songs, verse, games, and youth movements which embodied imperial dreams.

Imperialism, therefore, was not something that took place only abroad. The nationalism the Empire generated, the race antipathies it provoked, played a crucial part in British society, in particular in creating strategic solidarities within the country. National selfhood in Britain had traditionally been forged in opposition to an other over-seas. But whereas in 1688 this other was Catholic Europe, increasingly, as the Empire grew, identity was defined as against the inferior state of being which the colonized were said to represent. Broader imperial identity, superimposed on older regional identities and bracketing together different class groups, was reinforced by social stratification in the colonies, where class and racial divisions often coincided. This conflation of social privilege suggests a further possible reason for the emphasis on text in the Empire. Any white colonial officer, whatever his origins, was seen as forming part of an élite. His education, his military or administrative skills—in effect, his mastery of texts— became a key marker of that status.

At the height of the Empire, such was their confidence, such the resilience of their sense of self, that Britons could speak brazenly of their unique imperial strengths as a nation. In the opinion of the Colonial Secretary Joseph Chamberlain, 'the British race [was] the greatest of governing races that the world [had] ever seen'. W. E. Henley, whose poetry acclaimed imperial vigour, declared England to be the 'chosen daughter of the Lord'. By the time of the outbreak of the South African War (1899–1902), imperialism had evolved into a national creed to spread Britain's gifts, 'freedom, justice, the spirit of humanity', throughout the world.[23]

However, the intensity of such pronouncements could conceal an edge of anxiety. A greater defensiveness, too, was a distinguishing feature of high empire: a fear that all that had been gained could be as easily lost, a nervousness that immense power might weaken, or deeply corrupt. In his Inaugural Lecture at the University of Oxford (1870), Ruskin pleaded with British men to 'Reign or Die'. Thomas Hardy expressed dark disillusionment that Victorian progress could bring nothing more elevated than the 'scheduled slaughter' of the Anglo-Boer conflict ('Embarcation', 'At the War Office, London', 1899). As the new century approached, imperial self-confidence gave way to a greater cautiousness and, as Joseph Conrad starkly reflects in his turn-of-the-century narratives 'Heart of Darkness' (1899) and *Lord Jim* (1900), a self-consciousness about the damaging losses involved in empire.

It was certainly true that Britain's heavy dependency on the colonies had exacted its costs. Proud and splendid isolation in fact brought with it a dangerous complacency. In 1896, a year after the disastrous Jameson Raid had confirmed Britain's unpopularity among the Great Powers, Kipling spoke with foreboding of the 'Nations in their harness' going up 'against our path' ('Hymn before Action'). He was not wrong. The Great Depression of 1873–96 had shifted the economic power bases in Europe. Other nations were not only outstripping Britain in trade, manufacture, and technological development, they were also challenging its sway by amassing colonial possessions for themselves abroad. Britain's early ascendancy now left it unnervingly alone.

So despite its patriotic excesses, for Britain the turn of the century was a time also of growing self-doubt, in some cases of cultural panic. Civilization, wrote H. Rider Haggard, is a 'vainglory' that 'comes but to fade'. Though fears and doubts about empire fully surfaced only after 1914, expressions of anxiety about social regression and national decline were widespread. Movements that implied a loss of traditional authority—Irish nationalism, socialism, the New Woman—met with stern repression. Throughout the 1890s, popular and patriotic verse, always a gauge of imperial attitudes, stressed more than ever, and more aggressively, the importance of white colonial brotherhood and the rightness of British rule. W. E. Henley appealed in strenuous terms to the Empire as a cleansing warlike force, 'sifting the nations, | The slag from the metal', causing authority to 'flame' out across darkness. Culturally the Edwardian decade was marked, too, by retraction and a new inwardness—a preoccupation with the domestic, the local, the folk, the quintessentially English. The period witnessed an unprecedented efflorescence of children's literature—writing like E. Nesbit's *The Railway Children* (1906) or Frances Hodgson Burnett's *The Secret Garden* (1911) which, even so, bore the mark of Britain's imperial interests.

There was apprehension, too, at the effects of what was called miscegenation or racial mixing in the colonies—at creolization, 'going native', 'sinking' racially. As later chapters will show, these anxieties were stimulated by a more general preoccupation with degeneration and entropy. The progress promised by science in the mid-Victorian age now seemed a remote and fairy vision. In Britain the birth-rate was falling. The fear was that humankind might be regressing instead of striving onwards and upwards.[24] Percival Campbell, kidnapped by Indians in Marryat's *Settlers in Canada*, returns 'wonderfully' quickly to 'a state of nature'. His fate, like that of other of Marryat's characters who come close to 'going back', is intended as an object lesson in the fragility of the civilized state. Contact with the other created vulnerability.

As we see again in R. L. Stevenson's later tales, colonial literature was sensitive to these anxieties. The white degenerate began to replace the intrepid adventurers of a more self-assured era. In Kipling's 1890 novel *The Light that Failed*, anxiety about the ability of the British to live up to their imperial promise is unmistakable. The novel recites a litany of failures. Dick, the hero, loses his sight and his beloved, and dies in a suicide mission to a North African war zone. Fears about degeneration also found an outlet in colonial horror tales, or what has been named imperial gothic, in which the European hero comes under threat of reversion to a lower state, and barbarism threatens.[25] Conrad's Kurtz in 'Heart of Darkness' is an eloquent example of the white man of great promise who has, in spite of everything, regressed.

Alongside rivalry from without, there were threats to colonial power also from within the Empire, most notably with the outbreak of the Indian Mutiny or War of Rebellion of 1857. From this time British imperial policy began to concentrate on firm rule and showed greater caution in reform. It was more openly acknowledged that the strength and security of the Empire had to rest on force, that authoritative control and 'responsibility' alone would guarantee its permanence. James FitzJames Stephen, a high official in the Indian Civil Service and brother of Leslie Stephen, editor of the *Dictionary of National Biography*, described British government in India as absolute and belligerent, 'founded not on consent, but on conquest': 'our government implies at every point the superiority of the conquering races.' This was the period in which the stalwart colonial officer in colonial tales came into his own as the guardian of peoples and lord of his district. As Kipling reiterates time and again in his stories (*Plain Tales from the Hills*, 1888; *Life's Handicap; The Day's Work*), the officer's uncompromising integrity, strength under pressure, and selfless 'day's work' guaranteed the good management and stability of the Empire and incarnated its highest virtues.

In Britain itself, patriotism, called jingoism in its more rabid forms, was perhaps the most powerful medium through which the belief in the Empire was maintained. It, too, found a major outlet in texts— again in adventure literature, school books, and, a form very popular towards the end of the century, music-hall songs. In the 1870s, Disraeli, the then Prime Minister, worked to consolidate imperial sentiment by popularizing the Empire in the press and in imperial societies. In a series of gigantic national exhibitions, such as the Colonial and Indian Exhibition of 1886, other cultures were displayed in the form of tableaux against which ordinary British citizens might measure their own culture's sophistication.[26] The novelist Anthony Trollope reflected broad national opinion when, in his colonial travelogues (*Australia and New Zealand*, 1873; *South Africa*, 1878), he observed that the Empire was being ruled to the best advantage of its countless inhabitants. Some twenty-five years on, with the outbreak of the South African War, the *Pax Britannica* had become a popular faith, empire an inalienable part of British culture. In his bellicose poem 'The Song of the Sword' (1890), Henley described British imperialism as an absolute force and a universal good. The British sword, 'Hilted with government', transformed the 'waste places' of the globe into 'sweetness', 'teeming with peace'.

Wealth, sweetness, glory: justifications for empire

Having reviewed imperialism and imperial writing in very broad terms, I now turn to look more carefully at justifications of imperial power. The imperialist ethos that mobilized virtually an entire culture, and compelled attention in story and symbol, demands closer attention. How was it that a colonizing nation managed to weave an interpretative net over much of the earth's surface? Theories of racial and cultural supremacy obviously played a key role in validating imperial rule. Imperialist discourse, one may well say, was indistinguishable from racism. But did racial ideologies act alone? How else was empire legitimated? As we shall see when colonial representations are examined, the texts through which colonial power projected itself provided points of focus for its motives and values. But how were those motives and values explained?

Motives and justifications for imperialism can perhaps best be seen as having formed a complicated interlocking matrix, comprising many layers. Within this matrix, justifications—such as the need to 'civilize' natives, or the appeal to the technological superiority of the West—could transmute into motives. And motives might overlap, the one becoming conflated with the other. In British East Africa at the end of the nineteenth century, for example, strategic pressures (involving the sea-route to India) converged with anti-slavery sentiment and economic speculation to encourage colonization.

As is well known, the Victorians had a genius for fashioning moral ideals which matched their economic needs: they stapled duty on to interest, Christianity on to profit. Enterprise, it was believed, would secure the happiness, prosperity, and salvation of dark tribes sunk in barbarism. In 1835 Macaulay strongly supported giving a European education to Indians because of the attendant benefits of encouraging 'civilized' behaviour and hence profitable trade among former 'savages'. The missionary David Livingstone justified his work in Africa by appeal to the 'two pioneers of civilization', Commerce and Christianity.

In G. A. Henty's *With Clive in India* (1884), Charlie Marryat, one day to be captain in the East India Company, observes that 'every one who went to India made fortunes'.[27] While allowing for the layering of imperial ideologies, the centrality of the wealth-making drive is hard to miss in most arguments for empire. Prosperity, material improvement, treasure: as the Romans and Spaniards well knew, these were the most desirable prizes of expansion. Throughout most of the nineteenth century, it was to the profit motive that Britain might attribute its position at the centre of a world economy. The Empire had become a great complicated web of economic exchange and flow of goods and money. As Kipling suggestively described it in his poem 'The Song of the English' (1893), Britain had built for itself an industrial loom spanning the globe, in which the shuttles flying to and fro were the ships of the British merchant marine.

Theories regarding the determinative primacy and consistency of capital's drive for colonies have been vigorously debated. Yet, on the whole, the specific economic bases and benefits of global colonization—whether in the form of export surpluses, taxation, employment, or investment—are widely accepted. Financial interest, the British Liberal J. A. Hobson wrote at the start of the twentieth century, tended to govern the forces of colonial expansion, even where these were generated by groups with mixed motives, such as politicians or philanthropists. The 'motor-power' of imperialism may have been provided by sectional interests, but its 'governor' was 'the struggle for profitable markets' (*Imperialism: A Study*, 1902). Indeed, touched in some way by the benefits and luxuries of the Empire, many Victorians believed that possessing colonies promoted British industry and improved the value of life. 'Trade follows the flag' was the imperialist Cecil John Rhodes's maxim.

As well as Hobson's, one of the best-known early critiques of empire as economic exploitation is V. I. Lenin's *Imperialism: The Highest Stage of Capitalism* (1917), in which he attributed expansion to late capitalist accumulation. In 1867, forty years before the publication of Lenin's book, however, the Indian nationalist Dadabhai Naoroji had begun to explore these lines of thought in his 'drain' theory concerning the extraction of wealth from India by Britain.[28] In 1897 the South African writer Olive Schreiner, too, in a pessimistic parable entitled *Trooper Peter Halket of Mashonaland*, indicted the ruthless profit motive underlying colonialist annexations.

The greed of empire may have assumed a particularly virulent form in the later nineteenth century, yet as far back as early settlement in

North America, colonization had been marked by rationalizations imbuing wealth-making with virtue. The industry of colonizers was said to grant legitimate ownership of the land they worked. This thinking would later find its way into racist justifications of white rule. In the late seventeenth century, in his *Second Treatise of Government* (1690), John Locke argued that 'subduing or cultivating the earth, and having dominion . . . are joined together'. For Livingstone a century and a half later, the ideology of work remained persuasive. Work, he wrote on an expedition to the Zambezi, improved lands and souls. Land improvement and enterprise were antidotes to the slave trade. In his travels he kept an eye open for fertile lands, resources which might draw the attention of European capital. Despite his resistance to stereotypes of the savage, it was Livingstone's conviction, as it was Mary Kingsley's, that Africans would benefit immensely from uplifting labour and participation in trade under European supervision.

Versions of such thought, both sophisticated and crude, combining motive (wealth) and justification (civilization), were used to give colonial masters virtually unbounded rights over the lands and subjects they claimed. In his South African travelogue, Anthony Trollope showed himself to be a convinced proponent of the creed that 'labour only can civilize'. Where religion, philanthropy, and liberal ideas had failed, work on European lines was the only salvation for African people living in 'idleness and dependence on the work of women [*sic*]'. Especially during the period of formal imperialism, the goal of 'civilizing the natives' through profitable work and/or Christian rule became ubiquitous as an argument in favour of colonization. Edwin Arnold, who differed from many in regarding Indians as 'civilized', none the less saw imperial rule as a task of improvement committed 'by Providence to the English race' (*India Revisited*, 1886). Economic and moral arguments in favour of setting people to work in the colonies operated with mutually justifying force. Even conscripted labour and indenture could be defended as benefiting both lands and pagan souls. In the post-slave trade essay 'The Nigger Question' (1849), Thomas Carlyle, too, took for granted that labour was improving, and if invested in land created rights of proprietorship. For this reason, he stated, it was within the rights of the white man in possession to compel the black man to work 'his' land.

Assumptions regarding the improving power of work shaped,

and were reinforced by, colonialist characterizations of the diligent colonial officer and, his converse, the degenerate, lazy native. Stereotypes of the other as indolent malingerers, shirkers, good-for-nothings, layabouts, debased versions of the pastoral idler, were the stock-in-trade of colonialist writing. In contrast, the white man represented himself as the archetypal worker and provident profit-maker. He built railway grids, administrative centres, cities. He raised the stone, cleaved the wood (Kipling, 'The Sons of Martha', 1907). Significantly, the three shipwrecked boy heroes of R. M. Ballantyne's *The Coral Island* (1858) are concerned from the beginning of their time on the island not to waste their days in idleness and play. They want for very little; the climate is good and there is adequate land. Yet, like colonial officers in the making, like Crusoe or the Boy Scouts of the future, they work assiduously, filling their hours with building, mapping, and exploration.

Given the great size of the Empire, motives as widespread as those of prosperity and civilization were mediated in different ways depending on context, time, and circumstance. Commercial interests, for example, which had prepared the way for scientific and geographic exploration, were in their turn supported by the technological developments which exploration encouraged. By the time of Captain James Cook's voyages in the second half of the eighteenth century, the Enlightenment interest in classifying the world had itself developed into a strong incitement for exploration. The 'edge of the world', in the phrase of George Bowering's fictional Captain Vancouver, was being turned 'day by day into facts. Fathoms, leagues, rainfall, names' (*Burning Water*, 1980). A large scientific party set out on Cook's first expedition of 1768–71 on board the *Endeavour*. On their departure John Ellis, a naturalist, wrote to the Swedish botanist and classifier Linnaeus (Carl von Linné): 'No people ever went to sea better fitted out for the purpose of Natural History, nor more elegantly.' Yet, contrary to its own self-estimation, the Linnaean systematization of all plants on earth was not a purely disinterested scientific project, non-exploitative, orderly, even stylish. Even though scientists assumed a neutrality in their work, that neutrality took for granted a European understanding of the world, and the supporting presence of European military and economic power. In addition, research supplied useful information which might be used for the exploitation of new lands.

As Anthony Trollope again perceived, the Empire and the development of colonies also provided means of ensuring social stability at home. It was not only that an imperial patriotism projected class hostilities beyond the borders of the nation. Colonies also encouraged emigration and so provided an answer to Malthusian anxieties about population increase. In the past, Trollope observed baldly in *Australia*, Britain 'took distant spots on the globe from foreign nations' to gain in power, or because 'wealth was to be obtained for ourselves at home, and wealth deducted from our enemies abroad'. Now it was rather the case that 'new hives [were] wanted for new swarms'. Imagery such as this had remained compelling across the century. In 1812, six decades before Trollope's reconnoitring colonial visits, the poet Robert Southey had used a similar image to advocate emigration. In his essay 'On the State of the Poor' he wrote: 'It is time that Britain should become the hive of nations, and cast her swarms; and here are lands to receive them'. Both at home and abroad, the *Edinburgh Review* commented in 1850, colonization was 'an enterprise which would convert . . . paupers into customers'.

And, in fact, the imperial enterprise did convert Britain into a society of avid consumers. Imperial developments had created among the British public an entirely new menu of needs and desires. Consumer demands in turn stimulated the quest for markets, sprinkling the kitchens and parlours of the Victorian world (and its novels) with exotic products and pleasures. As well as their interest in Indian shawls, the middle classes, and soon also the working classes, developed a taste for tea, and with tea went, variously, sugar, treacle, jam, pudding, Bakewell tarts, Eccles cakes, buns. During the course of the nineteenth century, sugar consumption in Britain increased by an astronomical 700 per cent. Whether rural or urban, Northern or southern, privileged or poor, the British day had become unthinkable without its rituals of tea and dessert, with all their 'colonial' trimmings of spicy biscuits, raisin-rich scones, sticky-sweet puddings, and chocolate cakes.[29]

And with the passing of time, the Empire developed its own forms of self-validation. Being in charge had created a momentum, encouraged by a widely pervasive sense of imperial rightness. The Empire had come to seem inevitable, a benign force of fate. By definition, any extension of British influence would widen the skirts of light, would increase the total quantity of good in the world. Whether through influence or coercion, the Empire distributed to those in need values which upheld a fair and democratic culture. England's destiny, said John Ruskin in his Inaugural Lecture, was to rule: she took with her to the farthest places her flame of 'beneficent glory'. Therefore—in lines that the Cape Colony magnate Rhodes would cherish—Ruskin urged that England 'found colonies as far and as fast she is able'.[30]

The faith that White Men bring, Kipling agreed, was freedom, the righting of wrongs—though 'failing freedom, War' ('The Song of the White Men', 1899).[31] The English conquered, he again pointed out, in order to educate; they might even manage to turn natives into judges and engineers ('Kitchener's School', 1898). As late as 1934 the liberal Edward Thompson, though troubled by the divisions between Indians and the British under the Raj, listed as among the special virtues that 'went to the building up of the British Empire and its retention by a minute force': a 'high sense of duty, incorruptibility, a passion for improving, a recognition of social responsibility', as well as the installation of 42,000 miles of railway, and 60,000 of metalled roads—paid for, it might be added, by lakhs in Indian taxes (Conclusion, *Rise and Fulfilment of British Rule in India*). So it followed, as Kipling perceived, that the work of the Empire was in itself valuable: a job that was heroic because dogged and unpraised. The 'old, grim, thankless task of ruling, heedless of praise or blame', the *Quarterly Review* defined it in 1919. As the often-quoted poem 'The White Man's Burden' (1899) reiterated, the role of the imperialist was that of enlightened worker, to serve, to tend, to care, without reward. The colonial officer ideal is embodied in Kipling characters such as Tallantire or Strickland, men who are adaptable but disciplined and ever-vigilant in their devotion to their task.

Again, the idea of emulating the imperial successes of the classical past—or more simply, of appearing imperial—might provide incentives for colonial work more taken for granted than overtly stated. In their plans for enlightened service and development the British discerned the makings of a new Rome. The Romans had laid roads; the British now built railroads and laid telegraph cables. Their rule exhibited inspirational continuities with the past. Benjamin Jowett, Master of Balliol at the time of high imperialism, advised that men destined for the Indian Civil Service be schooled in the classics and moral sciences to 'train [their minds] for the highest purposes of active life'.

Their education should be designed to fit the magnitude and responsibility of their task. And indeed, in practice, the Raj was staffed by a team of a thousand or so Oxbridge-trained intellectuals. A colonizer's work, therefore, could be justified because it was imperial, which meant historically important, involving good government, Palladian-style expansionism, and peace under the law. It was work that could, once again, be portrayed as selfless and serious and grand.

As Victorian colonial writings show, these ways of thinking became circular through sheer force of conviction, supported by self-obsession and bombast. It was possible to justify the Empire because it was self-evidently responsible, above blame, just—and it was just, it could be claimed, because it was British. In Philip Meadows Taylor's *Confessions of a Thug*, the thug Ameer Ali's long trail of murder and theft is cleanly rounded off with his imprisonment and appeal to British justice: 'you will not deny me a fair hearing', he trusts, 'and the justice you give to thousands'.[32] This is one instance among many in colonial literature of the colonized corroborating the self-image of the colonizer. The thug's entire tale, narrated to a sahib in authority, is symbolically enclosed within the framework of the British justice system. The British—so ideologies of racial and national superiority spelled out—were natural imperialists, born rulers like the Romans, men who upheld a free and fair legal system, who were above all responsible and benevolent, the best rulers a colonized people might hope to have. Similar assumptions are in place—though they are also subtly questioned—in Leonard Woolf's *The Village in the Jungle* (1913).

Kipling's and Henley's imperialist hymns distilled the spirit of this faith in nation and Empire. Despite its minor key, 'Recessional' (1897) by Kipling is unembarrassed about calling on God—'Beneath whose awful hand we hold Dominion over palm and pine'—to stick to the British side. British Empire to Kipling meant the world-wide reign of justice, and the 'Queen's Peace overall'. For Henley, British global might was one of the great Constants, commensurate with God's 'Will', surrounding the earth in the manner of the 'universal seas' (*Rhymes and Rhythms*, 1889–92). When war with the Boers threatened in 1899, Henley urged:

> Ever the faith endures,
> England, my England:—

Take and break us: we are yours,
England my own!
'Pro Rege Nostro', from *For
England's Sake*, 1900

Or, again, as Cecil John Rhodes contended: 'we are the first race in the world' and 'the more of the world we inhabit, the better it is for the human race'.

Within this closed world of imperial belief, opposition was virtually inadmissible. Britain was set on a path of progression that led in one direction only: upwards. Given the dominant picture of things, any signs to the contrary could make little sense. Hardy met with social disapproval for his criticism of British aggression in the South African War. Socialists who opposed the war were attacked from all sides. Fabians such as George Bernard Shaw, and Beatrice and Sidney Webb, found jingoism repugnant, and advocated pacificism at home, yet did not oppose expansionism abroad where it was perceived to further the spread of social improvement. Shaw wrote: 'until the [socialist] Federation of the world becomes an accomplished fact, we must accept the most responsible Imperial federations as a substitute for it' (*Fabianism and the Empire*, 1900).

Relatively late in imperial terms though it is, Kipling's *Kim* (1901) deftly demonstrates how unassailable the circularity of imperial faith could be. Though the novel appeared sixteen years after the formation of the Indian National Congress, it cannot admit to the possibility of native resistance. Its single mention of the Indian Mutiny, which is critical of those who revolted, is made by a veteran soldier who remained loyal to the British. Colonial rule, we are again led to think, is accepted by the colonized himself. What greater proof could there be that the Empire is right; is the best of all possible worlds?

Reading the strange: an empire of the imagination

As suggested, literary texts helped sustain the colonial vision, giving reinforcement to an already insular colonial world. For a Victorian writer to resist the prevailing representations of empire would have meant resisting the very self-perceptions on which mid- to late nineteenth-century society grounded itself. In a society steeped in imperial ideologies, however, such a move was unlikely. Whether they were themselves travelled, or whether they were resolutely London-based (as was W. E. Henley, disabled by tuberculosis for much of his life), writers formed part of a society that was unflinchingly imperial. They wrote in the interpretative shadow of earlier colonial and exotic fictions. The rest of the chapter focuses on this thickening of representation under the late Empire, and on the relative inwardness of colonial symbolic processes. As the first sections have anticipated, through the nineteenth and well into the twentieth century, perspectives on other lands continued to be directed through the prisms of inherited tropes: Utopia, or the lawless wilderness; the Noble Savage or the unregenerate Primitive; the Garden of Eden and the Holy City. For Britain the glorious figure of Britannia was regnant over all. The interlinked symbolic codes of imperial writing created a textual environment which, while interactive, was also self-repeating, and often self-enclosed. The enclosedness mirrored the insularity of the arguments legitimating empire.

The abundant metaphors and similes inspired by the *Arabian Nights* in nineteenth-century literature amply testify to the literary and generative nature of colonial description. Their prevalence also offers an instance of orientalist thought: the way in which the West perceived the East as taking the form of its own fantasies of a paradisiacal Orient. So intensively was the *Nights* mined for tropes of richness and delight that it became itself, as a phrase, a signifier or shorthand for magic and the exotic. Before the explorer Richard Burton produced the first unexpurgated version (1885–8), extracts had been frequently translated in Victorian Britain. The interest in the *Arabian Nights* again points to the European practice of consulting Asian texts the better to comprehend the beyond. Europe colonized foreign stories as well as foreign lands. Thus, far from excluding interaction with other cultures, self-reiteration in fact incorporated foreign influences.[33]

To note but a few examples, the *Arabian Nights* are referred to in Wordsworth's *The Prelude* (1850), Thomas Carlyle's *Sartor Resartus* (1833), Charlotte Brontë's *Jane Eyre*, in Anthony Trollope's *Tales of All Countries* (1861), in *Sesame and Lilies* (1865) by John Ruskin, in several of Dickens's novels, including *Edwin Drood* (1870), and in

Mary Kingsley's travel writings. De Quincey's recollections in *The Confessions of an English Opium-Eater* (1821) are, not surprisingly, saturated with *Nights* imagery. When in *Vanity Fair* Becky Sharp yearns for fabulous fortune, she thinks of turbans, elephants, and the Grand Mogul—imagery garnered from the pages of the *Arabian Nights*. The *Nights*, then, provided metaphors for marvellous and unintelligible realities, for fancy and escape, childlike imagining and sudden transformations, opulence and sensuality. In *Our Mutual Friend* (1864–5), the *nouveaux riches* Veneerings 'have a house out of the Tales of the Genii, and give dinners out of the Arabian Nights'. In *Cranford* (1853) by Mrs Gaskell, Mr Peter returns from India bearing stories said to be even more wonderful than those of Sinbad the sailor.

Working within a tradition of dense textual referencing, colonial*ist* writers—that is, those who addressed themselves to colonial experience specifically—also had their Arabian dreams. To W. E. Henley the East was this 'Book of rocs, Sandalwood, ivory, turbans, ambergris'. In 1893 he published his *Arabian Nights' Entertainments* in praise of the power of the *Nights* to conjure childhood fantasy. Kipling too plucked his signifiers of the fantastical or the mysteriously beautiful from the *Arabian Nights* and Haggard's *She* (1887), amongst other sources. (A statue in an Egyptian temple he described as having 'the very face of "She" '.) In contrast, in 1882 Robert Louis Stevenson published a book called *New Arabian Nights*, a collection of sombre *fin-de-siècle* tales, a dark mirror-image to the libidinous delight present in the original *Nights*. In a second nod at the story-telling thrall of the *Nights*, Stevenson in 1892 brought together his Pacific tales under the title *Island Nights' Entertainments*. In these late tales of the South Seas, Stevenson employs the *Arabian Nights* signifier to evoke, interestingly, not only the local exotic of the islands, but the strangeness of the white man's presence in the region, and the exotic shapes of white dreams.

Stevenson's Pacific tales, in particular 'The Beach of Falesá' (1892) and 'The Ebb-Tide' (1893), fed into a colonialist lineage which connected him to Conrad. In reciprocal fashion, the latter writer was drawn to Stevenson's treatment of colonial themes. Conrad's work, like that of Stevenson, shows the tensions of a split heritage, divided between the demands of the adventure and the 'literary' novel. In his own writing, too, he would develop the Stevensonian subjects of colonial bad faith and fear of regression. As Chapter 2 will show in more depth, in several character studies of flawed Europeans—Kurtz, Kayerts and Carlier, Jim—he examined the contradictions of the white man's 'civilizing' mission.

Colonialist writers, therefore, intertextually inspired one another with images. H. Rider Haggard was as a boy a reader of the *Arabian Nights* and Edgar Allan Poe and spoke of himself as 'held' in a 'golden thrall' by *Robinson Crusoe*. He wrote *King Solomon's Mines* (1885) in response to a bet that he attempt to match the wonder and excitement of Robert Louis Stevenson's *Treasure Island* (1883). This and other of his adventure tales Haggard also modelled in part on the quest patterns of the explorer narratives in general circulation at the time. And Stevenson duly praised him for his 'fine, weird imagination'. Rudyard Kipling found inspiration as a young writer reading Haggard's *Nada the Lily* (1890). Edmund Candler, imperial travel writer and journalist, set out on his first journey to India in 1896 to discover, as he himself said, the world of Marlow's East, described in *Youth* (1902) as quintessentially mysterious, 'perfumed like a flower, silent like death'. Stevenson consciously drew motifs for *Treasure Island* from Defoe and Poe. His book also bears traces of, amongst others, Ballantyne's *The Coral Island*, and Captain Marryat's *The Pirate* (1836) and *Masterman Ready* (1841).

Developing as part of the mid-Victorian adventure writing boom, the subgenre of the Robinsonade (which included *The Coral Island* and *Treasure Island*, and extended to other European literatures) testified of course to the paradigmatic power of *Robinson Crusoe*, but also to the energy of metaphoric borrowings within a wider tradition of colonial romance. Motifs of shipwreck, resourceful settlement and cultivation, treasure, slaves, and the fear of cannibalism resurfaced time and again in boys' stories. In colonial texts more generally, the pairing of white master and black slave/servant became an unquestioned commonplace. As Joseph Bristow's *Empire Boys* shows, what changed was that, across the century, the boy heroes in the English Robinsonade grew incrementally younger, and ever more invincible—lively and ever livelier embodiments of British imperial self-confidence.[34]

Perhaps more than any other writer, Kipling was vitally alert to the potential for story, and for creative cross-connections between stories, in the self-absorbed world of the Empire, which for him meant first and foremost the Indian Empire. In his tales he evokes an atmosphere that is abuzz with narrative. He foregrounds the told quality of his own tales, or draws out the verbal idiosyncrasies of his narrators. Moreover, his short stories form their own network of cross-references. Certain characters—Strickland, Dr Dumoise—are carried over from one story to another. The parallels between situations in different stories are underlined. A narrator may point to an analogous incident in another tale—'I knew a case once. . . . But that is another story'. Kipling can be pictured writing in the midst of a hubbub of story-telling, a clubroom swapping of tall tales and 'true-life' adventures.[35] Many of his stories hold at their core the titbits of rumour and anecdote that did the rounds in Anglo-Indian clubs. There are stories, for example, concerning the appearance of a white man in native guise ('The Incarnation of Krishna Mulvaney', and Kim's own tale); or the anxieties of sexual relations between colonial officials and Indian women ('Without Benefit of Clergy' and 'Georgie Porgie' in *Life's Handicap*; 'The Gate of the Hundred Sorrows', 'Beyond the Pale', and 'Lispeth' in *Plain Tales from the Hills*, to quote but a few examples).

As did the writers of romance, explorers and settlers too read one another and were influenced by their reading. They conceived of newly mapped or settled places using the terms of reference laid down and tested by those who went before them. Watkin Tench, the First Fleet chronicler, developed a spatial vocabulary for New South Wales by drawing on Captain Cook's description of the area, though he also indignantly disagreed with it. According to what he says in *How I Found Livingstone*, Stanley prepared himself for his journey to meet Livingstone by reading the African travel writings of Richard Burton and John Hanning Speke. Mary Kingsley recommended that African explorers read books on 'primitive religion' before starting out on their travels, as she herself had done. Australian land explorers consulted each other's texts in order to help translate the landscape. Charles Sturt and Edward John Eyre, for example, read and discussed each other's views about the outback.

Earlier, colonization was referred to as at once a metaphoric and a cartographic undertaking. New spaces were interpreted visually and verbally, both as grids and triangulations, and as sentences retracing the travellers' routes. The common factor in these representations was the familiarity of the symbolic languages used: the dialogue with a known or translatable text. This in part is what is meant when colonialist discourse critics point out that, travelling to the outer regions of the world, Europeans were confronted with nothing so much as an image of themselves. As well as spoils, they brought back from their journeys writings, descriptions circumscribed by the way they understood the world.

Further instances of the colonial reliance on texts could be quoted in abundance. Enlightenment philosophical debates established in advance the way in which a late eighteenth-century explorer like Mungo Park would represent Africans as noble savages. Joseph Banks, the botanist who accompanied James Cook on his first voyage, compared Tahitians to ancient Greeks. John Hawkesworth, who wrote up the *Voyages* on their return, was in all likelihood himself influenced by his classical learning and his reading of romance when he upheld the well-known rumour that the Patagonians were men of titanic size. The excitement generated over the search for the source of the Nile can in part be attributed to its being a biblical river, which connected the African heart of darkness to a known antiquity. In the words of Speke, one of its European discoverers: 'as I had foretold, the lake [Victoria] was the great source of the holy river which cradled the first expounder of our religious belief'.[36] It was a river and a search which appealed to men who were schooled in the classics. In 1790 James Bruce, an earlier traveller in quest of the Nile's source, commented that this was 'one of the few phenomena in natural history' that the ancient philosophers too had spent time investigating.

In addition to creating imaginative interest, colonial writers obtained verisimilitude by building on existing written accounts. Reflecting this process, Rider Haggard in *She* has the story of Ayesha or 'She' communicated to Horace Holly and Leo Vincey by letters, writings on a potsherd, and the written narrative of Leo's dead father. G. A. Henty, the author of any number of imperial adventure tales for 'young colonists' and other boys, drew on newspaper reports, histories, and explorers' diaries to authenticate his accounts of colonial wars and empire-building. Captain Marryat in *The Mission, or Scenes in Africa* (1846) padded a scanty plot involving shipwreck and racial anxiety with detailed accounts of big game hunting very obviously gleaned from first-hand sources, not his own.

Half a century later, in an 1898 letter, Conrad confessed to William Blackwood that the action of his Malayan stories was 'backed' by travellers' tales, and gleaned from 'dull, wise' sourcebooks, not from experience. Texts also shaped Conrad's personal expectations of the world beyond Europe. As he notes in *Last Essays* (1926), his early reading as a boy in land-locked Poland—about the Spanish *conquistadores*, Livingstone, and the rajas of Borneo—gave him a taste for travel and the sea. In fantasy he saw himself as another Crusoe, surviving with fortitude on remote islands.

It is in the light of this textuality of empire that the theoretical term *colonialist discourse* is probably best understood. Colonialist discourse can be taken to refer to that collection of symbolic practices, including textual codes and conventions and implied meanings, which Europe deployed in the process of its colonial expansion and, in particular, in understanding the bizarre and apparently untranslatable strangeness with which it came into contact. Its interpretations were an expression of its mastery, but they also reflected other responses: wonder, bewilderment, fear. Colonialist discourse, therefore, embraced a set of ideological approaches to expansion and foreign rule. Sometimes called orientalist or Africanist, depending on the categories of representation involved, colonialist discourses thus constituted the systems of cognition—interpretative screens, glass churches—which Europe used to found and guarantee its colonial authority.

Contemporary postcolonial theories of discourse are typically associated with the work of Michel Foucault and Louis Althusser, amongst others, concerning the involvement of textual practices in relations of power. Such theories were influentially brought to bear on colonial writing by Edward Said in his analysis of Orientalist discourse, *Orientalism* (1978). Orientalism in Said's interpretation is the body of knowledge on the basis of which Europe developed an image of the East to accompany and justify its territorial accumulations. His book explicates at length what I have shown happening above—the ways in which European linguistic conventions and epistemologies underpinned the conception, management, and control of colonial relationships. Contrary to the impression conveyed by Said's references to monolithic power, his reading of empire should not, however, rule out comeback and remonstrance from the colonized or subaltern.

An important tenet of colonialist discourse theory, therefore, holds that empire was governed as much by symbolism as by real distinctions in the world. That is to say, because colonial authority expressed its dominance in part through the medium of representation, a colonialist work of imagination functioned as an instrument of power. Crusoe, we remember, made a servant of Friday by attempting to convert him into a copy of himself. Crucially, colonialist constructions of the other as in need of civilization were used to justify the dispossession of natives. On a specifically literary level, the study of literature was advocated throughout the British Empire as a means of inculcating a sense of imperial loyalty in the colonized. Or as the Government of India under Lord Bentinck decided, in response to Macaulay's highly influential Minute of 1835: 'the great objects of British [rule in India] ought to be the promotion of European literature and science among the natives of India'. Fifty years later, Sir Richard Temple, once the Governor of Bombay, again emphasized the importance of educating the Indian élite. 'English or Western education', he stated in his memoirs, 'has greatly elevated the character of natives who have come within its influence'.[37]

The travelling metaphor

On the basis of what has been seen up till now, the British Empire can be described as an interconnected intertextual milieu at once far-reaching yet closely enmeshed. It was a network which made possible an exchange of symbolic languages and habits between writers in different parts of the imperial world. Metaphors that translated other lands and peoples developed into conventions of seeing and reading which moved not only between texts (and paintings) but between colonized regions also. In effect, colonization seeded across widely separate and vastly different territories cultural symbols which exhibited a remarkable synonymity.

This *transferability* of empire's organizing metaphors is one of the key distinguishing characteristics of colonialist discourse—one that made possible the intertextuality of writing under empire. Itinerant and adaptive, focusing colonial myths, activating imperialist energies, what I will call the *travelling metaphor* formed an essential constitutive element of an intensely imagined colonial system. Because of metaphorical movement between different places, colonial territories came to be interpreted, as it were, as a series of reflecting mirrors, which repeated, reinforced, and at times reversed (though within the same symbolic system) cultural significations emanating from England and Europe.

Kipling again provides a telling example. Though his own complicated achievement constantly pulls against stereotype, he himself was a maker of defining images. In his heyday, which was also the heyday of formal empire, his characterizations of colonial life became the medium through which the British viewed their work not only in India, Burma, and Ceylon, but in Africa also. Maud Diver in *The Englishwoman in India* (1909) spoke of the 'inimitable skill and truth' of his portraits of Anglo-Indian women. Leonard Woolf, it will be seen, discerned the shapes of Kipling's stories lurking behind the 1900s charade of European life in Ceylon. The ideal which Kipling's verse disseminated across the globe was of the Empire as a school of practical skills and unrewarded duty—an Empire, in short, in which one perfected the art of being imperial, regardless of setting. His conception of selfless imperial labour set the criteria of a colonial officer's success throughout the rest of the Empire. Australian writers of the 1890s took up Kiplingesque images of unforgiving graft on the colonial fringe. And his catch-phrases and definitive expressions— 'the white man's burden', 'East is East, and West is West, and never the twain shall meet', 'He has smote for us a pathway to the ends of all the Earth!', 'somewheres east of Suez'—became part of everyday colonialist idiom, as George Orwell pointed out in his essay 'Rudyard Kipling' (1946).

Other colonial vocabularies too showed evidence of interchangeability. Since Columbus's time, it had been a European practice to use the term 'Indian' to name all native peoples of the Americas and the Pacific. By metaphoric association based on their perceived difference, peoples as geographically and culturally far apart as Caribs and Maoris were cast in the same perceptual mould. So, too, the term 'nigger' used by Europeans in India was exported to Africa. The device of the travelling name again underlines that prevailing quality in colonial interpretation of sameness bridging difference. From the point of view of the power which distributed the dominant meanings, one set of colonized was pretty much like another. It was possible to find homogeneity in areas as far apart as India and the South Seas.

A colonial power made of its possessions homogeneous and parallel worlds. Though the metropolis was rarely the sole maker of definitions, it acted as though it were—the source of architectural styles and dress patterns, and also of names, scientific understanding, histories, texts, for all the Empire. In English literature, as Macaulay believed, the intellectual and imaginative wealth of the world was laid up. One image among many which colonial writing projected from the centre represented potentially fruitful lands as pastoral Edens, a multiplicity of English meadows. With the help of this particular figure, which cropped up wherever fertile lands were found to develop, the British sprinkled across the world, both in text and in fact, a whole collection of green spots. Ranging all the way from New Zealand and Tasmania to Simla in India, the Kenyan Highlands, Zomba plateau, and the Jamaican hills could be found replicas of the Kentish garden county, geographically far apart yet identified as similar. Kate Erlton in Flora Annie Steel's On the Face of the Waters (1897) grows heart's-ease and sweet peas in her Indian garden. Her 'cult of home' wards off the disturbing strangeness of her surroundings: 'she loved to grow her poor clumps of English annuals more than all the scented and blooming shrubs which . . . turned the garden into a wilderness of strange beauty.'

The way to manage alterity was to homogenize it. The same thing happens to an extent in contemporary tourism. Trying to tempt her to travel with him, Dick tells Maggie in The Light that Failed that the world is a plenitude of sensuous pleasures, 'orchids that make mouths at you', stupendous sights, places of languor and opalescent colour. These warm Lotus Lands could be the South Seas, or Central America, or parts of India. But from the point of view of England they form a single exotic space. A like homogeneity was attributed by Richard Burton to the 'Sotadic zone' of sexual depravity and 'confirmed cannibalism' which he believed engirdled the globe, embracing all warm countries in its sweep.[38]

On the basis of its capacity to remain stable despite its many migrations, it is possible to characterize the travelling colonial metaphor as operating, not unlike a gene, as a *carrier* of dominant conceptual characteristics. It might be creatively adapted to new contexts in the course of its migrations—'Indian' or 'garden' in the West Indies meant something very different from 'Indian' in India or 'garden' in Australia. But the metaphor did not essentially change in interpretative intention as it travelled. Whatever their metamorphoses, 'garden' and 'Indian' were ways of mapping the known to the unknown, mingling into that unknown meanings derived from a very different environment. It was by means of this carrier device therefore that colonialist discourse was able to reproduce itself from territory to territory, administration to administration.

As carriers, metaphors also related colonial writings genealogically the one to the other. For example, the paradigm of desperate and glorious adventure on board ship (also a parable of white exploration into the unknown) links *Westward Ho!* (1855) by Charles Kingsley to Captain Marryat's rather earlier popular sea fiction for boys, *Mr Midshipman Easy* (1836) and *Masterman Ready,* and to Stevenson's adventure fiction. The same set of motifs reappeared, sometimes in ironized form, in Conrad's tales of mariners' solidarity and crisis at sea.

The tendency to construct synonymic connections between different regions, even where these were not immediately in evidence, was in great part a function of imperialist superiority. But transference between very different colonial spaces was facilitated too by the horizontal distinctions which separated Europeans from others across the imperial world. Colonial officers were drawn from the like-minded enclaves of the British upper and middle classes, reinforced by racial barriers in the Empire. Forging their careers, they traced routes that were socially and geographically fixed. As in the iconic career of the colonial officer (and writer) Hugh Clifford, the experiences of one man would be little different from those of his similarly privileged colleagues.

The repetition-across-difference also stems from the sheer spread of colonial power. The expanse of the Empire, because vast, heterogeneous, and confusing, encouraged the exchange of the dependable stock images between widely separate cultural and geographic spaces, blurring their differences. Moreover, though always in the face of resistance, the colonizer's aim was to impose a monopoly on discourse. Colonial spaces—from company offices to the guest-rooms of government houses to the libraries of hill-stations—became flooded with the same kinds of literature. The imaginations of readers across the British Empire were led along parallel grooves.

There was also the Raj, which functioned as practically an Empire on its own. Because of its size and importance, British India was not only central to the process of generating images of rule. The Raj itself made up a vast structure of social interconnections. In the

Indian Empire, said Kipling, 'You can never be sure of getting rid of a friend or an enemy till he or she dies' ('On the Strength of a Likeness', *Plain Tales from the Hills*). Everywhere India was held up as the example according to which others should build. Chiselled into the memorable shapes of Kipling's stories and poems, Indian images made up a rich source from which the greater Empire drew models of imperial power as well as its architectural designs. It was here, we now know, that the image of the gentleman colonial officer was honed. In the 1900s Lord Lugard sought to organize the administration of Northern Nigeria following the example of the Raj.

In sum, the global system of British imperial communications rested on a combination of factors: the social position of colonial officers, soldiers, and writers coupled with their geographic mobility; the need to translate foreignness into comprehensible terms; the energizing influence of the Raj; and the emphasis on book-learning among the ruling élite (as opposed, say, to the military prowess demanded by other European empires). To quote Kipling again: the Empire's great 'Knowability' rested on the fact that after twenty years' service, a man 'knows, or knows something about, every Englishman in the Empire and may travel anywhere and everywhere without paying hotel-bills' ('The Phantom 'Rickshaw', *The Man who would be King*). Even at its height the Indian Civil Service numbered its men in hundreds rather than in thousands. Itinerant as they were between corners of the Empire as far removed from one another as they were from Britain, men in the colonial services formed a relatively small group which itself forged the interconnections between regions.[39]

The careers of high-ranking officials exemplify these link-ups. The following list is representative but far from exhaustive. Sir Bartle Frere saw service as Councillor of the Governor-General in Calcutta (1858–62), and as Governor both in Bombay (1862–6) and in the Cape Colony (1877–80). As a Fellow of the Royal Geographic Society from 1867 he supported the African expeditions of both Livingstone and Stanley. Lord Kitchener served armies and administrations in Egypt, South Africa, the Sudan, and India. Lord Alfred Milner graduated from the position of Under-Secretary to the Ministry of Finance in Egypt, to High Commissioner of the Cape Colony at the time of the South African War. The British army itself saw action right across the Empire. Thousands of white volunteers came from Australia, Canada,

New Zealand, Ceylon, and other colonial possessions to fight against the Boers in South Africa.

Travelling officials could also be reporters of one sort or another, who recorded their observations of a new place in writing before moving on to another. Sir George Grey, whose career spanned the governorships of South Australia (from 1841), New Zealand (from 1845, and 1861–7, where he was a collector of Maori artefacts), and the Cape Colony (from 1854), explored Western Australia as a young man and kept a journal of his experiences. Governor Edward John Eyre of Jamaica traced a similar early career path, beginning as a magistrate and an explorer in southern Australia, where he published *Discoveries in Central Australia* (1845). Thereafter he took up positions as Lieutenant-Governor of New Zealand, under George Grey, Lieutenant-Governor of St Vincent (from 1854), replacement Governor in Antigua (1859), and finally Governor of Jamaica. It was Eyre who ordered the violent repression of the 1865 rebellion in that colony. Lord Frederick Lugard, the advocate of Indirect Rule during his period of authority in Nigeria, served in the Afghan War of 1878–80, in the Sudan (1885), in the Burmese Expedition of 1886, and in Nyasaland (1888). While working as the representative of the British East Africa Company in Uganda (1889–92), he set up a vigorous campaign for the development of this part of the Empire. Robert Baden-Powell, founder of the Scout Movement and author of the definitive manual for imperial boyhood, *Scouting for Boys* (1908), was known for his role during the siege of Mafeking, for which he was prepared by army training in India, and involvement in the Ashanti, or Asante, Expedition (1895–6) and the Matabele War (1896–7). Empire, as is clear from these biographical details, involved a fair amount of fighting with colonized peoples, often uninvited by them.

But the wide-ranging colonial careers of governors were by no means unique. Colonial writers too had experience of different parts of the world. Like explorers, they were sometimes acquainted with one another, and this again strengthened the interpretative connections between regions. Captain Marryat's long naval career took him from the First Burmese War of 1824–6 to Canada and the West Indies. R. M. Ballantyne worked for the Hudson's Bay Company. G. A. Henty was a war correspondent covering campaigns in West Africa and Central Asia. Rider Haggard was closely involved in the 1877 British annexation of the Transvaal. The friends Henley and Stevenson collaborated as writers. Kipling in his capacity as reporter and imperial raconteur travelled widely throughout the Empire. In Cecil John Rhodes, whom he met in South Africa, Kipling found an embodiment of his own colonial ideals. Rhodes in turn called him the 'purveyor' of his vision.

Kipling's 'The Mark of the Beast' (*Life's Handicap*) describes a New Year's Eve party where men from the uttermost ends of the Indian Empire foregather, and from which they will again disperse, some to annex Burma, 'and some tried to open up the Soudan and were opened up by Fuzzies in the cruel scrub outside Suakim'. With the Scramble for Africa, old India 'hands', veterans of the Mutiny or of the Indian Civil Service, spread out to this or that new tropical possession to help with the job of colonization. In Africa the resourceful men of the old Empire of India, it was said, could continue the good work of administrating natives. It was predictable that these men, continually coming together and dispersing, dependent on one another for company, would tend to see one place in terms of another, and to exchange assessments and terms of description along the way.

In distant lands, Conrad wrote in the 1895 Preface to *Almayer's Folly*, life comprises more than 'a yell and a war dance', yet 'the dazzled [European] eye misses the delicate detail'. In India, Kipling agreed, 'There are no half-tints worth noticing' (*Plain Tales from the Hills*). In her Preface to *The Story of an African Farm*, Olive Schreiner observed that tales of wild adventure in Africa depended on a view projected from afar, from 'Piccadilly or the Strand', untrammelled by the grey facts of the everyday. To the extent that it relied on the projection of interchangeable, standard-issue images, colonial perception finds a final correlate in the magic lantern show sometimes used by European travellers to impress or intimidate natives. Although travelling very light, David Livingstone carried with him on his journey to the Angolan coast a magic lantern, 'a never-failing source of interest and instruction': 'the simple savages never tired of looking at the pictures, many of them travelling miles to see them' (*Missionary Travels*). In similar vein, Mary Kingsley describes the French explorer De Brazza as distracting a group of hostile-looking Fans by 'arranging for a pyrotechnic display to take place without human aid'.[40] And in Henty's *By Sheer Pluck: A Tale of the Ashanti* (1884), Goodenough and his party placate a tribe of 'cannibal Fans' by impressing them with a chemistry show and magic lantern display featuring elephants and ships.

To colonize the world, British writers both in the field and at home projected their images, like the lantern's plates of coloured glass, on lands they claimed as new. The same images did for different places. Projection was a mode of cognition and of exerting influence across different colonial possessions. The context might change but the show itself was not adapted to suit local conditions. However, as the next two chapters will suggest, such images were not always effective in entirely blocking out the local backdrop. Glass churches could crack and magic lanterns fail. And, most disruptively, the 'savages' who stepped out of the background to show their interest in the white man's artefacts were simultaneously offering their own interpretations of the colonial caravanserai.

Further Reading

Thomas Assad, *Three Victorian Travellers: Burton, Blunt, Doughty* (Routledge & Kegan Paul, 1964).

Syed Hussein Alatas, *The Myth of the Lazy Native* (Frank Cass, 1977).

C. A. Bayly, *Imperial Meridian: The British Empire and the World 1780–1830* (Harlow: Longman, 1989).

Robin Blackburn, *The Overthrow of Colonial Slavery 1776–1848* (Verso, 1989).

Neil Charlesworth, *British Rule and the Indian Economy 1800–1914* (Macmillan, 1982).

Linda Colley, *Britons: Forging the Nation 1701–1837* (BCA, 1992).

Philip D. Curtin, *Death by Migration* (Cambridge UP, 1989).

Lance E. Davis and Robert Huttenback, *Mammon and the Pursuit of Empire* (Cambridge UP, 1986).

Geoffrey Dutton, *The Hero as Murderer: The Life of Edward John Eyre, Australian Explorer and Governor of Jamaica 1815–1901* (Collins, 1967).

David Ellis and James Walvin, *The Abolition of the Atlantic Slave Trade* (Madison: University of Wisconsin Press, 1981).

Eric Hobsbawm, *The Age of Empire 1875–1914* (Weidenfeld & Nicolson, 1987).

Peter Hopkirk, *The Great Game: On Secret Service in High Asia* (Oxford UP, 1991).

Ronald Hyam, *Britain's Imperial Century 1815–1914: A Study of Empire and Expansion* (Macmillan, 1993).

Denis Judd, *Empire: The British Imperial Experience, from 1765 to the Present* (Fontana, 1996).

Rana Kabbani, *Europe's Myths of the Orient* (Macmillan, 1986).

Suvir Kaul, *Poems of Nation, Anthems of Empire: English Verse in the Long Eighteenth Century* (Charlottesville: University of Virginia Press, 2000).

V. G. Kiernan, *European Empires from Conquest to Collapse* (Leicester UP and Fontana, 1982).

Ania Loomba and Martin Orkin (eds.), *Post-Colonial Shakespeares* (Routledge, 1998).

P. J. Marshall, *East Indian Fortunes: The British in Bengal in the Eighteenth Century* (Oxford UP, 1976).

Jan Morris, *Pax Britannica* (Faber, 1968).

Thomas Pakenham, *The Scramble for Africa 1876–1912* (Weidenfeld & Nicolson, 1991).

Lydia Potts, *The World Labour Market: A History of Migration* (Zed, 1990).

Walter Rodney, *How Europe Underdeveloped Africa* (Bogle L'Ouverture Publications, 1972).

Hugh Tinker, *A New System of Slavery: The Export of Indian Labour Overseas 1830–1920* (Oxford UP, 1974).

Gauri Viswanathan, *Masks of Conquest: Literary Study and British Rule in India* (Faber, 1990).

Eric Williams, *Capitalism and Slavery* (New York: Russell & Russell, 1961).

Eric Wolf, *Europe and the People without History* (Berkeley: University of California Press, 1982).

2

Colonialist Concerns

and as for the country, that marvellous kaleidoscope of ever-changing colours, it was merely a backdrop against which we existed in a manner that was to resemble as closely as possible the life of an English country gentleman in early Victorian England.
John Morris, *Eating the Indian Air*, 1968

'thou wilt return to the bold white *mem-log*, for kind calls to kind . . . in thy very death thou wilt be taken to a strange place and a paradise that I do not know.'
Rudyard Kipling, 'Without Benefit of Clergy', *Life's Handicap*, 1891

And so everywhere they went they turned it into England; and everybody they met they turned English. But no place could ever really be England, and nobody who did not look exactly like them would ever be English.
Jamaica Kincaid, *A Small Place*, 1988

The late imperial hero: *Lord Jim*

Having looked at broad trends and patterns in colonial writing in Chapter 1, I now turn to colonialist literature specifically: that is, the literature—narrative is the preferred form—more directly concerned with colonial experience. Such writing revolves constantly, even obsessively, around certain key themes: the introversion of the colonial mission, or *colonial drama*; the masculine aspect of that drama; the representation of other peoples; and the resistant incomprehensibility or unreadability of the colonized beyond.

By way of opening, a discussion of Joseph Conrad's sceptical novel of the late British Empire, *Lord Jim* (1900), will help to single out a number of the central preoccupations of colonialist writing under high imperialism, the period which defines my main area of concern. A Polish *émigré* who grew up under the shadow of Russian imperialism, Conrad wrote several stories and novels which engage with the matter of formal empire: 'An Outpost of Progress' in *Tales of Unrest* (1898), *Lord Jim*, 'Heart of Darkness' (1899). The slightly later *Nostromo* (1904) explores the relentless drive of new American imperialism to expand its material interests while *Victory* (1915) is a *Tempest*-tale of warped imperial purpose. Of these works, 'Heart of Darkness' has been most intensively discussed as a colonialist narrative. Like the *Arabian Nights*, it is now taken as paradigmatic. However, the reputation of 'Heart of Darkness' has tended to overshadow Conrad's other powerful tales dealing with life in colonial outposts. *Lord Jim* is revealing not only for underscoring the contradictions of the 'civilizing' mission exposed in 'Heart of Darkness' (which too is a Marlow narrative). It is interesting also for its wary if admiring attitude to heroic adventure in a maturing Empire. Jim, who wishes always to be 'an example of devotion to duty, and as unflinching as a hero in a book', is in fact flawed. He is a colonial idealist who, unlike his many predecessors in adventure fiction, cannot act. In the drama of colonialist self-making, the European realized himself by imposing his rule on another culture. The experiment fails calamitously in Jim's case.

Though a contemporary of Kipling, Conrad temperamentally belonged to a later historical moment—a moment in which colonial possession had become more problematic, raising spectres of European cultural failure. Published a year before *Kim*, *Lord Jim* is far less confident in its treatment of colonial mastery. The imperialism which in *Kim* is a Great Game, becomes in *Lord Jim* a troubling question of white honour. Reduced to inaction by the contemplation of beautiful dreams, and suffering intense self-consciousness, Jim is unmistakably a figure of the *fin de siècle*, if not of early modernism. Like Robert Louis Stevenson in his 1890s tales of the South Seas, and also in *Dr Jekyll and Mr Hyde* (1886), Conrad suspected a primitive and demoralizing other to reside within the white. *Lord Jim* can be seen as a defining tale of the doubt which threatened the project of European expansion.

Like Kipling's Kim, Jim is a young protagonist, concerned to define his own identity, enthusiastic about training for imperial service, and convinced of his ability 'to shine'. The novel begins with the aftermath of his abandoning the steamer *Patna*, on which he was serving as mate. Yet despite his culpability in this event—what Marlow calls his 'criminal weakness'—Jim believes that disgrace cannot ultimately stain him. His middle-class 'decency' and his status as 'one of us', a member of the British merchant marine, guarantees his blamelessness. And indeed, after a period of ignominy, Marlow and his contact Stein, another idealist, are willing to believe in Jim enough to give him a second chance. He is appointed as the representative of European commercial ventures in the Malayan archipelago.

The second part of Marlow's tale deals with Jim's time on the island of Patusan. Here, as on the steamer, his task is to exercise authority over a darker race, portrayed as less disciplined and in need of leadership. It is also his second chance to re-create himself in the *Boy's Own* image of his adolescent dreams. For a time he succeeds in fashioning a new biography of success. To the people on the island he becomes Tuan Jim—Lord Jim—a title of respect.

Aptly if somewhat ominously, Marlow several times points to the fictional aspects of Jim's undertaking. On Patusan Jim becomes the author of his own romantic hero story. The island has given him 'a totally new set of conditions for his imaginative faculty to work upon'. A 'legend of strength and prowess [forms] round his name'. His is a narrative of high adventure, a colonial drama which takes place on the archetypal Robinsonian setting for that drama, a tropical island. All the requisite elements of romance, daring, and danger are present: the ring given as token of trust, the noble native warrior, the degenerate white man who is a betrayer, and the threatened heroine, a half-caste 'princess' called Jewel. And as does Crusoe, Jim names the native to whom he is closest and she learns to speak like him.

To Marlow such successes have the look of a fine tale, 'something you read of in books': 'Romance [has] singled Jim for its own'. However, it is clear that for Marlow the aspect of romance does not inspire confidence. There is something questionable about a man's attempt to set a personal ideal of romantic glory above all else, including his responsibility to others. In 'Heart of Darkness' the degenerate Kurtz represents the malaise of the conquering West—the races that in Marlow's terms 'have emerged from the gloom' yet remain seduced by the crude appeal of power. As with Kurtz, Jim's fate symbolizes the dangers of the colonial mission, that self-regarding 'jump into the unknown' propelled by fantasy and cultural hubris.

It is not too surprising, therefore, that Jim fails to fulfil his romantic dreams a second time. His self-made legend is rendered fragile because of its ideological underpinnings. Not unlike Kim who despite all his dissembling is said to remain a sahib, Jim does not lose his European sense of self, though he is declared lord of his eastern island. He uses the local population to prove himself, but from his point of view their respect can ultimately be only second-rate. As demonstrated by Jim's dilemma, no matter how far afield it was performed, the drama of colonial heroism—which included Kipling's 'building great works for the good of the land' ('Only a Subaltern', *The Man who would be King*, 1987)—took western values for its standards of success. In this drama, natives remained natives: the simple children and the subtle savages in opposition to whom the colonialist defined his selfhood, first as a European, one of a 'superior kind', but also as a man. For masculinity too characterized colonialist action. As we see in Marlow's strong identification with Jim, which outlasts his suspicion and bafflement, the close bonds of a race-exclusive Empire were also strongly homosocial.

As comparison with other colonialist fictions demonstrates, Jim's predicament is the extreme example that tests a rule. Like any displaced European's, his life-narrative is split: his personal ideals remain centred in Europe but his experience is set on the colonial periphery. On the one hand, there is the authority defined in relationship with the native population; on the other, there is the self-consciously superior white man, in search of European approval, believing himself disconnected from native life. Significantly, when a group of unscrupulous Europeans comes to seek Jim out, he responds to them as of his own kind, with fatal consequences. The co-operation, even if superficial, loses him the trust of the island community.

Until the end of Jim's tale, Marlow continues in theory at least to uphold the ethics of group-loyalty and self-control that safeguard the western civilization he believes in. The same goes for his creator. Though empire in certain of its forms was aberrant, for Conrad the values on which the cultural mission of a colonizing Europe was built were not ultimately in question. But, at the same time, any reading of his work must allow for the ambiguity of his representations.

Alongside the prevailing belief in the people who have emerged from the gloom, there are also his character studies in the pride and self-delusion on which racial superiority rested. *Lord Jim* exposes the tautology of the colonial hero ideal—the assumption that the British hero is great because British, because 'one of us'.

Marlow comments revealingly that the colonial dream, the fanciful 'empire' of 'recklessly heroic aspirations'—though held for 'the sake of better morality' and 'the greater profit', and though sustained by a myth of the white man's worth—is in fact based on a fundamental hypocrisy. Apparently selfless acts—the civilizing mission, the expansion of responsible authority—are motivated by a 'sublimated, idealized selfishness'. But not only that. White colonial identity, the self manifested in the colonial drama, is also split and therefore critically weak. The European in the Empire rejects the native, yet he also requires the native's presence in order to experience to the full his own being as a white colonialist.

The colonial drama

To present-day readers, the worlds represented in colonialist fiction may seem strangely empty of indigenous characters. Although set in Borneo or Patagonia, the ventures and adventures of the colonizers, of white men, make up most of the important action. The available drama is *their* drama. Almost without exception there is no narrative interest without European involvement or intervention.

In the far corners of the Empire, the New Brightons and New Londons, the British introduced their language, methods of town planning, upholstery, cuisine, ways of dress, which were believed, as a matter of course, to be superior to other cultural forms. Churches and esplanades were constructed in imitation of parish churches and beach fronts back home. Plans for Houses of Parliament followed the lines of official buildings in the old country. True, certain foods and architectural styles were hybrid and syncretic. For example, Indo-Saracenic architecture, which was used during the later Raj for the construction of railway buildings and colleges, mixed and matched 'Hindoo' features—high-pitched roofs—and 'Mahommedan forms' — cusped heads of windows and stone arches—with 'the usefulness of scientific European design'.[1] But under the Empire such hybrids were represented as peculiarly a part of British colonial culture, safely adapted for use by the English, or, more specifically, in the case of the architecture, set up as an expression of British imperial magnitude and expertise.

Colonialist narratives participated in and reflected this imperial self-absorption, perhaps more prominently so than did other colonial writings, such as travellers' tales. In this way, therefore, as well as stimulating imperial fantasy, British colonialist fiction helped sanction and supervise—if anxiously, even paranoically—the demarcations of imperial power. Narrative presented a world in which British rule was accepted as part of the order of things: the natives were governed as they should be; the Queen Empress was on her throne; there was no question that her people occupied a central place in history. In this world, it almost goes without saying, British meanings and values were paramount. Everything of worth in the Empire, necessarily, was said to be British-made, created 'with a garnish of Red Sauce' (Kipling, 'On the City Wall', *The Man who would be King*). In the fiction—as in colonial existence—interest was grounded chiefly in the spaces of the cantonment, Civil Lines, European quarter, or hill-station. Regardless of geographic location, everyday life unfolded as a long procession of middle-class English social rituals. Stories are laden with tea-times, club life, sports, 'Gardens or bands or amusements', and their associated etiquette and patterns of behaviour. In a comment that is notable also for its nod at the British emulation of the Romans, Thackeray perceptively observed: 'Those who know the English colonies abroad, know that we carry with us our pride, pills, prejudices, Harvey-sauces, cayenne-peppers, and other Lares, making a little Britain wherever we settle down' (*Vanity Fair*, 1847–8).

In this paradoxically confined world of the Empire, any conflict which emerged would always in the first place have to do with the colonizer, with his attempt to shape his world in his image. His drama, the colonial drama, *was* the narrative. Narrative endorsed the struggles and triumphs of his self-making. Were further justification of his importance and authority needed, the irrelevance, contemptibility, or sheer unintelligibility of *that* world of the natives would demonstrate that *this* one was worthy of the greater interest. Many of the dominant, *constitutive motifs* of the colonialist narrative or drama which are reviewed in this section embody this sense of imperial centrality and certainty: the imagery of the racial divide and the dangers of cross-cultural contact; of the vigorous youth, and the technological and administrative proficiency of the European; and of the colonial gaze.

William Arnold's *Oakfield* (1853), a study of the white man in British India, highlights the exclusive focus of the colonialist narrative. The novel delivers a strong indictment of the moral character of the East India Company officers. Throughout the long tale Indians themselves are no more than massed, shadowy figures in the background. In fact, the non-European environment plays a part in the narrative only in so far as it corrupts. According to Arnold, the officers' unprincipled and dissolute behaviour is not out of keeping with the dull vacancy of all life in India. But it is European life which forms the centre of interest. As an officer comments, beyond official relations with sepoys and servants, the men 'see really nothing of the people'. There is 'an inconceivable separation' between 'us few English' and 'those Asiatics'.[2]

In like manner, in *Kim*, Kipling's treasure chest of imperialist mythologies, the boy hero is represented as occupying 'the middle' of the various Indian worlds he inhabits. He is indigenous to India and yet external to it because white. Whether travelling the Grand Trunk Road or plotting as part of the Great Game, he is in command of the scene, aware of all that is happening, 'more awake and more excited than anyone'. His Indian friends, the Pathan horse dealer Mahbub Ali, or the Bengali Hurree Chunder Mookerjee, never occupy centre stage in the same way. Vividly characterized as they are, Indians take on importance in the novel in so far as they exist in relationship with Kim, or in relation to their work for the Great Game, the Secret Service of British India. Again, in Rider Haggard's *She* (1887), the object of the quest undertaken by Holly and Leo Vincey is the ageless Ayesha, the white queen who lives at the heart of Africa, in the Caves of Kôr. In the core of darkness these men seek their own race image and origin.

To be sure, Philip Meadows Taylor's *Confessions of a Thug* (1838) and some of Kipling's short stories, such as 'In Flood Time' and 'Dray Wara Yow Dee' (*The Man who would be King*), do involve colonized protagonists and first-person narrators (as did the Bengali novels which had begun to emerge in the course of the nineteenth century).

Nonetheless, the rationale for the telling is provided by the implied European audience. The narrative frame and context, however qualified, remain those of the colonizer. In general, therefore, colonialist literature offers the spectacle of a society reproducing itself, ceaselessly representing to itself its own history and beliefs, repeatedly asserting its invincibility. This is so even where, as was briefly suggested in the first chapter, colonized peoples express resistance or indifference to colonial authority.

Thackeray's 'little Britains' may have been stratified by their own internal caste, class, and religious divisions, but in relation to the outside world, the native presence, they operated as a single unit. Perhaps the most binding imperative of colonial life was to stick to one's own. In E. M. Forster's *A Passage to India* (1924), Mr Turton observes: 'I have never known anything but disaster result when English people and Indians attempt to be intimate socially.' As we shall see again, keeping to oneself bore an openly racialized and sexualized aspect. In the Anglo-Indian novel and short story, contact between the races, in particular sexual contact, invariably brings trouble in its wake. At the time when Social Darwinist ideas were popular, it was generally believed that consort with dark peoples compromised white selfhood and threatened race purity. Especially in the second half of the nineteenth century, the post-Mutiny period, colonizers strove to maintain a strict divide between themselves and the local population. No matter how hard those who had been colonized might try to Europeanize themselves, colonial society whether in India or elsewhere was built upon this fundamental separation. There was, said Flora Annie Steel, an 'inevitable antagonism' between black and white (*On the Face of the Waters*, 1897).

Because the racial divide was so essential to sustaining notions of white superiority, even a slight modification of the rules of association—whether within the white community or in dealings with the local population—would threaten the structures which upheld the entire system. Indeed, for much of the later nineteenth century, any alternative to the command of the 'Supreme Government', as Kipling put it, was declared unthinkable—was either silenced or outlawed. Predictably, local self-government, a Kipling narrator comments, 'has destroyed the greater part of a native's respect for a Sahib' ('The Strange Ride of Morrowbie Jukes', *The Man who would be King*). An independent India, therefore, could be nothing more than a 'pretty' idea. In the story 'On the City Wall', though the Englishman unwittingly helps the ageing rebel Khem Singh to escape, the potential weakness in the system represented by that act is neutralized when the rebel gives himself up again. It turns out that Khem Singh is not merely attracted by the comforts—the aniseed brandy and 'nice warm bedding'—of a British prison. He has also discovered, significantly, that the days of rebellion are over: young men nowadays are joining 'native regiments or Government offices'. They seem more interested in receiving 'education of the English variety' than they are in revolt. British rule is once again confirmed in its inimitable sturdiness and rightness.

However, despite colonialist self-assertions of this sort, despite their manifest need for self-validation, it is important to acknowledge, if at this point only in passing, that European writers did at certain times and on certain occasions take account of the disturbing and/or creative potential represented by an encounter with the beyond. Once injected into the new environment, European cultural references could produce a very different complex of meanings from what had originally been intended. From the first days of colonization began the *mis*-translation or *imperfect copying* of cultural signifiers which forms a germinal impulse in postcolonial rewritings of colonial experience. But for colonialist writers, too, the migration and mutation of meaning could be a source of narrative or poetic interest. As an illustration, in Kipling's story 'False Dawn' (*Plain Tales from the Hills*), the social ritual of the riding-picnic is adapted to the Indian hot weather season by taking place at night and by moonlight. From this slippage, further confusion follows, in the manner of a midsummer night's dream. Lovers' identities are muddled and the codes of courtship seriously broken. 'It was like a scene in a theatre,' the narrator revealingly comments, 'I never knew anything so un-English in my life'.

Imperial confidence notwithstanding, the sense that standards and certainties could easily warp under pressure of an alien environment pervades colonialist writing. There was always the doubt that the British white man might not be fully in control. This was the negative interpretation of the possibility of mutation in foreign lands. Despite efforts at containment, the fear of other cultures, or of the primitive, found its way into texts, cropping up in all manner of images of *contamination*, infection, and bewitching. Constant anxiety was expressed about the degeneration allegedly caused not only by direct encounters with natives, but by the proximity to savage passions, or simply by the malign influence of the alien environment. In Anglo-Indian writing, in the work of Flora Annie Steel, Alice Perrin, and Maud Diver, for example, a major threat to life as it should be lived takes the form of the ennui and 'waste of nerve force' that accompanies Indian heat, dust, and disease. English men and women in India are plagued by encroaching tedium, 'an all-pervading atmosphere of inertia' and a miasmic 'tendency to fatalism', which corrodes their idealism and sense of connection with the home country. A later section examines in greater depth the representation of the other in colonial writing. What is important to note here is that, confident self-projections to the contrary, the confusions of the wild always retained the power to creep back into the colonial picture.

Where orderly empire was justified by the ability to work, idleness too was regarded as infinitely corrupting. In the colonial drama, anxiety at excessive relaxation, and the paralysing consequences of the languid life of the East, weigh heavily. Memorably, the serpent that lurked in the lotus-lands of the Pacific was ease, with its many attendant threats to physical and moral well-being. (In reality, the transmission of infections, including venereal diseases such as gonorrhoea and syphilis, was usually in the other direction, moving from European to, say, South Pacific Islander.) Conrad plays on the images and associations of South-East Asian idleness in Lord Jim. In Stevenson's 'The Ebb-Tide' (1893), the easy life on the far colonial periphery has become the refuge of demoralized Europeans. Both here and in 'The Beach of Falesá' (1892) any lingering desire to work is obstructed by native taboos or by the practices of already degenerate white men.

In contrast to these anxieties, in many a colonial drama, especially in the adventure tale, the *youth of the hero* served as a correlate for imperial energies and enterprise. Whether sailor, soldier, castaway, cadet, or trader, the young male hero was portrayed as a British 'lad of spirit', 'full of life and energy', who from an early age proved his integrity and fearlessness. For example, Jim Walsham in G. A. Henty's *With Wolfe in Canada* (1887) rescues men from a stormy sea as a young boy (whereas Jim in *Lord Jim* of course fails to do so). In their choice of youthful protagonists in *Lord Jim* and *Kim*, both Conrad and Kipling are very obviously positioned within this tradition of colonialist representation. Kim has not grown beyond adolescence when the novel ends. Jim dies while still a young man. Their timeless youth underlines the apparently unchanging or homogeneous temporal space imperial rule strove to create—a space in which change to the status quo was to be resisted.

In a world pervaded by Social Darwinist thinking, the young hero also symbolized the vitality of the so-called new races, poised at the evolutionary cutting edge. An emissary of progress, he embodied the best of the West, its life-force and virility, and also its much-acclaimed *rationality*, restraint, technological prowess, moral earnestness. In *Kim*, the young hero's chameleon-like abilities signify inventiveness, and acute powers of observation, essential qualities for the Empire builder and Secret Service spy. Kim uniquely raises faking and shape-changing to a near-perfect art form, but his resourcefulness he shares with other boy heroes of adventure fiction. Henty's Jim Walsham (*With Wolfe in Canada*), Charlie Marryat (*With Clive in India*, 1884), and Gregory Hilliard (*With Kitchener in the Soudan*, 1903) are involved in spying, decoding, and subterfuge, and like Kim are able to 'pass as natives'.

Most definitive perhaps as an organizing or concept-metaphor in colonialist narrative was the commanding perspective assumed by the European in the text, or what is called the *colonial gaze*.[3] The gaze was made manifest in the activities of investigation, examination, inspection, peeping, poring over, which were accompaniments to the colonial penetration of a country. In ethnographic description and scientific study, in the curious scrutiny of the colonized by the colonizer, there was much of the attitude of the voyeur as well as of the map-maker. In writing, the gaze appears as bird's-eye description, and is embodied in the high vantage point or knowledgeable position taken up by a writer or traveller as he re-creates a scene. In a review Edmund Gosse aptly described Kipling's art as 'a new kind of terrible and enchanting peepshow . . . we crowd round him begging for "just one more look" '.

Jim is pictured by Marlow on heights, white and solitary, removed from the people he rules, surveying them. The drama of the novel does not concern their lives but Jim's attempt to overcome past error in ruling them. His gazing, then, is part of what he must do to take their measure, to learn how best to manage them. To the same extent as the gaze depended on the colonizer's position in charge of a total system, it was also a potent expression of that position. To govern was to know; to see in the round, panoptically. From the first, in travellers' tales and explorers' journals, and then, more intensively, in eighteenth-century projects to classify all life on earth, the European cast himself as elevated observer, an arch-investigator in relation to whom the whole world was an object of scrutiny. Napoleon's invasion of Egypt in 1798, too, was prototypical as a project of in-depth examination. Napoleon founded an entire academy, the Institut d'Égypte, to accompany the expedition, its brief being to open the country—its languages, history, religion, society—to the searching light of European scholarship.

It became habitual for Europe to approach other cultures as *objects of study*, bodies of knowledge to assemble and to bring into shape. One memorable incident on his 1860–3 journey with James Grant to Lake Tanganyika was Speke's attempt to measure the 'milk-fed' proportions of the wife of the King of Buganda. The imagery of looking and measurement structures his description of the event. After first '[obtaining] a good view of her naked', Speke in his shirt-sleeves executed what he refers to as an 'engineering' process, taking the measurements of the woman's arms, thighs, and so on. As in so many other like situations involving western science and African bodies, what underlay the experiment, clearly, was the European's assumed right to scrutinize an African in this way.[4]

The interest in poring over others was seemingly inexhaustible. In colonial exhibitions towards the end of the nineteenth century entire native villages were put on show. In 1816 the precedent for such human displays had been set when Sarah Bartmann, a Khoi woman (called the Hottentot Venus), was exhibited to public audiences in Paris and London. Like Speke, Burton also took liberties on his 1850s journeys to Medina and Mecca, in disguise, and to the closed Somali city of Harar in East Africa. The description of the Mecca experience in particular represents the gaze both as conquest and as a form of research. While experiencing intense pride at gaining access to the forbidden, Burton also indulges his empirical curiosity: the black Kaaba, he 'narrowly observes', is made of 'an aerolite' (*Personal Narrative of a Pilgrimage* , 1854).[5] Both this and the Speke account, involving respectively sacred site and body, combined an attitude of scientific scrutiny with the sexualized challenge of the taboo.

The colonial look as authority made manifest, therefore, was also represented in motifs of *research*, scientific study, documentation, and survey. From the mid-eighteenth century, the European at large in colonial territory had seen himself in the character of the disinterested scientist, the rational and neutral gatherer of knowledge. Indeed the utilitarian James Mill, author of the influential *History of British India* (1817), justified his ability to pronounce on India by claiming that the subcontinent could best be understood by an informed outsider, one who had *never* visited India, such as himself.[6]

Colonialist fiction acknowledged the authority which the European scrutinizer wielded by giving narrative form to anthropological findings. In *Confessions of a Thug*, narrated 'for the information of those in England', the details which emerge are intended to satisfy the listening Englishman's appetite for local custom, and to provide the kind of knowledge that will make colonial rule more effective. In his 1858 Preface, Taylor remarked that the book was written as both an ethnological and a political study, 'to expose, as fully as I was able, the practices of the Thugs'. Horace Holly in *She* details some of the customs of the Amahagger tribe. The people, described as degenerate, act as a foil for the power and sophistication of 'She'. Colonel Creighton, Kim's mentor, is at once an ethnologist and a member of the Government of India Secret Service—the two roles are portrayed as complementary. Though his native-born and Irish origins do not give him the most pukka racial credentials, Kim himself accedes to a white tradition of overlordship in becoming part of the Great Game of British espionage. His job is to gather information while accompanying the lama on his spiritual search.[7]

Indian life in *Kim* is as rich and varied as are the myriad spectacles on the Trunk Road. Yet British authority, of which Kim is a part, is able to embrace this vastness within the grids of its bureaucracy and its intelligence and transport networks—the structures of its gaze. It is fitting within the terms of the novel that Kim's position as a European allows him the freedom to understand Indian culture in two ways, as a native, especially when in disguise, and yet as a detached observer. His eyes, like those of any European scrutinizer, sweep confidently and knowingly over the Trunk Road or the Himalayas. In like fashion, he has the power to ventriloquize the cacophony of Indian society, equipped by his ability to interpret different castes and sects in a manner that outwits Indians themselves. In ways that would be impossible for an Indian in Kipling's world, adolescent and omnicompetent Kim embodies British imperial authority. There may, certainly, be some tension buried in the sheer excess of his shape-changing—an implication that India can be thus contained in fantasy only. But undeniably he also represents an exuberant high imperial confidence, at once signifying and comprehending all-India.

For 'big and little boys'

The British Empire, it is plain to see, was a man's world, much more emphatically so than was Victorian patriarchal society back in Britain. From the beginning of the Empire, the expanding colonies had offered the 'mother country' a practice and testing ground for its manhood. Kipling's Raj, as he commented when a young journalist in Lahore, was filled with 'picked men at their definite work'. At every level, men ran the colonies.

To say so, of course, may be to state the obvious. Yet the masculinity of the Empire determined the character of colonial activity including writing in so many ways, that it is worth examining more closely. As Ruskin clearly saw, the fact was that England sent its 'energetic and worthiest' *sons*, its knights, not its daughters, to found colonies 'as fast and far as she [was] able' (Inaugural Lecture, 1870). 'How little our women know about India', the missionary Robin Alden comments in Edward Thompson's *A Farewell to India* (1931).[8] In out-of-the-way District Commissioners' offices as in big game hunting or in the gymkhana clubs of colonial towns, the forms of relationship and codes of behaviour were overwhelmingly masculine. As the fiction of the Empire shows, colonial society may have involved romance and love intrigue, but interest in such matters was passing when compared with the preoccupation of 'the day's work' performed by white men. Indeed, Robert Baden-Powell based the ethos of the Scout Movement on the belief that colonial frontier life was guaranteed to train boys to be *manly* men.

Illuminating research has been done in recent years on women's writing in the Empire, their accounts of travel, missionary work, and experience of settlement.[9] Focus has been on the way in which women placed themselves aslant male traditions of representation while yet endorsing the dominant cultural values of the colonial regime. For example, women travellers and settlers might take care to emphasize their femininity in order to compensate for their unconventional adventuring roles. Mary Kingsley insisted on wearing long skirts while trekking through Central African swamps—and is concerned to draw attention to this fact in her travelogue. However, at every level of imperial engagement women such as Kingsley, Isabella Bird, Lady Anne Blunt, and Emily Eden had to contend with the predominance of men, the definitive maleness of all that was done. A young middle-class man in search of a colonial career could rest assured that whatever choice he made would land him in the ranks of an exclusively male hierarchy. Wherever he might find himself in the Empire, he could rely on the maleness of imperial institutions: the British army, the Indian Civil Service, and other colonial administrations. Women, Marlow rightly observed in 'Heart of Darkness', were 'out of it'.

By and large, the intercolonial networks mentioned earlier were staffed by men—that is to say, by men's men, who worked almost solely with other men. As we see in the many pairings of men in colonialist writing, from the real-life newspaper-stunt meeting of Stanley and Livingstone to the fictional relationships of Holly and Leo Vincey, Marlow and Jim, Empire was not only where men as individuals defined their masculinity—or their honour, diligence, prowess. It was also where men bonded. Imperial masculinity rested on closely interactive homosocial relations. Horace Holly, adventurer and guardian of his beloved Leo—'few sons have been loved as I love Leo'—has a violent but not untypical aversion to women other than the otherworldly 'She'. His propensity, like that of his counterparts in reality, is more than indulged by the masculine project of penetrating Africa's cavernous secrets in the company of Leo and Job, following the instructions of Leo's dead father.

Empire was male also in inspiration. The examples which men followed in the imperial field, the ideals of valour and personal glory to which they marched, were those found in imperial histories, colonial tales of masculine achievement, and the Victorian reinvention of the chivalric code, as Conrad well noted. Boys' adventure fiction in particular formed a leading energizing genre of imperial struggle and sweat. Captain Marryat and R. M. Ballantyne, and the later, more militaristic Henty, as well as the *Boy's Own Paper* journal (est. 1879), catered for an audience already stimulated by the real-life accounts of colonial adventurers and explorers, like Mungo Park, or John Franklin of the north-west passage, or David Livingstone.[10] Evangelical organizations cannily adopted the genre to instruct young men in correct social and political attitudes. In the pages of boys' adventure fiction, British male strength and ability to rule were presented as justification in themselves for colonization: a hero's dreams and triumphs embodied the imperial vision. Not surprisingly, such evocations of vigour and success kept colonial administrations and armies well staffed with new recruits. By the end of the nineteenth century, the boys' adventure had evolved into an endlessly repeatable story of fearless campaigning and derring-do, all to magnify Britain's name, and its territories abroad. Henty's tales—*With Clive in India*, *With Wolfe in Canada*, and so on—became the best-sellers of the 1890s.

What were the ingredients of narrative that so had the power to quicken imperial fantasy? Usually the exploits of the adventuring hero took the shape of a quest, campaign, or rite of passage aimed at winning some final prize: victory against the natives, wealth, the achievement of identity, personal or national honour, and withal, status as a Briton and a man. As one might expect, women and romance did not feature much in the hero's life, except as the reward for a job well done, or to cap a triumphant return to England. In general, where women figured at all in the world beyond the seas it was as seductive distraction or baleful presence, unmanning and polluting for those who fell under her spell: Ustane in *She*, the Woman of Shamlegh in *Kim*, Kurtz's African woman, Paul Vereker's mother and grandmother in Alice Perrin's *The Stronger Claim* (1903). To show the persistence of these ideas, in John Buchan's significantly later *The Dancing Floor* (1928), a strange tale of primitive irruptions in the eastern Mediterranean, the wayward Koré Arabin drives a wedge between the 'uncommonly handsome' loner Vernon Milburne and his older mentor Sir Edward Leithen. In Orwell's *Burmese Days* (1934), Flory's Burmese mistress Ma Hla May works to sabotage his peace of mind, and his relationship with Elizabeth Lackersteen, his new-found English love. Predictably, if the hero's woman was black, the terrors of contamination and degeneration—or of excessive pleasure—were believed to be concentrated in her flesh.

In the world of the adventure tale, the important relationships were necessarily between men. In essence, to borrow another phrase from Kipling, colonialist narrative was 'the lore of men that have dealt with men'. In his tale 'At the End of the Passage' (*Life's Handicap*), colonial officials—a surveyor, a civil servant, a doctor, and an assistant engineer—travel long distances to keep each other company and to ward off the terrors of life in India. It was part of the imperial state of things that the Englishman out in the colonies, free of domestic responsibilities and white women, free to rule as he pleased, scornful of values other than his own, sought as companions those of his own kind. They alone would have the understanding, stature, and experience to match his own. Adventure fiction echoes this state of things. Colonial writings are full of scenes not merely of male bonding but of solidarity between men figured as self-mirroring and doubling. As did Stanley, as does Marlow, the white man in the wild sought and responded to men hewn in his own image, secret sharers, in Conrad's phrase, to confirm his own reality: Kim's friend the lama, Holly's ward Leo, Charlie Marryat's servant Tim Kelly in *With Clive in India*.

Though in a different sense, the effect of doubling applied to audiences also. The target public of imperial adventure tales was predominantly male. Haggard famously dedicated *King Solomon's Mines* (1885) to 'all the big and little boys who read it'. This meant that homosocial bonds were formed not only within but also by the adventure narrative: not only between protagonists—Ralph Rover, Jack Martin, and Peterkin Gay in R. M. Ballantyne's *Coral Island* (1858), Marlow and his hero friends, the list is long—but also between narrator and reader. The identification between men, inside the pages of colonialist fiction and out of it, helped to sublimate the uncertainties of a confrontation with colonized peoples. As the next section will show, the stress on sameness encouraged the portrayal of otherness—all that was not white and not male—as feminine. In the process, fiction reaffirmed the reasons for being out in the bush or blank veld, or isolated amid the torrid vastness of the Indian Empire.

In sum, the imperial adventure story, like the public school, raised ideological support for a male-led Empire, instilling in boy readers an image of self-confident British manliness, an ideal of robust character combining Christian honour with patriotism. As did the school, the adventure tale upheld the call to imperial duty, the Kiplingesque principle of service to mankind, and convictions of race pride. More practically, in Henty's case in particular, the fiction functioned as an information and instruction manual for future colonialists and English gentlemen. As Henty's titles show, his stories dramatize key moments in imperial history, most often through the medium of the fictional hero's involvement with a hero of Empire, such as Gordon or Wolfe. Troop movements and battle strategy are carefully detailed.

At appropriate points in the action, mostly between climaxes, 'How to do' sections offer tips on the handling of weapons or codes of martial conduct. Baden-Powell builds on this device of the imperial object lesson when in *Scouting for Boys* he uses stories drawn from the adventure and spy canon, such as by Fenimore Cooper and Arthur Conan Doyle, to teach scouting practices.[11]

It would be an oversight to end a section on the colonial male adventure story without noting that the popularity of this particular genre again underscores what was already discussed as the textuality of colonial experience, a textuality inscribed in a male hand. In the early Victorian period, as critics of the novel tell us, prose fiction was perceived to be the province of metropolitan women novelists. Now adventure stories, which generally sold extremely well, in part reclaimed for male writers and a male readership the province of the novel. Informing Victorian male youth as to what they might expect of the Empire, the writers of adventure directed attention beyond the close confines of the island nation, and beyond domestic realism. In so doing they provided an important imperial service: the rapid proliferation of their tales usefully printed images of colonial exertion and native life on the minds of future colonial officers. Even if in no other way, it would have been through the dissemination of boys' fiction, and the explorers' writings from which it drew inspiration, that the different parts of the Empire were imaginatively connected the one to the other.

Colonized others

In literature, as in colonialist politics, one of the most significant aspects of European self-projection was its representation of the people who inhabited the lands they claimed: the natives, the colonized, the subaltern. They too were interpreted by way of metaphoric or—the more precise term in this instance—stereotypic reproduction. The familiar labels at once marked and masked the unsettling strangeness that colonized peoples represented.

Throughout this and the first chapter, I have had to allude frequently to processes of *othering* as fundamental in colonization. The colonized made up the subordinate term in relation to which

European individuality was defined. Always with reference to the superiority of an expanding Europe, colonized peoples were represented as lesser: less human, less civilized, as child or savage, wild man, animal, or headless mass. Taking the form of both a retrospective and a synopsis, the present section places this symbolic complex of the other, the keystone of colonialist ideology, in closer focus. The discussion is intended to give general theoretical backing to the examples of othering already cited.

In a great many cultural contexts, identity is based on a distinction of the self from what is believed to be not self. It is endemic to cultures to negotiate with what is not known, or between peoples or subjectivities unfamiliar to one another, on the basis of convention. As will by now be apparent, over and above its economic and military might, what distinguished European hegemony (though may not have been unique to it) was its strong belief in the potential for universalization of its knowledge in science, politics, and religion; in particular, of its forms of rationality. European colonizers held the conviction not merely that the rest of the world could be understood in its terms, but that the rest of the world also could—and indeed should—be encouraged to interpret reality in a European way, according to a European language of reason.

As the J. G. Frazer biographer Robert Ackerman remarks, conceptions of the 'savage mind' as a cruder form of the 'civilized' were thick in the air during the mid-Victorian period.[12] Early anthropologists like Edward Tylor, William Robertson Smith, Andrew Lang, and Frazer himself readily categorized colonized peoples as 'primitives', inferior to Europeans. Given the powerful strategies of exclusion and repression on which they were built, nineteenth-century imperial projects required mechanisms of self-legitimation which, too, would work with power and effectiveness. As we saw in Kipling's 'On the City Wall', the representation of Indians (or Africans, black West Indians, Aborigines, etc.) as unfit to rule or to manage their own resources was one such ideological mechanism, or fretwork of mechanisms, one that worked with particular persuasiveness. According to this approach, the naming of other peoples—as irrational, barbarian, Indian, animal-like, childlike, effeminate—was simultaneously an act of evaluation, usually of downgrading. In certain colonial descriptions the presence of native peoples was entirely erased from the land they occupied.

Time and again the derogation of other cultures was used to validate the violence of invasion and occupation. Even before Darwin, colonization was represented as a survival of the fittest, in De Quincey's phrase 'winnowing the merits of races'. The struggle for survival dictated that the strong, or those best at imposing their power, were deserving of hegemony. Within the terms of colonialist representation, it was possible to style any incident of conquest as demonstrating the power of the invader and the inferiority of the conquered. Such characterizations provided the epistemic or ideological violence, to draw on the terminology of Gayatri Spivak, which aided and abetted the more overt brutalities of occupation.[13] The characterization of colonized people as secondary, abject, weak, feminine, and other to Europe, and in particular to England, was standard in British colonialist writing. In *Vanity Fair*, Jos Sedley's 'native servant' is usually described as a pathetic old-womanish figure of misery, wrapped in a shawl to ward off the English climate. Wali Dad in 'On the City Wall' is a young 'Mohammedan' with 'pencilled eyebrows' who composes pretty songs. Forster's Aziz in *A Passage to India* would later have similar fine features and exquisite sentiments.

But to understand more fully what lay behind imperial perceptions of race, we need to place these representations in historical perspective. Victorian classifications of difference and cultural superiority lead back to eighteenth-century Enlightenment perceptions of rational man. In the view of the late eighteenth century, the period of the early British Empire, the European was the leading exemplum of scientific humanity—which was believed to be humanity in its most achieved form. Master of himself, in command of reason as well as of new technologies of measurement and quantification—as are Kim and Colonel Creighton—he presumed the rest of the globe available for the operation of his intellect and curiosity. As imperial activity indeed showed, the world was regarded as so much raw material to fit into the white man's categories of knowledge.

As is clear from the foregoing description, such characterizations of the European were asserted in relation to an opposite, a 'rest' of the world, an other. Depending on context, this opposite took the form of woman or slave, servant or beast, and, with the onset of colonization, also became the colonized: a category of representation which subsumed within itself those other significations of difference. The feminized colonial other allowed the European the more intensively to realize himself—and in certain conditions, herself also. Images of the native, alien, or other, reflected *by contrast* Western conceptions of selfhood—of mastery and control, of rationality and cultural superiority, of energy, thrift, technological skilfulness. Europe ceaselessly reconfirmed its own identity and individuality by finding for itself around the globe subterranean or reverse selves, dark mirror-images: the Oriental, the Thug, the African, the New World Indian, the Quashee, Caliban, Friday, Jewel.

Taken together, all of this meant that the native improvement which colonization promoted could not in any circumstances take place at the expense of European superiority. Even if educated in the white man's schools, even if accepted as part of metropolitan intellectual life, as happened under French colonialism, the other could never, finally, become the European. As Chapter 4 will show more distinctly, this reality gave the lie to justifications of empire which appealed to native development, civilization, Europeanization, Christian conversion. For though the natives' lands were occupied in the name of civilization, they themselves, judged from the perspective of Europe, could not become completely civilized. Reason and authority were posited in relation to unreason, lack of civilization, disorder, which were located in the colonies. This basic distinction willy-nilly undermined the arguments of those who defended empire as 'uplifting' natives. Progress in the image of Europe might be advised, but the divide between Europeans and colonized peoples had to stay in place. Till the end of British Empire all rationales based on 'civilizing the natives' remained hobbled by this basic paradox. And, as we shall see again later on, it was not the only one. As Albert Memmi, Frantz Fanon, and others have pointed out, until the very last day of colonial occupation, the colonizer was haunted by the image of the native even as he, the colonizer, attempted to negate his dark presence. Like Jim, the European required that his existence be acknowledged by an entity whose full humanity he refused to accept.[14]

But the other was not merely a simple negative term set up in opposition to the colonizer's own self-image. It did not simply involve an antinomian pairing of white against black, or colonizer versus colonized. Colonial relations were always heterogeneous and shifting. Rather than representing an undifferentiated negative, the other was based on multiple distinctions. Depending on context and imperial interest, certain categories of people or cultures were deemed to be closer to the European self than others. Within the Empire, as Kim makes clear, the Irish were rated as superior to Indians while in India itself warlike Sikhs and Pathans were ranked above Bengalis. The fierce north-west border peoples of Kipling's 'The Head of the District' (*Life's Handicap*, 1891), for example, scorn the learned Bengali babu. On account of their military prowess, Haggard saw the Zulus as a people imbued with nobility: their status overtopped all other non-white peoples.

As was suggested in Chapter 1, ideologies of colonial supremacy and racism were complicated and layered. In part they developed as a rationale for market expansion and industrial development. In part they rose out of the cultural self-confidence of a newly industrialized society which interpreted its technological expertise as a fundamental sign of its superiority. And in part again, eighteenth-century belief in hierarchies of being, and the primacy of western scientific reason, contributed to the ideological complex that was the other.

On this basis, it is helpful to see the other as a historical palimpsest—or layering of interpretations—which combined different and changing ways of characterizing the alien condition. Whether in H. Rider Haggard, in 'Heart of Darkness', or in G. A. Henty's African stories, late nineteenth-century European representations of Africa, for example, combined apprehensions regarding social degeneration with fears of native unrest, possibly engendered by events in other regions of the Empire—most traumatically by the Indian Mutiny of 1857. These fears were in turn reinforced by the symbolism of African barbarism used in anti-slavery campaigns during the first decades of the century. To promote the Christianization of the continent, these campaigns had drawn on eighteenth-century perceptions of the savage, pictured as primitive and unregenerate even if noble.

As the writers Philip Curtin and Patrick Brantlinger have both convincingly argued, the effort to eradicate slavery at source by 'civilizing' Africans had as its ironic consequence this depiction of the victims of the slave trade as primitive, helpless, supine, and in need of 'improvement'.[15] The characterization or labelling of the other—that process already referred to as othering—can thus be described as a transvaluative response. In missionary and explorer writings, the image of Africa darkened in equal but opposite proportion to Europe's attempts to redeem Africans from darkness. This, then, meant that Africans could be characterized as responsible for their own degradation, a move which effectively absolved Europeans of a portion of their guilt for the slave trade. The imagery of the African continent as savage and degraded, a heart of darkness, therefore, predated Social Darwinist ideas regarding the differential development of cultures.

Also extremely influential in the process of figuring the other was the European symbolic complex called the Great Chain of Being. The Chain of Being, a system which purported to connect the highest forms of life to the lowest, went back to Renaissance times. In the Enlightenment period the figure was given particularly concrete expression by natural historians. Here again we see how the Victorian characterization of racial others can be traced back much further in time. From early on in the eighteenth century, men of science, scholars, and travellers sought to establish natural orders and measures, universalizing chains of succession that would embrace the entire natural world. As will be obvious, it was taken for granted that the apex of all such pyramids and chains was located in Europe. When it came to the classification of human beings, therefore, people from other cultures were ranked on the basis of their difference from Europeans, as degenerate or evolving types, filling the gaps between the human and the animal world.

Victorian popular evolutionary theory converted these taxonomies of difference into an evaluative ranking. Importantly, too, the idea of progress among species replaced the concept of a static chain of being. Briefly summarized, the belief that became current around the time Darwin's *Origin of Species* (1859) appeared—though Darwin himself was no Social Darwinist—was that cultural differences, ranged hierarchically, were based in nature, formed an intrinsic part of evolutionary development, and even pointed to several origins for the human race (polygenesis). The cultural traits and inclinations of peoples, graded relative to the West, were seen as bound up with their inherited physical characteristics. Alice Perrin's *The Stronger Claim*, for example, depicts 'half-caste' Eurasians as down-at-heel, characterless, and untrustworthy. Mr Jahans is a shifty auctioneer in damaged goods: his work, it is clear, befits his 'heritage'. Race classifications, therefore, could be used to explain not only biological variety but the superiority or inferiority of different cultural types ranged on a scale of evolutionary progress. A great gap, based in biology, was believed to separate white races from black. Differences between colonizer and colonized, European and other, gradually came to be represented in absolute terms rather than as contrasts or as shifting points on a scale.

The image of the evolutionary ladder which replaced that of the Great Chain of Being thus figured synchronically the differential advance of peoples. As was typically argued in Edward Tylor's *Primitive Culture* (1871), the founding document of British anthropology, within this system so-called primitive cultures were regarded as the fossilized survivals of earlier evolutionary stages. In his ascent Western man was believed to have moved through certain metamorphoses, the types of which could still be seen at large in other, less developed societies. The biological struggle for survival, in other words, offered an allegory of social development. The popular and often extremely crude versions of this kind of thinking which developed in the later nineteenth century went by the name of Social Darwinism. It was Social Darwinist thought that provided the undergirding for the imperialist syllogism whereby Europeans, defined as the fittest of all humanity, could defend empire not only on the basis of their fitness and ability to survive but as their *means* of survival.

As in *With Wolfe in Canada*, or *King Solomon's Mines*, images of racial excellence or inferiority based on the evolutionary ladder (not necessarily inflected by Social Darwinism) formed a staple ingredient of adventure fiction. But other writings of empire, too, spent energy painstakingly ranking different cultures in terms of their relative levels of development. Richard Burton, writing about his journey to Lake Tanganyika, took care to underline the advanced state of Arab civilizations when compared with those of Africa. Refusing to recognize the suffering inflicted on local people by the East African slave trade, he berated the Africans he encountered for being lazy, childlike, lost to barbarity (*The Lake Regions of Central Africa*, 2 vols., 1860). Like many others, Trollope in his colonial commentaries assessed other cultures specifically on the basis of their ability to survive European invasion. In his opinion, therefore, Africans had progressed further than Australian Aborigines. In his report on South Africa, Trollope further distinguished between *kinds* of native idleness, observing that Hottentots were 'not so apathetic as savages, not quite so indifferent as orientals'. *The People of India* (1868–75), an ethnographic survey of the Indian subcontinent, attempted a minute ranking and classification of Indian castes. Some thirty-five years after its appearance, the Fabians Sidney and Beatrice Webb, in their travel notes on India published as *Indian Diary* (1913), were still interpreting cultural, religious, and caste differences as evidence for the existence of an Indian hierarchy of intellectual and physical excellence. This was in spite of the fact that the Webbs, unlike many of their country-men and countrywomen, identified with those nationalists who sup-ported the gradual social and political evolution of India towards independence.

Kipling and Conrad, too, subscribed to theories of racial difference and supremacy, manifested in the main as the hierarchies of com-mand which dominate their narratives. Despite his failings, Marlow sees Lord Jim as possessing an internal nobility and quality of leader-ship that distinguishes him from the people of Patusan. Kim's Indian godfathers, all adult men, trained and competent in their work, unstintingly offer up their services and respect to the white boy. Different races have different predispositions to holding authority. Against this background the friendship between Kim and the lama is unique in bonding together the white boy and the other, the Buddhist priest, on a basis of mutual co-operation. But at the same time Kim's pragmatism and worldly knowledge—his white rationality—is repre-sented as a more successful strategy in dealing with a dangerous world than the spirituality of the lama.

In that colonization was a struggle for supremacy, not only of white against black, but between European nations, the scramble for territory took on the aspect of a conflict between competing virilities. From this it becomes clear how the ranking of cultures relative to a dominant and warlike Europe might have led to the feminization of other peoples briefly outlined earlier. The people of India, especially of Bengal, were typically characterized as passive, soft, seductive, lan-guid, and generally effeminate when compared to the robustly male personae of the colonizers. India was a 'woman-country', as the writer and commentator Maud Diver described it in *The Englishwoman in India* (1909). James Mill in his *History of British India*, and John Ruskin after him, in the lectures collected in *The Two Paths* (1858), described Hindu culture as febrile, decorative, delicate, all too femi-nine. Speaking a year after the Indian Mutiny, Ruskin related the softness of Indian art to native corruption and lack of moral disci-pline. In contrast, as Mill also saw it, Europeans excelled in plain, spare arts, in war, in government, and in law, 'rough' but more elevated masculine capabilities. It was in the context of such representations that European colonizers advocated hard work as a means of toughening the native male, masculinizing him.[16]

Alternatively, as happens in explorers' descriptions of Africa, a colonized land mass might be feminized rather than a people. Novelists, too, evoked the treacherous features of unknown terrain by drawing on metaphors of the engulfing female. In Haggard's *King Solomon's Mines* and *She*, aspects of African topography—the Sheba's Breasts mountains, the deep caves inhabited by Ayesha—unambiguously take on womanly form. This symbolism of the female body again captured salient traits of the racial other: of a body receptive to the male and, if not, then requiring subjection. Of course, as we saw in Haggard's representation of the Zulus, or in Kipling's attitude to the hill tribes of India, there were exceptions to the process of feminization. Colonized peoples might also be ranked relative to one another on a scale of masculinity, or of a lack thereof.

It is safe to say that few nineteenth-century colonial discourses would not have borne the imprint of a race vocabulary and racial ideas. Symbols of blood, race purity and taint, of kind calling to kind, and the lapse back 'into the native' were stacked up high in Victorian perception. Many of Kipling's stories, certainly, are preoccupied by race, in particular the misfortunes of sexual relations between Europeans and Indians. Though the narrative perspective is often critical of the sexual exploitation of Indian women by Englishmen, it is revealing that in 'Without Benefit of Clergy' (*Life's Handicap*), the most poignant of these tales, all evidence of the cross-racial relationship is gradually, indeed relentlessly, wiped out. The 'half-breed' child and then the Indian woman die, the house they occupied is destroyed. In the end, the Englishman Holden alone is the survivor of the experience, punished by the 'Powers', it seems, for having broken one of the taboos of his 'kind'. Similarly, in *The Stronger Claim*, Paul Vereker the half-caste breaks down under the effect of the warring elements in his own blood. He is afflicted by 'all the drawbacks of both nations, and the virtues of neither': 'it is the polarity of race, and the two were never meant to mix'. Not merely the prevalence but the conventionality of racial thinking is also strikingly demonstrated in the feminist settler novel *The Story of an African Farm* (1883) by Olive Schreiner. Otherwise a passionate plea for the freedom of the imaginative life and the rights of women to self-expression, the novel accepts white dominance as part of the order of things. A brief reading of the warring elements in this now liberal, now Social Darwinist work will bring this section on the layered construction of the other to a close.

The determined if doomed quest of its heroine Lyndall for self-expression has earned *The Story of an African Farm*, Schreiner's first published work, a high reputation as one of the earliest New Woman novels. It is also a notable instance of first-generation white settler writing in Africa. Separated from a cultural 'mother country' which at the time of writing she had not seen, yet which supplied her with descriptive metaphors, Schreiner was a native-born African who none the less felt herself to be an outsider in Africa. The described reality of her novel is South African, but the literary consciousness is rooted in Europe, not south of the Sahara.

Schreiner struggled with what we now perceive as the characteristic condition of colonial dislocation. The evocations of the dry Karoo landscape in *African Farm* are rightly celebrated for attempting to give imaginative validity to the non-European environment. At the same time the allegorical passages in the novel strenuously address Victorian theological and moral debates. Schreiner was well-read in Huxley, Spencer, and John Stuart Mill, amongst others. To engage with the social and evolutionary theories of these thinkers meant for her as for other writers of the time personal intellectual advancement and a valuable training in scientific thought.

The Story of an African Farm begins to give imaginative form to white colonial society, but it does so at the expense of marginalizing the black inhabitants of the land. Critics have attempted to counter this charge by arguing that Schreiner gives us a microcosm of African colonialist society in her sharply focused representation of cruelty and subordination in the white homestead. The abuse of authority in the household, in other words, offers an indirect comment on the violent repressions which supported colonial rule. However, it cannot be denied that, as is typical in the colonial drama, the action of *African Farm*, especially its dominant mode of questing, involves the white characters only. The novel is the story of their self-making. The exclusion mirrors in literary form the physical marginalization of Indigenous peoples by whites.

For Schreiner, an abstract language lamenting abuses of social justice is separate from a domestic vocabulary of race stereotype. 'There is no justice,' she comments. 'A black man is shot like a dog, and it goes well with the shooter.' But she also describes black people on the farm using conventional animal metaphors. The black characters—the Hottentot maid, the 'Kaffir' women who work around the homestead—are marginal if perceptive picturesque figures who provide local colour or act as foils to white action. Given her unconventional, non-metropolitan perspective, Schreiner's biases witness to the powerful hold of evolutionary precepts and representations of other peoples in the second half of the nineteenth century. It is all the more remarkable, then, that at one point early on in the novel Waldo muses on the 'Bushman-paintings' drawn on the Karoo rocks. He sees them as a trace or a hieroglyph of a lost black history once lived out in this desert land.[17]

Unreadable differences

The central characters in *The Story of an African Farm* are portrayed as solitary figures set against an arid backdrop. Displaced from their European origins, they confront the surrounding bleakness filled with the despair of their rootlessness, and find no succour. They lack a language or a faith with which to understand the alien environment. As a result the land in Schreiner's work seems to resist being adopted as a spiritual homeland.

Parallels for this settler lack of comprehension can be found elsewhere in colonialist writing. In nineteenth- and early twentieth-century Anglo-Indian literature—for instance, Flora Annie Steel's *On the Face of the Waters* or Maud Diver's *The Englishwoman in India*—India is consistently described as mysterious, grotesque, or malign, and in general hostile to European understanding. It presents a 'relentless placidity', 'vast, stupefying', even 'ghastly', reminding the British observer, as the caustic O. Douglas (Anna Buchan) noted in 1913, of 'the uncertainty of all things'.[18] In Conrad's East, in his Africa, or in the silver-mines of the South American country of Costaguana in *Nostromo*, the hero is stalked by a brooding nemesis, the threat of moral failure or the loss of rational control. It is a condition which appears to emerge in part out of the radical incongruity between the individual and the alien world in which he finds himself.

So far I have spoken of empire chiefly as an imposition—of power, of language, of ideology. But, as was briefly noted in Chapter 1, the act of taking possession should not be crudely understood as the obliteration of everything that was in existence before the arrival of the white man, or the projection of European imaginings to the exclusion of all else. Colonization rarely meant a complete take-over. Indeed, colonial power was far from a smooth extension outwards from a metropolitan centre—though this was naturally how it chose to represent itself. Nor was the colonizer unproblematically at home in the lands he occupied. The symbolism of the other, therefore, was not the product of confident authority alone. The native portrayed as primitive, as insurrectionary force, as libidinous temptation, as madness, was also an image redolent of extreme colonial uncertainty.

From the perspective of native society, too, colonization did not involve uniform mass exploitation or the total destruction of local power structures. It was not necessarily the case that the colonized had no choice but to live out the roles of servant or underdog that the colonizer inflicted upon them. In some cases they collaborated or in one way or another worked *with* the colonial power. In Bengal in the eighteenth century, as C. A. Bayly and Sumit Sarkar amongst others have argued, certain socio-economic groups—zamindars or rent-collectors, money-lenders, capitalist farmers—chose to co-operate with colonial forces, or benefited from their presence. From the time the first colonial colleges were established in Calcutta, young Westernized intellectuals sought an English education as a way of gaining the upper hand in power rivalries with traditional leaders. Like middle-class native élites in Nigeria, Kenya, or South Africa, they used colonial structures to further their own interests. Colonization, it is important again to emphasize, did not involve the simple propagation of knowledge, representation, social and political structures, and so on, outwards from a centre of dominance. To assume this would be either to attribute greater might and imperial confidence to the Europeans than they in fact possessed, or to see American, Indian, or African peoples and their lands as blank slates on which the British, French or Dutch easily imposed their plans and designs.

In reality, from the earliest times, there was both resistance to *and* co-operation with the colonial presence. As well as being a projection, colonial interpretation in certain situations involved a tentative or exploratory dialogue with the alien—most notably perhaps in late eighteenth-century orientalist scholarship. The many colonial wars which stud the careers described towards the end of Chapter 1—the

Zulu Wars, the Indian Mutiny, the Ashanti Wars, the conflicts with Caribs, Maori, Aborigines—begin to give an idea of the resistance Europeans experienced to their efforts to impose control. On the other hand, again, in some instances, the insertion of British power was aided and abetted by native landholders, merchants, and traders. Submission to British rule could well be calculated—was not in every case a passive act. For their part, as P. J. Marshall, C. A. Bayly, and others have shown, the British authorities in Bengal were manipulating on their own behalf a system of military and economic control and regulation set up in the Mughal period.[19] Both in India and on the West Coast of Africa at this time, they were able to find a foothold because of the fragmentation of local kingdoms or other state structures. They clambered into positions of authority on the scaffolding of existing powers, and did not simply inflict their rule on others.

Colonialist representation, too, encountered problems of dispersed and frustrated authority. Here, once again, we see that the projection of European images on other lands was never as all-enveloping or complete a process as the prevailing powers might have wished. Native strategies for appropriating the colonizer's language will be discussed at a later stage in this book. As far as the colonizers themselves were concerned, the effort to graft on to the colonized environment their own hermeneutic structures constantly met with difficulty. There was no necessary consonance between colonial imported metaphors and the colonized land. No assurance was available to the European that his transference of tropes would produce a perfect fit. Even if there had been such a fit—a perfect if unlikely match of imported word and other world—there were no known reference points against which constructions of the new reality might be checked for accuracy.

Distant lands, as I pointed out earlier, were brought into the colonizer's language by trial and error, in the process of their being explored and travelled. Though it might ultimately be ineffectual, writing strove to contain the disturbing effects of a new environment by attaching to that environment recognizable narrative and metaphoric patterns. Moving through unfamiliar country, travellers adapted the familiar concepts of hill, meadow, brook, and so on to give shape to their experience. They sought out features conforming to their own aesthetic schemes—misty tones, a heterogeneity of natural and geological features, the idealized landscapes associated with the seventeenth-century French painter Claude. So it was, as we now tend to believe, that the reality most feasible for a colonial culture to occupy was one of its own making, described in its own language. When Livingstone walked through Central Africa to the Angolan coast, the landscapes which he found worthy of description, and recommended for development, were those which were specifically green and 'refreshing' to his eye. Similarly, Charles Heaphy, a landscape artist in early colonial New Zealand, used English blues and greens to render the Antipodean scenery.[20]

And yet it was as likely as not that between their representations and the places Europeans sought to understand an alarming space existed, of misrecognition, of ignorance—who could tell? No matter how diligently colonizers translated unfamiliar landscapes, from their cultural and geographic standpoint the original script of that unfamiliarity was doomed to remain inaccessible. Even their acceptance of a self-constructed reality did not erase from view the tenebrous spaces, impervious blockages, and gaps in knowledge which persisted, despite all their efforts at interpretation. India, Africa, Australia continued to withhold their assumed essential core, frustrating the cool querying eye of scientist and governor alike. It is important not to underestimate the colonialist unease which was occasioned by this precariousness of their efforts at interpretation. Even at the time of the established Empire, difference or alterity remained shocking, vertiginous, a source of distress. For a system of domination founded on scrutiny, scientific observation, and the collection of knowledge, the inadequacy of Europe's descriptive capacity was threatening. It did not inspire confidence that colonial interpreters could not trust to the completeness of their vision.

The experience of the scientific observers aboard Cook's *Endeavour* offers an example of colonial interpretative difficulty: both of the experience of obfuscation and of the attempt to resist it. Having set out with the brief to observe accurately the beasts, fowls, and fishes of the South Seas, 'and in what Plenty', Joseph Banks and his colleagues soon discovered that the natural world they were documenting would not easily fit existing botanical classifications. Yet they persisted in their attempt. It was important as far as possible to give this recalcitrance structure and conceptual shape. European explorers in the Australian interior, like Eyre or Ludwig Leichhardt in the 1840s, also suffered the anxiety of interpretative blockage. They repeatedly found that their geographic terminologies did not suit the land they sought to name. They looked for mountains, rivers, lakes, bits of greenery, but the wide, brown uniformity of Australia did not allow for such differentiation. The land undermined their expectations: 'All was uncertainty and conjecture in this region of magic', commented Eyre on encountering yet another blinding waste of salt where inland seas had been anticipated.[21]

The insecurity surrounding colonial interpretation is widely reflected in imagery of the vastness and shapelessness of the other land. It is there in evocations of the terror contained in that shapelessness, as in Conrad's African forest, and of the distressing opacity of native peoples to European understanding, usually represented as their ignorance and dullness, their black magic and strange fetishism. In the deployment of such imagery, the colonizer's motive for documenting a new country—blanketing it with his own words—became two-edged. Apart from the desire to understand and control, there was also the need to avoid or delimit anything that eluded control. One way of doing this was to screen the incomprehensible as far as possible out of the picture. Another was simply to name the strange as strange, using metaphors which connoted mystery and inarticulateness. Intransigence, it was felt, might be contained by pointing to it. The strategy, in other words, was to admit, if guardedly, to the *unreadability* of the other.

But these devices did not get rid of the unease. Colonialist texts are littered with images of nameless threat and trauma: of inertia and impossible immensity, of places of engulfing darkness and overwhelming enigma, recalcitrant peoples, unbreachable jungles, vast wastelands, huge and shapeless crowds. Of India Kipling aptly observed: 'There is too much [of her] and she is too old'—as too was Haggard's 'She'. In Africa Haggard's heroes encounter as a matter of course swamps, mazes, and cavernous mountains. The image of female body as correlate for enveloping land came in handy. To reach Ayesha, Holly and Leo must move across volcanic concavities and into labyrinthine passages and caves. Yet the African travellers Stanley and Mary Kingsley too described their journeys as obstacle courses of enveloping swamps and treacherous paths (*How I Found Livingstone*, 1872; *Travels in West Africa*, 1897). It was as if travelling across Africa was constantly to lose one's bearings and one's balance; to be swamped and in danger of drowning. Imagery such as this was clearly aimed at managing the threat of the not-yet-interpreted by naming it as such. Yet the dark associations of this naming simultaneously conceded that the alterity, though masked, remained largely undescribable and horrific.

Rhetorical strategies to manage colonial unreadability can be organized into two broad groups. First, there was the practice of symbolic reproduction already discussed, where the intention to characterize a place expressed itself in defiance of the empirical evidence or conventional laws of association. As did the Australian explorers, colonizers created a viable space by repeating names and rhetorical structures from the home country regardless of their accuracy. As should be clear, metaphoric reiteration of this nature necessarily involved the editing out or occlusion of extreme otherness: what could not be translated was simply not a part of the represented scene.

Second, a development of the first, there was the strategy of displacement, a device whereby the intransigence or discomfort the colonizer experienced was projected on to the native. This is clearly demonstrated in the process of othering. Especially where they were resistant to his requirements, the European represented colonized people as unruly, inscrutable, or malign. Crowd imagery came in handy to suggest a lack of character and individual will. In *Burmese Days*, the mass besieging the European club makes a single 'deep, devilish roar'; in *A Passage to India*, Adela Quested, 'drawn into a mass of Indians', finds it is 'as if the heat of the sun had boiled and fried all the glories of the earth into a single mess'. A little differently, displacement in its more pronounced forms is characterized by its appeal to the Romantic Sublime. Here the unreadable subject is transformed into the sign of its own unreadability. What happens, typically, is that description admits defeat, submitting to the horror of the inarticulate. The native or colonized land is evoked as the quintessence of mystery, as inarticulateness itself.

For many writers on India, including the late-imperial Forster, the vastness and strangeness of the subcontinent was habitually evoked in terms of the unsayable: as Kipling observed, 'you can't focus anything in India' ('The Education of Otis Yeere', *The Man who would be King*). India became the sign of a universal Incomprehensibility. Western categories of description collapsed before it; it was not beautiful, it was too large. The Marabar Caves in *A Passage to India* denote nothing but their own vacancy of meaning. To William Arnold in *Oakfield*, the Himalayas, as gigantic as the Indian plains, defied 'individualizing personification'. India alone could signify its own mystery and complexity. The British were entirely alien to it. In an opening description of Bengal, Arnold noticed the 'almost fearful verdure', 'the ceaseless hum of animal life', 'the mud hovels of the swarming natives'. In 1909 Maud Diver came remarkably close to repeating these images when outlining the distinguishing features of India as 'the awful lifelessness of her vast dun-coloured plains, the smells and sounds of her swarming cities, the majesty of her incomparable mountains, the mystery that hangs over the lives and thoughts of her many peoples'.[22] Significantly in this context, Arnold's Oakfield finds himself struck by:

> the extraordinary fact of British dominion, so manifest everywhere; apparently so firmly planted in the soil, and yet so manifestly separate from it; so that while it was impossible to fancy the power being swept away, it was easy to look round and think of it as gone; the prominent feature in the picture, still, were it once removed, the picture would seem almost the same without it.[23]

Even within the fixed structures of the society in Kipling's stories, characters shut away from their own 'kind' often experience strange hauntings and fits of despair. In 'The Strange Ride of Morrowbie Jukes' and 'The Phantom Rickshaw' (*The Man who would be King*), men find themselves in limbo worlds, suspended between life and death. Their situations are analogous to the wider condition of colonial isolation. Some of Kipling's tales of ghostly persecution involve Indian protagonists, such as 'Gemini' or 'Dray Wara Yow Dee'. But an experience of haunting associated with acute alienation is peculiarly the territory of the white man in India. His conditions of work are hardship and loneliness: 'isolation that weighs upon the waking eyelids and drives you by force headlong into the labours of the day' ('The Judgement of Dungara', *The Man who would be King*). In 'Thrown Away' and 'At the End of the Passage' (*Life's Handicap*), boredom and heat lead men to delusions and suicide. Hummil in the latter story, hounded by nightmares that prevent sleep, dies, it seems, of a ghastly, otherworldly fear. The Great Indian Empire, is the comment, 'turns itself for six months into a house of torment'. Alice Perrin's collection of stories *East of Suez* (1901) builds on Kipling by supplying a catalogue of the further disasters, hauntings, and curses which the Orient is prone to inflict. India is itself a terror and a madness. To be touched by the place is to be possessed, as is the careless Fleete in 'The Mark of the Beast' (*Life's Handicap*), but to come no closer to her secrets. The African forest, too, relentlessly signals impenetrability to Marlow in 'Heart of Darkness'. The obsessive quality of Conrad's language in the novella betrays an inability to encompass this darkness in words. Even Mary Kingsley, whose travelogue persona was eminently matter-of-fact and sensible, was forced by what she saw as the indescribable immensity of the African forest repeatedly to resort to evocations of the Sublime. The 'endless walls of mangrove, unvarying in colour, unvarying in form, unvarying in height' reminded her of the stupendous vastness of the Himalayas: 'I just lose all sense of human individuality, all memory of human life, with its grief and worry and doubt, and become part of the atmosphere'.

Yet if never free of the threat of destabilization, colonial power had still to produce an illusion of permanence: hence the prevalence, even the overproduction under colonial administrations of reams of documentation, ethnographic and scientific studies, journals, accounts, censuses, dispatches, laws, etc. To colonize something was to pile writing, a grammar, a structure, upon it. From the earliest times, as we have seen, men of empire made books about their experiences, compiled dictionaries and lexicographic studies, noted down their speculations about native life and their theories of European rule, wrote their *England in Egypt*s, their *Glossaries of Revenue Terms*, their *Geographical Memoirs*. Just as travel writing declared an intention to make meaning, a desire to understand the beyond, so for any colonial authority inscription was a way of bringing into being the non-European environment. Textual projection—stories and poems as well as fact-sheets—was an attempt at both extensive comprehension and comprehensive control.

Further Reading

Robert Aldrich, *Colonialism and Homosexuality* (Routledge, 2003).

Nigel Barley, *White Rajah: A Biography of Sir James Brooke* (Boston: Little, Brown, 2002).

David Cairns and Shaun Richards, *Writing Ireland: Colonialism, Nationalism and Culture* (Manchester UP, 1988).

Rosinka Chaudhuri, *Gentleman Poets in Colonial Bengal: Emergent Nationalism and the Orientalist Project* (Calcutta: Seagull Books, 2002).

Graham Dawson, *Soldier Heroes: British Empire, Adventure and the Imagining of Masculinities* (Routledge, 1994).

Robert Fraser, *Victorian Quest Romance: Stevenson, Haggard, Kipling and Conan Doyle* (Plymbridge: Northcote House, 1988).

Henry Louis Gates, Jr. (ed.), '*Race*', *Writing and Difference* (University of Chicago Press, 1986).

Robert Giddings (ed.), *Literature and Imperialism* (Macmillan, 1991).

Sander Gilman, *Difference and Pathology: Stereotypes of Sexuality, Race and Madness* (Ithaca, NY: Cornell UP, 1985).

Mark Girouard, *The Return to Camelot: Chivalry and the English Gentleman* (London and New Haven: Yale UP, 1981).

Inderpal Grewal, *Home and Harem: Nation, Gender, Empire and the Cultures of Travel* (London: Leicester University Press, 1996).

Elizabeth Hallam and Brian Street (eds.), *Cultural Encounters: Representing Otherness* (Routledge, 2000).

Peter Hulme, *Colonial Encounters: Europe and the Native Caribbean 1492–1797* (Methuen, 1986).

Abdul JanMohamed, *Manichean Aesthetics: The Politics of Literature in Colonial Africa* (Amherst: University of Massachusetts Press, 1983).

V. G. Kiernan, *The Lords of Human Kind: Black Man, Yellow Man and White Man in an Age of Empire* (Weidenfeld & Nicolson, 1969).

Christopher Lane, *The Ruling Passion: British Colonial Allegory and the Paradox of Homosexual Desire* (Durham, NC: Duke UP, 1995).

Gail Ching-Liang Low, *White Skins, Black Masks: Representation and Colonialism* (Routledge, 1996).

Benita Parry, *Conrad and Imperialism* (Macmillan, 1983).

—— *Delusions and Discoveries: Studies on India in the British Imagination 1880–1930*, rev. edn. (1972; Allen Lane, 1998).

David Spurr, *The Rhetoric of Empire: Colonial Discourse in Journalism, Travel Writing and Imperial Administration* (Duke UP, 1993).

Brian V. Street, *The Savage in Literature: Representations of Primitive Society in English Fiction 1858–1920* (Routledge & Kegan Paul, 1975).

Robert J. C. Young, *White Mythologies: Writing, History and the West*, 2nd edn. (Routledge, 2004).

The Stirrings of
New Nationalism

The unprecedented severity of the storm, far from depressing
[Mhudi's] spirit, only served to inspire her with hope. . . . At
sunrise she stood near the side of a koppie, and saw the plains
spread out before her in one great prospect.

Sol Plaatje, *Mhudi*, 1930

In those balmy days . . . I was not English, but I considered
myself to be. I was a colonial, but did not consider myself to be
so. England belonged to me, her heritage, her war.

Derek Walcott, *Remembrance and Pantomime*, 1980

Datta. Dayadhvam. Damyata.
Shantih Shantih Shantih
T. S. Eliot, *The Waste Land*,
1922

Old Empire; new nationalisms

Colonial literature in its exploratory and expansionist phases proclaimed cultural superiority and rightness. However, as was suggested
earlier, the confidence which underlay colonial activity was not to last.
Conrad's dark colonial tales and Kipling's brooding hymn 'Recessional' (1897) were proved percipient in their foreboding. By the
beginning of the twentieth century Britain had begun to show signs
of severe imperial overstretch. The humiliations of the Anglo-Boer
War, in particular, laid bare the vulnerability of the Empire.

In contrast to mid-Victorian literature, an unmistakable new uncertainty, a large-scale disintegration of old absolutes, distinguishes the writing of early twentieth-century novelists like Virginia Woolf and E. M. Forster, and also, as Chapter 4 will show, the work of the slightly later George Orwell and Graham Greene. The note of questioning is present whether they address home or colonial subjects. While their doubting and pessimism are broadly regarded as symptoms of European modernism, it is also likely that the imperial retreat of this period contributed to or reinforced their uncertainty. And as if in confirmation of the European slippage in confidence, around the same time oppositional movements of resistance and self-affirmation were beginning to emerge in Britain's colonial territories. Across the Empire, during the first half of the twentieth century, colonized élites, articulate though embattled, began to organize cultural revivals, or raised their voices in protest at imperial power. White colonial nationalisms, too, were growing more confident and assertive.

As will become clearer as these chapters unfold, this situation should not be mistaken for a simple call-and-response, as if the weakening of the ruling power was chiefly responsible for enabling resistance. What we are talking about is once again a complicated nexus of historical causes and force fields. During the years when D. H. Lawrence was describing post-war London, the 'heart of the world', as collapsing, a 'vortex of broken passions, lusts, hopes, fears and horrors' (*Kangaroo*, 1923), differently positioned writers were learning to articulate a newly made cultural pride, often on their own initiative, and far beyond the gates of European authority.

It is helpful to chart a few key moments in this early nationalist period. In Australia (white) federation was achieved in 1901. The ensuing years saw, for example, the emergence of the 1905–8 Swadeshi movement in Bengal, the subsequent decline in moderate politics in the Indian National Congress, and the coming of the first Civil Disobedience movement (1921–2). Southern Africa, Kenya, and Nigeria experienced native protest and civil unrest sparked by the imposition of taxes and by mission reforms (for example, the Bambatha Rebellion, 1906; the Nigerian Women's Protest, 1929). In 1912 the South African Native National Congress, later the ANC, was formed. In the 1920s the rise of an African American mass movement under the auspices of the Universal Negro Improvement Association, with the Jamaican emigrant Marcus Garvey at its head, gave inspirational guidance to emergent black nationalisms in other lands. Across the colonized world, writers were speaking vehemently, with new confidence, about the validity of their own experience. Members of small, highly educated and committed élites, they cast their message across a wide textual spectrum, producing anthropological studies, social history, translations, and journalism as well as poetry and fiction to promote their cause.

This early moment of anti-imperialist nationalist—or more accurately, *nativist*—resistance was in many cases a relatively sedate preliminary to the more overt political liberationism which followed.[1] However, it laid the ideological and strategic bedrock of later developments. As with earlier Irish nationalism, the movements sought, in the first instance, an inversion of imperial values, if not of structures. Their messianism drew support from other utopian and/or millennarian ideologies of the time (Marxism, Fabianism, theosophy, evangelical versions of Christianity). The message they communicated was distinguished by a strenuous defence of the virtues of native culture, characterized as rich, pure, and authentic (hence the term nativist). The idea was that a people's identity, though long suppressed, lay embedded in its cultural origins and was recoverable intact, unadulterated by the depredations of colonialism.

So it was that culture—in the form of reinterpreted history, religious revivals, elegiac and nostalgic poetry and music—developed into an important front for nationalist mobilization. To this end literary conventions and discourses inherited from the colonizer were appropriated, translated, decentred, and hybridized in ways which we now name postcolonial but were in fact at the time anti-colonial, often opportunistic, tactical, and *ad hoc*, and which formed an important means of self-expression. Though very gradually at first, given imperial constraints, colonized writers began to come into their own. Starting before the Great War but especially during decades following, writers like Rabindranath Tagore (India), Claude McKay (Jamaica), Raja Rao (India), and Solomon Plaatje (South Africa) took up the Western genres of the novel, sonnet, and short story to articulate their own perceptions of cultural space and experience.

What this signified, crucially, was that from the early twentieth century the virtual white monopoly on imperial writing was broken. Europeans steadily and surely lost the sole charge of the pen that (bar a few exceptions—Henry Derozio, Toru Dutt, J. Africanus Horton,

Edward Wilmot Blyden, amongst them) colonial privilege had for years guaranteed as theirs. Even before the post-Second World War period of official colonial independence, the terrain of (what was still strictly speaking) colonial writing became markedly more diverse, fragmentary, and complex. It is this realignment of colonial perspectives that forms the subject of this and the next chapter. This means that the focus now becomes dual. Retreat and disillusion on the side of empire were accompanied by resistance and reconstruction on the part of those who spoke for the colonized. Two different modes of discourse about colonial experience emerged in juxtaposition if not in dialogue, as the time of high imperialism passed.

To illustrate, *Untouchable* (1935), a first novel by the Indian nationalist writer, Bloomsbury fellow-traveller, and BBC broadcaster Mulk Raj Anand, ends with the Dalit protagonist contemplating the possible end to his travail offered by promises of reform and 'modernization'. In stark contrast, the final scenes of E. M. Forster's study of latter-day colonial India, *A Passage to India* (1924), hold out little hope either for social interaction between Europeans and Indians, or for Indian national independence. British rule is represented as irrelevant; Anglo-Indian society as hopelessly solipsistic. Yet India's tenebrous immensity offers no viable alternatives to the novel's agonized liberalism. Indians appear to lack the pragmatic wherewithal to rule themselves. *Burmese Days* by George Orwell, which appeared ten years after Forster's novel and around the same time as *Untouchable*, seals its own message of imperial fatuity with the suicide of the liberal protagonist Flory. On the one hand, then, we see expressed the idealistic hope of renewal, the vision of the emergent colonial nationalist, which is the chief subject of the present chapter. On the other hand, we have humanism under threat, *Weltschmerz*, the pessimism of late imperial culture. This will form one of the main points of focus in Chapter 4. In broad perspective, colonial territories were working out their own demands for, and interpretations of modernity.

But early nationalist views did not rule out the prospect of interaction with Europeans. In fact, in literature as well as in other cultural forms, specific areas of exchange emerged. The interest shown by European modernism in the 'primitive' and in mythic structure, for instance, corresponded to some extent with the investigation of traditional myths by colonial nationalists. In other words, different quests for origins, and for pathways from tradition into the modern world, developed in tandem with one another. In mapping the oppositional textual terrain of the early twentieth century, it is important to keep an eye on these interactions and likenesses as well as on the contrasts. As I shall suggest in more detail later on, there is an intriguing coincidence in the fact that metropolitans began to acknowledge the presence of others around the same time as colonized writers were appropriating European genres, symbolic conventions, and modern structures to express their own identity.

In order to obtain some purchase on a vast field, the discussion of early colonial nationalist writing begins by looking at its general make-up and constituency. What were the thematic and generic preoccupations of writers? What was the relationship with the colonial centre in terms of which they still tended to define themselves? As part of the dual focus, towards the end of the chapter European and native literatures will be examined in conjunction with one another. At this time, metropolitan modernist writing formed both a counterpoint to and a correlate for what was happening away from the centre. But it is also true to say that artists from a variety of colonial spaces themselves contributed to the twentieth-century modernist moment. Though the distinction of centre and periphery remained a felt reality, within certain cosmopolitan movements cultural divisions began to grow blurred.

Mhudi: adapting the colonial gaze

In a letter written in 1920, Solomon T. Plaatje, the South African black writer, linguist, historian, and founding member of the African National Congress, stated that he was working on a novel, 'a love story after the manner of romances; but based on historical facts'. Between episodes of warfare he promised to introduce 'plenty of love, superstition, and imaginations'. It would be 'Just like the style of Rider Haggard when he writes about the Zulus'.[2] This novel, which was completed in 1917 and appeared as *Mhudi* in 1930, was the first such work by a black African to be published in English. Representing history in the form of prophetic vision, combining different literary conventions and linguistic registers drawn from Shakespeare, the Bible, and African oral forms, *Mhudi* is a hybrid text that significantly unsettles the careful discriminations made in colonialist discourse. With its embedded plea for black land rights, the novel is also a highly political text, a fictional accompaniment to Plaatje's 1916 indictment of black dispossession, *Native Life in South Africa*.

Mhudi can be read as paradigmatic of emerging trends in colonial nationalist writing in several ways. In the first place, despite its warnings of coming doom, the ending like that of *Untouchable* is upbeat, idealistic, forward-looking. As in a conventional romance, the final scenes involve marriage and the reaffirmation of the bond between Mhudi and her husband Ra-Thaga. There is also a consolidation of friendship between individual African and Boer. Then, too, *Mhudi* underlines its own pioneering intervention in colonial discourse with a tactical use of structuring motifs. These cluster around the figure of the black heroine. Mhudi travels boldly across lion-infested landscapes, a lone female pioneer, in some ways like, yet also of course extremely unlike, the white explorer hero.

Plaatje may have professed to be imitating the Haggard tradition of adventure writing, but he was also working in counterpoint to that tradition: transforming through appropriation. As does Chinua Achebe's later *Things Fall Apart* (1958), *Mhudi* considers black society in transition, poised between a past heroic age, free from white domination, and a new period of colonial contact and incipient injustice. Plaatje's intention, as his Preface suggests, was to present a statement of cultural self-worth or 'race pride', which is also subtly inflected by gender liberation, in response to the biases of white colonial history.

The novel is syncopated by sweeping scenic descriptions and bird's-eye views of battlefields. More than any other feature, perhaps, these panoramic scenes, obvious take-offs of the penetrating colonial gaze, signal the intention of this early nationalist narrative to write athwart the conventions of colonial representation. To adopt the bird's-eye position was to arrogate to oneself, even if momentarily, the cartographic and metaphoric authority of the colonizer. Mhudi's commanding vision, captured in the epigraph to this chapter, summarizes what was entailed when nationalist writers took up the colonizer's position. First, importantly, the trope of the gaze asserted the right of nationalists to conceive of their land on their own terms, that is, to represent what they claimed as their own, to invent independently, to take narrative and also political command.

But, secondly, implicit in the act of appropriation was also the difficulty of failing to innovate sufficiently, that is, of repetition *despite* displacement. How did this express itself? Nationalists worked with the colonizer's vocabulary of power even while creating oppositional categories of meaning. In the effort to be more themselves, therefore, they ran the risk paradoxically of mirroring the authoritative poses of the colonizer. Forced to participate in the dominant culture in order to make their case, writers could find themselves supporting the symbolic system that impelled their resistance in the first place. This problem, called *approximation*, emerges as a recurring feature in most reverse or counter-discourses, including anti- and postcolonial writing.[3] As will be seen again in the chapters that follow, it is a problem that raises important questions about the viability of resistance. Does appropriation inevitably commit a writer to approximation? How is this avoided? What is to be gained from operating within the colonizer's structures? How useful is imperfect copying or imitation-with-a-difference as a mode of self-assertion? The discussion of anti-colonial resistance will keep circling around these difficult issues.

The cleavings of colonial nationalism

With the rise of colonial nationalist movements, imperial history manifested a certain poetic justice. As things turned out, colonial rule furnished the terms of articulation for what it most sought to deny: the self-representation of subject or marginalized peoples. In the nineteenth century, the expansion of European nation-states in the form of colonialism had spread far and wide a rhetoric of cultural self-determination. It was this rhetoric which later activated colonial opposition movements. The ethos of national autonomy that Europe itself had propagated contributed to balking colonial expansion.

Yet, of course, the emergence of colonized movements of self-determination was at first a contingent development. Especially early on, the prospect of ultimate success for nationalist groups could not but be uncertain. For some indeed it appeared unthinkable. None the less, it was a predictable if unanticipated response to colonization that those who bore its burden of occupation would develop their own desire for national sovereignty and self-expression.[4] Colonial rule, that is to say, produced the conditions for its own delegitimization.

Across any number of colonial territories, nationalism in the twentieth century became the platform for mobilizing against the occupying power in the name of a common culture, language, or history; or, in many cases, by appeal to the experience of colonial occupation itself.

Mixing, upturning, and dismantling negative representations, the strategic line of attack taken by the colonized was to turn the identities ascribed to them into positive self-images. In this the Negritude writers—francophone Africans and West Indians like Léopold Sédar Senghor (Senegal), Aimé Césaire (Martinique), or Bernard Binlin Dadié (Ivory Coast)—are often singled out as an early typical case. Working in Paris in the late 1920s, the 1930s, and the 1940s, these nationalist artists made cultural capital out of their own othering by colonial France. They glamorized that which had been downtrodden; they gave spiritual vitality to degrading stereotypes. Negritude therefore meant celebrating all that had been identified as negative and inferior by the colonizers—the instinctual and the mysterious of darkest Africa.[5] The poetry rejoiced in the 'earth-loving' sensuality, visceral rhythms, and ancestral mystique of an imaginary pre-conquest Africa.

With this in mind, we might want to think of anti-imperial cultural nationalism as performing, as it were, a double process of *cleaving*. That is, cleaving in both senses of the word: *cleaving from*, moving away from colonial definitions, transgressing the boundaries of colonialist discourse; and, in order to effect this, *cleaving to*: borrowing, taking over, or appropriating the ideological, linguistic, and textual forms of the colonial power. While British writers who addressed colonial experience dwelt on themes of retreat and disillusionment, nationalist colonial writers were responding, often in English, in English metre, and English idiom, with expressions of cultural pride.

When did this cleaving begin? For the sake of clarity and convenience, the world-wide spread of anti-colonial nationalist feeling in the twentieth century can be officially dated from 1919 when the rights of dependent nations were officially acknowledged at Versailles. (Of course, much earlier than this, in 1775, the War of Independence of the thirteen American states had established the groundwork for national movements to come. The United States was also the country that forced self-determination on to the agenda at the 1919 Peace Talks.) Divided by this watershed date, two early phases of nationalist activity in the British Empire can be distinguished. There was the initial, truncated and tentative pre-First World War phase, predominantly represented by Indian Swadeshi resistance to British rule, and by small groups in the so-called white colonies. The phase which followed, more organized, and in some cases more strident, was bracketed by the two World Wars.

The 1914–18 period and its aftermath, in particular, brought cataclysmic changes. Already by 1916, the much-praised technical and scientific superiority of the West, its working faith for over a century, had produced carnage on a scale never before imaginable. As Europe surveyed the devastation of its ideals of progress, the success of the Bolshevik Revolution of 1917 set an oppositional example for those who felt the yoke of oppressive power. Thereafter, in 1922, after an uprising, long unrest, and a civil war, the Irish Free State was declared. In India, revolutionaries such as those involved in the Ghadr movement attempted to exploit 1914–18 international hostilities in order to strike off their British bonds. The hardship caused in the subcontinent by the war also fed into the anti-imperialist upsurge which began under Mohandas Gandhi's leadership in 1919. Also, after 1919, students from across Europe's different empires began to travel to the metropolis in increasing numbers, drawn by the criticisms of colonialism offered by radical schools of thought. African students organized a number of Pan-African congresses on European soil during the inter-war period, and after 1939.

If the shock of 1914–18 had brought a retreat from militant European nationalism, the Second World War, fought against a racist ideology, undermined the surviving rationales of empire. In 1918 Indian and African soldiers had come home from the war inspired by the new radical movements abroad. Now the conflict saw the further mass politicization of the African colonial troops who were involved in military action alongside whites. In the Indian subcontinent the example of collaboration between Subhas Chandra Bose's Indian National Army and the Japanese in the final years of the war proved inspirational for some, while the use of Indian army units to restore French and Dutch colonial rule in South-East Asia significantly heightened anti-imperialist sentiment. For Britain, the militant Quit India upsurge of 1942 had emphasized the importance of a negotiated transfer of power. Two years after the cessation of hostilities, in 1947, came the independence of India and Pakistan, the first 'non-white' British colonial territories to achieve this status.

However, even as I periodize in this way, two key points must be borne in mind. One is the contradiction of drawing on dates from European history to discuss anti-colonial writing in a global context, especially as many ethnic, class, and race groupings in the colonies declined to participate in European struggles or to fight on the side of Britain. The second point, related to this, is the fact that the roots of colonial nationalism and anti-colonial resistance ramified further back than the turn of the century. In 1857, for example, the Rebellion or Mutiny of Hindu and Muslim soldiers in the Indian army had seriously shaken Anglo-Indian nerves. And, as mentioned, the resistance put up by the nationally minded Boers in South Africa from 1899 to 1902 bruised British imperial prestige.

As might be expected, the growth of local nationalisms followed different historical trajectories in different parts of the British Empire. Moves towards autonomy and self-assertion ranged from white constitutionalism to Indian passive resistance to pockets of militant radicalism. British responses to such moves also differed widely. Early on, under Queen Victoria, it had already been possible for British settler societies such as in Australia and Canada to secure a measure of independence by virtue of the close relationships they shared with the 'mother country'. The fate of the 'non-white' colonies was not so happy. After their landslide election victory, the Liberals in 1907 granted the white colonial territories self-government, bulwarked within a system of British protectionism. This encouraged feelings of settler self-sufficiency and patriotism, feelings which were further sharpened by colonial participation in the war of 1914–18. There were parallel developments in nationalist organization in the non-white Empire. But despite their participation in the war, political self-representation in these regions did not come in for consideration.

The belief was that the so-called Dominions might achieve independent nationhood in the context of a relationship with Britain. In complete contrast with this, though having sent 1.5 million men to war, India was denied Dominion status in 1919. In the Raj as elsewhere in the tropical Empire, self-aware, articulate élites were growing into political maturity in the expanding cities and new colleges. But their demands for greater autonomy were deeply mistrusted. The historian J. A. Froude commented in 1887 that liberties were brought into 'disrepute' if conceded to those who 'require[d] to be restrained'. His thinking was not unrepresentative. Whereas settler nationalisms in most cases received official sanction, nationalist movements in the non-white Empire, labelled as subversive, met with open hostility from colonial administrations and from London. British resistance to colonized unrest was brutally demonstrated in the Amritsar massacre of 1919.

Yet, though Britain may have discriminated, there were, as we shall see, important similarities between different strains of colonial nationalism. The 1890s nascence of Australian literary nationalism, especially as expressed in the pages of the Sydney journal the *Bulletin*, anticipated to some extent the movements for self-expression that would emerge in other colonized places. Inspired by the socialist and republican politics which marked urban life in the region, artists such as Henry Lawson and A. B. ('Banjo') Paterson developed a distinctive Australian colloquiality in their work. They promoted the mateship of the bush—an ethos of undemonstrative loyalty shared by men—as characteristic of their nation in formation.

An especially symptomatic effort on the part of the *Bulletin* writers was to foster authenticity. Young, predominantly native-born, they believed themselves to be in tune with the Australian environment. And therefore, they trusted, they were in a position to represent it. They were the 'knights of Romance' who would 'utter [Australia's] message'. This meant that for the first time Australian writers were self-consciously developing images of their country to replace those generated in Europe. In their attempt to evade English perceptions of nature and society—preconceptions dull and heavy as an English dinner, in the description of the *Bulletin* editor A. C. Stephens— they spun a myth of Australia's frontier days and lamented the lost heroism of that time (Henry Lawson, *In Days When the World Was Wide*, 1896).[6]

The typical nationalist quest for self-truth, as this outline suggests, was marked by a struggle to give shape to an everyday (here Australian) reality in resistance to images of the beautiful and the normal transmitted by colonial literature. An integral part of this process was the attempt to develop the literary forms appropriate for such expression. In stories like 'The Union Buries Its Dead' and 'The Drover's Wife' (*Short Stories in Prose and Verse*, 1894), Henry Lawson honed a sere realism and a vernacular narrative voice to capture what he saw as the definitive Australian life of harsh endurance in the bush. In his pioneering work *Such is Life* (1903), Joseph Furphy, too, concentrated on hard Australian specificities: the 'hot, black clay', the 'glassy haze', the 'barefaced incongruity' of outback life in the Riverina region. A stern 'annalist' for whom 'the monotonous variety of this interminable scrub [could have] a charm of its own', Furphy extracted from the campfire discussion of bullock drivers a recognizably Australian idiom.[7]

But the *Bulletin's* labour of national self-definition was not, of course, unique. Late nineteenth-century East India, for example, experienced a near-parallel movement of self-recovery. Around the same time as Lawson and Furphy were hymning Australia, the Bengali poet Rabindranath Tagore, even if speaking out of a very different context, and not in English, worried about the 'absurd farce' of Indians absorbing through their colonial education British ideas and words 'which enter into no chemical combination with the lives we live'.[8] His own attempt to combat this influence entailed combining Bengali poetic forms with English Romantic conventions. In poetry and stories Tagore along with other Bengali writers glorified the natural environment of Bengal as the locus of Hindu authenticity.

Laid alongside the example of Tagore, the case of the *Bulletin* writers shows two important features which were representative of colonial nationalist projects elsewhere. First, tradition as wrought in their hands was clearly something *made*: a composition or construction. The ethic of mateship, or the typical Australian signifiers of egalitarianism and the sun-soaked bush, did not spring fully formed from the Australian earth but were self-consciously fostered. Special attention was given to reclaiming the nineteenth-century bush ballad. Henry Lawson himself admitted to an element of invention in his 1892 correspondence with Paterson in the *Bulletin*. The real life of the bush, he pointed out, could be desolate and soul-destroying. Nostalgic evocations of rural locale were in the main city-based creations (as also in the case of many Bengali writers). They were also, he might have added, shaped by influences from abroad (see Henry Lawson, 'Up the Country' and 'The City Bushman', *In Days When the World Was Wide*, 1896; A. B. Paterson, 'In Defence of the Bush', *The Man from Snowy River*, 1895).

A second symptomatic feature, still sometimes overlooked, was that the white Australian nationalist upsurge in the 1890s was based on the massive exclusion of the Aboriginal population from the 'true' Australian landscape and way of life. At a time of political volatility in the country, patriotism had created a common cause in bringing together different classes of whites. This is exemplified in the ideals of bushworker and frontiersman, which took cultural homogeneity as given. The movement for Australian federation called explicitly for 'a nation for a continent', a white nation safeguarded by repressive legislation in which the severely reduced population of 67,000 Aborigines was not counted. This exclusion was reflected in the pages of the *Bulletin*. Its nationalist myth of Australia was guilty of a negation of the native presence which many twentieth-century white writers would reiterate and reinforce. Likewise in South Africa, the Union of that country in 1910 was founded on racial segregation and an exclusive symbolism of white reconciliation (between Boers and English-speaking whites).

Although they might have differed in other respects, nationalist movements elsewhere in the Empire were distinguished by related tendencies: in particular, the invention that went into the making of 'true' national character, in literature as in other forms of cultural life. Emphasis was placed upon such truth or authenticity as a way of combating the effects of imperial or metropolitan disregard. But self-representation also exacted its costs. In practice it did not mean that everyone obtained a voice. Early anti-colonial nationalist movements were in almost every case orchestrated by male élites, even in those places where white settler communities were absent. As well as invention, the exclusion from self-expression of the less empowered by those who had established for themselves a public voice marked colonial nationalisms world-wide.

Native, settler, creole

Differential experiences of self-determination under colonial rule draw attention to an important distinction which emerged early on in writing from the Empire. It was a distinction which first expressed itself in what are called the settler contact zones, where colonist Europeans and indigenous populations came into direct interaction with one another. Here the material and cultural position of the white *settlers*, or their descendants, the *creoles*, was clearly demarcated from that of the *native* population. In using terms such as native or creole, it is important to remember that empire constantly invoked racial and cultural categories such as these against the perceived creeping corruptions of mixing and miscegenation. Yet for my purposes, native–settler–creole distinctions[9] usefully highlight the asymmetrical relations of power which developed in the colonial contact zones, and the different political and literary traditions which evolved as a result.

In postcolonial studies, native colonial self-determination, the testimony of the colonized, is usually and justifiably taken as the more typical of marginalized experience. Why this is so can be easily demonstrated. In the white colonies, such as the prototypical South Africa or Australia, a system of internal colonization rigidly separated settler society from the native population. In the face of a threatening, too-proximate black presence, such separations were enforced not only geographically, as in native reserves, but legally and economically also. Seen in the context of the Empire as a whole, Indigenous peoples were, in this sense, doubly colonized or marginalized. In the South African Union, in New Zealand, and in the West Indies, British settler autonomy, especially in its vulnerable formative phases, was constructed in opposition to those who were regarded as the barbarian or the 'outsider within'. Settler demands for new visibility rested upon burying the evidence of such rival presences on the land.

Yet even as it marginalized, white colonial society was itself marginalized. It remained subordinated to London and rankled beneath the burden of what is sometimes called 'cultural cringe', after A. A. Phillips's 1950s phrase. In response to this situation, settler and creole writers became concerned to legitimate from their particular geographic and cultural perspective a subjectivity distinct, even if adapted, from Europe. Like later black nationalists, though less militantly so, they felt the need for an authenticating history. They cast about for myths of origin: tales of early pioneering, sagas involving settlers, trekkers, or bush-cutters in the interior. And they too attempted to hammer out on the anvil of their experience a language more closely moulded to their environment. As the Canadian critic E. K. Brown once commented, the mark of any colony was the lack of a 'spiritual energy', a belief in self.[10] It was in settler societies, and prototypically in nineteenth-century Ireland, therefore, that the first distinct phase of colonial national consciousness in the Empire at large can be said to have begun. Enabled by their status, European-educated creole élites—in Australia (as with the *Bulletin* writers, or Miles Franklin, or Henry Handel Richardson), Southern Africa (Olive Schreiner), the West Indies (Thomas MacDermot and, to an extent, Jean Rhys)—honed techniques of self-representation.

However, to allow that creole responses dominated the early nationalist period should not be to ignore near-contemporaneous moves towards cultural retrieval by native middle classes in other regions. In the 1880s and 1890s, as was already glimpsed, Bengal was the site of an urgent new nationalism to which Bankim Chandra Chatterjee, Rabindranath Tagore, and others gave a vernacular literary expression. To resist the dilution of indigenous cultures under British rule, Bankim developed Bengali as a narrative medium. *Anandamath* (1882), his most popular novel, gave inspiration to the Swadeshi resistance movement against the partition of Bengal in 1905. Dedicated to Mother India—'our only mother. We have no other mother'—*Anandamath* contained the rousing song 'Bande Mataram' (Hail Mother) which was taken as an anthem by protesting Indian nationalists.

Somewhat later, from the 1910s, fired by African American movements of self-determination, West Indian writers such as Claude McKay and Aimé Césaire began to proclaim African cultural dignity. Race pride, they believed, was to be recovered in the excavation of 'ancestral origins'. McKay textured his novels, *Home to Harlem* (1928), *Banjo* (1929), and *Banana Bottom* (1933), by incorporating black vernacular traditions, or as he put it 'the necromancy of [black] language'. Unconventionally for its time, his early poetry was written in Jamaican creole. *Banjo*, subtitled 'A Story without a Plot', is noteworthy for its inversion of European stereotypes of African people, in the manner of francophone Negritude writing. The novel stages discussions about black identity and Marcus Garvey's 1920s Back-to-Africa movement (directed at African Americans) as a series of lively café scenes between black vagabonds in the Marseilles docks. McKay proclaims the value of what Europe has dismissed as primitive, the 'rough rhythm of darkly-carnal life'. Drawn from across the Black Atlantic Diaspora, his displaced wanderers deploy the tactics of exile, noise, and cunning to effect a benign occupation of the French seaboard.

Yet, whether settler or creole, colonial nationalists often tended to have more in common with their middle-class counterparts in other colonies struggling for self-representation than with the disenfranchised masses of their own countries. Not unlike European nationalists of the previous century, they arose from urban-based intelligentsias or relatively privileged minorities in countries undergoing highly uneven economic development. Their biographies often ran in parallel: an élite colonial schooling; scholarships abroad; jobs in the lawcourts and the civil service. Therefore they shared ways of looking at the world. As we shall see, symbols of resistance, nationalist signs, and models of emancipation circulated among movements in the Empire in a manner reminiscent of the transfer of colonialist metaphors of old.[11]

The inspiration and guidance that India found in the example of Ireland went particularly deep. The basis for the contact lay in the contiguity of the national movements, as Lord Salisbury well saw when in 1883 he spoke of the threat which 'any species of [Irish] independence' posed to the security of the Empire at large. Though the Indian National Congress was formed in 1885, it was especially after 1905 that Indian nationalist radicals began to establish links with their Irish counterparts. Irish strategies of both parliamentary pressure and armed insurrection were investigated by Indian nationalists such as Bal Tilak and Aurobindo Ghose. Significantly, the *Gaelic American* was seized by Indian customs along with radical publications, the *Indian Sociologist* and *Bande Mataram*. As he notes in his autobiography, Jawaharlal Nehru interested himself in the formation of the Sinn Féin movement.[12] To him, the 1916 Easter Rising represented a model of indomitable nationalism. Writers, too, felt the pull of Irish contact. Both Tagore and Mulk Raj Anand found helpful correspondences for their own work in Irish literature, especially in its folk influences and Gaelic insertions. Tagore endorsed his one-time collaborator W. B. Yeats's call for writers to go back to legends and myth: 'I share his ideas of inheriting the past—if it is made relevant for the present' ('A Conversation', with Mulk Raj Anand, 1928).

Perhaps the most powerful commonality held between settler/ creole and native writers was the problem of self-fashioning: finding a position of cultural integrity from which to speak. Whether European or non-European by origin, the quest of colonials across the Empire was to hone conceptual languages which might give shape to their lived experience, their own sense of home and belonging. As we have seen, native writers, like their settler counterparts, did not in most cases speak for their people as a whole, as they claimed. Yet their intention was, emphatically, to redeem their own cultural ways from colonial denigration. Across geographically separate regions, writers were interested in exploring historical beginnings and aetiologies as the basis for a new selfhood, in order to bludgeon the damage of the colonial past. That which was perceived as source they named authentic. Bent to the construction of a 'real' or rooted identity, both settler and native writers found themselves in situations of conflicted collaboration with European cultural forms—the nation, identity, 'civilization'.

The double vision of the colonized

To be true to oneself in borrowed robes: this was the core dilemma of the colonial nationalist, most particularly of the colonized native. The full dimensions of the question of self-articulation become clear when we consider that not only the language and literary traditions transmitted by a colonial education were British, but also the institutions and political ideologies through which autonomy was asserted were derived in part from European research and European templates. In India, for example, the historical recovery work done by William Jones and other orientalists was foundational for the nationalist movement. The Europeans' interpretation and integration of Hindu myths, laws, and rituals to form a coherent system gave substance and shape to Indian romanticization of the past. From the moment of their genesis, therefore, nationalist élites were caught in a situation of *split perception* or *double vision*. Bilingual and bicultural, having Janus-like access to both metropolitan and local cultures, yet alienated from both, the élites who sought to challenge aspects of imperial rule also found they might gain advantages from making compromises with it.

Undeniably, the Empire would not have survived as long as it did without the early co-operation of colonized élites. Frantz Fanon, a key theorist of anti-imperial nationalism, rightly observed that the colonized man breathed the 'appeal of Europe like pure air' (*Peau noire, masques blancs*, 1952; *Black Skin, White Masks*, 1967). European ways were believed to bring income, status, and the possibility of sharing in power. Nationalists in particular reached for that which was progressive, 'modern', and improving in a Western sense as vehicles of political mobilization. Typically, a black *Who's Who* published in South Africa in 1930 featured 'New Africans', spokesmen of a new black consciousness (of which Sol Plaatje was an early representative), who were selected for inclusion on the basis of their being 'progressive', 'hardworking', 'Christian', and bent on 'self-improvement'. Plaatje himself was typical of nativist politicians when he invoked not only British liberalism but also the civilizing ideals of the colonial mission to voice his opposition to South African land law.[13]

The better to advance their position, native nationalists across a wide geographical spectrum adopted the persona of enlightened English gentleman—more correct, more colonialist, more English in fact than the real item. Yet in so doing they inevitably ran up against the cleavings of the colonized situation. Even as they raised their status within the imperial system, imperial ideology marked them as inferior. In this the promise of imperial identity—all subjects equally placed beneath the magnanimous rule of Queen Victoria—was shown up for its hollowness. As the next chapter demonstrates in more depth, no matter how hard native nationalists—and also settler colonials—struggled, they could never be exactly British. Allegedly civilized through the beneficence of colonial rule or by virtue of cultural inheritance, they were not deemed civilized at source. Even in their efforts to be the same they were marked as different. They mimicked Europeans and were ridiculed for their mimicry. This is starkly exemplified in Kipling's portrait of the inept yet 'cultured', 'more English than the English' Bengali babu, the charmer of drawing-rooms, in the story 'The Head of the District' (*Life's Handicap*, 1891). White colonials, too, were said to lack concrete identity, as in the case of Lawrence's Australians in *Kangaroo*. They belonged neither in Britain nor in their 'adopted' homes.

In short, colonial writers, positioned between diametrically different cultural worlds, were able to borrow from several traditions, yet belonged to no one. In the face of their uneasy marginality or supplementarity, they would turn in time to what might be called their own—their own experience of environment, migration, or invasion, as the case might be—to find a position for self-reconstruction. As discussed in Chapter 5, the mode of return and renewal, of recuperation generally, remains crucial in postcolonial writing today.

Generic choice in nationalist writing

Culturally in exile, the effort of nationalist writers was to retrieve or invent edenic homelands, lost spiritual traditions set in an unspoilt pastoral past. W. B. Yeats, in his incarnation as Irish nationalist, sought in native traditions the regeneration of his nation from the effects of English rule. 'I would have Ireland re-create the ancient arts', he wrote, '. . . as they were understood when they moved a whole people' ('Ireland and the Arts', *Essays and Introductions*, 1901, 1961). Claude McKay regarded black folklore, melody, and verbal artistry as a taproot into the 'legendary vitality' of (a masculine) black culture, its strongest guard against 'the civilised machine' of modern life (see *Banjo* and *Banana Bottom*).

As this might suggest, an important line of approach available to both creole and native writers in search of identity was the conversion of apparent deficiencies into definitions of self. They learned to exploit the resources of their own half-and-half status. The condition of placelessness—the 'mongrel education' of the colonized, as Nehru describes his own upbringing, became the impulse for narratives of reconstructed belonging. Writers attempted to transform their experience of cultural schizophrenia into a restorative dream of home, a healing myth of origin, or a consolatory lyric combining diverse melodies. The approach can be traced both in nationalists' choice of subject-matter—childhood, homecoming, separation, and return—and in their generic and stylistic responses to the European colonial inheritance.

A bilingual position poised between cultures allowed access to two kinds of rhetoric, at least two traditions of public speech. Mixing and crossing languages, forms, and styles, colonized writers evolved polysemic—truly *creolized*—modes of expression. The genealogy of the Indian novel in English gives an idea of what this formation of a colonial *hybrid* or *contact text* involved. Its growth was informed most obviously by the influence of the English nineteenth-century novel, usually first encountered by writers as a school text. Works by Walter Scott, Wilkie Collins, Disraeli, and the now unknown G. M. W. Reynolds were popular. But equally important in building this new form were indigenous and themselves hybridized narrative traditions: tales from the *Arabian Nights*, the embedded story-telling conventions of the *Mahabharata* and the *Ramayana*, the medieval oral narrative structures of the Puranas.[14] Earlier in the nineteenth century, too, the Indo-Anglian poet Henry Derozio had experimented syncretically, combining English metre and rhythm with Indian themes. Over in West Africa, the literary culture of the 1920s (which provides an informing backcloth to the work of writers like Chinua Achebe and Cyprian Ekwensi), again formed a rich mix, in this case of improving mission literature, popular European novelists like Marie Corelli, advice journalism, and oral tales.[15]

A significant consequence of their imaginative work, therefore, was that nationalist writers began bit by bit to intrude upon the generic provinces of colonialist discourse: the adventure and quest tale, the colonial or New World pastoral, and, as we shall see a little later, historical narrative. Writers were now taking the initiative in the representation of their geography as edenic, natural, wild, a site of myth and ritual, to be either reclaimed or mourned. Plaatje of course made an allusive nod in the direction of H. Rider Haggard while proceeding to write his own nationalist romance about nineteenth-century Africa. In his 1890s short stories, Tagore painted pastoral scenes of a peaceful, bucolic Bengal, to give shape to his patriotic feelings for the region. In *Banana Bottom*, McKay depicts his heroine Bita Plant's return to Jamaica from Europe by staging pageants of dance and obeah ritual against a country background of fertile fruit-bearing valleys. Bita Plant was as a child raped in the lush 'peasant fields' where she is now happily reunited with her community. The home environment becomes a paradise regained.

Generic intrusion had the potential for powerful transvaluation. Reworking from their own historical positions Europe's fantasies of New Worlds, or high-flown propaganda for colonial settlement, nationalists converted the stereotyped images and generic codes which once had labelled them into sources of positive being. Their techniques of intrusion and conversion followed two main lines of approach. First, writers might combine genres associated with colonialist culture, such as the exotic romance and the pastoral, with the special grittiness or quiddity of their own cultural experience. Romanticizing the past, they none the less tried to represent their societies accurately from within. As we shall see later on, 1960s novelists in Nigeria such as Chinua Achebe, Flora Nwapa, Elechi Amadi, and Onuora Nzekwu would take this path.

Or, in an earlier nativist response, writers might choose to keep colonialist divisions in place while inverting their meaning. That is, as did the Negritude poets, they drew upon the dualisms that defined the colonial other, but at the same time contested the stereotypes of barbarian and savage: they negated these negations. Claude McKay proclaimed pride in 'Congo-sounding laughter', 'jungle jazzing', the close 'biological kinship [of those of African origin] to the swell of primitive earth life'.[16] Tagore, writing in Bengali, laid stress on the sensitivity, spirituality, and harmony of Indian culture, as against the harsh pragmatism and realism of Europe. Again, colonialist East/West dichotomies were kept in place but their associations were reversed.

W. B. Yeats's evocations of an ancestral 'romantic Ireland' represent a forerunner of compensatory nationalist re-creations. Though his involvement in active nationalist politics was always touched by ambivalence, Yeats like later postcolonial writers drew upon his reading of myth and legend to forge an image of traditional Ireland. Like them, he valued the artifice of nostalgia, and sought to shape the future by redescribing the past. He believed in cultural retrieval, 'the reawakening of imaginative life', as a strengthening force for a nation. In poetry and essays he crafted a utopian Irish past of peasants and warriors, a myth-fantasy which was quite clearly the opposite of materialist Britain, yet drew on the conventions of English pastoral. Such retrospective imaginings recall the nationalist energies of Tagore and Gandhi. Gandhi too fostered an image of a pre-industrial homeland, a pastoral India fashioned on the lines of Ruskin's *Unto this Last* (1862), which like Yeats he had read and cherished. As well as its revivalist make-up, Yeats's romantic Ireland bears other representative features. First, it is élitist: a feudal land ruled by aristocrats and warriors. Second, the gendering of his image of Ireland, as illustrated in *Cathleen ni Houlihan* (1902), would characterize other nationalist movements also. Ireland for Yeats, like the African continent for the Negritude writers, or India for Bankim, was female. Another concern Yeats shared with colonial nationalists elsewhere was that of language choice and usage. Adopting English, the colonial tongue, writers even at this early stage sought to rework its meanings and structures. Yeats's belief was that Ireland's heroic history should be sung in a tongue at least adapted to the people's heritage, or in his words, 'in English, [but] with the accent of their own country'.

But the nationalist vision of the homeland did not necessarily signify unrelieved harmony. Another oppositional strategy was available to writers whereby they collapsed together or mingled the polarities which underpinned colonialist rhetoric. Thus their work might simultaneously debunk and idealize the past, placing negative alongside positive terms, New Worlds beside dystopias, the noble savage shoulder to shoulder with the barbarian and the slave. This is vividly demonstrated in the Martinican Aimé Césaire's *Cahier d'un retour au pays natal* (1939; *Notebook of a Return to the Native Land*, 1983), a 1930s Negritude poem which became a model of defiance for younger anti-colonial writers.

In the course of this long surrealist work, the poet strives to come to terms with a black history of degradation and martyrdom, a memory 'encircled with blood'. The process is encapsulated in his imagined return to his native island. The quest demands an unconditional acceptance of everything that the past has brought, both its shame and its heroism. The poet recalls from ancestral memory, alongside totemic symbols of hummingbird, dolphin, stars, and a dreamlike 'Congo resounding with forests and rivers', scenes of blood-letting and subjection. Juxtaposed with the image of the powerful sea-swell, suggesting the coming of new force to the island, there is also the grief of the island's slave history.

Along with nativist or nostalgic pastoral, historical narrative, too, was used to counter the negative images of colonial rule. In a nationalist historical romance, the past, officially represented as a tale of colonial successes, could be told from a different angle. Here again a writer might adopt a nostalgic mood, as exemplified in Thomas Mofolo's *Chaka* (1925), or the historical romances of Bankim, or parts of Henry Handel (Ethel Florence) Richardson's reconstructions of nineteenth-century Australia in the trilogy *The Fortunes of Richard Mahony* (1930; published as *Australia Felix*, 1917, *The Way Home*, 1925, and *Ultima Thule*, 1929). In Bankim's *Anandamath*, a fabulistic Bengali retelling of late eighteenth-century resistance to the East India Company, the forests of Bengal are evoked in romantic terms, as a type of fragrant Arden.

But, as in Césaire and Richardson, the view of the past or the homeland could be ambivalent. *Australia Felix* opens with an old Ballarat digger's 'desperate homesickness' for the old country and his exile's hatred for the new. The scene is one of mud and denuded earth, the 'havoc' that mining has made of Australia's 'green-spread crust'. In Christina Stead's Australian novel *Seven Poor Men of Sydney* (1934), the 1920s city is both 'radiant' and an underworld of poverty and frustrated idealism. Even as the characters haltingly seek an imaginative language to describe their reality, they are hemmed in by parochialism or urban alienation: they 'cannot even speak their difference to each other'. In reclaiming black history, *Mhudi* does not turn its face from the vengeful wars which took place between communities in southern Africa around the time of white penetration. Achebe's *Things Fall Apart* and *Arrow of God* (1964) continue this trend, dramatizing in the histories of Okonkwo and Ezeulu the internal divisions which racked villages in the Niger delta, and helped prepare the way for the white man's incursion.

Both the pastoral romance and the historical novel allowed colonial intellectuals to participate in the narratives of the imperial centre, but obliquely, cunningly. The anti-representational and fantastical aspects of romance encouraged the conception of alternative worlds, other possibilities of being, self-recovery, consolation. Writers like Bankim, Plaatje, or Raja Rao, who retained links with oral culture, were drawn to the ways in which the stylization of the written romance overlapped with the patterns of oral narrative. In contrast, the documentary or realist mode of historical narration, like the socio-historical reportage of Mulk Raj Anand, prompted a different kind of rewriting, a careful scripting of the near past, or of one's own lived reality. Writers could claim agency in giving conceptual shape to their history, culture, and society.

Both approaches also permitted *retrospect as aspiration*. Both were concerned with recovering an identity fragmented, displaced, or discredited under colonialism in order to reconstitute cultural integrity and, in this way, to construct a vision of an independent future. Of his work Bankim commented that without a history recounting their 'greatness', Bengalis could 'never rise to their full stature'. Tagore repeatedly pointed out that history had the power to revivify the wasted self-esteem of Indians. The African writers of independence, as we shall see, took a similar line. The past and the land, the land as embodiment of the values of the past, provided sources of authenticity, primarily for the nation emerging from its history of colonial occupation, but also, more specifically, for its intellectual élite. That the land was in more cases than not pictured as maternal, or as abused and adored female body, while leadership was figured as masculine, points to the dominant gender configurations of early colonial nationalist movements.

As well as being overwhelmingly male, nationalist leadership at this time was, as we saw earlier, middle-class, highly educated—also urbanized, liberal-minded, cosmopolitan, and often more proficient in European than in indigenous forms of expression. Crucially, élites were separated from the knowable communities that formed the locus of their newly crafted identity. Nostalgia and reconstruction, therefore, helped legitimate or—as the case might be—camouflage the more 'advanced' of an élite's progressive or modernist attitudes. To lay accent on the unity and restored identity of a hitherto unrepresented people was to rally the nationalist cause, to champion the people, and also, significantly, to claim a part of their wholeness.

Metropolitans, modernists, and nationalists

Even as the new colonial writers harked back to the past, therefore, they opened up a future. While constructing for themselves homelands of the imagination, they were also moving closer in their literary and political sympathy to the cosmopolitan but still imperial European metropolis. Indeed, ironically, the romantic focus on cultural reconstruction signalled a self-conscious modernity, and hence a means of obtaining recognition on the international stage.

Coinciding with these developments in the colonial world, European modernism had begun to give acknowledgement to the so-called primitive arts. During the first decades of the twentieth century, there was growing recognition in the capitals of Europe that the cultures brought into view by colonization had something of substance to offer a society increasingly less confident of its own truths. Concern about self-representation in the Empire, therefore, resonated with the new climate of questioning in the West. What emerges here is a seeming conjuncture between, on the one hand, the modernist crisis over meaning, and the consequent widespread European interest in *other* (often colonized) cultures, and, on the other, colonial nationalists' early struggles to find a progressive if nostalgic literary voice. Cultural and aesthetic influences, it would appear, moved in two directions across the divide between the metropolis and the colonial margins.

Given its seeming importance to both sides, what in more detail did this conjuncture of interests involve? To explore this question, it will be necessary to widen the scope of attention. Early nationalist writing must be located in an expanded international mapping in which end-of-era colonial and modernist discourse—the work of D. H. Lawrence, the Woolfs, T. S. Eliot, E. M. Forster, and others—is juxtaposed with responses from colonial territories. This wider context displaces what is called the 'diffusionist' interpretation of early twentieth-century cultural movements: a cartography of Europe as still the maker of the world's meanings, and the native as the passive recipient of its interpretations.

Clearly, the new colonial writers stood to learn much from the techniques of dislocation which distinguished the modernist avant-garde. For expatriate and colonized artists, modernist urban reality correlated quite closely with their own experience, doubly or triply alienated from origins. But it would be wrong to speak of their rela-tionship to cultural movements in the centre as merely derivative. It may be that the emergence of new colonial writers, their presence in avant-garde circles in the West, and in particular the challenge their self-expression posed to European cultural authority, all contributed to the volatile new cosmopolitan climate. Certainly, even if outspoken and self-confident colonial artists were at this stage still few and far between, the heterogeneity and vigorous modernity they represented corresponded to modernist interests in the displaced, the fragmented, the inverse, the miscellaneous.

From the 1910s onward, drawn irresistibly to the cultural freedoms of the metropolis, colonial writers like Katherine Mansfield, Claude McKay, Mulk Raj Anand, Jean Rhys, C. L. R. James, came to form part of the 'complex and open milieu' of the new cosmopolitan city. Resident in London or Paris, they participated in the hubbub of metropolitan experimentation; they helped constitute the cultural collage that was the modernist urban avant-garde.[17] This intrusion of other cultural presences into metropolitan consciousness could not but have intensified those experiences characteristically associated with modernism: 'making new', the sense of historical liminality, interests in subjective and multiple perspectives and in the fluidity of consciousness. Perhaps, too, the colonials' culturally translated art provided models for the multilingual, generically mixed utterance that modernism favoured. Moreover, the preoccupation with displacement and loss of identity shared by the new colonial writers corresponded to the breakdown in universal systems of understanding with which metropolitan modernists were concerned. Exile, deracination, urban disorientation, the fragmentation of absolutes, alienation in a variety of different forms, all these defined existence for twentieth-century writers throughout the world, both those from the emergent nations and those based in the colonial centre.

The modernist movement, of course, is characteristically regarded as metropolitan and Euro-American. But this description neglects the contributions to modernist art from the British and also the French colonies (in particular, in the latter case, from the Negritude poets). In modernism, cross-fertilized influences, transplanted cultural forms— not in every case transferred by Europeans—displaced western precepts and conventional beliefs. Salman Rushdie has observed that writers of the colonial contact zone, inhabitants of fractured, hybrid, upturned worlds, polyglot by necessity, were in a sense modernists *avant la lettre*. They 'have been forced by cultural displacement to accept the provisional nature of all truths, all certainties, have perhaps had modernism forced upon [them]' ('Imaginary Homelands', 1982). Relatedly, Paul Gilroy and Toni Morrison have designated the African slaves of the New World the first moderns on the basis of their painful but ultimately transformational interaction with, and adaptation to, different cultures.[18]

The point, however, is not simply to assert that colonials were precursor modernists. It is rather to recognize that aspects of colonized and colonial expatriate reality were distinctively, perhaps in some cases even definitively modernist. It is also to observe that modernism as a body of discursive practices was not simply imposed on the Empire in the form of influential trends or school curricula. We see in modernism signs of colonial writers critically engaging with the writing of the centre—its surrealism, its fragmentary forms. They appropriated its influences selectively, interpreting these to match their own experience.

And metropolitan modernism, in turn, was deeply influenced by the new aesthetic perspectives which Western expansion across the globe had laid bare. In the mishmash of ethnologists' findings, in the *mélanges* that were museum displays, hybridized menus, and plant collections, in language borrowings and the formation of dialects and creoles, the crossing and collision of cultures in the colonial process had created the possibility of differently angled perceptions, new and rejuvenating interpretations. During the first half of the twentieth century the cultural values of other peoples, which had formerly been neglected or held in contempt, began for the first time significantly to unsettle European preconceptions, pointing to different but valid ways of knowing.

In any number of different forms the West experienced this arrival of the Stranger in its midst: in the rise of cultural anthropology; in late nineteenth-century theosophist preoccupations with Eastern spirituality; in fauvist and primitivist styles of painting; in theories of the unconscious mind. What was once otherworldly was now encouraged to interact creatively with western forms of understanding. Henri Bergson's ideas concerning different, coexistent flows of time undercut certain fundamental concepts of duration, succession, and simultaneity. Freud and Jung looked to myths and fetish objects from other cultures to illuminate the European psyche. For modernist artists—not only Picasso, but also André Derain, Jean Dubuffet, Henri Matisse, and others—the masks, carvings, and ceremonial artefacts which might be discovered in European collections held rich potential for new aesthetic speculations. Especially significant for their acceptance of non-western representational styles and modes of colouration are Paul Gauguin's 1890s search for the honesty of 'barbarism' over the subterfuges of 'civilization' in the South Seas; Post-Impressionists' interest in Japanese prints and Javanese friezes; Picasso's iconoclastic *Demoiselles d'Avignon* (1907) and experimentation with African mask motifs in the years following. In Australia in the 1920s, the artist Margaret Preston, influenced by Bergson, cited Aboriginal art forms as the 'foundation of a national culture for this country'.[19] As the scholar of comparative religion Mircea Eliade once commented, early twentieth-century explorations in religion, surrealism and 'depth-psychology' had begun to corrode the barriers which in colonial times had separated the 'backward' world and the 'modern' West.[20] Investigations into non-European myth across a broad spectrum exposed areas of lack and occlusion in European conceptual systems.

Resulting from these explorations, the suspicion arose that the European self might have certain characteristics *in common* with the other. Early anthropologists, among them J. G. Frazer, author of the influential comparative study *The Golden Bough* (1890, 1911–15), sought to demonstrate that western religions rested on a common ancient base: diverse cultures might well be linked by underlying ritualistic themes. These various new developments, working from different points of view, undoubtedly posed a potential cumulative challenge to nineteenth-century conceptions of European centrality and superiority. But the apparent threat to the West represented by such a challenge also held out hope. In societies where institutions and beliefs inherited from the past were increasingly called into question, the symbolic systems of once-discredited other cultures offered consoling new modes of form–giving, new kinds of spiritual connection.

Writers, too, opened themselves to 'enlightening' influences from lands conventionally perceived as degenerate or dark. In his Introduction to Tagore's self-translated *Gitanjali* (1912), Yeats commended the poetry's simplicity, courtesy, intensity of mood, and cultural wholeness, noting that nothing in years had so 'stirred his blood'. Tagore, who was strenuously promoted in Europe at this time, was also taken up in the 1920s by Wittgenstein, who sought religious insight in his work. India represented to thinkers and writers the possibility of new spiritual awakening. Already in the late nineteenth century the young Yeats's psychic explorations had brought him to Indian literature, where he found organizing motifs for his own work. Asia, he believed, with its ceremonies and its religious gravity, had much to offer Europe. The meaningful structures he perceived in Eastern traditions—their underlying ancestral matrix—laid the first foundations of the myth-system he would construct for himself in *A Vision* (1925).

So the early colonial nationalist quest for mythic identity developed alongside European explorations in new belief systems: mysticism, the occult, back-to-nature movements. And both kinds of investigation were powerfully reinforced by the experience of 1914–18. The technologized slaughter of that war revealed the immense capacity for destruction of a mechanized civilization obsessed with dominance. Gandhi, for example, was relentless in his condemnation of mass production and the materialist West. But D. H. Lawrence, too, struggled to avoid what he saw as the strangulating grip of industrial Europe. As Chapter 4 will show, in novels like *Kangaroo* and *The Plumed Serpent* (1926), he sought in distant—to him primitive and hence more vitalistic—societies impulses for Western regeneration. Around the same time, T. S. Eliot was involved in developing his own influential doctrine concerning myth. Mythic structure as found in the Irish cosmopolitan Joyce's *Ulysses*, he believed, was a way of giving form to the futility and anarchy of a post-war world. In *The Waste Land* he assembled shards of disparate rituals and religious systems— the fertility cults described by J. G. Frazer and Jessie Weston, fragments of the Upanishads—in the belief that these formed part of a lost but more meaningful cultural whole. A poet who had studied Sanskrit and Pali in order to read Indian philosophy, Eliot observed in his notes to *The Waste Land* that the 'Buddha's Fire Sermon [from the *Maha-vagga*] . . . corresponds in importance to the Sermon on the Mount'. Europe, writers began gradually to observe, needed to 'own' its other, its repressed, to save itself from moral and spiritual breakdown.

It is now a critical truism that modernism was in large measure a movement comprising outsiders and exiles. (T. S. Eliot, James Joyce, Wyndham Lewis, Mina Loy, Ezra Pound, Leonard and Virginia Woolf, and Lawrence, were national, gender, sex, or class 'exiles'.) Their expressions of estrangement shaped structures of feeling in wider metropolitan society. But as cultural migrants, their concerns were potentially also aligned with those of the new provincial or colonial writers. Admittedly, certain tendencies in modernism may appear to resist this interpretation. In particular, there was the intellectual élite's dread of the mass and working-class insurrection, which amplified their sense of alienation. Indeed, their fear may to an extent be attributed to the new visibility and increasing restlessness of colonial subjects. The incursion of other peoples in the West, therefore, was not in every case embraced. Nor, as will become clear, did it necessarily lead to sharing or equal cultural exchange.

However, the fact remains that modernist writers, like the colonials, spoke out of a reality of social displacement or disintegration. They, too, expressed a consciousness of being removed from source, or truth, or reality (as left-wing or avant-garde, as regional or female, lower middle-class, gay). Emergent nationalist or creole writers may have placed primary value on the search for identity or a reintegrated subjectivity. In contrast their metropolitan counterparts were concerned with the dispersal of the self, and the disintegration of meaning generally. But the two groups shared a strong sense of cultural insecurity, a mistrust of orthodoxy, and an interest in alternative values.[21]

Seen in this light, the culturally alienated colonial writer becomes representative of a much broader movement. The quest for home and history of McKay or Césaire, or the expatriate restlessness of Rhys, Mansfield, or Christina Stead, both reflected and helped to shape modernist questions about subjectivity, language, and belief. Like the European modernists, these migrants tended to have high regard for the authority of the cultural past—western or otherwise. Yet, chafing at the limits they experienced within tradition, they sought also to remake it. Further out from the centre, writers who did not migrate, or only briefly, such as, respectively, R. K. Narayan (India) or Morley Callaghan (Canada), were none the less preoccupied with problems similar to those of the metropolitan expatriates. Their search for non-British, local or indigenous forms of cultural expression related to the crisis in meaning-making experienced by their London- and Paris-based counterparts.

Yet merely tracing correspondences between interests in the metropolis and in its outlying districts can appear to leave too much, as it were, to mere coincidence. In that the new colonial writers themselves represented dissent and difference from source, their contribution can perhaps be interpreted in a stronger sense. Can they be seen as forming a constitutive part of the modernist movement rather than as being merely its symptom, or sympathetic effect? What, more substantively, did their contribution entail?

As already suggested, by their presence, as by the difference of their perspectives, emergent colonial artists, both native and creole, represented for their period a kind of interference, even if modest and careful, in the sphere of western cultural hegemony. Though their influence may not have been great at this stage, they went some way towards effecting a displacement of conventional perspectives. In their own practice writers helped constellate an international modernism. Their writing, as well as their experience as early migrant writers, crossed the cultural forces of the centre and the periphery. Jean Rhys's *Voyage in the Dark* (1934), for instance, interleaves scenes of urban spiritual dereliction with homesickness for the West Indies. Permeated by a yearning for the wholeness promised by Dominica, the centre of Rhys's childhood history, the novel evokes a Caribbean exotic on the basis of an insider's memories while in metropolitan exile. From the vantage point of an alienated colonial, the imperial capital is thus observed at once from within and without.

It was especially from the time of the First World War that colonial artists and writers working in the metropolis—Mulk Raj Anand, Aimé Césaire, Claude McKay, Katherine Mansfield, Sol Plaatje, William Plomer—enacted and depicted cultural difference within the purlieus of European culture, even if only in isolated pockets at first. Like Rhys, Mansfield (as we shall see) and Anand, who haunted Bloomsbury circles between the wars, re-created, from the point of view of London, their distant homelands in their fiction. Their art intersected the capital and the colonies. Therefore, whereas critical accounts of modernism have taken for granted European agency in the search for alternative meaning, it is surely also the case that emergent colonial artists must grasp some of the credit for both representing and demonstrating plurality to western eyes.

Taking into account not only the involvement of colonial writers but also the new hybridity of aesthetic influence, modernism is therefore revealed as the beginning of a process of global transculturation in literature that has continued to effloresce. It constituted the first stage in a broad movement of twentieth-century cultural displacement, a development which the Sri Lankan-born Canadian writer Michael Ondaatje has described as colonial bastardy (see *The English Patient*). In modernism the colonial world was confirmed in its status as province to the Western city. *There* was the place that the artefacts came from. *Here* was where the definitions that counted were still made. Yet in modernist writing, too, the Empire made the first moves to write back to, and in so doing to displace, the centre. Despite imperialist intentions to transplant English culture abroad, in practice colonization brought cultural cross-fertilization and eventual hybridization.

It remains true to say, however, that even while modernism was infused with perspectives from elsewhere, emergent writers from colonial territories also stood to gain from contact with the metropolis. This applies in particular to those local élites who, educated in colonial schools, were injected with western ideas and sentiment. The theories of Freud, Marx, and Nietzsche suggested to them useful decentring strategies, ways of dismantling dominant patterns of European thought. 'Making new', the iconoclasm of James Joyce, Virginia Woolf, T. S. Eliot, or of surrealism, was liberating: modernist writing made available symbolic languages for interpreting the rapidly changing reality of colonial territories. From the 1930s, for Bengali poets such as Bishnu De, the fragmented structures of Eliot's work, and later those of Auden, suggested ways of giving conceptual shape to local urban experience. Poets in Canada during the same period—A. J. M. Smith, Robert Finch, Dorothy Livesay—learned from Yeats, Eliot, and Pound how to accommodate the conversational rhythms of their own vernacular. A later generation of West Indian poets, too, lent an ear to Eliot in their attempt to reconcile European poetic forms with creole. The allusive, disjunctive style of modernist poetry would also suggest to African writers at the time of independence ways of representing the stark contrasts of their postcolonial experience. As Wole Soyinka put it, from the 1950s onwards Nigerian poets sought to 'regroup images of Ezra Pound around the oil bean and the nude spear'. Eliot's validation of tradition, Yeats's fabrication of a private symbolic system, and modernist re-evaluations of alien myth systems in general plotted strategies of self-justification for nationalist writers, even though enclosed within European epistemic structures.[22]

Again, for Césaire in the 1930s, surrealist techniques based on Freudian and Jungian ideas helped to create an 'insurrectional', 'hell-bound' poetry with which to undercut imprisoning forms of western conceptual thought. Mulk Raj Anand described himself in Joycean terms as forging with the help of modernist techniques 'the uncreated conscience of [his] race'. He identified with British writers whom he saw as 'knocking down the walls': Forster and his criticisms of British society; Joyce's 'word-coinage'; D H. Lawrence's atavism; Virginia Woolf's fascination for the numinous in language. Marrying Freud to Hinduism in a characteristic move, Anand said of his time in Bloomsbury: 'I wanted to liberate the unconscious via the Shakti–Shakta Tantric thought and dig down to the depths' (*Conversations in Bloomsbury*, 1981). Though he did not like to write as a 'foreign novelist', Anand's countryman and contemporary Raja Rao also admitted to the European (though non-English) influence on his work of, amongst others, Yeats, Gide, and French symbolist poetry. He spent much of his writing life in Europe.

Anand's and Rao's European sojourns may seem incongruous but were not untypical. For many colonial writers, native or settler, migration to the metropolis, usually Paris or London but increasingly also New York, signified a necessary cultural pilgrimage. As Fanon said, the colonial capital was perceived as the Tabernacle, the source of ultimate knowledge (*Black Skin, White Masks*). For élites from different parts of the Empire, the journey to that source afforded a common rite of passage, binding writers together. Its streets represented escape-routes from the stifling provinciality of, as the case might be, New Zealand, Canada, or the West Indies. Already in 1899, Henry Lawson, though bearing 'a heart full of love for Australia', was advising the young writer 'to go steerage, stow away, swim, and seek London, Yankeeland, or Timbuctoo—rather than stay in Australia till his genius turned to gall, or beer' (' "Pursuing Literature" in Australia').

It was indeed a consequence of the colonial replication of the centre in the periphery that, relative to the metropolis, the latter was doomed to appear derivative, prosaic, slow. In vivid contrast, the twentieth-century western city was at once the environment and the symbol of the future. Here the avant-garde found the freedom to test the boundaries of the conventional. Here new technologies of travel and communication created a rich, confusing simultaneity of experience. For colonials and metropolitans alike, the city made possible a modernist aesthetic. It was a fashion, a lifestyle, a cultural imperative. It was also the place where audiences tended to be more tolerant of otherness and nationalist dissent than was society out in the Empire. For those in the centre, the challenge of newly emergent voices represented no real political threat—or not yet. It was therefore to the progressive venues of the cosmopolitan city that nationalist artists, writers, and activists came to call attention to colonial injustice, and to understand their oppression at its cultural source.

Yet the parallels I have drawn need some qualification. To interconnect writings does not mean conflating them. The new nationalists differed from the early urban modernists in at least two important respects. First, the cultural resources upon which they drew to express their alterity, even if reconstructed, were to them more accessible, or more present, than the 'primitive' references of their European counterparts. They were not exotic to themselves. Second, if metropolitan culture of the early twentieth century laid accent on the experience of alienation, and began to distrust the capacity of language to mean, it was, in contrast, imperative for the new nationalists to continue to make sense. Their need was to (re-)create a meaningful identity and history, though to do so in a new way.

Mansfield and Rao: between worlds

Dilemmas of cultural exile unite the work of native and creole writers, and link it, too, with what was going on in metropolitan literary circles. To bring this chapter to a synoptic close, illustrations of two possible positions in the area of emergent colonial writing will be taken from Katherine Mansfield, the New Zealand pioneer of the modernist short story, and Raja Rao, one of the first Indian novelists to write in English.

During her relatively short career as a writer, Katherine Mansfield embraced the personae both of modernist artist as outsider and of colonial outsider as modernist. An expatriate in Europe, she spoke for a condition of psychological and physical exile. Her short stories reflect the glancing surface realities of the modern city. Yet at moments, and increasingly after 1916, they hark back to the brightly coloured worlds of her South Pacific childhood. Her work also evokes the frangibility of women's existence, out of place both in the competitive male world of the frontier and in the metropolitan centre.

Fleeing the confinements of colonial Wellington, Mansfield as a young writer sought a place for herself in avant-garde London. The impressionistic scene-painting and intensely focused subjectivity which she developed in her stories were soon recognized as distinctively modernist. But even if self-consciously acquired as part of a cosmopolitan aesthetic, the restlessness of the writing, reflected in its fragmented linearity, also connects with Mansfield's position as a transient in Europe. Significantly, her characters often inhabit a void: they are vagrants, lacking social and cultural co-ordinates. Historical associations in the stories are generally vague, as if recoverable in memory only.

As with character, so also with narrative voice: Mansfield did not speak for a definable region; her narrative consciousness was not rooted. Notoriously, she tried out other people's styles. In an almost stereotyped instance of colonial copying, she once 'translated freely' from Chekhov, mimicking in order to find her own narrative approach. Her favoured generic form, the short story, allowed her to develop the technique of sharp, rapidly flitting observation which suited her transient state. The form did not demand the sustained attention of a novel.

Mansfield's chosen environment was the modern city. Yet, no doubt prompted by her experience of cosmopolitan rootlessness, she also attempted as she grew older to re-create from memory her New Zealand homeland. As she wrote in her journal (22 February 1916), she sought to make her 'undiscovered country leap into the eyes of the Old World'. This imagined return is reflected in the long short story draft *The Aloe* (1915–1916). Written as an elegiac exercise following her brother's death in the First World War, *The Aloe* is a tale of displacement. It depicts a house-moving from an already transitional zone, the New Zealand shoreline near Wellington, to an 'unknown country', a hinterland where nature seems at once recognizably English and yet alien, wild and intense: the dew is drenching, the flowers grow lustily. *Aloe* accents the otherness of its world by evoking a child's atmospheric perceptions of space. To the girl Kezia nature is alarming, filled with threat and violence.

Aloe's fractured conversations are unmistakably reminiscent of Virginia Woolf's narrative style. However, it might equally be the case that the difficulty of representing the cultural difference of her material inspired Mansfield to develop darting and fragmented observations. Significantly, in the later revised and neatened work 'Prelude' (1917), she cut some of *Aloe's* specifically colonial details: the store full of 'big untidy men' which is covered everywhere 'either with fly paper or an advertisement', the Young Ladies Academy with its teacher '(from England)', the reference to a Maori war.

Throughout *Aloe* an otherness persists in obtruding, in particular in the secluded spaces of the women-dominated family homestead. Women's fantasies in the story are rebellious, part of the 'violent sweet thing called life' which is exorbitantly expressed in the natural world. It is at the very axis of that wilderness world, in the centre of the garden, that the hypnotic presence of the aloe is found. In this symbol Mansfield concentrates her perceptions of her own and her country's difference. Unambiguously an object of female longing, the plant with its animal-like qualities contains a strong native energy yet is in fact a foreigner, an African desert bloom. In this newly tamed South Pacific garden, it represents a force that the colonial bourgeoisie cannot fully control.

Kanthapura (1938) by Raja Rao works at two closely connected levels. It takes the form of a transcribed or 'literary' oral tale that narrates the Indian independence movement as experienced in a single village. At the same time, the story of that community's efforts to withstand the exploitation of workers on the nearby Skeffington Coffee Estate can be read as a parable about Gandhian passive resistance politics. Pastoral romance, Hindu myth, and traditional narrative techniques blend with contemporary history in such a way as to create a contemporary fabulistic tale of nationalist struggle. Opposition to British rule, for example, is likened to the destruction of Ravana by Rama, and to Krishna's slaying of the serpent Kal.

The pastoral in *Kanthapura* relates to its politics. In the context of Gandhian resistance, efforts to champion old village ways bear an explicitly political edge. This becomes especially clear when we remember that the Gandhian political system was based on a vision of India as a vast network of villages, not as a nation-state. In the novel, the village followers of the local Congressman Moorthy are encouraged to resist the programme of mass agricultural production enforced by the British. To tell their story Rao assumes the lyrical speaking voice of an older woman in the village. This technique has several purposes. It naturalizes the return to traditional ways and, as a result, legitimates the more radical, or less traditional aspects of Gandhian policy. Moreover, the presence of a female narrator underlines the feminized Gandhian approach of submission and non-aggression.

In his Foreword to the novel Rao describes the difficulty of articulating colonized subjectivity in the language of the colonizer. His words have become a classic statement of the postcolonial experience of appropriation. He notes that, to adapt English to match the Indian 'emotional make-up', he has tried to transliterate the language, to 'infuse' it with the 'tempo' of Indian life. Yet the Foreword ultimately accommodates rather than rejects the culture of the Raj. For though Indian 'thought-movement' may look 'maltreated in an alien language', the attempt will none the less be to 'convey [its] various shades' in the English tongue, modified by patterned repetitions, Hindi words, and mythic allusions which ground the tale in the oral tradition. Later generations of nationalist writers developed like techniques. Rao romanticizes traditional narrative, representing it as ahistorical, interminable, unstoppable, flowing out of a depthless past into an unfathomable future. But even if in translated form, this is, paradoxically, a version of the colonialist image of India as infinitely large, populous as the sands of the sea-shore, massive enough to withstand all suffering.

In the tale itself the signs of cultural retrieval are unmistakable. Kanthapura, a generic village situated somewhere in southern India, is carefully mapped out, restored in textual form. There are the Brahmin and Pariah quarters, the temple, the shop, the representatives of various walks of life. Mohandas Gandhi is introduced as a mythic figure, 'his forehead . . . brilliant with wisdom'. His village analogue, Moorthy 'our Gandhi', is represented as 'a saint, a holy man'. Character hue conjoins the metaphysical and the contemporary: history is filtered through legend.

The village unity which is achieved towards the end of the novel carries a distinct political message: 'there is neither caste nor clan nor family' when it comes to resisting the government. As in *Mhudi*, despite the final burning of Kanthapura, the concluding emphasis is on harmony: the narrative voice is sustained until the last refrain-like sentence. Rao has composed a narrative in which story-line, generic structure, and nationalist resistance politics mutually reflect on one another. Though without entirely rejecting European cultural influences, Gandhi called for a reinterpreted Hindu tradition and a return to simpler pastoral forms of life. *Kanthapura* is a reconstructed oral narrative told in a nostalgic pastoral mode, though in English, about a traditional village. The novel therefore performs its own politics: narrating in a suitably community-based style, incorporating exhortations to self-help, disseminating Gandhian epithets, but without jettisoning what was once the colonizer's tongue, the language which helps to undergird, as will be seen, the nationalist imagination in India.

Further Reading

Richard Allen and Harish Trivedi (eds.), *Literature and Nation: Britain and India 1800–1990* (Routledge, 2000).

Derek Attridge and Marjorie Howes (eds.), *Semicolonial Joyce* (Cambridge UP, 2000).

Dipesh Chakrabarty, *Provincializing Europe: Postcolonial Thought and Historical Difference* (Princeton UP, 2000).

Laura Chrisman, *Rereading the Imperial Romance: British Imperialism and South African Resistance in Haggard, Schreiner, and Plaatje* (Oxford UP, 2000).

John Darwin, *The End of the British Empire: The Historical Debate* (Oxford: Blackwell, 1991).

Terry Eagleton, *Exiles and Emigrés: Studies in Modern Literature* (Chatto & Windus, 1970).

Olisanwuche Esedebe, *Pan-Africanism: The Idea and the Movement* (Washington, DC: Howard UP, 1982).

Michel Fabre, *From Harlem to Paris: Black American Writers in Paris, 1840–1980* (Urbana: University of Illinois Press, 1991).

Simon Gikandi, *Maps of Englishness: Writing Identity in the Culture of Colonialism* (New York: Columbia UP, 1996).

Ulf Hannerz, *Transnational Connections: Culture, People, Places* (Routledge, 1996).

E. J. Hobsbawm, *Nations and Nationalism since 1780: Programme, Myth, Reality* (Cambridge UP, 1990).

Stephen Howe, *Anti-colonialism in British Politics: The Left and the End of Empire 1928–1964* (Oxford: Clarendon Press, 1993).

C. L. Innes, *A History of Black and Asian Writing in Britain, 1700–2000* (Cambridge UP, 2002).

George Padmore, *History of the Pan-African Congress* (1947; Hammersmith Bookshop, 1963).

David Richards, *Masks of Difference: Cultural Representations in Literature, Anthropology and Art* (Cambridge UP, 1995).

Bill Schwarz (ed.), *West Indian Intellectuals in Britain* (Manchester UP, 2003).

Angela Smith, *Katherine Mansfield and Virginia Woolf: A Public of Two* (Oxford UP, 1999).

Harish Trivedi, *Colonial Transactions: English Literature and India* (Calcutta: Sangam, 1994).

Richard White, *Inventing Australia: Images and Identity 1688–1980* (Sydney: Allen & Unwin, 1981).

Robert J. C. Young, *Postcolonialism: An Historical Introduction* (Oxford: Blackwell, 2001).

4

Metropolitans and Mimics

'But surely [savages] have old, old religions and mysteries—it *must* be wonderful, surely it must.'

'I don't know about mysteries—howling and heathen practices, more or less indecent. No, I see nothing wonderful in that kind of stuff. And I wonder that you should, when you have lived in London or Paris or New York—'

'Ah, *everybody* lives in London or Paris or New York'—said the young man, as if this were an argument.

D. H. Lawrence, 'The Woman Who Rode Away', 1928

The leap from one imagination to another can hardly be made; no more than Desdemona could understand truly the Moor's military exploits. We own the country we grow up in, or we are aliens and invaders.

Michael Ondaatje, *Running in the Family*, 1983

A stranger here, with the nerves of a stranger, and yet with a knowledge of the language and the history of the language and the writing. . . .

I felt that my presence in that old valley was part of something like an upheaval, a change in the course of the history of the country.

V. S. Naipaul, *The Enigma of Arrival*, 1987

Colonial and anti-colonial transformations

The twentieth-century recognition of the non-West by the West was earlier described as regenerative, a recognition of reciprocal affinities. It represented a new accessibility of what had once been disavowed as strange. But if viewed in terms of relative *power* and *status*, the semblance of reciprocity recedes. Colonized and creole artists may have been included in metropolitan culture as migrants, yet they were rarely accepted as full participants in that culture. Far from bringing disruption, the foreign and the 'primitive' were enlisted by Western tradition as instruments of its own internal renewal.

From the European point of view, colonial writers did not shed their peripheral character. As we saw, the nineteenth-century novel had mapped a world-picture in which Britain stood at the centre of things. Although it uncovered parallels between centre and periphery, early twentieth-century metropolitan writing did not interfere with this general picture. European sovereignty remained largely unquestioned, as did the cultural authority of the West. Even though artefacts from other cultures were placed side by side with western symbols in modernist art, colonial artists did not enjoy the same status as their British, French, or American counterparts. In the early decades of the twentieth century these unequal relationships reflected at a microcosmic level the still dominant if less secure colonial situation.

The last chapter took a wide-angle view of early twentieth-century shifts in the writings of empire. I shall begin now to look more closely at European expressions of self-doubt and disaffection. To gain insight into Indian, African, and West Indian efforts to write in opposition to empire, it is important also to examine the self-absorption of the colonies' metropolitan interlocutors, the voice of cultural authority against which nationalist self-articulation was defined. This fairly extended overview will then lead into a more general theoretical discussion of anti-colonial discursive resistance: of the epistemological and linguistic difficulties involved in displacing colonialist perceptions.

As has been seen, the two main groups of writers who responded to empire at this time—metropolitans on the one hand and representatives from non-European cultures on the other—were concerned with overlapping issues. Yet the positions from which they represented those issues remained divided. They spoke out of different social and economic contexts, and different worlds of knowledge. True, the 'voyages in' of colonial artists signified at times a transformative interference in western perceptual languages. But it is important not to mistake the cross-cultural conversation that emerged for a true shift in the terms of European cognition, or for a relationship of sharing or equal interchange. At every turn, in public life, in educational institutions and cultural forums, colonial writers still faced discrimination and restrictions upon their self-expression, whether as artists or as human beings. Given this situation, the question to explore is: how were the opponents of colonialism to articulate their resistance? What was involved in rejecting imperialist definitions? Which is to say, how did a native or nationalist writer located in a colonial system, often operating from within colonial categories of knowledge, begin to challenge European dominance and at the same time avoid being enlisted as part of the West?

Woolfian uncertainty

The case of Leonard Woolf as colonial officer offers a preliminary insight into the constrictions with which European writers in a late Empire had to grapple. He experienced intensely the difficulty of dissent in a colonial system that continued at this time, if less confidently, to expand. During a six-year stint as a colonial officer in Ceylon (1905–11), Woolf was exposed to, as he described it, the hypocrisy of 'humanitarian' colonial rule, its humbug and puffed conceits. As with Conrad, the observations recorded in his letters, and underscored in the apologia contained in the (later) autobiography *Growing*, now read as prescient of the wider European disillusion that was to come.

Woolf began his career in Ceylon embodying the Kiplingesque ideal of colonial diligence. 'I work, God, how I work,' he wrote to Lytton Strachey, describing his job as a police magistrate; 'I have reduced it to a method & exalted it to a mania.' After 1908, when he was assigned his own district, he made it 'the most efficiently governed in the colony': he 'managed to have an unprecedented amount of salt collected'. But his diligence did not prevent critical perception. Anticipating the change of heart experienced by both George Orwell and E. M. Forster, Woolf came in time to see through the contradictions and artificiality on which colonialist society was built. 'We treat them [the colonized] as inferiors', he wrote, but 'tell them that they are their own equals.' The British colonizers, as he saw them, self-consciously modelled their lives on Kipling's tales, acting as 'tougher, more British' and more snobbish than it seemed at all practicable to be.

Woolf's disenchantment catalysed his attitudes about the Empire. Though it took the cataclysm of 1914–18 to force his inner divisions to the surface, already in 1910, he noted, his profession had become 'consciously distasteful' to him. Administering an incongruous system of justice in an alien society produced in him 'an ineradicable and melancholy disillusionment' with empire. In his novel about Ceylon, *The Village in the Jungle* (1913), white authority seen from the village point of view is so remote as to be otherworldly. Colonialist justice is a grim farce of irrelevance and misunderstanding which leads eventually to the extinction of the community.[1]

Yet Woolf's colonialist critique does not cancel prejudice as much as exist side by side with it. In this his experience is again prototypical of what would follow, for disillusion did not bring early liberal colonialist critics to question the first principles of empire. Woolf's descriptions of Ceylon feature degenerate natives graded on a scale of development in the usual way. The Tamil was 'just what the oriental is popularly supposed to be, but with many more queer little traits—subtle & quick-witted'. Somewhat like Sidney and Beatrice Webb on their Indian travels (*Indian Diary*, 1913), Woolf could not conceive of indigenous society in its present state as able to govern itself independently, without British guidance. *The Village in the Jungle*, which Woolf himself regarded as emblematic of his growing anti-imperialism, describes native characters in terms of animality and inertia. The novel is, not without reason, considered remarkable for its evocations of indigenous life and local speech patterns. But it also repeatedly falls back on the colonialist topos of displaced savagery, the conventional symbolism of the jungle as disembodied evil. The environment is made to represent a fear of other people.

Virginia Woolf's writing also houses persisting imperialist attitudes alongside anti-colonial sentiment. This is despite—or perhaps indeed because of—the fact that she did not herself experience the Empire at first hand. Her work is of course widely renowned for its iconoclasm. She managed to distil into her acerbic observations on social authority something of the spleen which Leonard Woolf had brought back with him from Ceylon. Yet, particularly earlier on in her career, she too relied on habitual forms of colonialist perception even while delivering indictments of the British Establishment.[2]

In *Mrs Dalloway* (1925), Woolf explores questions of authority, foreignness, and deviance in a group portrait of London high society. Developing the psychological exploration of the Empire-building ruling class in *Jacob's Room* (1922), the novel probes the condition of late imperial malaise. Though it is never centre-stage, Empire impinges directly on the lives of the characters. It is several years after the Amritsar massacre (1919), but Lady Bruton cannot sleep for its 'wickedness'. Peter Walsh, just returned from India, represents the condition of the transplanted colonial, alien yet identified with Britain. Though he does not feel at home in London, Walsh still experiences 'moments of pride in England'.

For Woolf in *Mrs Dalloway* the pathology of British world power is deeply embedded, expressed in 'prying and insidious' ways in the 'public-spirited, British Empire, tariff-reform, governing-class spirit' with which the specialist Sir William Bradshaw and Walsh in their different ways are identified. The spirit according to Woolf takes two forms, 'Proportion' and 'Conversion'. Proportion signifies law and order, Conversion the means of its enforcement—including international wars, the discipline imposed on the shell-shocked First World War soldier Septimus Warren Smith, and the oppressions involved in empire. Beneath disguises of civility, a coercive imperialist authority links metropolitan centre and colonial periphery. In 'the heat and sands of India, the mud and swamps of Africa, the purlieus of London', Woolf comments, Conversion 'offers help, but desires power; smites out of her way roughly the dissentient, or dissatisfied'. As she was to spell out over a decade later in her anti-war essay *Three Guineas* (1938), Sir William's brand of forbidding patriarchal ferocity was manifested not only in Fascism, but in the Victorian Establishment which staffed the 'splendid Empire'. In the fictional counterpart to that essay, the wish-fulfilling and prophetic *Between the Acts* (1941), Miss La Trobe's haphazard dramatization of English history again underscores Woolf's abiding belief that unities (symbolizing political as well as creative authority) are difficult to achieve and almost impossible to sustain without doing damage to the onward flux of life. As in *Mrs Dalloway*, but perhaps more outspokenly so, the force of Empire, requiring 'protection and correction', is described as wielding its 'truncheon' over 'thought and religion; drink; dress; manners; marriage too'.[3]

And yet, with Virginia as with Leonard Woolf, the critique of imperial wrongs does not preclude a kind of complicity. Woolf in *Mrs Dalloway* is concerned about the self-importance and exclusivity manifested in the English upper classes. But the novel replicates exactly the imperial geography of centred metropolis and largely invisible periphery which sustained that exclusivity. The action is set in the upper-class social world of the West End of London, the epi-centre of the circles of sound with which Big Ben—symbol of stand-ardized time—measures the day. There is irony in Peter Walsh's smug self-satisfaction when expressing admiration for the city: 'A splendid achievement in its own way; after all, London; the season; civiliza-tion.' Yet the novel can imagine no alternative to that 'civilization', nothing beyond imperial rule.

This ideological bloc or blindness—a self-repetition on the part of the self-critical—appears again and again in the work of Virginia Woolf's contemporaries covered in this chapter. Not only the Woolfs but also later deeply critical and pessimistic writers like Orwell and Greene would uphold colonial perspectives even as they sought to challenge them. As readers will observe, their self-reiterations under-line the immense moral and imaginative effort which was required for the transformation of colonialist discourses. This was a time when the Empire still remained in place. In fact, the colonial holdings of Britain and also France were strengthened after the First World War. From 1920, annual Labour Party Conferences supported the Wilsonian principle of self-determination for India, yet Britain's per-ceived obligations as an imperial power prevented the practical appli-cation of such resolutions. As Orwell forthrightly reflected in the essay 'Not Counting Niggers' (1939), throughout the inter-war period Labour struggled in vain to develop a coherent anti-colonial policy, compromised at almost every turn by the benefit to British workers furnished by colonial exploitation.

Just as did politicians and policy-makers, dissenting metropol-itan and/or colonialist writers found themselves locked into deeply contradictory positions. Part of the dominant group despite their most earnest inclinations, they partook of its values and symbolic languages as well as of its privileges. Whatever their political persuasion, they continued still to assume the attitude of dominant member in the colonial relationship. They tended to believe, for instance, that any impetus for change in the Empire should, when it was necessary, come from the centre, from Britain.

Transcultural modernism?

Twentieth-century metropolitan writers acknowledged the challenge to their intellectual preconceptions represented by contact with other cultures. But no matter how cosmopolitan or transnational their interests, a distinct—and perhaps inevitable—cultural and political fixity remains a characteristic of their work. The relativism that was part of international modernism was hemmed in by world-wide grids of imperial authority. As is still the case today, though in a different form, writers were bound to relate to a colonial, globally dominant West. Even if denying any share in an expansionist colonialism, modernists attempting to approach Europe's others did so in terms of European cultural assumptions. Experimentation in the colonial centres rarely turned into anti-colonial critique. The aesthetic encounter of 'the west and the rest', therefore, may ultimately have amounted to little more than decorative *proximation*, a coming together without a significant displacement of terms.

While not losing sight of the contribution made by colonials to the fragmented vistas of modernist art, it is important to recognize the extent to which their acceptance by metropolitans was in many cases a matter of marginal annotation, even of embroidery. The 'mythical method' of building on ethnological findings and 'primitive' symbols did not generally mean that western ideological categories were thrown into question. Modernist allusion by and large remained exactly that—a corroboration of European points of view. Even where habits of thought fundamental to a European sense of superiority were examined, the habits themselves had a way of persisting. Beliefs in European centrality, technological achievement, and patterns of development held firm, as did an objectifying interest in the curious and exotic. Western codes remained human norms, the measure of how the world should be. It is not for nothing, therefore, that T. S. Eliot sets the shattered social landscapes and polyglot murmurings of *The Waste Land* (1922) in London, not on the Gangetic Plain. By and large the citation of foreign cultures was an expression of Europe's concern with itself. Colonized cultures were catalytic agents for metropolitan self-questioning.

These qualifications raise an important question concerning the place of white metropolitan modernism relative to nineteenth-century colonialist discourse. What we are considering here is not so much the expanded modernism of Chapter 3, but, more specifically, First World War modernism, and its later 1920s and 1930s expressions. Metropolitan writers, like Forster or Lawrence, appeared willing to take other cultures more on their own terms, but in exploring new outlets for expression, the other retained many of its stereotyped identifications as barbarian hero or civilized savage, withal inchoate, dark, and strange. Seen in this context, there may be grounds for characterizing metropolitan modernism as a latter-day colonialist discourse even in its apparently revivifying recognition of 'exotic' arts.

Remembering that the pre-Second World War metropolis rested firmly on colonial economies, it is not surprising that culture, too, continued to be vigorously imperial. Adventure stories remained lustily in print. In 1926 the Under-Secretary of State for the Colonies could still enjoin Britons to 'keep our life distinct from other races'. Intellectual and administrative approaches may have been changing gradually in the 1919–39 period, but the organs of public opinion—popular magazines, schoolbooks, cinema—remained colonialist in orientation. Though a nationalist sympathizer, even Edward Thompson, the writer and missionary teacher of English at the Wesleyan College, Bankura, in Bengal (1910–23), could observe in 1931 that the 'English [have] shown India strength, patience; fortitude, fairness' (*A Farewell to India*, 1931). In general, British metropolitan and white colonial societies in the first half of the twentieth century expressed hostility when it came to anything more than superficial changes to the imperial status quo. The Woolfs or George Orwell may have been repelled by the reported or lived realities of the Empire. Leonard Woolf certainly was disgusted at its economic cynicism (*Economic Imperialism*, 1920; *Imperialism and Civilization*, 1928). D. H. Lawrence and Graham Greene were in their different ways witheringly critical of the European way of life. None the less the cumulative effect of their extracultural interests was effectively either to alienate or to assimilate what was unfamiliar. As the Victorians had long ago discovered, textual incorporation and categorization reduced the threat of extreme difference, containing the rival interpretations of reality which emergent colonial élites were beginning to assert. In lieu of complete elision, both stereotyping and the illustrative citation of foreign cultures represented ways of dealing with a world in which colonized peoples were beginning to make their presence more disturbingly felt.[4]

This is not to say that the modernist quest for alternatives was not experienced as urgent. I noted earlier that the First World War, if nothing else, represented for Europe a mass cultural trauma that blew apart notions of white supremacy. Yet writers could no more wish colonialism away than they could wish for the demise of their society. British colonial power itself survived at this time by either assimilating or suppressing nationalist movements in the Empire. In a way, as already suggested, writers' self-projections and incorporations mirrored colonial policy. The citation of native cultures on canvas or in poetry mimicked on a figural level the absorption of the non-European world by the West. Writers who stuck loyally to a colonialist idiom, such as Joyce Cary, exhibited a defensiveness connected to that which sustained the colonial system. While the position of the native colonized remained subordinate and peripheral, imperial power survived by dint of self-replication, preserving existing structures, resisting change. Any new openness in western writing therefore emerged in spite of lasting imperial constraints. By juxtaposing metropolitan continuities with the anti-colonial upsurge which is covered in Chapters 3 and 5, and reviewed again below, the following three sections will aim to demonstrate how gradual change in the Western narrative in fact was.

Lawrence, Forster, Thompson, Cary

Although not critical of empire as such, Lawrence's work is well known for its rejection of the destructive, 'bullying', materialist-industrial complex of Europe. He was commended by Mulk Raj

Anand for his interest in the spontaneous, the instinctual, and (by familiar analogy) the non-western. In the 1920s, in quest of what he hoped would be new sources of energy and 'sense-awareness', Lawrence embarked on a 'savage pilgrimage' (as Mansfield termed it) to the outer reaches of European settlement, the contact zones: first 'the East', Ceylon; then Australia, temptingly antipodal; and finally New Mexico, seat of 'prehistoric humanity'. Not unlike Gauguin or Picasso, he sought to draw on the cultures of the other for instruction in atavism and sex-mysteries, 'marvellous innate beauty and life-perfection' (Foreword, *Fantasia of the Unconscious*, 1922).

However, as is clearly exemplified in his Mexican novel, *The Plumed Serpent* (1926), what is telling in Lawrence is that ultimately, after instinct has been admired, the 'befeathered and bedaubed' native comes across as hardly less mindless and primitive than in earlier European colonialist fictions (see, for example, 'The Mozo', *Mornings in Mexico*, 1927).[5] In the short story 'The Woman Who Rode Away', the white woman encounters not transcendence but a vengeful and deadly blood-ritual in her attempt to meet with native Mexicans. The primitive confronted Lawrence with the shades of deeply embedded cultural nightmares, associations of, as he put it in *The Plumed Serpent*, 'violence and crudity . . . a touch of horror'.

And yet, to some extent, *The Plumed Serpent* does attempt to unsettle dominant categories. The form of the novel is itself experimental, a hybrid combination of quest tale, truncated travelogue, and religious exhortation. As the negative image of Europe, Mexico is sought out as a place of regeneration, an antidote to its destructive automatism. Lawrence's surrogate Kate Leslie submerges herself in a Mexican rural life that represents a range of enchantments but also horror, 'a richness of physical beauty' and 'a sort of demon world'. It is also significant that at several points in the novel Lawrence allows a calibration of cultural difference which counterposes conventional dichotomies. For example, Kate is not English but Irish and this, it seems, gives her some insight into Mexican darkness. The movement of national regeneration or cult of Quetzalcoatl in which she becomes involved presents an acute portrayal of a nationalist revival movement, which adapts tradition in a distinctly modern way. As interpreted by Don Ramon and his followers, their neo-Aztec movement lays emphasis on a resurgent masculinity, the recovery of pre-conquest myths, and the need to recapture the libidinal mysteries or 'second strength' the gringos destroyed. Yet, in Lawrence's view, the movement sabotages that energy by expressing itself also in militaristic ritual and formulaic doctrine. It remains governed by the 'mental-spiritual consciousness' of Europe.

Lawrence's ambivalence about the Quetzalcoatl scheme, and the attempt to 'substantiate' ancient mysteries, probably explains the incomplete ending of *The Plumed Serpent*, which leaves Kate's lengthy internal debates about commitment 'to the old way of life [in England], or to the new', unresolved. Lawrence uses the European woman as the test case: on the basis of her response the revival experiment stands or falls. However, she can arrive at no point of certainty. She is called upon to uphold Lawrentian sensuality or sex-mystery as the 'clue to all living'. But because Mexico retains for her an 'unspeakable malevolence', she may renounce it altogether. As in the story 'The Woman who Rode Away', European consciousness and Central American darkness remain opposed in nature and inclination. Yet, at the same time, as Lawrence's gradations of otherness intimate, the novel does hold up for deeper scrutiny the familiar struggle between the primitive—the 'great blood-creature'—and Western rationality. As also in the ambiguous relationship between Ramon and Cipriano, it is an opposition in which the one kind of awareness is ceaselessly threatening to annihilate, or to superimpose itself upon, the other (see 'The Border Line', 1924).

In the post-war years Lawrence's rejection of a mechanical Europe and his search for alternatives represented a symptomatic disquiet and a real need for change. Moreover, he pointed to the unreadable aspects of otherness in a way that was unusually non-judgemental for his time. To Lawrence different forms of understanding were not naturally commensurate with one another. The native was not assimilable, as and when European will might dictate: 'The Indian is completely embedded in the wonder of his own drama. It is a drama that has no beginning and no end, it is all-inclusive. It can't be judged, because there is nothing outside it to judge it' (*Mornings in Mexico*). In this regard it is significant that *Kangaroo* (1923), Lawrence's autobiographical novel about Australia, is curiously prescient about white settler identity under pressure of an indecipherable geography. A mark of the novel's insight into otherness was its importance for the Jindyworobak writers of the 1930s (who are discussed in Chapter 5). Even as he succumbs to overdrawn stereotypes of the uncouth colonial creole, Lawrence in *Kangaroo* considers at some length—again uniquely for the time of writing—the potential for the transformation of European influences in this 'new' and also ancient Australian world, in which he includes, though obliquely, the presence of the Aborigines.

Under the influence of the 'nameless past' of the land white Australians, according to Lawrence, have developed their own 'foreign' identity. In a manner anticipating later postcolonial theorists, he acknowledges the potential for two forms of otherness, the extreme difference represented by Aboriginal Australia and the more proximate otherness of white Australians. As well as allowing for this calibration of difference, he admits to the existence of cultural experience which is simply out of Europe's range—experience that it cannot conceptualize. As an image of this extreme difference, Lawrence evokes the near-'invisibility' of the Australian landscape, '[lurking] just beyond the range of our white vision'. It is a strangeness Lawrence chooses neither to abandon nor to develop. Unlike other late colonialist writers, he does not fret over or seek to represent this indeterminacy. He allows the bush its impenetrability. There is nothing out there but a 'terrible ageless watchfulness', a 'formlessness' that can be perceived only on the borders of European consciousness, or in Lawrence's words through 'clefts in the atmosphere'. The strangeness of the land remains elusive, resistant to Western perception: it is 'far-off, just as far-off when you are in it: nay, then furthest off'.[6]

In *A Passage to India* (1924), the subcontinent, too, remains 'far-off' to the resident European. E. M. Forster's attempt in this novel to understand the difference of India by way of a western vocabulary of liberal tolerance has received much critical acclaim, not least in India itself. Throughout the narrative, Indian sophistication in spiritual matters shows up the so-called superiority of western intellect. But the novel ends on another admission of native opacity. India is constructed as a place of continual European bafflement. This is slightly different from *Kangaroo* in which otherness, because it is recognized as disruptive and unrepresentable, is left to its inarticulacy. Forster by contrast does try to signify India, and to do so in conjunction with the West, as a mystifying—if also a self-regulating—confusion opposed to the West's control. The panoply of imagery of the Orient is seemingly so accessible as to be irresistible. India is a moral obfuscation, a vast and tenebrous chaos. As Forster confirmed on a return visit in 1946, the country was 'as before' 'monotonous, enigmatic, and at moments sinister' ('India Again', *Two Cheers for Democracy*, 1951).

The ambivalences of *A Passage to India* stem from its unresolved critique of the individualistic humanism that was Forster's own system of belief. It was a system which acknowledged a 'common humanity with Indians' yet which offered him no satisfactory way of dealing with the larger antinomian conflicts inherent to colonialism. As an illustration of his own divided opinions on India, Forster in a 1944 essay agreed with the Victorian writer William Arnold that 'Until the point of divergence between Eastern and Western mentality has been discovered, co-operation is impossible' ('William Arnold'). Forster's work itself, as Virginia Woolf once rightly remarked, makes up a 'contradictory assortment'. Suspended between the polarities of social naturalism and mystic symbolism, *A Passage to India* is a collection of dissonances. The novel seeks to reject the apparently intractable opposition of hardening British overlordship pitted against increasingly more defensive Indian resistance. To do so it offers a liberal option: an 'aristocracy of the sensitive' in the form of homosocial bonding across the colonial divide. British political dishonesty is to be condemned, India is chaotic; but individual Britons and Indians, like Fielding and Aziz, are occasionally able to rise above the divisiveness to affirm human value.

However, Forster also recognized that during a period of crisis—such as after Adela Quested's alleged rape—the injunction 'only connect' could not be sustained. A much deeper structural integration was needed, but was not for the time being imaginable. The dimensions of economic and political change lie beyond the range of *A Passage to India*. Though Indian anger at the time of the trial gives the impression that 'a new spirit seemed abroad, a rearrangement', British rule in the novel remains suspended in a continuous present. Aziz's later nationalism is a singular phenomenon, not connected to a wider movement. Clearly, though his interest in its obliquities is real, Forster could not yet release himself from an explanation of India as little more than an impenetrable 'muddle'.

As is apparent from Forster's account of his first visits to India in *The Hill of Devi* (1953), the country by turns appalled and fascinated him. In *A Passage to India* he attempts to approach the culture at the level which most intrigued him, as a testing ground of other spiritual options, a great temple of religious symbols. However, he makes clear that the pluralities of the Hindu pantheon, or even the dignified quietude of Islam, hold out no meaningful answers for the questing Westerner. The suspicion that this is inexorably the case, that India can offer nothing more than moral confusion, lies behind the experience of infinitely recurring nothingness represented by the Marabar Caves. The experience is repeated in the concentric circles of sky which encompass the action of the novel, and, at the microcosmic level, in the petrified bubbles of vacuum which make up the Caves. The various religious symbols India offers are subsumed in a complex figure of infinity that is also a void, a figure which again bears close resemblance to familiar colonialist tropes of unreadability.

The main difficulty with this symbol of negation in so far as it is made to encircle India is that the entire land is thus declared unknowable and formless, much like Conrad's Africa. India relentlessly resists European understanding; within its vast empty spaces historical autonomy or nationhood is not imaginable. Here 'everything that happens is said to be one thing and proves to be another' (*The Hill of Devi*). So, whilst giving vent to his heartfelt liberal discomforts, Forster leant on tried-and-true colonialist preconceptions to represent those discomforts. *A Passage to India* remains a historically important novel for its scathing exposition of social and ethical calcification under the Raj. In *Howards End* (1910), too, in the portrait of the Wilcoxes, active in the Imperial and West African Rubber Company, Forster exposed the stunted sensibility of the colonial ruling classes. And yet, despite his hopes for conciliation, towards the end of *A Passage to India* he returns to a well-worn cultural opposition, where the Mediterranean is described as the seed-bed of the human and the humane against the 'monstrous and the extraordinary' of what lies to the east.

Even though convinced that he shared a 'common humanity' with Indians, a critic of the Empire like Edward Thompson also did not escape the colonialist ideological bloc: what can also be described as a failure of political imagination on the part of European colonial sceptics. At one and the same time Thompson believed that India was in need of a change of authority, and that the world could not find better rulers of India than the British. Thompson's novel *A Farewell to India*, which is really a series of internal monologues written at the time of his own leave-taking, is unique as a European text not only for its focus on anti-British dissent—in particular the Civil Disobedience

movement (1930–2)—but also for its perceptive delineation of different political approaches, more and less radical, within the Indian
nationalist movement. The Thompson persona, Robin Alden, is said
to appreciate even the 'bloodier manifestations' of nationalism
for their 'grimness, humour and scholarship', though he also condemns them for their 'dishonesty'. As he makes clear in the novel,
Thompson believed that Britain had long outlived its usefulness in
India. The Raj has inflicted a 'long humiliation' on Indian people;
beneath its 'power and dignity' lurks an 'unforgivable snobbishness
and narrowmindedness and hardfaced folly'. Britain is now caught in
a false position, simply marking time in the subcontinent, its rule
reduced to a sham.

Yet despite this perception, neither Thompson, nor the British
authorities as he portrays them, can forge a change and plan for an
independent system of rule. The reason, quite simply, is that there
appears to be no viable alternative to the Raj. Thompson is deeply
sceptical of the militant, 'doctrinaire', and 'ruinous' nationalism now
dominant in India, a force which he repeatedly characterizes as par-
taking in the dark, impersonal powers or *bhuts* buried in the Indian
soil: 'something dull, stupid, brute, malignant, invulnerable'. The
description could well be Forster's. In stark contrast to this elemental
force stands, as ever, British 'decency' and 'austerity', and in particular the selfless good work which has for years been done by unsung
colonialists in out-of-the-way hamlets.[7]

It is apparent from his writings on India that Thompson was
deeply divided as to the Indian question. He found himself split
between the official role of paternalistic 'Englishman' (as he himself
characterized it), and his feeling for the country, as one who had
'found his roots and home in this India'. His portraits of individual
Indians are clear-eyed, precise, and compassionate, often attuned to
the distinguishing complexity or foible of a particular personality.
He was among the few European writers at this time who openly
presaged the inevitable end to British authority, 'the white beast that
has ranged the planet with such vision and cruel strength and ruthless purpose'. At the same time contemporary nationalism represented to him 'greed and righteousness . . . knit together'. Even so,
while taking into account his misjudgements, certainly as pertain to
Gandhi, we must grant Thompson his attempt to see further than the
Manichaean divide of the colonial conflict, which he described as

'a fight between God and Satan'. Though in some ways classically colonialist, his words on this subject have a certain pertinence for present-day analysts of empire, including postcolonial readers:

> Frankly, I don't understand what I've been watching in India during these last twenty years. I wonder if they'll understand, a century from now. No, of course they won't, though they'll write about it as slickly as they do now, these fools that simplify the whole process. . . . A fight for freedom against the oppressor! They neither see our soul, nor India's soul. (*Farewell to India*)

Forster's timeless India postpones the possibility of political transformation. Edward Thompson, when in India, could not imagine alternatives to British rule. As late as the mid-1930s, Joyce Cary represented the British as a constant, unbudgeable presence in another part of the Empire, Northern Nigeria. Cary's colonialist novels—*Aïssa Saved* (1932), *An American Visitor* (1933), *The African Witch* (1936), and *Mister Johnson* (1939)—reproduce many of the predictable significations of Africa: the continent is a metaphysical space, a Conradian moral hollowness, a depraved 'jungly' zone, ultimately debilitating for Europeans. Empire is the place where white purpose is honed, where character can be made. It is also the place where British power and influence are accepted as givens.

No doubt Cary's novels suffered a cultural time-lag. They were based on observations taken as a colonial officer in the 1910s. It may also be that during the decade when the ruling-class consensus about colonization was gradually disintegrating, his reaction was defensive: an attempt to preserve the coherence of a familiar world. It is further true that his writing is often ironic. White characters' racist remarks often reflect their own ignorance or lack of perception. *Mister Johnson*, for example, was intended as a satire of colonial Nigeria. Rudbeck, the Assistant District Officer, proves himself by using the error of his servant Johnson to his own advantage. And *The African Witch*, Cary emphasized, was *not* written as 'a picture of contemporary conditions in West Africa'. Most importantly, on a linguistic level, he has set an example for later African writers. In a novel like *Mister Johnson*, he transposes the layering of languages in Nigeria (pidgin, Hausa, English, etc.) into what is a creatively heteroglot text.[8] But even taking into account his own self-confessed peripheral stance as a writer—like Lawrence's Kate he was Irish and not an English colonial officer—the effect Cary creates is to preserve the way things are, an effect which his ironies ultimately only help to reinforce. In the midst of a volatile political situation, his African novels, as retrospective accounts, uphold and also clarify the workings of a long-established colonialism.

The native characters in *The African Witch* are ranged on a standard-issue scale of progress according to their political, religious, or cultural affiliations—'ju-ju' or Christian, 'primitive' or enlightened nationalist. Though he is elsewhere more careful about the complexity of social determination, in this novel Cary invokes the nineteenth-century belief that racial heritage was character. Aladai the nationalist protagonist is finally powerless against the resurgence in his psyche of 'the lower brain—the beast blood'. The novel re-enacts the old colonial conflict between savagery and civilization, where savagery justifies occupation and the occupiers, the District Officers, retain the upper hand. Against this background, resistance is explained away as primitive savagery.

The climate of intense political polarization of the 1930s, it seems, reinforced the polarities of Cary's own vision. *Mister Johnson*, his most successful novel, traces the gulf of consciousness dividing Africans from Europeans. The eponymous hero, like Aladai, is a 'demi-évolué', 'sharp as a sharp child', lacking in reason. He is also an exile from Southern Nigeria and thus appears doubly ridiculous, from the point of view of both the whites and the local Hausas. The action concerns his always already doomed attempts to Europeanize himself in the image of the ADO Rudbeck. Johnson's utter devotion to the white man, which is expressed as dedication to his road-building project, proceeds through embezzlement, and ends in murder.

The irony of the tale is that Rudbeck himself has condoned Johnson's actions for the sake of the road. The novel exposes the pathos of Johnson's end, but at the same time it refuses to allow the trespassing that his imitation of the white man represents. Not only his fate but the road he helps build illustrate the social and political confusions that ensue when boundaries between native and European break down. One of Johnson's last parties presents a rich multicultural display of Hausa mime and Yoruba girls 'dancing an American fox-trot'. However, these crossings, when not ridiculous, are represented as dangerous. The road, which connects communities, also increases the crime rate. Civilization, far from improving a man like Johnson, in fact corrupts African society at large.

'No change of place'

In Cary, but also in the other writers discussed above, in spite of their differences, colonialist symbolism demonstrates a distinct tenacity. The colonial system of self-projection—also sometimes called the 'Empire of the Same'—maintained itself by way of strategic but relatively minor readjustments.[9] Indeed, it may be that limited shifts in attitude (modernist self-questioning, literary incorporations of the alien) helped to preserve more fundamental continuities.

In the Empire, the 'entre-deux-guerres' period—the time of later modernist writing—was characterized above all by anxiety about change. Where nineteenth-century British imperialism had been expansive, confident, adventuring, its twentieth-century formations were by contrast conservative, defensive, administrative. True, the hyperdestructive impact of the First World War had exploded the image of white global mastery. After 1919 the example which was made of a once-expansionist Germany was sobering. Imperialist hubris now appeared anachronistic, also excessive. But these perceptions were confined to élites and did not by any means have the force to dismantle empire. Colonialism kept its defenders, who pointed out the advantages of modernization to the colonized. The British Establishment—Woolf's forces of Conversion—asserted that a post-Versailles Empire was for the good of people world-wide. On the part of colonial authorities the response to change was a stubborn adherence to the codes of law and order of the past. If colonialism had once represented adventure, campaign, and widening dominion, it had now become more of a duty, even a job of repair and maintenance. Even so, world rule was still believed to represent a worthy task. Moreover—to emphasize another important continuity—that task and duty remained a predominantly male preserve, associated with masculine attributes of rigour, toughness, and self-discipline.

In a sense, as Alan Sandison has suggested, in the twentieth century the Social Darwinism of Victorian imperialists rebounded on its heirs.[10] The imperative to progress implied the wasting of those who stood still. In the world after Versailles, colonial boundaries, once flexible and extendable, now fixed and closed, demanded safeguards, an ever more vigilant securing. What had been won had now to be responsibly protected. As part of the overall picture of retraction and defensiveness, it is significant that Cary and Orwell of the 1930s generation of British colonialist writers were returned and—in different ways—disillusioned colonial officers, as Woolf their predecessor had also been. And the new colonial travellers, like Waugh and Greene, were journalists, not adventurers, literary men on publicity stunts in search of copy, parodically repeating the adventuring poses of the past.

Where no expansion, fragmentation. In a very graphic way the Darwinist logic seemed to hold true. As the 1920s and 1930s passed, a number of developments—political threats in Europe, the effects of the 1929 Depression, the upsurge of the Labour movement, the emergence of increasingly more vocal nationalist movements in the Empire—reinforced concerns about security. Starting in India, the signs of potential crisis led the British colonial establishment to reaction, police reinforcement, repressive emergency laws, and military intervention. The threat of imperial reversal brought dogged reassertions of colonial values. A similar trajectory—reaffirmation in the guise of limited change—can be traced in the colonialist writing of the time.

With the ending of the age of the explorer, the heyday of the adventure tale gradually ended also. Travel writers like Peter Fleming, Evelyn Waugh, and Graham Greene were self-conscious and parodic inheritors of the *Boy's Own* type of narrative. They effectively proclaimed its obsolescence, lampooning stereotyped styles.[11] And yet in their work the motifs of colonial adventure—danger and ardour, the encounter with primitive tribes, the authority of the European—show surprising staying power. Their cynical antics become a form of wistful retrospection, once again suggesting an unwillingness or an inability to change. Seemingly, in a world disturbingly prone to cataclysm, there was self-protection to be found in the caustic pose. As I will show in more detail, while colonialist idioms were questioned, they also survived—indeed, survived by being questioned.

Particularly in the 1930s, the predominant literary mode accompanying the scaling down of the colonialist venture was irony, which aptly relies on reversal. Literalizing or trivializing colonial commonplaces, an ironic style underscored the new banality of an administrative Empire: dark comedy, parody, pessimistic reportage, anti-adventure, and anti-epic cut open colonialist presumption. In the late imperial context, however, irony could work as a support for, as well as a scourge of, imperial stasis. Though the ironic work signals self-criticism and doubt, at the same time it also declines to mend what it has taken apart; it does not suggest alternatives.

In short, irony was favoured in late colonial writing because it tended to reproduce rather than to upturn existing structures in the world. Virginia Woolf's *The Waves* (1931), for instance, is an ironic elegy which marks the demise of the (absent) Kiplingesque hero Percival in India. The novel lays bare the tight homosocial and patriarchal bonds which have supported imperial society. However, for Woolf, as for her six main characters, other forms of social organization are not yet imaginable. European civilization in the novel is conceived in contrast to the murky disorder represented by the East. Neither world seems open to change. Even as they interrogated, mocked, or despaired, therefore, dark parodic effects formed part of the self-constituting project of imperialism. It was another case of the antithetical, or of seeming inversion, as a function of the same.

Admittedly, the 1930s period in British writing generally speaking carries associations of rebellion. The younger generation of mainly liberal and radical writers politicized earlier modernist repudiations. They sought to jettison the whole package of surviving British Establishment values—from 'Patriotism, religion, Empire' to 'Old School Tie' and 'honour', as Orwell listed them in 'Inside the Whale' (1940). However, though these writers, with Auden at their head, energetically welcomed the ruin of everything that was—economic and political empires, the glory of the West, the bourgeois order—by the end of the decade those who had stayed the course conceded a certain defeat. Even in the case of corrosively self-critical writers like Orwell and Greene, anti-imperial as well as anti-bourgeois protest was contained within a European cultural framework. Once again, writers' rebuttals continued to reflect aspects of their middle-class imperial world.

In their efforts to reject the old order, the 1930s generation could not of course have been uninfluenced by a climate in which pressure groups on the left were campaigning for colonial freedoms, and political critiques of empire and race issues were by now fairly widely available. Joining Winifred Holtby's clear-eyed journalism about South Africa in the late 1920s and early 1930s ('General Hertzog's Native Policy', 1927; 'Jan Christiaan Smuts', 1934, amongst others), and Leonard Woolf's writings for the Labour Party, the later 1930s produced several hard-hitting radical critiques of the Empire which advocated both economic reform and extended political rights for the non-white colonies (for example, Leonard Barnes's *The Duty of Empire*, 1935, and *Empire or Democracy?*, 1939).

However, as one commentator has it, the dissent that there was, even on the left, remained a 'tiny, and not very dissonant, voice'. Many of the pre-1939 debunkers of the British system, Valentine Cunningham points out, belonged to a 'bourgeois cousinhood' or Old Boy network which differed hardly at all from that which sustained the colonial officer élite of an earlier generation. As the following discussion of individual texts will suggest, leading writers of the time were at once more aware of, and yet necessarily also tolerated, the comfortable enclosures of a tenaciously colonial British world. Bourgeois, Britain-centred, and basically still imperial in their perceptions, the 1930s writers did not come close to committed anti-colonial critique. In theory they sought challenges to the system, but in practice they stayed just this side of cultural frontiers. Most of their work, therefore, both illustrates and enacts the difficulty of escaping the confines of British male class privilege and its assumptions of global authority. A similar closedness would characterize also those British narratives of empire that were chronologically postcolonial, such as Paul Scott's *The Jewel in the Crown* (1966) and his other retrospective novels about a very late and jaded Raj. In the 1930s and after, despite efforts to get free, 'There is no change of place', said Auden.

Still a closed system: Orwell, Greene, Waugh

George Orwell's colonial writings—the novel *Burmese Days* (1934), the opening of the confessional Part Two in *The Road to Wigan Pier* (1937), essays such as 'A Hanging' (1931) and 'Shooting an Elephant' (1936)—are central to a discussion of limits and closure in late colonialist rhetoric. Orwell is remarkable both for his contempt regarding the bankruptcy of the civilizing mission, and for his collusion with that same mission. It was a collusion of which he was conscious, and with which he struggled.

As in the case of Leonard Woolf, Orwell's own colonial experience—serving in Burma from 1922 as an Assistant Superintendent of Police—was a passage into disquieting political awareness. He describes in 'A Hanging' how the task of having to work as an instrument of imperial justice revealed to him the 'machinery of despotism'. Colonial discipline, he learned, was an 'unjustifiable tyranny' (*Wigan Pier*). He returned to England after five years '[hating]' Empire 'with a bitterness'.

Orwell's self-declared purpose in *Burmese Days* as in his subsequent work was to expose the hypocrisy of the British Establishment. The novel is repeatedly interrupted by anti-imperial invective. Yet if the work condemns, cursing 'Pox Britannica', it also holds back from a full assault. It thus shares in the hesitations of Edward Thompson, Orwell's near contemporary in British East India. As did Thompson, as did Woolf, Orwell in later writings returned to his experiences of 'futility at the white man's dominion in the East'. But in *Burmese Days*, though he is outspoken and deliberately oppositional, his sympathies remain divided.

By inaugurating a more critical, disaffected approach to colonial experience, *Burmese Days* joins company with writing by Orwell's contemporaries Waugh and Greene. Acerbic, tough-talking, given to exaggeration and aggressive criticism, this writing is markedly hardline when compared to the liberal uncertainties of Forster. Orwell in fact criticized Forster for his 'humanitarian' blindness to the economic logic fundamental to colonialism ('Rudyard Kipling', 1946). But the otherwise distinct approaches of these two writers did share a quality of inflexibility when it came to the Raj. Whether consciously or unconsciously, for Orwell as for Forster, the closed world of the British Empire did not permit political or social shift. Within the perimeters of this world, as Cary's novels made clear, neither the European nor the colonial could find much room for realignment. This fixity is also well illustrated in Waugh's writing which, for all its insouciance, is solidly based on an underlying British conservatism.

Burmese Days represents in miniature outlying British East India. By bringing together a number of emblematic characters who interact in predictable ways, Orwell demonstrates that the Empire is a system preserved by the rootedness of formality and habit. As a closed system it provides a hothouse atmosphere for the spread of ideological contagion: 'they could go on week after week, year after year, repeating word for word the same evil-minded drivel, like a parody of a fifth-rate story in [the nineteenth-century gentleman's magazine] *Blackwood's.*' Flory's expostulation outlines not just the fictionality—again as in Leonard Woolf—but also the suffocating confinements of the Anglo-Indian world: all who are involved are implicated in the general hebetude. The disgusted colonial officer is himself a captive of the system.[12]

Anti-colonial refusal is built even into the structure of *Burmese Days*. The novel lacks any semblance of a colonial hero. Certainly the indecisive and dissolute Flory is not one. At many points, textual echoes show awareness of a colonialist tradition. There are the Conradian references to the decay of the white man in the East, and the pictures of Club life filtered through Kipling. Traces of Forster emerge in details of imagery and character situation—the oppressive sky as a figure for the limitless unknown, the inescapable difficulty of friendship between natives and Europeans. But Orwell cites in order not only to situate his narrative against a textual background but also to subvert that heritage. For instance, he undermines the conventional representation of cross-racial liaisons: instead of surviving his dalliance unscathed, Flory the white man suffers and dies; Ma Hla May his Burmese lover gets the opportunity to condemn him publicly.

Despite the attempt at counter-narrative, however, Orwell does not ultimately diverge significantly from a colonialist semiotic. Traditional assumptions retain their hold. The scenes concerning the defence of the Club draw uncritically on imperial legends of stalwart white minorities threatened by dark hordes, heroic tales of Rorke's Drift, and Gordon at Khartoum. It is also telling that, much like Forster, Orwell includes no nationalist figures in the main plot, though the Club is well aware of the country being 'rotten with sedition'. The potential for liberation offered by such forces is sabotaged by the story: stereotypically, the leaders are unscrupulous. Here we might recall that Orwell in Burma, like Flory, represented and serviced the colonial system of law and order he also despised. Kipling-like and Woolf-like, he believed in putting in his day's work to keep the Empire running smoothly.

As Orwell himself lucidly remarked: 'when the white man turns tyrant it is his own freedom that he destroys' ('Shooting an Elephant'). The individual colonial officer had little choice but to represent the imperial power in whose name he acted. In *Burmese Days* Flory tries to save the Club from attack in spite of his loathing. As Albert Memmi made clear some twenty-five years after Orwell, should colonial power be under threat, the white colonialist, whether he disagreed with the principles of the system or no, would be invoked by it, called upon to perform as part of the colonizing force (see Ch. 2).

Burmese Days is distinguished from earlier colonial writings by its knowingness—its anti-adventure cynicism, its penetrating insights into the less than honourable mechanisms of empire. Flory the anti-hero, the little man of modernism transplanted to the colonial town, bears the painful self-consciousness of one aware of imperial wrong-doing yet impotent against it. His failures underline the pointless circularity of the colonial system. As he observes, medical 'progress' is introduced to colonized peoples to combat diseases the imperialists themselves have brought. 'Civilization' is merely the replication of imperial culture across the globe. Colonial society appears to have a vast capacity to reinvent and perpetuate itself in different lands. Yet, the inventiveness having grown repetitive, Orwell with *Burmese Days* signals the closing down of an entire genre of imperial heroics, as well as, by implication, the system that sustained it. Flory's suicide is a concluding comment on a world that will either approach entropy through endless reiteration, or require destruction to be changed. This is so despite the fact that Orwell could not himself, in 1934, envisage that change.

At a time of imperial self-doubt and retrenchment, the secret was to stick to certainties. Reiteration, circularity, and inertia characterize the societies portrayed by what we might term the die-hards of colo-nialist discourse. Orwell's treatment of the Empire—the inability to visualize a post-Empire world alongside the moral disillusionment— is corroborated in the dissolute foreign worlds of Graham Greene. In Greene as in Orwell colonial spaces seem to occupy a timeless dimen-sion supported more by humdrum ritual and a time-worn idiom than by imperial faith.

In true Marlow style, Graham Greene's mid-1930s travelogue *Jour-ney without Maps* (1936) represents a journey into uncharted Liberia as a voyage into the self. Unwrapping a Conradian and Freudian lexicon of interlocking quest, trial, evolutionary, and psychoanalytic images, Greene gestures frequently at the metaphoric baggage that the European colonialist carried into the world of the other. In much of his travel writing as in his fiction, Greene like Orwell paid his respects to his literary precursors—in particular the writers of imperial adventure and quest narratives. Conrad was obviously a dominant model, but other antecedents are recognizable. Scobie in *The Heart of the Matter* (1948), a novel based on the *Journey without Maps* experience, has Allan Quartermain for a boyhood hero.

As in Waugh, Greene's salient duality is canniness: a deep self-awareness about inheriting a tradition of imperial writing which, post-war, has lost its relevance and edge, but remains imaginatively powerful. In *Journey without Maps* he investigates the archetypal connections between the movement through the African environment and the excavation of a personal and racial past. The journey is approached as a script, a path struck through a rhetorical tradition as well as through physical terrain: Africa, Greene points out, signifies strangeness, the unconscious, a painful absurdity, 'the shape . . . of the human heart'.[13]

The effort to make his preconceptions explicit does not of course prevent Greene's African archetypes from exerting their usual suggestive power. Unlike Conrad or Cary, Greene in *Journey without Maps* looks at African 'darkness' in a positive way. However, as we have come to expect, the reversal does not dissolve the stereotype. Civilized and primitive retain their customary meanings. Colonial antimonies are as distinct as ever. The African continent remains the heartland of libidinal darkness. In *The Heart of the Matter* Sierra Leone is developed into a metaphor for human seediness, a place of moral degradation and spiritual dereliction, where even the (white) man of integrity is corrupted. Greene's self-consciousness therefore does not dilute the conventional symbolism through which the alien is represented. Africa is not only a place of 'unexplained brutality'. In *Journey without Maps* it is also a reflector for the psychological state of Europe, and a possible catalyst for its healing. Nor is the continent unique in upholding customary associations. In *The Lawless Roads* (1939), Greene adopts wholesale Lawrentian evocations of native Mexican life as a 'cruel anarchy' and a recurring cycle of violence: 'Everything is repeated there, even the blood sacrifices of the Aztecs: the age of Mexico falls on the spirit like a cloud.' The persistence of this kind of imagery again demonstrates the difficulty of transcending the dominant languages of empire, even if, as in Greene's case, colonialism's gains are ambivalently viewed, and the attempt is to take other cultures on their own terms.

In the caricatures of Evelyn Waugh late colonialist cynicism achieves what is perhaps its culminating expression. Waugh's tales of colonial places—*Black Mischief* (1932), *A Handful of Dust* (1934), and *Scoop* (1938)—transform the conventional motifs of empire into the stuff of mock-exotic and pseudo-epic. Slapstick and grotesque effects parody public-school heroics. The trend is consistently towards deflation. The grand themes of the civilizing mission, or of the white man's self-discovery, are converted into jokes. But Waugh's devices do not mask the underlying social and political structures of his world. A lasting conviction of British superiority is the immovable axis around which his caricatured worlds of freakish foreigners and colonized mimics spin. His difference from earlier colonialist discourse, therefore, is essentially one of approach. He was fascinated by 'distant and barbarous' places, he once wrote, because here 'ideas, uprooted from their traditions, [have] become oddly changed in transplantation' (*When the Going was Good*, 1946). And yet London unquestionably remained the centre of his cultural universe. The British may have lost some of their imperial acuity, but no others, he believed, least of all Africans, were in a position to take their place.

In the aristocratic social milieux with which Waugh was largely concerned, the great houses are in decay, the symbols of 'Edwardian masculinity', racing flasks and tobacco jars, look 'sombre' and out of place (*A Handful of Dust*). Service abroad is no longer the essential beginning to an important career. William Boot in *Scoop*, a retiring man who can rarely be made to leave the confines of the English countryside, is sent out as an African foreign correspondent by mistake. In *Black Mischief* Basil Seal goes to Azania out of dilettantish curiosity, because he has nothing better to do. The familiar colonial scene has an outmoded, ramshackle look. Empire no longer means authority, efficiency, national faith. Colonial scenarios are now pastiches, made in the image of, but not the real thing. The artificiality is underlined by exaggerated effects and ironic contrasts. William Boot takes to Africa the supplies of a Victorian explorer, conspicuously dated: cleft sticks, an 'overfurnished tent', and 'a portable humidor' (*Scoop*). The accoutrements of a bygone colonial age are still in place but the power of the ruling class is eroded.

The keynote in Waugh's novels is once again canniness and disaffection. Their subject, colonial endeavour, has lost its gloss of idealism, but in the absence of compelling alternatives has not been relinquished. The guiding imperial notions of mission, purpose, modernization, and racial solidarity occur as quotations, or solecisms; are shown up for being anachronistic, illusory, or ridiculously out of place. To Seth, self-proclaimed Emperor of Azania in *Black Mischief*, progress is a question of appearance and orotund assertion—troops wearing boots (though it is known this will lame the men); 'Light and Speed and Strength, Steel and Steam, Youth, Today and Tomorrow'. Familiar images from imperial tales—the uncomprehending native, for example—appear in the main as stock signifiers of context. As in Greene, though more ostentatiously so, the terms of reference are largely concentrated not in the present imperial world but in the past writing of empire. At the same time, the alternatives to British Empire are equally prone to foolish excess. The Fleet Street farce in *Scoop*, set in a post-independent African republic, mercilessly parodies windy nationalist rhetoric.

A Handful of Dust contains Waugh's most cunning exposé of the artifice and self-absorption involved in the colonial drama. In the Brazilian tropics the aptly named Tony Last, desperately seeking to escape his past, is hoodwinked by a half-caste man who demands that he read to him every day from Dickens. Able neither to return to Europe nor to obtain the Lawrentian spiritual release he seeks, the white man finds himself a captive of European narrative, imprisoned by the classical fictions of his culture's own making, and also by colonialism's repressed heritage of racial mixing. In feverish dreams Last sees the lost Indian City, the object of his questing, taking the form of the neo-Gothic Great House that he has lost back in England. The white man is returned to the shapes of his own past, which is itself a historical fantasy.

Waugh uses his stereotypes knowingly, but in order to do so must keep their Manichaean references intact. To be sure, in *Scoop* nepotism marks the worlds of both London and the African state Ishmaelia. But for the purposes of sardonic commentary, the worlds of the primitive and the civilized are if anything more starkly in opposition than in earlier narratives. The one is sunk in world-weariness, the other in an irredeemable primitive chaos. Race hierarchies remain in place throughout. Waugh mercilessly spoofs the possibility of Africa as being a place of moral or political value. The worth or absurdity of characters is defined relative to an always superior Britishness. In *Black Mischief*, embodied in the symbol of the steadying policeman familiar from Conrad's 'Heart of Darkness',

British colonial authority alone is capable of restoring law and order to the barbaric shambles of Azania.

The anti-colonial conundrum

Colonialism was not different from other kinds of authority, religious or political, in claiming a monopoly on definitions in order to control a diverse, unstable reality. As previous chapters have shown, dominance was gained first by the constant incorporation and suppression of difference, and then also by a vigorous reiteration of authoritative meanings. Predictably, given what we have seen of the closures and circularity of colonialist discourse, deviation from the norm would be difficult. European writers certainly experienced this. But so too, and more intensely, did those who organized and wrote in direct opposition to colonialism: colonial nationalists, whose protest is often taken as definitive, but also creole writers, traditionalists who sought a return to pre-colonial ways, nativists, anarchists, socialists, and other radicals.

In Chapter 3 I looked at colonial writers' first strivings to find utterance. This was juxtaposed with the discussion in the first sections of this chapter concerning the relative failure on the part of British writers to move beyond a colonialist perspective. I will now examine in more detail the epistemological leap involved in opposing empire, in particular for those who were oppressed by it; and investigate, specifically, the theoretical conundrum of colonized self-representation. Given their experience of denigration under the Empire, in what ways were the native opponents of British rule to respond: how were they to articulate their refusal and at the same time to formulate their own selfhood and voice? As Ezeulu in Achebe's *Arrow of God* (1964) might have put it, if the colonized found the white man sitting squarely on a stool in their own house, how were they to drive him away? By overturning the stool (of one materially stronger than they), by leaving the house (and thereby giving up the struggle), or by sitting down beside the white man in conversation (and in an act of compromise)?

Constructed as secondary to the colonialist, educated in their own unfitness, attempts by writers from the 'rest' of the Empire to resist colonial authority were always vulnerable to containment. Writers sought the freedom to name the world for themselves. Yet how were they to legitimate this search? Any effort by colonials to alter dominant terms, to claim independent nationhood, to transvalue negative identities, to forge a sense of self, would either be forbidden, as subversion, or adapted to the dominant idiom, and so neutralized. As we saw to some extent in the work of Solomon Plaatje, and is also evident, for example, in the blank verse plays of H. I. E. Dhlomo, the 1930s South African Zulu intellectual, writers could find themselves approximating a colonialist idiom, working with the system which had impelled their protest in the first place. How then were they to proceed? How were those marginalized under colonialism to achieve convincing self-expression—self-expression that, while reflecting their conditions of life, had also to be intelligible to the colonizer?

Britons critical of colonialism, it was said earlier, seemed doomed to repeating the colonialist attitudes of the past. Yet for native or colonized opponents of empire, too, an ironic reiteration was the order of the day. The main difference, clearly, was that in their case the repetition of Europe's political and cultural vocabularies was a response even more closely hedged around with contradiction. Paradoxically, most decolonizing movements were predicated upon cultural narratives they simultaneously sought to deconstruct—the narratives, that is, of European humanism, secularization, internationalism, and also modernization or 'improvement'. Seeking self-representation, colonial nationalists incorporated Europe's ideals of subjectivity, progress, and independence, and its rhetoric of rights. It was an incorporation that could appear, on the surface anyway, to undermine the validity of their own fledgling struggles for autonomy.

Not only ideologically, but in many other respects, the world of the middle-class colonized was dominated by empire. The rituals of public life, the languages of instruction and commerce, the legal procedures to which people had access, their means of self-advancement, all these were colonial, which meant that the superiority of the European was taken for granted throughout. More, resistance and identity movements gave expression to the largely imaginary identities that Europe in the process of colonization had attributed to others—the images, say, of Africans as impassioned singers and craftsmen, or of Indians as ascetic seers. The Indian National Congress at first petitioned for no more than greater Indian participation in the civil and military services of the Raj, and in the lower ranks of European business, changes which, where accepted, simply preserved colonial hierarchies. Though, as Benedict Anderson has argued, nationalism may have found its real efflorescence on the colonial periphery, even the nationalist ideals which colonized peoples used to claim independence were often first received in forms communicated by Europe.[14] Ashis Nandy has rightly commented that 'the West' was 'everywhere, within the West and outside: in structures and in minds'.[15]

As is the case for postcolonial critics like Frantz Fanon, Ngugi wa Thiong'o, and Chinweizu, the colonialist consciousness or 'mental colonization' of nationalist élites is usually attributed to the colonial education they received. In the colonies as at home, English-language and -literature instruction played a key role in naturalizing British values. As Chapter 1 already suggested, the groundwork for an English-based education in the colonies had been laid in nineteenth-century India, in response to Thomas Babington Macaulay's influential 'Minute on Education' of 1835. By the early twentieth century, students across the Empire were being instructed as to the world-excellence of English literature and western systems of rationality, and the deficiencies of their own. Thus the knowledge which made possible the colonized's advance within the colonial system, and which furnished the terms of their protest, acted also to waylay or entrap them.

This picture of western encirclement is worth recalling for it underlines once again what I described as the double bind—the cleaving *to* and *from* Europe—involved in the colonized search for agency. Admittedly many oppositional forms, such as Gandhian *satyagraha* (non-violent resistance to injustice), were hybrid, following neither purely modern nor purely traditional models. Still, it was *generally* the case, especially in literature, that native élites found themselves developing new styles of identity in terms supplied by their antagonists. To them, European cultural centrality was axiomatic. Like the white writers of the late Empire, they were to some extent creations of a colonial world; they worked within its systems of understanding, its interpretative circles. From their point of view, as for white writers, colonial interpretations of the world operated as closed frameworks in which any change had to take place within the terms set by that framework. In other words, reinterpretation had to be predicated on the previously interpreted. How then were native colonials to discard the modes of thought which dominated school syllabuses and set cultural standards? If writers were, in the words of Salman Rushdie, 'to tell the untold stories', how were they to go about this when their own cultural viewpoints were by and large ignored?

Questions such as these concerning self-representation were difficult. But the colonial world was not quite as closed as it might seem. Imperial regulatory systems were sometimes less vigilant than we might imagine following the accepted view of colonialism's all-encompassing, unavoidable power. Moreover, after 1919, colonial nationalists were up against a defensive, and not an expansive colonial power. Across the Empire, nationalist dissent was both a symptom of, and a factor contributing to, the new vulnerability. Even though within policed limits, it was possible for anti-imperialists to voice their protests actively. Only a few decades later, when Indian independence in 1947 was followed by African and Caribbean independence from the late 1950s, the old-style colonialists conceded the day to those who called for national self-determination.

However, to achieve autonomy people had first to find the means to articulate it. To win self-determination they had to develop ways of dealing with the negation, self-alienation, and internal hatred produced by colonialist rule. It was at this point, where they were confronted by their own self-contradiction, that many had creative recourse to the very predicament that entrapped them: self-repetition or mimicry. Precisely because they could never be quite white or right enough, native colonials were able to transform the condition of mimicking the colonizer's moves into a strategy of resistance. Adopting and adapting the white man's tongue, they learned to speak up for themselves. We see this situation clearly demonstrated in the parodies of Shakespeare and Kipling—convention-bound yet slanted, mock-heroic, subtly disobedient—of the 1930s Jamaican poet Una Marson; in Nirad Chaudhuri's delineation of British colonial beneficence in *The Autobiography of an Unknown Indian* (1951) and other writings; more generally in the autobiographies of early nationalist intellectuals; and indeed in the work of all once-colonized writers who have used the novel, the forms of European poetry, or the English language to describe their lives. Where other channels of self-expression were closed, the imitation of dominant symbols—in literature, song, or nationalist pageantry—at the least enabled native or colonized writers to give voice. In this way they began gradually but steadily to represent their own marginalized views of the world— and so, by and by, to turn their margins into (constellations of) 'centres'.

To disavow dominant colonial myths and languages, the colonized had in the first place to inhabit them. European conceptual traditions in history, philosophy, literature, etc., which downgraded that which was non-European, had first to be displaced by an act of repetition, even 'slavish' copying. Success lay in the camouflage and subterfuge. In a book like *Mhudi*, loaded with biblical and Shakespearian rhetoric; or in an Indian nationalist poet's studied reworking of a classically exotic East; in the careful anthropological annotations of *Banana Bottom*, or again in the honed English sentences of the much later *The Enigma of Arrival* (1987), writers like Sol Plaatje, Sarojini Naidu, Claude McKay, and V. S. Naipaul challenge the dominant culture on its own ground and in its own terms. From the position of their otherness—their different and often feared place of enunciation— native colonials were then able to begin to unsettle the perspectives that organized the colonialist world.

J. M. Coetzee's *Foe* (1988), a postmodern rewriting of the Robinson Crusoe story, gives a neat symbolic shorthand for the colonized process of self-articulation. In this novel, the Friday character, who lacks a tongue, mutely represents the colonized problem of making meaning. He dances in a circle, he plays one tune on the flute, he writes one character only, o, the empty set, the empty mouth. In a situation where there is no access to the media of cultural authority—the voice, the pen, the book—the forms of expression available to Friday are either silent or repetitive, or both. Yet, by enacting his own exclusion, by tracing the circles of interpretation, which shut him out—by writing o—Friday begins to signify. Making meaning using his master's tools at first signifies very little. But at the same time, in this very show of dumbness, the muted man takes the initiative in representing himself, his own imprisonment, by himself.[16]

To be sure, the mimicker might be accused of being the white man's artifice, a Maharajah of Chhokrapur, inept classicist and would-be polymath in J. R. Ackerley's *Hindoo Holiday* (1932), or an endlessly smiling Mister Johnson. Yet, as the postcolonial theorist Homi Bhabha has explained at length, the act of doubling the white man's image in effect displaced the representations of authority. While never under-estimating the magnitude of the task, and the effort and danger of the undertaking, we can see here how imitation became a kind of remak-ing, the creation not of a simple copy but of something subtly but distinctly new. Where colonial writers began to represent themselves in literary forms adopted from Europe, they effectively sidestepped the position of silent object in colonialist representation. Mimickers reflected back to colonizer a distorted image of his world; they under-cut his valorized categories of perception. Their rhetorical mode was essentially oxymoronic. They were speaking mutes, Man Friday talking back, the Hottentot Venus looking back. In celebrating their denigrated cultures, 'barbarians' or 'provincials' who had once been labelled inarticulate were speaking out in crafted, complex ways. Learning to borrow selectively and unsupervised from Europe, those who 'had no culture' took the initiative in interpretation.

Postcolonial criticism helpfully relies on the post-structuralist concept of language as indeterminate, multilayered, and historically contingent to illuminate how anti-colonial resistance might work in texts. Authority, we know, whether colonial or otherwise, usually takes care to supervise its meanings. Yet despite its best efforts, mean-ings remain partial, unstable, susceptible to permutation and transla-tion. As the next chapter on postcolonial writing will show, when the colonized signified, they exploited this instability. Due to their differ-ential position in any discursive situation, they constantly enacted and re-enacted what post-structuralism calls the contestability of signs. From the perspective of their cultural heterogeneity or hybrid-ity, they generated diverse possibilities of interpretation. Though ven-triloquizing the colonizer's voice, though identifying themselves in the vocabulary of their oppression, they also mixed up and upturned dominant meanings. Their cleaving *to* colonial definitions of self was therefore *at the same time* a cleaving *from*.

Like the lodger character Haynes in the Caribbean C. L. R. James's series of yard-life observations called *Minty Alley* (1936), the middle-class native writer occupied an in-between position, sandwiched between colonialist society and the oppressed. Educated in a European system, observing local goings-on in Jamaica from a distance, James's Haynes dwells on borderlines. Spying through cracks in the wall, his vision is always divided into strips. Like Claude McKay, or C. L. R. James himself, the colonial nationalist writer, working within a cosmopolitan mould, represented in truncated and translated form, in the colonizer's language, his or her cultures of origin. Or if not, if the writer strove for complete assimilation, that assimilation none the less rose out of a position of antithesis, which inevitably had the effect of shifting accepted meanings.

It was of course possible for the transformative effects of colonial and/or nationalist mimicry to be suppressed by ridicule or by punishment. Yet, after the mid-twentieth century, few chose to stand in the way of colonial nationalisms, whether these took the form of *proximation* and *assimilation*, or, later, more radically, of *reversal* and *resistance*. As Chapter 5 will discuss, during the years of nationalist independence struggles in India and Africa, a time when assimilation was increasingly associated with collaboration and privilege, the second more combative approach won favour. Europhilic 'native agents' drew criticism for the compromise that seemed to be involved in their borderline positions.

However, at least in the medium of language and literary form, assimilation, or *subversion by imitation*, has remained for nationalists and other anti-colonials an important mode of resistance. It is a mode constantly enacted in the bending and 'misshaping' of the English language by postcolonial writers around the world today. And yet, during the initial stages of anti-colonial mobilization, where culturally hybrid writers produced variation out of what looked like accurate copying, this too was oppositional. Transposing English novelistic conventions into an Indian, African, or Caribbean context expanded what it was possible to say within the framework of those conventions. Because conducted from within colonial structures, assimilation was at this time perhaps more subversively effective than a more mechanistic nativist reversal.

Even today, as when Aboriginal writers in Australia adopt the white man's narrative conventions, or a Pacific writer like Sia Figiel turns an anthropological gaze on herself, mimicry remains a powerful strategy. Certainly, the poet Derek Walcott has suggested, when early élite or 'patrician' writers refracted European styles through the irony of their differential positioning, this offered strengths which were not at that stage obtainable elsewhere.[17] A more violent rejection in the same context could merely have reinforced colonial lines of conflict. Antagonism was a risk that pioneer spokespersons, patronized by the colonizer, could ill afford. Though the experience was 'bitter perhaps', early writers found in European literature the continuity of tradition which in their own cultures they had sometimes lost. And through manipulating these inherited forms, and combining them with their own conceptual structures, they were able, bit by bit, to begin to create imaginative spaces beyond the ambit of European definitions. Their slow, molecular transformations prepared the material which would foster more overt and sophisticated—and, in some cases, more aggressive—reverse discourses.

Oblique angles: R. K. Narayan and V. S. Naipaul

But if this is the theory, how in practice did the oblique approach emerge in texts? The secret, as we saw, was to preserve appearances— or to mimic standard responses—while yet speaking as other. Where the colonial claimed interpretative agency, centre v. margin relationships were disturbed. Either/or binaries were converted into situations of both/and, mingling opposites. As he records in *The Enigma of Arrival*, when the Trinidad-born British writer V. S. Naipaul domiciled himself in Wiltshire, he transformed the landscape by the sheer 'oddity' of his existence in it. His alien presence changed the aspect of the place even as he sought to adapt to it. Rather than a confrontation of extremes, there was an eventual blending, and remoulding, on both sides.

As the phrase suggests, subversion by imitation is reflected mainly in the unspoken and the understated within texts. It emerges in ironies, double meanings, unlikely juxtapositions and disjunctures. Muted opposition of this sort can be demonstrated in the work of two writers of colonized experience, V. S. Naipaul and the Indian R. K. Narayan. (Neither writer, however, is in fact strictly colonial in period, both having published widely since independence.) Though their approaches were always rather different, both, significantly, avoided the stance of overt repudiation. The comic pastorals of R. K. Narayan, taken here from his early period, emphasize the continuity and harmony of small-town India. His work deals with the colonial presence mainly by avoidance. In comparison to Narayan,

V. S. Naipaul's responses are more pessimistic and ironic. His 1961 novel *A House for Mr Biswas* is a cusp narrative, which opens out into the independence and post-independence period. The story of Mr Biswas's existence from birth to death, structured by his search for a house, represents in the form of an individual life the historical process leading up to Trinidadian independence. As a writer enamoured of British culture, and scornful of formerly colonized societies, Naipaul is central to any discussion of assimilation and the duality of postcolonial identity.

In R. K. Narayan's early novels, Indian self-sufficiency is brought to the fore through the simple device of ignoring the British presence. The British were still in power when he first began to publish, yet in his novels they are marginal. If they appear at all, as in the first scenes of *Swami and Friends* (1935), or in *The Bachelor of Arts* (1937), they act merely as aggravating but avoidable hindrances to Indian purposes. From the beginning Narayan has of course drawn on a legacy of British rule, the English language, as his narrative medium. But, though he does not adapt Indian speech-rhythms, unlike Raja Rao, he does use the language to demarcate a very non-English cultural space, defined by its own beliefs and practices. Beginning with his first novel, *Swami and Friends*, Narayan has employed the English language and English literary conventions to map the social life of the south Indian town Malgudi across a long series of subsequent novels.

Although the 1930s and 1940s novels were written at a time of intense nationalist activity, they dramatize a world that existed quite independently of the colonial power. An important organizing principle in all Narayan's work is the recuperation of a distinctly Indian way of life, occasionally associated with the activity of the Congress movement. The English teacher of the novel with the same title (*The English Teacher*, 1945) leaves his soul-destroying profession of 'mugging up' Milton, Carlyle, and Shakespeare to begin a life of retreat and meditation. Chandran in *The Bachelor of Arts*, a younger version of the English teacher, also graduates away from the study of English, the 'dead mutton' of 'classifying, labelling, departmentalizing', and moves towards 'a proper synthesis of life'.[18] Tellingly, it is the same transition and cultural change of heart—a move from dependency to self-reliance and greater wholeness—that India as a nation will also make.

Although Narayan's novels take care to avoid explicitly political subjects, nationalism and a mythic Hinduism are embedded in the narrative. The writer evokes a quietist Indian way of life that gives way before and so eventually absorbs the forces of history, rather than reacting destructively against them. Orientalist scholars and late nineteenth-century orthodox Hindu nationalists promoted comparable images of India as passive, feminine, all-accepting, truth-seeking. Railways, for example, Narayan accepts as central to Indian life—they are 'in the blood' (*The Guide*, 1958)—whereas Christianity or a systematized study of English are not, though may be tolerated as part of the social landscape. Narayan adapts the structure of the novel to accentuate this sense of serene randomness and continually unfolding action, without perceivable climaxes. *The Bachelor of Arts* is a 'slice of life' biographical tale, meandering, episodic. It ends without denouement or conclusion, as though the action will soon continue: individual narratives form part of the wider haphazard pattern of Malgudi life. Writing from within this randomness—Forster's Indian muddle—Narayan reveals its internal comprehensibility, or if not that, its capacity for survival despite interference from outside.

Though he began publishing in 1957, V. S. Naipaul's work can be more accurately described as post-colonial and, especially, metropolitan than as colonial or, even more, subversive. He approaches literature as a means of laying claim to a British cultural heritage experienced but never fully understood as a colonial schoolboy. From the time that he arrived in Britain all his effort was to distance himself from the West Indies. His work, however, is rarely set in Britain. Most of his novels and travel writings are devoted to minute dissections of the cultural paralysis (recalling Joyce) and the hypocrisies (recalling Conrad) of once-colonized nations. His willed alienation, though often singularly hostile, bears the symptoms of a first-generation colonial seeking distance from origins and the freedom of self-expression. Indeed, he has himself acknowledged that his identification with English culture is a product of growing up on the colonized periphery. In several works Naipaul gives perceptive analyses of colonial self-estrangement (such as in 'Prologue to an Autobiography', *Finding the Centre*, 1984). As he sees it, writers from the formerly colonized world must search for the means to give conceptual shape to their experience. English, a foreign import, is the authoritative medium of expression, but, though freely and widely used, it comes accompanied by a normative but 'alien mythology', 'quite separate from everyday things'. In *A House for Mr Biswas*, the Ideal School of Journalism, based in London, requires Mr Biswas to write about English seasons he has never experienced: unsurprisingly he is 'stumped'. The authority of the imported idiom robs the society of relevance: things seem shallow, provisional, without history. The once-colonized country clearly needs its writers to supply the imaginative coherence that was undermined during colonial times. But because of physical and psychological deprivations, such as those suffered by Mr Biswas throughout his life, colonial writers lack the confidence and the means to develop their skills.[19]

In reciprocal fashion, Naipaul observes, colonials who migrate to the capital do not escape alienation, though their condition is manifested in a different way. Their education gives migrants an insider's knowledge of metropolitan culture. Everything has a strange familiarity 'like something . . . always known'. However, they must learn to overcome the fracture which divides their lived experience from their fantasy of metropolitan life. They must, as we are by now aware, make their adopted language their own by speaking of such fractures, bringing the discordances into prominence in their work. Naipaul has confessed that his own internal split of 'man' and 'writer' could be healed only once his suppressed 'colonial-Hindu self' had been made to surface in his writing.

Focused on the strivings of an insignificant and impetuous West Indian to find fulfilment as a writer and a householder, *A House for Mr Biswas* comments on the dilemmas of colonial dispossession, the need for a 'portion of the earth' to call one's own. As background to Mr Biswas's struggle, the novel also recounts the experience of the acculturated Indian immigrant community in colonial Trinidad before and after the Second World War. Their history is one of transition, between languages, classes, castes, generations. Compiling a fictional record of his community, Naipaul copies but also subtly adapts the language and literary styles taught him as part of a colonial schooling. The narrative forms a rambling rag-bag picaresque with tragicomic dimensions, in which ambitions are consistently deflated, and difficulties endured if never overcome. Figures of authority are caricatured; popular and classical texts offer incongruous moral principles. Given its scope, the novel invites the name of epic, yet the weakness and failures of its protagonist, the relentless tendency to bathos, and the final death of the hero, resist the term. We see Naipaul situating himself in relation to a European tradition, but at an oblique angle, using his borrowings ironically, often to suggest distance from source. The ironic distance and the mockery are faintly reminiscent of Waugh, or Orwell, but are obviously delivered from a very different cultural point of view. It is in fact in Conrad that Naipaul has found his literary mentor, discovering a common lot with a writer of empire who himself experienced the lack of an originary tradition, and who used English to give expression to a translated and transnational vision.

Further Reading

Homi Bhabha, *The Location of Culture* (Routledge, 1994).

Edward Kamau Brathwaite, *History of the Voice: The Development of Nation Language in Anglophone Caribbean Poetry* (New Beacon, 1984).

P. J. Cain and A. G. Hopkins, *British Imperialism: Crisis and Deconstruction 1914–1990* (Harlow: Longman, 1993).

Amit Chaudhuri, *D. H. Lawrence and 'Difference'* (Oxford: Clarendon Press, 2003).

Chinweizu, Onwuchekwa Jemie, and Ihechukwu Madubuike, *Toward the Decolonization of African Literature: African Fiction and Poetry and their Critics* (KPI, 1985).

Michael Echeruo, *Joyce Cary and the Novel of Africa* (Harlow: Longman, 1973).

Michael Gorra, *After Empire: Scott, Naipaul, Rushdie* (University of Chicago Press, 1997).

Martin Green, *The English Novel in the Twentieth Century* (Routledge & Kegan Paul, 1984).

Allen J. Greenberger, *The British Image of India: A Study in the Literature of Imperialism 1880–1960* (Oxford UP, 1969).

Abdul JanMohamed, *Manichean Aesthetics: The Politics of Literature in Colonial Africa* (Amherst: University of Massachusetts Press, 1983).

Carola M. Kaplan and Anne B. Simpson (eds.), *Seeing Double: Revisioning Edwardian and Modernist Literature* (Basingstoke: Macmillan, 1996).

Bruce King, *The New English Literatures: Cultural Nationalism in a Changing World* (Macmillan, 1980).

Steven Matthews and Keith Williams (eds.), *Rewriting the Thirties* (Harlow: Longman, 1997).

David Medalie, *E. M. Forster's Modernism* (Basingstoke: Macmillan, 2002).

Peter Morey, *Fictions of India: Narrative and Power* (Edinburgh UP, 2000).

Rob Nixon, *London Calling: V. S. Naipaul, Postcolonial Mandarin* (Oxford UP, 1992).

Edward Said, *Reflections on Exile and Other Literary and Cultural Essays* (Granta Books, 2001).

Sara Suleri, *The Rhetoric of English India* (University of Chicago Press, 1992).

D. J. Taylor, *Orwell: The Life* (Chatto & Windus, 2003).

John Thieme, *The Web of Tradition: The Use of Allusion in V. S. Naipaul's Fiction* (Aarhus: Dangaroo, 1987).

Chris Tiffin and Alan Lawson (eds.), *De-Scribing Empire: Post-Colonialism and Textuality* (Routledge, 1994).

Independence

I am wholly what I am. I do not have to look for the universal
. . . My Negro consciousness does not hold itself out as a lack. It
is. It is its own follower.

> Frantz Fanon, *Peau noire, masques blancs*, 1952; *Black Skin,
> White Masks*, 1967

the real language problem: how to bend it shape it, how to let
it be our freedom, how to repossess its poisoned wells.

> Salman Rushdie, *The Satanic Verses*, 1988

If . . . you sing the country, celebrate the country, then it's your
country. These are the titles of ownership.

> Les Murray, *The Daylight Moon*, 1992

The time of independence

In Raja Rao's *Kanthapura* (1938), the women of the village respond
to imperial police brutality with long-suffering passive resistance.
In Mulk Raj Anand's *Coolie* (1936), there are bold but unrealized
plans for a Bombay workers' strike against the colonial authorities.
These 1930s colonial novels contrast strongly with later postcolonial
examples of the genre. In Ngugi wa Thiong'o's *A Grain of Wheat*
(1967), for instance, a hero dies while carrying arms in the Kenyan
anti-colonial struggle. Throughout the novel, his memory is cherished as an inspirational example for those who survive to create
the new nation. Only a decade earlier, in 1957, the year in which
Ghana became the first sub-Saharan state to win independence, this
literary apotheosis of an African revolutionary would hardly have

been imaginable. Between the 1930s, when Rao and Anand began to publish, and the 1950s and 1960s, when African and Caribbean writers won prominence, the terms and the tone of anti-colonial argument had undergone a tidal shift.

There had been, as was seen, movements of resistance in the Empire before the Second World War. However, opening with the transformational moment of Indian and Pakistani independence, the post-1947 period incontrovertibly represents the high period of decolonization—and the focus of this chapter. The mass achievement of statehood by formerly colonized peoples at this time spelt the demise of the empires of Britain, and also of France, the Netherlands, and Portugal. Nationalists across a wide political spectrum, discouraged by the piecemeal success of assimilation policies, took a more confrontational approach than in the past.

Speaking at the brink of midnight before India's Independence Day, Jawaharlal Nehru heralded the moment as historical and rare, an earth-changing move from an old world into a new 'when the soul of a nation, long suppressed, finds utterance'. This demand for utterance, for self-representation and self-respect, was spoken with steadily increasing urgency, in some cases with militancy, across three and more decades after 1945. In the early 1950s, asking the searching question, 'What does the black man want?', Frantz Fanon, the leading anti-colonial thinker, radically invoked the self-determining powers of colonized peoples. His pioneering psychological essay, *Black Skin, White Masks* (*Peau noire, masques blancs*), called for the colonized to resist decisively 'the arsenal of complexes'—paranoia, feelings of inferiority—created by the colonial system. By the mid-1950s the decolonization movement, which had begun with demands for constitutional change before the war, had gathered into what looked for a time like an unstoppable force, a great global wave of angry opposition to colonial rule.

Of course, periodization forces us to draw lines through processes that are incremental, stochastic, and often far from clear-cut. Postwar anti-imperialism was not in all respects new. Revolutionary tactics had, for example, been adopted in India as early as 1905. Though the changes that took place after 1947 were profound, there were certain predictable continuities with the anti-colonial politics and writing of the first half of the twentieth century. Like their elder brothers, nationalist writers and leaders in the 1950s and 1960s tended still to be male, middle-class, and privileged. Moreover, as we shall see, their chosen medium of expression in many cases remained the colonizer's tongue. In culture and in politics, those who spoke up for the colonized, and sought to reclaim territory from the colonialist, still acted the part of what George Lamming has called overseers. They were middlemen, spokespersons for the people, yet alienated from them, and also, because of their privilege, prone to co-option by the West (*In the Castle of my Skin*, 1953).

But, accepting the continuities, no one could deny that there was at this time a marked intensification and radicalization in nationalist activity. The key difference was the extent of support for outright, and even violent opposition. In the decolonizing nations—especially perhaps in African countries like Ghana, Kenya, Tanzania, and the French colony of Algeria—the call was for freedom in the broadest sense. In politics this meant nation-state independence and new institutions, while in the economic realm it entailed control over productive resources and, in some cases, national ownership. As leaders, intellectuals, and writers proclaimed more and more vigorously, what was needed to effect these goals was belligerent defiance, absolute opposition, liberation struggle. Compromise had not dislodged colonial governments, or bucked their intransigence. From the 1920s onwards, but mightily in the 1950s, nationalist groups gave support to distinctly more combative political methods: non-co-operation; concerted demands for, as Gandhi phrased it in 1930, 'purna swaraj' (complete independence); active resistance on all fronts, economic, cultural, and political, with the option for some nationalist movements of armed struggle.

The year 1952 in particular marked the beginning of a more militant phase in the decolonization process. In 1952 the first incidents of the 'Mau Mau' or Land and Freedom revolt in Kenya took anti-colonial struggle into the arena of armed resistance. Two years later the four years' civil war against French colonization in Algeria broke out. Anti-apartheid protest in South Africa also intensified during the 1950s, even as apartheid was being constituted as official state policy. Within the next decade Africa experienced a continental shift of independence successes: in Ghana (1957), Nigeria (1960), Tanzania (1961), Algeria (1962), Kenya (1963), Zambia (1964). Across the Atlantic, Jamaica and Trinidad and Tobago gained their independence in 1962, Barbados in 1966. Beyond the bounds of European empire, the Chinese revolution in 1949 was followed by key opening moves in the Cold War: the Korean War, the Suez Canal incident, and the Cuban revolution. These developments too would have important repercussions for independence politics and the fate of the new Non-Aligned movement of nations (consolidated at the 1955 Bandung Conference of Asian and African countries). Anti-imperial nationalisms and nation-states became important counters in the jockeying for influence between the two superpowers.

It was at any number of different levels, therefore, that anti-colonial nationalists waged the fight for freedom. Of particular concern for us here is the mobilization of culture, and of writing in particular, as a weapon of political liberation. This, too, was an important marker of the decolonization moment: writers' attempts to enlist their work in the anti-colonialist cause. In his major work of revolutionary politics, *Les Damnés de la terre* (*The Wretched of the Earth*, 1961), Fanon called for the entire structure of colonial society to be changed 'from the bottom up', violently. To decolonize thoroughly meant that the indigenous be forcibly substituted for the alien, in literature as in life.

Fanon's theories were specifically geared to the Algerian anti-colonial struggle. However, especially in *The Wretched of the Earth*, his characterization of resistance was influential in other contexts, though in Africa and the Caribbean more than in India. Unlike earlier Negritude attempts to reverse racist stereotypes, Fanon argued, the struggle against the colonizer should take as its aims not only complete national autonomy but the transformation of social and political consciousness. The colonized had to 'insult' and 'vomit up' the white man's values. Culture, therefore, was chosen by Fanon, amongst others, as a foremost arena of transformation, a site where psychological and spiritual freedoms might be won. By drawing upon their internal cultural resources, he theorized, nationalists might claim representation *on their own terms*. Mobilizing the enduring strengths and insights of their own communities, those which had withstood invasion and occupation, they would be able to eject the colonizer's presence and change their lives.

Many writers in English from Africa and the Caribbean took up the call to include literature as a moving spirit in the nationalist struggle. Anti-colonial resistance became for them a rallying cause, an enabling context, and a focal subject. There was widespread agreement that the role of culture was to help transform social life, and that, in turn, social transformation had the potential to regenerate a marginalized culture. To George Lamming, 'the education [or re-education] of feeling' in creative literature constituted a basic, sustaining force in a liberation struggle ('A Visit to Carriacou', 1982). Especially during the 1970s and early 1980s, Ngugi insisted in essay after essay that, in its own sphere, the pen might do the work of the gun; a play might pack the power of a hand grenade (*Barrel of a Pen*, 1983). It seemed that the mimicry of earlier writings, even though subtly subversive, had been unable to displace what remained an entrenched opposition between native and colonizer. To change this situation, writing now had to take sides. Writers, therefore, were invoked as the beacons, soothsayers, and seers of political move-ments. It was seen as a writer's role to reinterpret the world, to grasp the initiative in cultural self-definition.

From this it becomes clear that the post-1945 moment of anti-colonial and (usually) nationalist upsurge produced the first litera-ture which unambiguously invites the name *postcolonial*: that is to say, it was a literature which identified itself with the broad move-ment of resistance to, and transformation of, colonial societies. In the rest of this chapter, it is this literature which is placed in the fore-ground. In particular, the sections which follow look at the literary activity of self-making and nation-building, its defining modes and preoccupations: the ways in which writing—in particular perhaps the novel—was used to project autonomous identity, to re-create tradi-tional, communal relationships within new national formations, or otherwise to promote socialist or collectivist forms of social bonding. A 'writer', as Caryl Phillips observes in an essay, 'can infuse a people with a sense of their own unique identity and spiritually kindle the fire of resistance' (*The European Tribe*, 1987).

Although the nation in certain situations took on wider definitions of race, or of a community identified by its racial oppression, in general the independent nation-state at this time was seen to repre-sent the most achieved form of self-realization for oppressed peoples. Following the incisive analysis of Benedict Anderson, in postcolonial criticism the process of national self-making in story and symbol is often called *imagining the nation*. What this phrase implies is that the nation as we know it is a thing of social artifice—a symbolic forma-tion rather than a natural essence. It exists in so far as the people who make up the nation have it in mind, or experience it as citizens, soldiers, readers of newspapers, watchers of television, students, and so on. Every new instance of independence, therefore—and some might say each new stage in the process of winning independence—required that the nation be reconstructed in the collective imagination; or that identity be symbolized anew. As we shall see, fictional narrative, with its potential to compose alternative realities and inscribe new origins and historical trajectories, provided a rich medium for the purpose.[1]

As nationalist writing in this period is usually considered paradigmatic of the postcolonial, in what follows literary imagining will be considered first and foremost with respect to the *decolonizing nations*. Later the distinguishing features of the *settler* context will also be reviewed. Though far less embattled, and therefore less angry, white creole writers did share certain preoccupations concerning identity, language-use, and cultural authenticity with their non-settler, anti-imperialist counterparts. This chapter therefore divides into two unequal sections: the first addresses the literature of once-colonized peoples, while the second takes up the writing of settler societies.

The much-rehearsed contrast between the two kinds of postcolonial writing can finally be summarized as a question of *difference* and *continuity*. Indian, African, Caribbean, and latterly Pacific nationalist writers focused on reconstituting from the position of their historical, racial, or metaphysical *difference* a cultural identity which had been damaged by the colonial experience. The need was for roots, origins, founding myths and ancestors, national fore-mothers and -fathers: in short, for a restorative history. For the settler nations still experiencing profound *continuities* with the home or mother country, the problem was rather to manufacture a difference of identity out of the incongruities and contingent experiences of living in a strange new land. If the first group sought to establish a continuity diachronically, with the past, the second group sought contiguity, a congruence with locale and geography, continuity in space.

But areas of convergence remain. True, for the anti-colonial black nationalist, forging an identity usually involved some form of resistance struggle. It meant claiming a humanity denied under colonialism, combating the destructive inheritance of racism, negating cultural negations. Settler descendants by contrast might have been considered poor cousins or second-class citizens within the white Empire, but they were never denigrated in the same way as were peoples of colour. As in the emphatically paradigmatic case of apartheid South Africa (till 1994), the settlers' eventual right to self-determination was rarely a matter for dispute. In fact, they more often than not became lower-rung or secondary colonizers in 'their' new lands, local oppressors of the indigenous inhabitants.

And yet in the case of both creole and colonized groups, if to differing degrees, national self-images represented a tussle for dominance, and depended on fabrication. Both groups reconstructed their histories in the manner of collages, made up of fragments and off-cuts of cultural memory and myth. Both also drew on the proto-typical story of American independence, which was the first to merge demands for political self-determination with a quest for cultural and geographic authenticity. The black colonized in particular called attention to the coherence and validity of their own cultural ways; the descendants of settlers concentrated on their experiential differences from Europe. But both groups sought homes, belonging, a place to call their own, a spiritual possession or repossession of the landscapes in which they found themselves.

The postcolonial search for self-definition

Dissenting intellectuals of the decolonizing era faced a stern imaginative challenge. As the previous section suggested, making a *post-colonial* world meant learning how to live in and represent that world in a profoundly different way. But this was far from easy. While they may have taken a more oppositional stance *vis-à-vis* empire than their predecessors, the new generation of nationalists continued to wrestle with the problems of colonial dependency. As before, national ideals and cultural values tended to be moulded in the image of the West. Of growing up as a black South African in the 1920s Peter Abrahams wrote that, prior to hearing 'the crystallizing call of Harlem', he 'desired to know himself' in terms of the standards set by Shakespeare and English poetry (*Tell Freedom*, 1954).[2] Again, a double act was required: to remain vigilantly critical of the legacy of colonialism, but also, because it could not be entirely eliminated, to discover how to accommodate that legacy even while reinterpreting it.

To conceive an independent national identity, postcolonial writers concentrated on developing a symbolic vocabulary that was recognizably indigenous—or at least other to European representation—and yet at the same time intelligible within a global grammar of postwar politics. In particular, they enjoined one another to tap into the African or Indian wellsprings of their cultures in order to offset the borrowed influences of Europe. Amilcar Cabral, the lusophone West African leader whose work, like that of Fanon and the Ghanaian leader Kwame Nkrumah, was extremely influential at this time, spoke in *Unity and Struggle* of the central importance of 're-Africanizing' minds (*Unité et lutte*, 1975). A group of Nigerian writers in the 1960s (including Chinua Achebe, Elechi Amadi, Flora Nwapa, Nkem Nwankwo, Onuora Nzekwu) told stories of Igbo family and compound life which not only championed traditional ways but figured communal and—by implication—national togetherness *from within*, using symbols of recognizably local derivation.

More and more the trend was to the cultural revivalism that we saw emerge in Bengal and Ireland at the end of the Victorian period. It was believed that in the recuperation of oral and mythic traditions might be found a wealth of signifiers to achieve *authentic* self-definition: songs and tales testifying to indigenous cultural richness; or metaphysical systems, predating the colonizers, that had eluded their interpretative grasp. In the following sections I shall examine various specific forms of such recuperation, in particular, efforts at historical, mythic, and linguistic retrieval. But first, as a preliminary, I will review in a general way the nationalists' quest for self-generated or authentic forms of expression.

Like Bankim in the late nineteenth century, nationalist writers, casting about for cultural and political examples to follow other than those bequeathed by Europe, looked to anti-colonial uprisings in other parts of the world. They investigated histories of anti-imperialist struggle and their own legends of ancestral valour against invading powers. In this spirit, Mazisi Kunene's *Emperor Shaka the Great* (1979), which rewrites Thomas Mofolo's earlier interpretation of the Zulu king, is dedicated to 'the heroes and heroines of the African continent . . . who shall make her name great'. As they record in their autobiographies, African nationalist leaders like Kwame Nkrumah and Kenneth Kaunda turned to Indian mass political protest to find templates for African liberation struggle. Gandhi is also an example for anti-colonial opposition in Ngugi wa Thiong'o's *A Grain of Wheat*. But equally significant during this period in providing models to conceptualize resistance—and in exacerbating other anti-colonial conflicts—were the 1960s emergence of the civil rights movement in the United States, the Vietnamese defeat of the French, and American setbacks in Vietnam. In the decolonizing world and in the West, responses to these developments inaugurated a new politics of social transformation.[3] It was at this time that activists began to insist vehemently on the linkage between political and cultural resistance. Nationalist literature became increasingly more combative, cause-led, and, often, unashamedly polemical.

As Ngugi wa Thiong'o amongst others describes, one of the more damaging effects of colonization was the psychological dissonance and alienation experienced by colonized peoples ('Literature and Society', *Writers in Politics*, 1973, 1981). In the colonized world, whether native or settler, high culture and significance were believed to come from elsewhere. 'Reality and Rightness', muses the narrator Tee in Merle Hodge's *Crick Crack, Monkey* (1970), 'were to be found abroad'. Neither the official language, nor the literature of the colonizer encountered as part of a colonial education, corresponded to native experience, which by contrast appeared the more marginal, the more degraded. Knowing Dickens, colonial schoolchildren might feel more confident about describing the fog of London than their own weather. But at the same time, that fog, that other world of England, was unreal to them. His young son, Ngugi notes with consternation, thinks that the daffodils of Wordsworth's poem are 'just little fishes', while the schoolgirl Alofa in Sia Figiel's *Where We Once Belonged* (1996) imagines the mythic flowers as dancers living in the sky. Jamaica Kincaid's Lucy, a Caribbean *au pair* working in the United States, is entirely unable to relate to daffodils' overdetermined Northern beauty (*Lucy*, 1990). Naipaul observes in *The Enigma of Arrival* (1987) that though as a young man in Trinidad he knew of the 'lowing herd winding o'er the lea' from Gray's 'Elegy', the cows he had in mind were those featured on condensed-milk tins: 'we had no herds like that on my island'.[4] Trying to give meaning to their culturally dislocated lives, many writers turned in vain to descriptions of the world disseminated as part of a colonial upbringing: Jane Austen's comedies of manners, heroic images from British history, the Romantics' songs of praise to European nature, illustrations of luminous skies, bluebells, and dappled shade featured in school readers or in advertising. As Ngugi again comments, colonial subjects were expected to evaluate the world according to the way it was seen by Europeans, and so were presented with a 'distorted image' of themselves ('Literature in Schools', 1976).

To mend the obfuscating and self-cancelling disjunction between language and lived reality, colonized writers had to begin to imagine the world from their own point of view. It was the writer's task, Ngugi remarks, to assert 'the right [of the once-colonized] to name the world for ourselves' ('Moving the Centre', 1991). Chinua Achebe, too, has spoken of the imperative need for writers to help change the way the colonized world was seen, to tell their own stories, to wage 'a battle of the mind with colonialism' by 're-educating' readers: 'I think it part of my business as a writer to teach . . . that there is nothing disgraceful about the African weather, that the palm-tree is a fit subject for poetry' ('The Novelist as Teacher', 1965). Literature had to represent the struggles, passions, and landscapes that lay close to colonized hearts. Most pertinently of all, it should begin by dramatizing moments of indigenous resistance. In Achebe's own *Things Fall Apart* (1958), which records the fragmentation of Igbo communities following colonial encroachments, Okonkwo, one of the titled men of Umuofia village, refuses to conciliate the Christian missionaries. In Ngugi's *The River Between* (1965), another story about division in an African community brought about by Christianization, the younger generation shows 'determination to have something of their own making, fired by their own imagination'. Muthoni, who is from a converted family, controversially rejects what she regards as the white man's rules concerning women's initiation; Waiyaki, the young leader, starts 'self-help' schools for the people to 'build together', to 'champion' their own cultural ways.[5]

Part of the effort to repudiate a European vision also involved suturing the divisions inflicted by colonial history. Any number of postcolonial writers have addressed the sorrow of broken cultural lineages and fragmented memory under empire. Derek Walcott mourns in 'Laventille':

> We left
> somewhere a life we never found,
> customs and gods that are not born again
> *Collected Poems*, 1986

In her poem 'Eulogy', haunted by the 'ruptured tones' of the Middle Passage casualties, Grace Nichols struggles with the question 'how can I eulogize your names?' The names of her African forebears themselves are lost (*i is a long-memoried woman*, 1983). This colonial state of bereavement has many times been described by writers in terms of orphanhood or urchinhood, bastardy, familial rift—metaphors underscoring the loss of communal moorings, the destruction of an essential umbilical cord with history. (Consider Neil Bissoondath, *Digging up the Mountains*, 1985; Jamaica Kincaid, *A Small Place*, 1988, and *Lucy*; Peter Carey, *Oscar and Lucinda*, 1988; Ben Okri, *The Famished Road*, 1991; Michael Ondaatje, *The English Patient*, 1992; Caryl Phillips, *Crossing the River*, 1993; Romesh Gunesekera, *Reef*, 1994; Arundhati Roy, *The God of Small Things*, 1997; etc.) To mend these breaks, as we shall see, post-independence novelists and poets, like their early twentieth-century counterparts, attempted to find and describe networks of racial and ancestral affiliation, to unearth generational memory. Such attempts to reconnect are reflected, for example, in Walcott's historical excavations and naval explorations in *Omeros* (1991), Elechi Amadi's evocation of Igbo war history in *The Great Ponds* (1969), itself inspired by Achebe's historical retrievals, and in Manju Kapur's narration of emotionally complicated mother–daughter lineages in *Difficult Daughters* (1998).

Again and again nationalist writing emphasized the importance of unity *within*, cleaving to one's own. Apart from anything else, the act of reinforcing communal unity was perceived to be politically astute. After colonial policies of divide and rule, the key to success as an independent nation-state was cultural oneness (though once again the nation was not in every case invoked as the basis for unity—continentalism and racial bonding, as in Pan-Africanism, were also favoured). Already before the Second World War, the inaugural text of modern Kenyan nationalism, Jomo Kenyatta's *Facing Mount Kenya* (1938), had repeatedly underlined the wholeness and completeness of traditional Gikuyu life. In Raja Rao's *The Serpent and the Rope* (1960), India is represented as a spiritual and cultural unity, the 'Guru' of the world. In the name of national unity, as is demonstrated by Ngugi's 1960s and 1970s novels, it became acceptable to project particular class and cultural identities and regional loyalties on to the nation as a whole. What helped nationalist élites in quest of unity was that the imperatives of resistance tended for the present either to suppress or to mask internal differences.

Assertions of unity had additional structural advantages for writers, preparing a homogeneous cultural ground out of which national symbols could be extracted. As this implies, *synecdoche*, in particular, supplied the rhetorical connective tissue of early postcolonial literature. In a nationalist novel or poem, part could signify whole and singular plural because they were, by definition, so much alike. A writer might, for example, choose to reflect the history of a whole section of the national community in the experience of one character—Mumbi in Ngugi's *A Grain of Wheat*, 'G' in Lamming's *In the Castle of my Skin*, Rushdie's Saleem Sinai in *Midnight's Children*. As James Olney describes, two of the distinctive genres of the independence period assumed link-ups of this sort: the communal biography (such as those of the Igbo novelists listed above), in which the cultural life of a particular group was made to represent a broader history; and the symbolic autobiography.[6] The latter genre embraced personal histories, reminiscences, prison memoirs, as well as collections of speeches charting a political career, and again bore a wider national reference. As narratives of parts of the nation, of individuals, and of communities—of bits of national history, personal moments, and local struggle—such nationalist texts also undercut by way of contrast the *grand récit*, and the all-encompassing rhetorical figures, of colonialist discourse.

A host of biographies and autobiographies by or about national figures appeared at this time. In such works it was taken as self-evident that the experience of the writer or subject—usually the leader of a mass nationalist movement—was in some way typical. His (almost invariably his) development captured in cameo form the emergence of the self-conscious nation. As in Jawaharlal Nehru's *An Autobiography* (1936), Kwame Nkrumah's *Autobiography* (1957), or Kenneth Kaunda's *Zambia Shall Be Free* (1962), the life was offered as an emblem of the nation's coming-into-being. In fiction the assumption was much the same. Thus Okonkwo and Ezeulu of Achebe's early novels *Things Fall Apart* and *Arrow of God* (1964) encapsulate salient aspects of Igbo identity, in particular the apparently fatal propensity for single-minded resistance and endurance. (This propensity is mirrored—though there are also significant divergences—in women's tales located in the same community, like those of Flora

Nwapa's eponymous Efuru, 1966, and of Nnu Ego in Buchi Emecheta's *The Joys of Motherhood*, 1978.) As will be obvious, however, the symbolic life-story had the potential to muzzle just as much as to give utterance. Reinforced by the personality cults surrounding charismatic leaders in these politically charged times, the homology between personal and national biography could exclude from the idealized nation such groups as women, peasants, untouchables, and already marginalized landless and ethnic communities.

Finally, as yet another way of preserving unity, or continuity with the past, nationalist writers did not lose connection with the teachings of the generation which had gone before, in particular those of a radical tendency—Aimé Césaire, C. L. R. James, Jomo Kenyatta. These elder brothers' visionary poetry, and anthropological and historical reassessments—James's important work of recovery, *The Black Jacobins* (1938), Kenyatta's *Facing Mount Kenya*—gave valuable guidance to those in quest of a self-defined black identity, or of strategies of anti-colonial overthrow. Seeking alternative political traditions, striving for the transformation of their societies, many also turned to the revolutionary politics of Marxism and radical socialist nationalism. Writers who made this move include, of the older generation, C. L. R. James and George Padmore, and of the post-war group of writers, George Lamming, Alex La Guma, Ngugi wa Thiong'o, and Fanon himself.

As the historian Stephen Howe has explained, both before and after 1939, black radicals based in Britain shared a close but deeply complicated relationship with the Communist movement. C. L. R. James was a Trotskyist; George Padmore served as a prominent official in the Red International of Labour Unions. The anti-imperialist, anti-capitalist impulses present in Marxist thought gave support to their critiques of empire, though their commitment to internationalism was often much greater than that of their European counterparts. Before too long, however, black radicals were forced to come to terms with the compromises and havering of the European Left regarding anti-colonial issues. Fanon succinctly encapsulated his own partial disengagement from Marxism in *The Wretched of the Earth*: 'Marxist analysis should always be slightly stretched every time we have to do with the colonial problem' (where, that is, race reinforces class divisions).[7] In the 1930s, European Communists tended to give priority to Russian interests over and above the demands of colonized people. Not all were willing to condemn the 1935 Italian invasion of Abyssinia, which was perceived as having been a feudalist state. Even before the 1939–45 war, therefore, African, Caribbean, and Indian Marxist sympathizers, disillusioned and increasingly mistrustful, concentrated on developing their own independent body of radical thought, including Pan-African socialist nationalism. As an ideology that proclaimed the unity of peoples of African descent, and stressed the importance of anti-imperial nationalist struggle as a force for world revolution, Pan-Africanism posed an important challenge to the European Communists' assumed monopoly of revolutionary strategy.

In the post-war period, Marxist-Leninist thought was adapted by anti-colonialists to endorse the view that literature, or culture in general, could be a crucial site in the struggle to change the conditions of life. Throughout the 1980s, a decade of fierce anti-apartheid conflict in South Africa, what is called cultural work (to distinguish it from the élitist term, literature), especially theatre and performance poetry, was seen by many as invaluable in so far as it could be used as a medium for political mobilization and instruction.

Historical excavations

After empire, it was clear, the history of the colonized needed repair. Amilcar Cabral expressed it this way: 'The national liberation of a people is the regaining of the historical personality of that people, it is their return to history' (*Unity and Struggle*). As we also find in feminist scholarship and literature, historical retrieval, including the reclamation of oral memory, was believed to be the process through which historically damaged selves could be remade. Whether in fiction, narrative poetry, literary epic, or transcribed oral tale, once-colonized writers could represent themselves as subjects of their own past. To cancel colonial stereotypes, they searched for evidence of a rich and varied pre-colonial existence, tales of military victory against colonial forces, portraits of defiant or self-determining leaders—the early Jamaican rebel George William Gordon for Vic Reid; Harry Thuku and Waiyaki for Ngugi; the spirit-medium Nehanda in the case of Zimbabwean writers in the 1980s and 1990s. Again, their smaller-scale writings—stories of a colonial childhood, prison note-books, revolutionary reminiscences—worked against the more monu-mental histories of the imperial powers. Empire, of course, had been grounded in imposing inscriptions of all kinds.

The urge to rewrite the past grew particularly acute where Europe represented the pre-conquest period as a blank, unmarked by any sort of significant action or achievement: that is, most of Africa, the Caribbean, and Australia in the case of Aboriginal writers. As Chapter 1 suggested, Europe's colonial officers had favoured scribal over oral cultures. In India, China, and South-East Asia, the orientalist interest in sacred texts had underscored the antiquity of these cultures, though at the same time emphasizing their decline. In relation to Europe's modernity, the East came to signify stasis, timelessness, backwardness. The governing topos of colonialist representation in the Old Empire, therefore, was predominantly one of degeneration: the region had an ancient history, but tended now to entropy. In contrast, the 'New' Empire was believed to have been an area entirely *without* time before the coming of the European. It was a *terra nullius* lacking all traces of history.

As for early nativist writers, the antidote to such negation lay in the activity of recollection or, as Achebe said, 'ritual return' and 'atone-ment', for which fiction offered particularly fertile terrain. In the first place, the novels of remembering which flowered from the time of independence—*Arrow of God* or *In the Castle of my Skin* or Ayi Kwei Armah's later *The Healers* (1978)—dramatized indigenous culture in new ways. But in so doing, these works also adjusted the perspectives from which the past had traditionally been viewed, fundamentally unsettling a world-picture in which the colonized had always occu-pied the fringe. For Achebe, novelists had it in their power to demon-strate that the African past was no 'long night of savagery' but, like everywhere else, was filled with significant human interaction—conflict, tragedy, friendship, ceremony ('The Novelist as Teacher'). As is evident in his study of the fiercely patriarchal Okonkwo, or in Amadi's depiction of the warrior-leader Olumba in *The Great Ponds*, or in Armah's millennial *Two Thousand Seasons* (1973), native char-acters could now be portrayed not as the passive onlookers and victims of European action, but as subjects of their own history: fighting amongst themselves, plotting, making mistakes, failing or succeeding. Whether the period in question was pre-colonial, or, as was more often the case, the time of encounter, historical retrieval thus represented a way of making reparation. Writers established a restorative connection with that which colonialist discourse had denied—the internal life of the colonized, their experience as historical actors.

Many more postcolonial narratives than can comfortably be enumerated here have plots which are based on history. Especially in the early post-independence era, this was the history concerned with colonial times, the build-up to independence and its immediate aftermath. Vic Reid's *New Day* (1949), an early Jamaican nationalist novel, is bracketed by the Morant Bay Rebellion of 1865, which Governor Eyre crushed, and the 1944 achievement of self-government. Between these two nodal points, the growth of a new Jamaican self-consciousness is charted through the medium of Johnny Campbell's reminiscences. He participated in the early uprising; now he sees its historical fulfilment. His tale, Reid writes by way of an Author's Note, offers 'as true an impression as fiction can of the way by which Jamaica and its people came to today'.

Chinua Achebe's chronicles of the Niger delta just before and at the time of colonial invasion also present a view-from-within of his people's past. It is fitting therefore that *Things Fall Apart* assigns to the status of footnote the white man's presumptuous history mentioned at the end of the novel, the District Commissioner's *Pacification of the Primitive Tribes of the Lower Niger*. Ngugi's *A Grain of Wheat*, set during the four days leading up to Uhuru in 1963, telescopes the emergence of the Kenyan, or in this case Gikuyu, nation from earliest times. The focal point of that history, the Mau Mau struggle, is told in the form of recollection by a group of historically representative characters, both collaborators and heroes of resistance. Nayantara Sahgal's *Rich Like Us* (1985) is once again a later novel, but here too fictional lives run in parallel to history; domestic plots reflect national events. Rose and Mona, Ram's English and Indian co-wives, for example, forge a new amity at the time of Indian independence.

For purposes of analysis, the importance of nationalist historical fictions may be summarized under three headings: *control, self-making* or *selving,* and *form-giving*. First, as I have noted, for the colonized to tell a history meant *assuming control*—taking charge of the past, of self-definition, or of political destiny. No longer was history something that came only from outside. Whereas colonized peoples had previously been relegated to early historical periods frozen in time, or to the realm of the timeless, in histories and historical narrative they claimed and gained access to temporality. They represented themselves as governing the course of their own lives. It is important, too, that, as part of this attempt to explore agency, writers investigated the part their own people had played in colonial occupation. To resist the stereotype of passivity, troubling questions had to be asked. Did the colonized bear any responsibility for colonization? As Achebe put it: where, if at all, did they go wrong, where did they make themselves vulnerable to subjection ('The Novelist as Teacher')? He provides his own answers to these questions in his study of Igbo divisiveness, *Things Fall Apart*, and also in *Arrow of God*.

Historical atonement, the account of a community's coming-into-being, was fundamental, too, in the process of nationalist *self-making* or *self-imagining*. The examples of the past, elaborated as allegory, or simplified as object lesson, could be used to crystallize the ideals of liberation. More freely perhaps in a historical fiction than in a conventional history, a disappearing, threatened, or neglected way of life could be re-created and preserved. Narrative had the capacity to project communal wholeness, to enact nationalist wish-fulfilment in text, and to provide role models.

However, in certain situations, especially in the Caribbean, and in the case of the First Nations or Indigenous peoples of countries like Canada and Australia, any attempt to uncover the past meant dealing not only with the noise of conflicting memories, but, in certain cases, with near-silence. In the West Indies, in Neil Bissoondath's pessimistic phrase, the past amounts to no more than a 'big, black hole'. It is not merely that Caribbean history has been misrepresented or partially erased. The Middle Passage, the splitting-up of transported peoples, the legacy of indenture and colonial rule, had the combined effect of crushing a wealth of cultural memory. A grimly ironic sign of this loss is that the Barbadian schoolchildren described by Lamming in *In the Castle of my Skin* do not understand 'the meaning of slave'. In Australia, where whites in Victorian times confidently looked forward to Aboriginal extinction, the effect has been similar. In certain parts of the country, as Mudrooroo records in *Doctor Wooreddy's Prescription for Enduring the Ending of the World* (1983), a tale of the Tasmanian Aborigines' loss of home and ritual, indigenous historical memory has been almost completely obliterated.

In such situations, narrative comes into its own as a means to rekindle memory. For a people shipwrecked by history, a story of the past, even if wholly or in part a fiction, again offers a kind of restitution. Especially because of its chronological structure, a novel or a narrative poem has the potential to forge imaginary connections between the reduced present and the legendary past. Where pre-invasion histories may be obscure, such as in Africa, the West Indies, Australia, or the South Pacific, a creative work can also embellish the sketchy evidence of myth and archaeology. Imaginary and actual returns to Africa, site of the betrayal into slavery but also of rich ancestral memory, feature prominently in the work of Caribbean writers such as Kamau Brathwaite, George Lamming, and Derek Walcott, as also in the Caribbean-born black British author Caryl Phillips.

Postcolonial fiction therefore gives structure to, as well as being structured by, history. Here we come to the idea of historical narrative—indeed of narrative in general—as a process of *form-giving*. The space–time framework and patterns of causality in a narrative work not only impart coherence to a fragmented history, but also help organize and clarify foundational moments in the anti-imperial movement: the initial emergence of political self-consciousness, say, or the explosion of resistance. In a nationalist novel or play, such as Ngugi's *Matigari* (1986/1989), or *The Trial of Dedan Kimathi* (1976, written jointly with Micere Mugo), as earlier in Raja Rao's *Kanthapura*, a story of anti-colonial heroism may be highlighted, elaborated, and made memorable; national triumphs can be underscored and praised.

As this might suggest, post-independence narrative also has the capacity to establish new metaphors of nationhood: not only to rewrite history, but to create and to frame defining symbols for the purposes of imagining the nation. Perhaps most iconic amongst such narratives is Salman Rushdie's *Midnight's Children* (1981), which comprises a medley of images and stories drawn from Indian myth, legend, Bombay talkies, history, bazaar culture, and conventions of pickle-making, images which separately and together are made to correlate with national self-perceptions. '[T]here are so many stories to tell,' comments the narrator and hero, Saleem Sinai, 'too many, such an excess of intertwined lives events miracles places rumours.' India itself, as the novel makes clear, is an excess. By implication therefore, almost without the reader realizing it at first, *Midnight's*

Children itself develops into a complex figure for the plenitude of India—and has indeed been multiply cited as such. Ngugi's *A Grain of Wheat* and *Petals of Blood* (1977), Shimmer Chinodya's *Harvest of Thorns* (1989), and Walcott's *Omeros*, too, serve as repositories of national symbols. In *A Grain of Wheat* the encompassing unity of place and time (the village setting, the four days leading up to independence) brings together individual life-histories in a structure of communal solidarity not unlike that which the new nation-state is to offer at a macrocosmic level. The story provides a channel through which to conceive the process of national coming-into-being.

Fictional returns

If the postcolonial quest was to establish control over the past and to give it form, it would seem to follow that the organizing themes of the literature, too, would be concerned with going back and with retrieval. From the foregoing, it becomes apparent that the many acts of remembering that characterize post-independence writing partake in an overarching metanarrative of *journeying* and *return*. In the words of Ayi Kwei Armah in *Two Thousand Seasons*, the search is for paths to a 'necessary beginning', the start of a different history, 'to work out better directions, to follow better visions in our salvaged lives'.

Palace of the Peacock (1960) by Wilson Harris, a rewriting of Conrad's 'Heart of Darkness', offers a model of the postcolonial journeying tale. In the novel a dreamlike voyage upriver into the Guyanese hinterland turns into a ritual of spiritual reconciliation for each of the group of travellers involved. In the course of the journey oppositions of past and future, and of colonial besieger and besieged, merge. Warring minds are synthesized into an interdependent whole or, to use Harris's terms, a complex 'ancestral womb' which can be read as a symbol for the new Guyana. Motifs of similar travels and journeys—the pilgrimage, the great march, the Middle Passage, the road or path connecting disparate realities or contrasting states of being (town and city, past and present/future, life and afterlife)— underpin the plot or provide a symbolic framework in a great number of postcolonial texts. These include Wole Soyinka's *The Road* (1965),

Ama Ata Aidoo's *Our Sister Killjoy* (1977), Ngugi's *Petals of Blood*, Achebe's *Anthills of the Savannah* (1987), the poetry of Kamau Brathwaite and Derek Walcott, Anita Desai's *Journey to Ithaca* (1995), and Tayeb Salih's postcolonial classic in Arabic *Season of Migration to the North* (1966/1969). Among a younger generation of writers, Chenjerai Hove's *Bones* (1988), Michelle Cliff's *No Telephone to Heaven* (1988), Ben Okri's *The Famished Road,* Amitav Ghosh's *The Shadow Lines* (1988) and *In an Antique Land* (1992), Yvonne Vera's *Without a Name* (1994), and several of Caryl Phillips's novels, are in their many different ways preoccupied with journeying.

A writer may also choose to focus on specific episodes in the greater narrative of journeying: the idyllic childhood and the dawn of self-consciousness; or the time following, of severance and departure, and the loss of roots, home, or motherland. Childhood moments are memorably recalled in Peter Abrahams's *Tell Freedom* (1954), Ezekiel Mphahlele's *Down Second Avenue* (1959), Merle Hodge's *Crick Crack, Monkey,* Wole Soyinka's account of the syncretic experience of an Abeokuta upbringing in *Aké* (1981), Jamaica Kincaid's *Annie John* (1985), a series of wry episodic reminiscences about growing up in late colonial Antigua (and thus a 'prequel' to *Lucy*), Amit Chaudhuri's *A Strange and Sublime Address* (1991), and Romesh Gunesekera's *Reef.* Tales of wandering, migration, exile, and banishment are often featured—not by accident—in the work of Caribbean and also South African writers, such as Alex La Guma. V. S. Naipaul's novels from *A House for Mr Biswas* (1961) and *The Mimic Men* (1967), to *Guerrillas* (1975) and *A Bend in the River* (1979), recount different incidents in what is essentially a larger narrative of wandering and displacement embracing his entire *œuvre*. Sam Selvon in *The Lonely Londoners* (1956) casts a humorous if caustic eye on the West Indian migrant experience in 1950s Britain. In more recent times, as recounted in Chapter 6, novels of postcolonial migration—'extra-territorial' tales straddling different cultural worlds—have so proliferated as to have formed a definitive genre of post-independence writing. Beginning with the violent propulsion of two Indian men into southern England, Salman Rushdie's *The Satanic Verses* (1988), for example, offers a pair of contrasting tales about cultural exile: one involving miserable alienation, the experience of Saladin Chamcha; the other unwished-for integration, which is Gibreel Farishta's story. The adventures of both heroes end with their return home to Bombay.

And, indeed, the culminating event in the journey narrative is that of homecoming, a moment which appears under a range of moods, extending from celebration to disillusionment. Early examples are Lamming's *Of Age and Innocence* (1958) in which West Indian expatriates struggle to involve themselves in the politics of their home island, Achebe's *No Longer at Ease* (1960), a novel recounting the acculturation of a 'been-to' Nigerian who has returned home after a period of study in Britain, and Wole Soyinka's related *The Interpreters* (1965), in which a group of friends, all intellectually sophisticated and socially privileged, seek a role in the new Nigeria. In Caribbean writing, dreamlike and mythic images of African homecoming often figure a desire to reconnect with the past after a long history of dispossession. Brathwaite's poems of the later 1960s (*Rights of Passage*, 1967; *Masks*, 1968; and *Islands*, 1969) repeatedly retrace the slave routes between Barbados and West Africa. Circling around the unspeakable moment of betrayal into slavery, the poet tries to imagine from the point of view of a 'stranger' the African rituals lost during the Middle Passage. In a dream Achille in Walcott's epic *Omeros* walks the Atlantic back to Africa. More recent African and Caribbean journeys back are less visionary. To take a rough selection, Buchi Emecheta's *Double Yoke* (1982), Joan Riley's *The Unbelonging* (1985), Caryl Phillips's *A State of Independence* (1986), and Ngugi in *Matigari* all represent the return to the homeland as an emotional crisis, the end of a nostalgic dream, or a harsh encounter with a reality of continuing social and political hardship.

In their myriad narratives of journeying we see how postcolonial writers have managed, through a process of mass imaginative appropriation, to hijack one of the defining stories of imperial expansion: the traveller's tale, the voyage into mystery, to the heart of darkness. Tales of occupation and settlement plotted from the colonial centre to the colonies have been supplanted by journeys *from* the hinterland *to* the city—with the extra inflection of the final moment of homecoming and return. Another reverse narrative in the same genre is the pilgrimage into a spiritual reality obscure to Europe. Incorporating indigenous cultural material, defiant of western authority, the postcolonial quest seeks mastery not in the first instance over land or other peoples, but of history and self.

Of karma and Caliban

From an early time, the adaptation of indigenous myth represented another important mode of retrieval. Poets like the Ugandan Okot p'Bitek, or the West Indians Louise Bennett and Merle Collins, but also more self-consciously literary and allusive writers like Wole Soyinka or Christopher Okigbo, have been heirs to still-vital oral traditions. Other writers have grown up in cultures with a long history of writing in the vernacular, such as existed in India. Using conceptual structures drawn from local tradition they therefore tried to integrate the cultural life of the past with their post-independence, westernized reality. As the novel was, unlike the poem or the play, perceived to be an imported genre, writers tried to graft it to non-European surroundings with the help of native forms. In a nationalist climate, the belief embedded in indigenous myth, too, recaptured attention. Writers came to recognize that the gods, daemons, half-children, warriors, and strange beasts of local legend and oral epic still held explanatory power, despite the efforts of missions and schools to eradicate them. Figures from myth could not simply be dismissed as outworn fetishes or heathen embarrassments. They offered a rich resource for cultures seeking redefinitions of locale, community, and identity.

Working in the medium of a highly decorated English, Soyinka from the start of his career drew on Yoruba mythic concepts to structure his novels, poems, and plays. The god Ogun, destroyer and creator, frequently appears in his work, as catalyst of action, agent of destiny, or purifying force. Some years before, in the early 1950s, Soyinka's fellow countryman Amos Tutuola raided Yoruba oral culture for the fantastical characters and amazing metamorphoses which fill his stories in 'broken' English (for example, *The Palm-Wine Drinkard*, 1952, and *My Life in the Bush of Ghosts*, 1954). Ghanaian playwrights, such as Efua Sutherland in *The Marriage of Anansewa* (1967), or Ama Ata Aidoo in her play *Anowa* (1965), have drawn on Akan legend, most notably the Ananse story-telling tradition, both to shape their work and to ground it in a known cultural background. More explicitly than in his early stories, the plots of R. K. Narayan's 1950s and 1960s novels are patterned on concepts of karma and Hindu spiritual progression. Almost in spite of himself, Raju in *The*

Guide (1958) comes to embody, in the right sequence, the traditional roles of student, householder, hermit, and *sanyasi* (holy man). Raja Rao's *The Serpent and the Rope* is loud with resonances from the epic tale of Rama, the god who moves through phases of marriage, exile, and the loss of his consort, as does Rao's hero. In *Midnight's Children* the honeycombed structure of multiple mini-narratives reflects the digressive form of the *Mahabharata* and *Ramayana*. Characters like Clare and the avenging Christopher in Cliff's *No Telephone to Heaven* replay in their West Indian context classic roles drawn both from a creolized Yoruba mythology and from the English 'Great Tradition'. The Kathakali dance cycle offers Arundhati Roy a rich allusive background against which to situate the reductions of the postcolonial present in *The God of Small Things*.

Crossing the adventures of indigenous gods with European realism, superimposing images from other worlds on Westernized city landscapes, post-independence writers relied on an intensely practical hybridity—the blending of their different cultural influences, an upfront and active syncretism—to unsettle the inheritance of Europe. In postcolonial discourse the term hybridity, usually attributed to the challenging work of Homi Bhabha, could be seen to refer to a bewildering array of different kinds of mixing. In relation to much post-independence writing, however, the fact is that novelists, playwrights, and poets probably had little option but to be syncretic. No matter how determined were writers' efforts at reclamation, in a postcolonial society coming to terms with the corrosion of tradition during colonial occupation, cultural purity was not on offer. Indigenous myth could not give automatic access to a national essence or 'soul'. Yet, far from syncretism being a disadvantage, the powerful mutating energies of mixed genres like the myth-based novel or the Caribbean or African modernist poem made available symbolic languages with which to signify the vivid contrasts of, for example, expanding post-independence cities like Bombay, Kingston, or Accra.

The impact of European modernism on writers from Soyinka through to Rushdie and Ben Okri vividly illustrates not only the *impurity* of influence in postcolonial writing, but also the fact that cultural mixing was intrinsic even to the processes that led writers to myth in the first place. Montage effects and mythic adaptations were, as we know, championed by Anglo-American modernist poetry. This poetry, in particular the work of T. S. Eliot, formed a staple part of the university syllabuses with which most of the writers of independence came into contact. In literary circles from Ibadan to Wellington modernist techniques were popular. Writers turned to their own spiritual traditions, therefore, both as the source of a new national identity, and also as a mythic resource with which to structure poetic collages. Modernism was certainly not the only such influence on these writers, yet it did offer a particularly commodious vocabulary with which a post-imperial world might be represented. Soyinka and Okigbo, for example, found in modernist fragmentation and 'difficulty' a way of expressing their alienation in a teeming, culturally divided Nigeria. For Ngugi, Conrad's epistemological complexities suggested how moral and social dilemmas in the new Kenya might be portrayed. In a slightly different way, a Caribbean poet like Kamau Brathwaite was encouraged in part by the conversational movements of Eliot's early poems to experiment with patois or nation-language, mixing formal and demotic styles. Eliot's influence in postcolonial writing has continued. As an epigraph to her 1980 novel *Clear Light of Day*, a meditative tale about remembrance and personal change, Anita Desai uses an image of transfiguration taken from 'Four Quartets'. Eliot's evocations of multidimensional time underline Desai's layered chronology in the novel.[8]

There is in effect no end to the hotchpotch of cultural and mythic influences that is postcolonial writing. For example, as well as borrowing from Swift, Conrad, Kafka, and Bulgakov, Ngugi has moulded to fit the Kenyan context biblical archetypes picked up as part of a colonial education—Moses leading the Israelites to the Promised Land, the martyrdom of Christ. His adaptation of European cultural myths for nationalist purposes reminds us that postcolonial borrowing was, and is, not innocent, nor merely gestural. Representing the present in symbols derived from the indigenous past was a decolonizing strategy, but the same was true of the adaptation and mutation of colonial Europe's defining tales. For the once-colonized to interpret Homer or Shakespeare or Dante *on their own terms* meant staking a claim to European tradition from beyond its conventional boundaries. Take-over or appropriation was in its way a bold refusal of cultural dependency. It signified that the powerful paradigms represented by Europe's canonical texts were now mobilized in defence of what had once been seen as secondary, unorthodox, deviant, primitive. The colonized laid claim to the right of speech by what Lamming calls 'error' or 'blasphemy': a flagrant contravention of colonial cultural rules, a wrenching of dominant assumptions. This annexation or error, as he says, was the 'privilege of the excluded Caliban' (*The Pleasures of Exile*, 1960).

As Lamming implies, the texts that were regarded as the icons of European culture, and especially those that symbolized its claims to authority, became the object of repeated native/colonized appropriations: *The Tempest, Robinson Crusoe*, 'Heart of Darkness'. Lamming's *The Pleasures of Exile* and *Water with Berries* (1971), Kamau Brathwaite's *Islands*, David Dabydeen's 'Miranda/Britannia' poems in *Coolie Odyssey* (1988), and the Mauritian Dev Virahsawmy's play *Toufann* (1991) invert and appropriate the perspectives of *The Tempest*, most prominently by identifying with the bitter cursing of Caliban. Derek Walcott's poems 'Crusoe's Island' and 'Crusoe's Journal' (*Collected Poems*), and his play *Pantomime* (1980), take Defoe as a semi-ironic emblem for states of contemporary life in the Caribbean. Inverted writings such as these stage a contest to read reality in a different way from before—from an angle unimaginable to the colonizer. *Omeros* transports the *Odyssey*, Dante's *Divine Comedy*, and elements of James Joyce's *Ulysses* to the fishing communities of the St Lucian seaboard. 'Heart of Darkness' informs Naipaul's *A Bend in the River* and David Dabydeen's *The Intended* (1991) as well as Harris's *Palace of the Peacock*; Conrad's *Under Western Eyes* shades into *A Grain of Wheat; Arrow of God* gives the reverse, African angle on the road-building scenes of Cary's *Mister Johnson*.

Disruption can also, of course, take place at the level of structure and narrative voice. As Salman Rushdie emphasizes in *Imaginary Homelands* (1991), post-imperial narrative constantly negotiates between different registers, between high and low voices, and contrasting realities, past and future, First and Third World, élite and mass. As we see in Aidoo's *Our Sister Killjoy*, Nuruddin Farah's *Maps* (1986), Shashi Tharoor's *The Great Indian Novel* (1989), Caryl Phillips's *Cambridge* (1991), or Rushdie's own work, to mention but a handful of texts, the postcolonial writer flamboyantly crosses, fragments, and parodies different narrative styles and perspectives. Local contexts are reflected in the inclusion of pidgin English, untranslated words, obscure proverbs. The writer introduces a noise of voices that resists easy decoding. A similar effect is created where a work cites cultural information—jokes, fragments of oral epic, indigenous film, vernacular histories—which cannot be deciphered without background knowledge.

Another contrapuntal technique is to foreground the roles of formerly marginalized historical actors—a sweeper, a peasant, a slave, an island child, a guerrilla fighter, a fisherman. Alternatively the view from inside, from the group, from below, from beyond the civil lines, is conveyed by a communal narrator or a choric voice. Olive Senior's *Summer Lightning* (1986) is told from the point of view of a West Indian child, as is Jamaica Kincaid's *Annie John*. Roy's *The God of Small Things* gives the 'two-egg' twins' perspective on regional and family trauma. The Zimbabwean Yvonne Vera's central women characters are repeatedly wounded by a national history that denies them entry. And *Things Fall Apart* famously strings together a collection of mini-narratives concerned with the experience of women, *osu* (or outcasts), and slaves in the Umuofia community. In all such experiments with perspective and dissonant techniques we see writers exploiting the subversive, impious tendencies already present in the novel. The polyphony which results has encouraged post-structuralist critics to see in postcolonial narrative an amplification of the dialogic quality which the critical theorist Mikhail Bakhtin once defined as the particular property of the novel.[9] The implications of the convergence between Western literary theory and postcolonial narrative will be considered in Chapter 6.

A foreign anguish?

The crux of post-colonial debates about cultural authenticity, hybridity, and resistance is most prominently drawn at the point of language choice. This, alongside the recovery of history, was one of the issues of greatest significance in the nationalist writing of independence, and a key source of contention in the effort to define identity.

Fanon observed that to use a language meant 'to assume a culture' (*Black Skin, White Masks*). Therefore, to be cut off from a mother tongue implied a damaging loss of connection with one's culture of origin. Under colonization—most recently in certain African colonies, and most destructively in the Caribbean—the suppression of vernacular languages in favour of English was used as an instrument of imperial rule. In African schools, as several writers recount, the mastery of the colonizer's tongue was taken as a measure of a student's self-improvement and Europeanization. So it is not surprising that, with independence, the use of English came to be criticized as a form of national betrayal. For a national élite to express itself in a European language entrenched cultural and class divisions at a time when the need for wholeness was paramount.

However, in spite of the incursions of a colonial education, in Africa and also in India, writers did by and large retain knowledge of at least one vernacular language. The situation was rather different in the West Indies where, as the poet Nourbese Philip has expressed it, 'English' signifies a permanent dispossession, a 'foreign . . . l/anguish' (*She Tries Her Tongue*, 1989). In the reminiscences of the narrator in Walcott's *Omeros*, 'what began dissolving' during the time of slavery in the West Indies were the languages from the other side of the Atlantic: 'Everything was forgotten. . . . The deaf sea has changed around every name.' The Caribbean '[yearns] for a sound that is missing'.

Although West Indian writers have developed vibrant native forms of literary expression through borrowing from creole speech, even so the loss of African and Carib/Arawak mother tongues is keenly felt. The borrowed, non-standard, yet paradoxically native English of the West Indies has acted as a reminder to its speakers both of their marginality relative to the metropolis, and their alienation from their cultural roots. Especially at the time of decolonization, the use of English (or French in the French Caribbean) appeared to neutralize efforts at communal self-definition. For, as Jamaica Kincaid has written, 'The language of the criminal can explain and express the deed only from the criminal's point of view' (*A Small Place*).

Ngugi wa Thiong'o was for some time one of the more committed critics of the use of the colonizer's language in post-independence writing, and, in more recent years, of the encroachments of the state on artists' work.[10] As he has strenuously testified, he has made it his life's project to resist the 'spiritual subjugation' that English represents (*Decolonising the Mind*, 1986). To him, the colonial language still holds embedded colonial values, so constraining expression and perpetuating cultural inferiority complexes. Curiously like Naipaul, Ngugi highlights the displacement suffered where literature fails to reflect local reality and where local reality is defined by a foreign language. But his remedy is very different from Naipaul's: not imitation, if with subtle variations of approach, but outright rejection. From 1979 Ngugi attempted to break with English as a literary medium, to return to his mother tongue, Gikuyu, and to promote intra-African translation pathways. Along with this, like the African critic Chinweizu, he has also sought to resist Eurocentric approaches to literature in the African academy.[11]

From the time of independence, the debate about decolonizing language, in which Ngugi's case is often cited as touchstone, has embraced a wide variety of concerns. Writers weigh the advantages offered by English as a world language against the diluting effects on identity of using not only the former colonial tongue, but the language which has, more recently, served as the medium of Hollywood's cultural hegemony, of the West-based popular music industry and the Web—in short, of the American imperium. Those who use English worry about the limited accessibility to local populations of literature written in what remains to many a foreign language. Knotty questions of political and cultural orientation crop up. Does literature in English signify a lasting colonial dependency, a cultural correlate for the neo-colonial economic relations which continue to exist between the metropolitan centre and the formerly colonized periphery? Do postcolonial writers find themselves in the position of producing literary 'raw material'—which conveniently needs no translation—for the critical and academic industries of wealthy Northern countries? Can those who write in European languages claim to speak to and for their own people?

As with other attempts to diminish the effects of the colonial encounter, such questions come up against the ineradicable historical fact of that encounter. In Upamanyu Chatterjee's phrase, English is an 'unavoidable leftover' of colonization (*English, August*, 1988). Projects of linguistic retrieval cannot hope to return colonized vernaculars to a pre-colonial state. The situation in the West Indies thus becomes the extreme that illustrates a general condition. As writers widely concede, it is not possible any longer to escape the effects of a globalized culture produced in part by colonization. Already early in the 1960s, Chinua Achebe publicly declared his willingness to make use of the historical incursion of English. He gave his support to the language for two main reasons. First, English as a lingua franca helped maintain national unity in Nigeria, a country where over 200 languages are spoken. And, second, English was in his view so much a part of Nigerian life as to qualify as an African language: 'spoken by Africans on African soil, a language in which Africans write [which therefore] justifies itself' ('The African Writer and the English Language', 1964; 'The Song of Ourselves', 1990). Though in a very different national context, the critic Aijaz Ahmad in India takes a line similar to that of Achebe. To subtract English from South Asian cultural life, he observes, would be as absurdly pointless as boycotting the railways.[12] English has simply become one of the languages of the subcontinent. Especially following the efflorescence of the Indian novel in English since the 1980s, the language has also been fully accepted as a creative medium. Its elimination in favour of Hindi, once a political objective, is now no longer an issue.

Many postcolonial writers have fallen in with Achebe's opinion concerning English. For them the choice of the language as an international medium, though with the potential for multifarious local adaptations, is a foregone if never entirely comfortable conclusion. Few turn up their noses at the large readership and more affluent market to which they have access by writing in English. Cultural authenticity or linguistic purity, writers tacitly accept, is in any case not on offer in their mixed, heterogeneous worlds. And the English language itself, shared amongst a varied group of postcolonial nations, is showing interesting signs of its many transcultural migrations. English in India, for example, spoken by over 20 million people, coexists and intermingles with regional languages or *bhasha*. Nigerian English has taken on some of the resonances of pidgin.

The option widely favoured by writers is to participate in the processes of indigenization already taking place: to make a virtue of historical necessity by manipulating English to suit their own creative needs.[13] Alternatively, writers may justify their choice of language by emphasizing how the various conflicts and anomalies of the postcolonial condition are vibrantly displayed within the hybridized medium itself. But the point on which they agree is the need to dismantle the authority once commanded by English. If a colonial language embodies a colonial vision, then the aim must be to dislodge that vision. To borrow the terminology suggested by Ashcroft, Griffiths, and Tiffin in *The Empire Writes Back*, it is important to encourage a situation in which a multiplicity of 'Englishes' are able to coexist, as opposed to a world in which one metropolitan English is dominant over other 'deviant' forms.

English has perhaps attracted special support because of its perceived malleability. Far from enforcing the cultural centrality of its historical homeland, the language, itself an Anglo-Saxon and Norman 'blend', has proved to be a generous and accommodative traveller. It has been grafted on to different cultures, adjusted to local conditions, mutated, and mongrelized. It has also promoted feelings of solidarity among nationalist middle classes. In large multicultural nations such as India or Nigeria, English is paradoxically the one language which allows communication and cultural exchange between élites in different regions.

In this way, what Britain saw as one of its cultural monuments— the tongue that Shakespeare knew—has been broken up and thrown about, creating any number of splinter forms which are no longer recognizably 'English'. Like the incorporation into Jamaican or Indian daily life of cricket or jelly-and-custard desserts, Marie biscuits or ginger beer, the development of multiple literary and spoken Englishes illustrates the fecundity of postcolonial adaptation. It is a process which can also be termed cultural boomeranging or switchback, where the once-colonized take the artefacts of the former master and make them their own. As Narayan emphasizes, English is to him an absolutely 'swadeshi' language: 'English, of course, in a remote horoscopic sense, is a native of England; but it enjoys, by virtue of its canny adaptability, citizenship in every country in the world' ('To a Hindi Enthusiast', *A Writer's Nightmare*, 1988). He has been echoed by the Indian poet Kamala Das, who also writes in Malayalam. To her, English represents a valid personal choice: 'half English, half Indian', the language with 'its distortions, its queernesses' is there for the taking ('An Introduction', *The Old Playhouse and Other Poems*, 1973).

Yet it is a point worth emphasizing that few of those who speak in support of English envisage its adoption in unmediated form. Walcott notes in 'Crusoe's Journal', 'parroting our master's style and voice, we make his language our own'. English is 'conquered', Salman Rushdie writes, by acculturation: 'we can't simply use the language in the way the British did . . . it needs remaking for our own purposes' ('Imaginary Homelands', 1982). To loosen it from its colonial past, as they would the novel, writers must subject English to processes of syntactic and verbal dislocation. By adopting local idioms and cultural referents 'an English' is acclimatized, made national. Raja Rao, we remember, filtered Indian speech-rhythms into his 'alien' English in order to reflect 'the spirit that is one's own'.

Hosts of writers have experimented in similar ways. Chinua Achebe and fellow Nigerians like Flora Nwapa and Gabriel Okara early on incorporated a transliterated Igbo or Ijaw idiom, respectively, into their narrative English (Flora Nwapa, *Idu*, 1970, and *Efuru*; Gabriel Okara, *The Voice*, 1964). A decade or two later, recalling the example of Tutuola, Nigerian writers like Festus Iyayi and Ken Saro-Wiwa introduced pidgin English into the conversational interstices of their novels. In both his English and his Gikuyu writing Ngugi has cross-fertilized Gikuyu oral formulae, English speech habits, and biblical rhetoric. In Rushdie's *Midnight's Children*, the susurration of the Bombay crowd is intermingled with advertising doggerel, 'quotations' from filmic and religious texts, parodic asides in Indian English officialese. The language used by Agastya and his friends in Chatterjee's *English, August* is, as they themselves excitedly announce, an 'Amazing mix. . . . Hazaar fucked. Urdu and American . . . I'm sure nowhere else could language be mixed and spoken with such ease'.

As will be seen in more detail in the next chapter, postcolonial women novelists, poets, playwrights, and autobiographers represent an important special case of such language transformation. Speaking from the borderline and transgressive positions which they occupy, they have forged their own singular voices and styles of self-expression. Writers like Louise Bennett, Flora Nwapa, Anita Desai, Bessie Head, Nayantara Sahgal, Olive Senior, Erna Brodber, Tsitsi Dangarembga, Shani Mootoo, and Sia Figiel, amongst many others, have drawn domestic, private, and secret languages out of the excluded (and secluded) spaces of women's experience: the rhymes of childhood and madness, lovers' pleas, ritual speech and incantations. From the 1940s, led by her commitment to 'the free expression of the people', Louise Bennett dramatized in her poetry the voices or 'moutability' of 'Jamaica ooman', both street sellers and social matriarchs, 'high, low, miggle, suspended' ('Bans o' Ooman!', 'Moot Taxes', *Jamaica Labrish*, 1966). More recently, taking a more intimate, and certainly less garrulous approach, Lorna Goodison, another Jamaican poet, has hymned what the poetry of male writers has excluded from attention—in her case, the liminal moments of women's lives, their experiences of desire, love, motherhood, and the mystical (*I am becoming my mother*, 1986; *Heartease*, 1988).

'I must be given words to refashion futures like a healer's hand', writes Kamau Brathwaite ('Negus', *Islands*). Walcott has repeatedly spoken of the need to form an Adamic language of nouns for the Caribbean, pure, new naming words to re-create the St Lucian world in all its pristine particularity. Driven by their lack of a true 'nation-language', Caribbean writers—perhaps more intensively than other postcolonials—have concentrated on adapting local languages or patois (*patwa*) in order to free their 'trapped, curled [tongues]' (Brathwaite, 'Sunsum', *Masks*). 'Deprived of their original language', Walcott comments, 'the captured and indentured tribes create their own'—one based on acceptance, not anger ('The Antilles: Fragments of Epic Memory', *What the Twilight Says*). Louise Bennett has been joined in her vernacular experimentation by Sam Selvon, George Lamming, Earl Lovelace, Olive Senior, Oonya Kempadoo (a far from complete list)—all of whom have used dialect to fashion colloquial and communal textures in their writing. In his 1960s poetry Brathwaite mingled creole voices with Akan myth and vocabulary to mould a Barbadian idiom. As Édouard Glissant's theory of *créolité* in the francophone Caribbean too celebrates, for these writers a layered, mixed language is both a reflection of the region's fragmented history and a recognition of the distinctive richness of their islands' intermingled cultures.

Converting there into here: postcolonial settler writing

So far this chapter has shown that the quest by African, Caribbean, Indian, and Pacific writers for a self-constituted identity combined the rediscovery of historical roots with attempts to remake or modify English. But such quests, anxieties of imperial influence, and voyages of discovery were not confined to so-called Third World writing. In the former settler colonies also, the period of decolonization represented a time of growing cultural self-assertion and national self-consciousness—what George Woodcock, the founding editor of *Canadian Literature* (1959), called 'the rising up of national pride' ('Possessing the Land, 1977). Excluding Ireland and the eighteenth-century experience of the United States, the white nations did not, of course, take up the weapons of political resistance. There was no anti-colonial struggle to speak of, no fight for independence. But Australian, New Zealand, and Canadian (settler or creole) writers did share with their counterparts in the decolonizing nations a desire to shake off the relationship of colonial dependency. Debates arose about national indigenity or the lack of it, about the nature of belonging, the anomaly of being native in what was still seen as alien land. Though *never* as severely marginalized, settler writers experienced in their own way anxieties about the cultural mimicry produced by metropolitan domination. And they too began increasingly to seek an identity distinct from Britain.

Ironically, national self-consciousness in Australia, New Zealand, and Canada, especially that which began to emerge from the 1950s onwards—as well as the striated selfhood of white South Africans—had at its root a perception of non-identity. There was something about the new world reality that did not fit. Settler colonials saw themselves as essentially cultural migrants, overburdened with values and attitudes which belonged in an older or other world. Their education, literature, religious practices, cultural precepts, and institutions all reinforced the impression of being Britons abroad, ex-centric to what had become their native land. Lacking meaningful connection with their surroundings, they seemed constantly to be working around absences—of cultural roots, of home, or of a sense of location in the here and now. In South Africa, where the pervasive sense of lack and distance was reinforced by racial conflict under apartheid (established as state policy in 1948), such agonies of white alienation, as in Nadine Gordimer's *The Conservationist* (1973) or J. M. Coetzee's *Age of Iron* (1990), were symptomatically severe.

A settler writer's dilemma of belonging attached in particular to the disjuncture, which many in the 1950s and 1960s still felt, between the colonial or metropolitan language and the so-called exotic geography of the home country. The difficulties of naming experienced by early travellers and colonists persisted, if in a different form. For writers, sensibility remained poised uneasily between aesthetic vocabularies imported from Europe and viewed as superior, and an environment regarded as peripheral, strange, unknowable, or hostile. The lack of fit hampered efforts to write of the land, or to come to terms with it imaginatively. According to his own description, Patrick White grew up with the impression of being permanently at a remove from Australian reality ('The Prodigal Son', 1958). The maxim 'Only the British can be right' governed his upbringing. Many shared his experience of alienation. Ian Mudie, one of the Jindyworobak poets, spoke of white Australians as being 'merely aliens in our own land', not 'orientated' to the continent, lacking a 'frame of native reference'. 'All the books we read were full of trees we had never seen,' Thomas Keneally once remarked, Australians are 'educated to be exiles' in their own land.[14] In Canada a sense of rootlessness was also prevalent. In *The Bush Garden* (1971), the critic Northrop Frye described Canadian identity in the 1950s and 1960s as a '*via media* or *via mediocris*', divided between regional loyalties and the colonial cultural authority, and also between British traditionalism and American modernity. In its attempt to square these rival claims, Canada had settled for bland cultural compromise and conventionality—Frye's term is 'imaginative dystrophy'.

Now that the world-wide stirrings of nationalist awareness had brought these uncertainties into prominence, how were settler disjunctures and crises of confidence to be mended? Canadians, the novelist Margaret Lawrence observed in the 1970s, needed to 'write out of what is truly [theirs] in the face of an overwhelming cultural imperialism' directed from both Britain and the United States ('Ivory Tower or Grassroot?'). Reiterating a question Frye had posed— 'Where is here?'—Margaret Atwood in *Survival* (1972) also argued that Canada had to make itself known to itself, to develop a distinct self-consciousness, to conceptualize its 'here' in relation to a colonial 'there' always regarded as more sophisticated. However, given a history lived in relative consonance with Britain, how might settler writers go about developing the defiant cultural pride and spiky self-awareness they so needed? Patrick White suggested a point of necessary focus: geography, he noted, 'is what makes us'. The explorer and the writer must fashion 'fresh forms out of the rocks and sticks of words' ('Citizens for Democracy', 1977; 'The Prodigal Son', 1958). Taking a leaf, ironically as it happened, from US cultural nationalism, Northrop Frye similarly believed that the basis of Canadian identity and self-expression was to be found in the nation's obsession with its vast natural world, the 'Great North'. For Atwood in the early 1970s, the symbols which defined the national psyche rose out of experiences of suffering, endurance, and survival in the wild. It is symptomatic of the settler condition that for both Canadian writers identity was to be extracted from experiences of negation or loss. Colonial lack, in other words, could be converted into a source of self-definition.

For other writers, too, it was the case that the settler experience of displacement and alienation generated organizing themes for their art, and means of defining the self. As the post-1960 literary upsurge in Australia and Canada showed, an awareness of disjuncture could under certain conditions act as a stimulus to the imagination. Unlike African, Caribbean, or Indian writers, settler colonials did not generally have ready access to a culture or metaphysic distinct from the metropolis. Other than in South Africa (where, in any event, relatively few whites were radically involved), what was also absent was the catalysing experience of political resistance, most obviously the crystallization of identity in the crucible of a nationalist struggle. In time, however, white writers began to discover potential for self-definition even in the unlikely juxtapositions of their displaced condition.

In Australia and Canada, as elsewhere, the 1960s, marked by relative economic stability and the widening of educational networks, was hospitable to the emergence of new writing. Grant and subsidy systems had begun to expand or were being instituted for the first time (the Canadian Council Grants started in the late 1950s). Small presses and new imprints emerged. Anti-Vietnam resistance and anti-American sentiment raised awareness of cultural imperialism. Predictably enough, not only those ideas about civil rights which were emanating from the United States but the nationalist movements which were forming across the decolonizing world both gave encouragement to a local politics of self-assertion. From the mid-1950s in Canada there had been strong pressure for regional (as opposed to British) content in educational curricula. The nation, as Atwood said, was becoming more interested in looking at itself through the medium of a home-grown literature. Her own *Survival* is symptomatic of the changes that are described in its pages.

In Australia, the nationalistic climate that developed after the Second World War had stimulated the writing of poetry that was self-consciously Australian. Now, as memories of the 1943–4 Ern Malley hoax which mocked poetic obscurity receded, and as educational opportunities broadened, modernist poetry too began to find a significant following in Australian urban centres.[15] In debates testifying to the lively self-consciousness of the local literary scene, the nationalist journal *Poetry Australia* and the modernists' *New Poetry* offered conflicting interpretations of Australian poetry and what it meant to be Australian. A little later, in the early 1970s, the period of Gough Whitlam's premiership further encouraged the development of national literature and literary self-awareness, in particular with the formation of the Australian Council in 1973 to promote cultural activity. In Canada in the early 1960s, *Canadian Literature*, the first literary magazine to concentrate entirely on Canadian writers, helped establish the beginnings of an infrastructure within which new writing and criticism could be fostered.

In Margaret Atwood's emblematic novel *Surfacing* (1972), the woman narrator tries to decipher the wild by divesting herself of the trappings of urban or 'civilized' life. Exploring her own personal history on the land, she seeks a language with which to conceptualize her being in it. To resolve the dilemmas of settler displacement, writers experimented with a variety of techniques. These ranged from piecemeal experiments with vocabulary to a more thorough revision of conventional perceptions of the land. The first and most obvious strategy was to ground ill-fitting cultural equipment in the 'new' geography by incorporating indigenous referents, local plant and animal imagery, and details of local habits and customs which had become characteristic of settler life. Precedents for this approach had been set earlier in the century. Following models suggested by the 1930s Jindyworobak movement, the poet Judith Wright, for example, began in the 1940s to discard images of Australia as an ahistorical space inimical to life. Instead she represented the land as humanly viable, its geography made complex by historical and spiritual associations. The work of convicts, the dancing of Aborigines, the solitary dreams of bullock drivers enrich Wright's Australian earth: 'the long solitary tracks' of the outback are etched with past journeys, crowded with memories and dreams ('Bullocky', *Collected Poems*, 1971). In 'Nigger's Leap, New England', Wright reads into dust and rocks the silenced history of Aborigines pursued to death by whites.

'Not all the botany | Of Joseph Banks . . . | Could find the Latin for this loveliness', wrote the 1920s and 1930s poet Kenneth Slessor, describing Australia as first seen by Captain Cook and his crew ('Five Visions of Captain Cook', 1931). Quoting the names of local flora and fauna in order to root an alien language in a new land was one thing. More questionable was the attempt to use Indigenous or First Nations people or their cultural artefacts as authenticating symbols. To hone an image for the harsh North, the Canadian poet George Bowering in his poem 'Windigo' extracts from native Canadian culture a mythic being, the fearsome Windigo, a creature with a heart of 'hard ice' (*Touch*, 1971). However, this method of borrowing, though obviously effective, shared problematic features with conventional colonialist representation, in particular the tendency to make free with the cultural resources of native peoples in order to achieve European self-definition. In the case of South Africa, declared a republic a year after passing through the fire of the 1960 Sharpeville massacre, many liberal and radical writers viewed such citation (as deployed in the Afrikaans poetry of N. P. van Wyk Louw, for instance), as politically unacceptable. As in the homeland system, the apartheid state reified ethnic difference as a ground on which to discriminate against non-whites. Instead, black and some white writers, such as those associated with *Drum* magazine in the 1950s, turned to the syncopation of urban space as the stimulus of their aesthetic.

The late 1930s and 1940s Jindyworobak movement in South Australia constitutes an early representative attempt by white writers to indigenize their work. It was notably preceded, however, by Katharine Susannah Prichard's attempt in her novel *Coonardoo: The Well in the Shadow* (1928), first published in the *Bulletin*, not only to dramatize the 'primitive imagination' of the eponymous 'gin' heroine, but also to capture the 'significance' of Aboriginal legend and dance.[16] Yet, differently from Prichard's still-objectifying gaze, the Jindyworobak poets sought to develop a specifically mystical relationship with their country by joining together 'colonial and modern influences' and 'primeval' Aboriginal mythology. The word Jindyworobak itself was an Aboriginal word meaning 'to annex, to join'. Deliberately hybridizing their own European traditions, poets imported into their writing knowledge gleaned from anthropological texts about Australian Aborigines, in particular the Aboriginal concept of Alcheringa or Dreaming. And yet, though they named the Aborigines 'true ancestors' of the country, Jindyworobak poetry in effect merely reinforced the indigenes' marginalized situation. The assimilation the poets sought was a matter of metaphor only—metaphors which were confined to white texts. More than this,

Aboriginal peoples at this time still lacked official representation in the Australian nation. Even as the Dreamtime was developed as a mythic complex in settler writing, therefore, those whose myth it was continued to be denied a political and a poetic voice.

In 1930s New Zealand, after the Depression, the writer Frank Sargeson, the mentor of Janet Frame, tried to simplify the style of his short stories in order to convey the idioms of working-class and rural New Zealand life (*Conversation with my Uncle*, 1936). More readily accessible than native myth for white writers in search of authenticity were the vernacular traditions emerging within their own cultures. This 'middle voice' is described by Les Murray, Australia's self-elected bard of the demotic, as 'the real matrix of any distinctive-ness [Australians] possess as a nation' ('The Australian Republic', 1973). '[W]e are a colloquial nation', he writes, 'most colonial when serious' ('Cycling', *The Vernacular Republic*, 1982). Murray believes that when poets adopt the vernacular, they at once resist the 'colonial hangover' and identify with a self-respecting 'ordinary' Australia, the 'vernacular republic'. The vernacular, therefore, is a mode of poetic validation.

Murray's ideal of the demotic nation again builds on the concept of the Dreamtime, and, as in The *Boys who Stole the Funeral* (1980), includes symbols from Aboriginal myth and initiation ritual. How-ever, it also embraces other marginalized strains in the culture: Irish oral traditions, populist conventions of 'anti-bullshit' conversation. Murray brings into his language the terse 'ritual speech' used by farmers, the Scottish idiom of his ancestors, fragments of various local oral cultures, and Aboriginal place-names, now 'pronounced in English' ('The Mitchells', 'Their Cities, their Universities', 'Cycling in the Lake Country'). Along with other Australians, and writers in other colonial spaces, Murray agrees that the apparently 'limitless country' resists speech; that it 'will be centuries before many men are truly at home in this country' ('The Fire Autumn', 'The Noonday Axeman'). But from this position he goes on to approach the land as a palimpsest, detecting like Judith Wright traces of human history—the 'rough foundations of legends'—in its surface textures: 'it is the earth that holds our mark longest' ('The Noonday Axeman', 'Toward the Imminent Days'). The medley of utterance which the land has witnessed—expletive, tale, and song—forms part of that palimpsest.

Like their non-settler nationalist counterparts, settler writers have also relied on narrative as a mode of national form-giving. In the novel they are able to organize into meaningful shapes the 'multiple borderlines, psychic, social, and geographic' which, in Marshall McLuhan's words, make up the post-imperial decentralized Canadian world ('Canada: The Borderline Case', 1977). For instance, in two big novels of the 1950s, *The Tree of Man* (1955) and *Voss* (1957), Patrick White dramatized the inaugural moments of, respectively, Australian settlement and the exploration of the interior. In both, White underscores the need to develop ways of living in and conceiving the new land, of inhabiting it imaginatively. As he sees it, learning to belong to a new country essentially involves stripping away the (colonial) past, and a reduction to 'the essentials of tree and shrub'.

Like Atwood in *Surfacing*, Thomas Keneally, too, in his Australian novels, examines acts of symbolic inhabitation, key moments in the process of national coming-to-consciousness and rooting-in. *Bring Larks and Heroes* (1967) deals with the dystopic founding of Australia as a British penal colony in the late 1780s and 1790s. The controversial novel *The Chant of Jimmie Blacksmith*, published in 1972, the year the White Australia policy was formally ended, looks at the unofficial side of national formation, at who gets excluded or killed when a nation is formed. It is set during the foundational period of white Australian federation, a time when only whites and not Aborigines were counted in the national census. In the history of 'Half-breed Jimmie', Keneally lays bare the contradiction between, on the one hand, white Australian ideals of nationhood and self-determination and, on the other, the treatment of Indigenous peoples by whites.

Lastly, a settler writer's culturally displaced existence might itself provide materials for self-expression. It was possible, in other words, to use the contingency of settler existence—what Michael Ondaatje, adapting Conrad, has called 'the extreme looseness of the structure of things'—to signify that same contingency or looseness (*In the Skin of a Lion*, 1987). Charting the maze of migrant biographies that makes up their society, contemporary Canadian writers in particular have drawn on this source of signification. But there is an early illustration of the same tendency in the mythic realist Frederick Philip Grove's *A Search for America* (1927), which is a tale of apprenticeship in the craft of self-improvization. The novel demonstrates that the identity of a colonial immigrant in a new country is made up at random, using whatever cultural materials lie closest to hand—outmoded codes of ethics, newly adopted social habits, survival tips from strangers. Identity, it appears, is no more than a product of historical accident, or, as the Canadian novelist and poet Robert Kroetsch writes: 'Identity . . . is at once impossible and unavoidable' (*Excerpts from the Real World*, 1986). In similar vein, Patrick Lewis, the Anglo-Canadian protagonist of Ondaatje's *In the Skin of a Lion*, finds that his biography is made up of moments of contact and interconnection with the lives of migrant Canadians—'Macedonians, Finns, and Greeks'. His personality is not something that exists in itself, born of the Canadian soil.

Paradoxically, for settler writers, their inauthenticity in the landscape becomes a source of meaning. Some would go even further than this assertion. For Kroetsch, for example, the incommensurability of reality and language is more than merely the foundation of Canadian self-definition. Rather, that intersection of indecipherable environment and late twentieth-century global culture which is so distinctive of Canada, he suggests, also epitomizes the postmodern dislocation of language and world. With its mismatches and strange conjunctions, in other words, Canadian culture articulates the postmodern. Kroetsch's own poetry and parodic picaresque novels (such as *The Studhorse Man*, 1969, and *Gone Indian*, 1973) relentlessly undermine structural continuity and coherence. He is anxious to show that what we understand by the real world, be it in Canada or in Scotland, comes to us notationally, perfunctorily, in scraps and 'excerpts'; conventional assumptions and stock perceptions are under continual threat of breaking down into nonsense. His *Excerpts from the Real World* jumbles together clichéd sayings, 'classic' prairie scenes, and touristic images of land anthropomorphized as lover's body. In *Selected Organs* (1988), the poet bp Nichol, too, brings together impressionistic sketches of his own disparate body-parts to form an 'interim autobiography': 'collected workings I think of as me'. In Canada, as it is represented by both critics and writers, incongruities and fragmentations that could be called postcolonial also exemplify aspects of the postmodern condition: the uncertainty of meaning, the dissolution of universals, the indeterminacy of selfhood.

As the next chapter will explain further, it is at this point that contemporary settler cultures most clearly betray their distance from what we have called the decolonizing world. For Third World nations, decolonization can never be focused primarily at a discursive level. Where, in many cases, autonomy has yet to be won; where power hierarchies inherited from the colonizer have remained more or less intact; where in the face of state corruption and repression national independence has proved a farce—the struggle for selfhood is much more than the subject of self-reflexive irony. In a Third World context, self-legitimization depended, and depends, not on discursive play but on day-to-day *lived* resistance, a struggle for meanings which is *in* the world as well as on paper.

Further Reading

Bill Ashcroft, Gareth Griffiths, and Helen Tiffin, *The Empire Writes Back: Theory and Practice in Post-Colonial Literatures*, 2nd edn. (1989; Routledge, 2002).

Margaret Atwood, *Strange Things: The Malevolent North in Canadian Literature* (Oxford: Clarendon Press, 1995).

Basil Davidson, *The Black Man's Burden: Africa and the Curse of the Nation-State* (James Currey, 1992).

Helen Gilbert and Joanne Tompkins, *Post-Colonial Drama: Theory, Practice, Politics* (Routledge, 1996).

Barbara Harlow, *Resistance Literature* (Methuen, 1987).

Stephen Howe, *Anti-colonialism in British Politics: The Left and the End of Empire* (Oxford: Clarendon Press, 1993)

Linda Hutcheon, *Splitting Images: Contemporary Canadian Ironies* (Oxford UP, 1991).

Kadiatu Kanneh, *African Identities: Race, Nation and Culture in Ethnography, Pan-Africanism and Black Literatures* (Routledge, 1998).

Tabish Khair, *Babu Fictions: Alienation in Contemporary Indian English Novels* (New Delhi: Oxford UP, 2001).

Viney Kirpal, *The Third World Novel of Expatriation: A Study of Émigré Fiction by Indian, West African and Caribbean Writers* (New Delhi: Sterling, 1989).

Neil Lazarus, *Nationalism and Cultural Practice in the Postcolonial World* (Cambridge UP, 1999).

John McLeod, *Beginning Postcolonialism* (Manchester UP, 2000).

Brian Matthews, *Federation* (Melbourne: Text Publishing, 1999).

Judie Newman, *The Ballistic Bard: Postcolonial Fictions* (Arnold, 1995).

Rob Nixon, *Homelands, Harlem and Hollywood: South African Culture and the World Beyond* (Routledge, 1994).

Lewis Nkosi, *Home and Exile* (Harlow: Longman, 1983).

Salman Rushdie, *Imaginary Homelands: Essays and Criticism 1981–1991* (Granta, 1991).

John Thieme, *Postcolonial Con-Texts: Writing Back to the Canon* (Continuum, 2001).

Ngugi wa Thiong'o, *Decolonizing the Mind* (Heinemann, 1986).

Robert J. C. Young, *Postcolonialism: An Historical Introduction* (Oxford: Blackwell, 2001).

Postcolonialism

Where will it end? Like most of our leaders, he creates a problem, then creates another problem to deal with the first one—on and on, endlessly fertile, always creatively spiralling to greater chaos . . . It was around that time that I learnt of the Rastafarian's survival.

Ben Okri, *Stars of the New Curfew*, 1988

When I turned back . . . I was struck with wonder that there had really been a time, not so long ago, when people, sensible people, of good intention, had thought that all maps were the same, that there was a special enchantment in lines; I had to remind myself that they were not to be blamed for believing that there was something admirable in moving violence to the borders and dealing with it through science and factories, for that was the pattern of the world. They had drawn their borders, believing in that pattern, in the enchantment of lines.

Amitav Ghosh, *The Shadow Lines*, 1988

Whatever our view of what we do, we are made by the forces of people moving about the world.

Gayatri Spivak, *Death of a Discipline*, 2004

Postcolonial literatures (anglophone, francophone, lusophone, etc.) proliferate and change constantly, even as postcolonial critical studies in the academy continue to grow apace. This chapter aims to outline 1990s developments in the area, in particular with respect to the prominence of two constituencies of postcolonial writers relatively overlooked at the time of independence and into the 1970s—women and Indigenous peoples. A third group, migrant and/or diasporic writers, also demand attention, as their situation is increasingly regarded as representative, if not iconic, of postcolonial writing in general.

A further noteworthy development over the 1980s and 1990s was the convergence between postcolonial critical approaches and post-structuralist theory in the Western academy, to the extent that the sign was in many instances privileged over the real. As theory has played a central role in organizing both the perception and the reception of writing after empire, the chapter will end by considering this situation of convergence—though it will reappear (albeit under a more globalized aspect) in the Afterword. A particularly important concern will be the possibility of a 'dependency relationship' developing between literature from the so-called periphery and metropolitan theory.

'Distinct actualities': postcolonial women's writing

Until the early 1970s, from the point of view of many of the authoritative critics in the field, the writing of women represented an unknown continent in both colonial and postcolonial nationalist discourses. As I observed earlier, women were by no means absent from colonialist activity, either as travellers and settlers or as writers, diary-makers, log-keepers, though they were not canonized in the same way as were male adventurers and adventure writers. Women travellers like Mary Kingsley, Gertrude Bell, Isabella Bird, Florence Dixie, Emily Eden, Lucie Duff Gordon, Flora Shaw, Freya Stark, and Harriet Ward, as well as 'settlers' such as Louisa Lawson, Susanna Moodie, Catherine Parr Traill, and Phyllis Shand Allfrey, shared certain colonialist attitudes (most obviously, stereotypical responses to Indigenous peoples). But they also experienced different practical and discursive constraints from men in the colonial field. Moreover, their work was read and mediated in ways other than those associated with their male counterparts.[1]

However, if they experienced discrimination in the masculine world of the Empire, still European women more often than not formed part of the same race and social group as their male consorts and counterparts. By contrast, native or subaltern women were, as it is called, *doubly* or *triply marginalized*. That is to say, they were disadvantaged on the grounds not only of gender but also of race, social class, and, in some cases, religion, caste, sexuality, and regional status. Far from being eradicated, the grim irony of the independence period was that the pressures of national liberation reinforced many of these forms of exclusion. Gender divisions in particular were often brought into greater prominence.

The feminization of colonized men under empire had produced, as a kind of defensive reflex, an aggressive masculinity in the men who led the opposition to colonialism. Nationalist movements encouraged their members, who were mostly male, to assert themselves as agents of their own history, as self-fashioning and in control. Women were not so encouraged. They were marginalized therefore both by nationalist political activity and by the rhetoric of nationalist address. Whether we look at Bankim's *Anandamath* (1882) and the rallying symbols of the Bengal Resistance, or at the African writing of independence—Peter Abrahams's *A Wreath for Udomo* (1956), for example, or Soyinka's *A Dance of the Forests* (1960)—it is clear that, whereas men are invoked as the definitive citizens of the new nation, women are cast as icons of national values, or idealized custodians of tradition.[2] (Gandhi, who promoted a feminized style of politics, is an exception here, though he, too, favoured traditional images of women.) The kinds of narrative chosen by writers at the time of independence reflected this male-centred vision of national destiny: the quest tale, often autobiographical, featuring an individualist hero who embodies the process of national overcoming; the nostalgic reminiscence in which a mother-figure symbolizes the integrity of the past.

From the early 1970s, however, this gendered picture began to change. To be sure, native or nationalist women writers *had been present* on the literary landscape *throughout*, even if they were often critically disregarded, as the many examples cited in Chapters 4 and 5 will have indicated. Key historical developments affecting the shift towards a new acceptability were, crucially, the political and cultural initiatives taken by Third World women, and minority women in the First World, to define their own positions in relation both to nationalist and neo-colonial discrimination, and to Western feminism. As Obioma Nnaemeka writes with respect to Africa: 'we do not need to look too far into the annals of African history to see the inscription of feminist engagements'.[3] The resurgence of the women's movement in Europe and the United States, too, offered inspiriting instances of demands for legal recognition, identity, rights, and so on, on the basis of sameness *as well as* difference. Literature, again, was a powerful medium through which self-definition was sought. As in the case of earlier generations of male nationalists, for a woman to tell her own story was to call into being an image of autonomous selfhood. The written word, as the Zimbabwean Yvonne Vera urges, opens a terrain of relatively free expression to women, into which taboos and secrets may be released.[4]

A telling example of women's narrative self-embodying comes from 1980s South Africa where, during the years that apartheid repression was at its height, autobiographies by black women first began to appear in significant numbers, a development marked in particular by Ellen Kuzwayo's path-breaking *Call Me Woman* (1985). This was later followed by, amongst others, Emma Mashinini's *Strikes Have Followed Me All my Life* (1989) and *A Bed Called Home* (1993) by Mamphela Ramphele. On the one hand, black South African women struggled to withstand the system of multiple discriminations that was apartheid. On the other, they tried to stake out a place for themselves in the always still male-dominated liberation movements. The autobiographical form allowed them to mould and voice an identity grounded in these diverse experiences of endurance and overcoming, of both typicality and singularity. The life-story was also seen as a way of forging political solidarity, reaching out to black women caught in similar situations. In general, as Third World women sought words and forms to fit their experience, this meant in part identifying with, but in part also distinguishing themselves from the narrative strategies—the autobiography, the quest novel—used by other groups seeking representation. Sharing, or professing to share a platform with black women were, most obviously, male nationalists, but also, as importantly, white feminists.

As far as Western, and usually white, feminism was concerned, postcolonial women critics and West-based women critics of colour—among them, Avtar Brah, Barbara Christian, Carolyn Cooper, Madhu Dubey, bell hooks, Chandra Mohanty, Molara Ogundipe—have challenged its basis in liberal humanist thinking, and its assumptions of a shared marginality centred in gender.[5] Up until the late 1970s, at least, feminist analyses of power placed emphasis on a *common* experience of oppression, to the extent that important cultural differences, and differential experiences of powerlessness, were often ignored. Agency and rights were, for example, defined from a white American or European point of view with a stress on the individual, and frequently in patronizing ways. An unfortunate result of this was that stereotypes of the Third World as less liberated, less advanced, or mired in tradition and superstition, resurfaced. The decisive intervention made by black/ex-colonized women writers and activists was to insist on the *diversity* and *layeredness* of women's experience, and on the validity of forms of self-expression and community other than those prevalent in the West. Social determinants of class, race, national affiliation, religion, and ethnicity, they pointed out, necessarily cut across and made more problematic a politics of identity based solely on gender. And their writing, they argued, demanded a different complexity of response than did the writing of Western women or once-colonized men.

As this implies, while autobiography has been important for the achievement of self-representation, for speaking from seeming silence, postcolonial women's writing has not been confined to studies from life. In novels, short stories, poems, plays, postcolonial women have for decades sought to overturn preconceptions of Third World women's experience as uniformly degraded, passively oppressed, or lacking in powers of self-determination. Claiming a historical validity for the ordinary, they have situated their work alongside, and overlapping with, conventional narratives of a national, public history. For this reason it is important to note that the task of addressing this writing in a separate section, as I am undertaking here, is aimed at acknowledging a new critical pre-eminence and should *not* be seen to bracket away and homogenize the wide spectrum of differences to which women's literary work attests.

Our Sister Killjoy (1977) by the Ghanaian writer Ama Ata Aidoo, for example, was a significant early testament to a black woman's self-assured and resistant otherness. The protagonist Sissie finds she cannot identify with the needs of Maria, her European friend, yet she also distances herself from the self-centred and overly optimistic political interests of her African 'brothers'. In the course of her tale, Sissie journeys from Africa to Europe, and then, significantly, goes back again. The narrative form is clearly borrowed from the nationalist quest tradition but is also experimental—truncated, non-sequential, and interleaved with poetry. Relatedly, the Indian writer Shashi Deshpande's nuanced work—*That Long Silence* (1988), *The Binding Vine* (1993)—conveys through the widespread use of conversation and stream-of-consciousness women's experiences of day-to-day resilience living with, and within, a traditional family-centred ethos.

Given its stress on the multiplicity of difference, a crucial structural feature of much postcolonial women's writing (though not exclusive to it) is its mosaic or composite quality: the intermingling of forms derived from indigenous, nationalist, and European literary traditions. Coming from very different cultural contexts themselves, writers emphasize the need for a lively heterogeneity of styles and speaking positions in their work. They practise what Gayatri Spivak has described as a 'frontier style', favouring cross-hatched, fragmented, and choric forms.[6] Story-telling can often be self-consciously many-voiced, or interrupted and digressive in the manner of an oral tale. Flora Nwapa's *Efuru* (1966) and *Idu* (1970) are both created out of the languages of everyday life of the eponymous women characters. In each case the entire tale is told through medium of the rumour and ritual which take place in the women's compounds of Igbo communities. In her episodic novel *Where We Once Belonged* (1996) Sia Figiel adapts the Samoan tradition of participative story-telling, *su'ifefiloi*, to narrate from the perspective of a growing girl those mores and customs which a Western anthropologist might deem 'typical' but which to the girl constitute, if forbiddingly, 'how things are'. *Our Sister Killjoy*, too, combines declamatory poetry, novelistic, prose, and epistolary address in a way which recalls a polyphonic oral performance.[7] The writing of Bessie Head, Merle Hodge, Keri Hulme, Michelle Cliff, and Erna Brodber, amongst many others, embraces incantation and song, word-games, dream-sequences, and dramatic interchanges, all techniques which work against the unifying viewpoint more typical of European realism, and also, again, of 1960s nationalist novels by male writers.

Yet far from launching themselves into a dialogic free-for-all, which might give very little sense of social context, postcolonial women writers from India, the Caribbean, the Pacific, and across Africa are equally concerned to bring to the fore the specific textures of their own existence. Both as women and as postcolonial citizens they concentrate, as Trinh Minh-ha has expressed it, on their own 'distinct actualities'.[8] Often this signifies a political commitment, a way of noting the validity of the buried, apparently humble lives of the women who have gone before them and who perhaps helped to make their own achievement possible. At first in emulation of African American writers, but increasingly independently, the writers retrieve in their work suppressed oral traditions, half-forgotten histories, unrecorded private languages, moments of understated or unrecognized women's resistance. To the more general postcolonial interest in multiplicity, therefore, they add the concept of women's many-centred, constellated power, the emphasis being *at once* on the importance of diversity *and* on occupying an enabling position from which to articulate selfhood. It is because of these complicated and fascinating ways in which their writing has addressed, redressed, and distressed the historical legacy of compounded oppression and survival that it has become almost emblematic of postcolonial writing as a category. At the same time however, importantly, the writers as well as postcolonial women critics remain wary of their 'too good to be true' canonicity.[9]

The concept of women's dispersed power is embodied in Tsitsi Dangarembga's *Nervous Conditions* (1988), a novel which is nowadays unsurprisingly regarded in many pedagogic contexts as a postcolonial text *par excellence*. *Nervous Conditions* is both a post-independence *Bildungsroman* and a retrospective account of Zimbabwe in the 1970s, as experienced by a diverse group of women characters. Feminizing Fanon's findings on colonial cultural alienation, Dangarembga represents different forms of black women's estrangement and self-possession. The boldly defiant Lucia, called a witch in her own community, seeks to become literate in the white man's culture. Yet the anorectic distress of the young, Anglicized Nyasha reveals that the 'modern' and western can be as psychologically oppressive for a woman as is traditional society. Between these two poles stands the frontier figure of Tambudzai, Nyasha's cousin and the novel's narrator. Tambudzai has from early on struggled to escape both the 'poverty of blackness' and the 'weight of womanhood' by educating herself. She experiences Christian mission life as a process of both 'reincarnation' and self-splitting, in which she is forced to inhabit borderlines, at one and the same time losing, and yet retaining loyalty to, the traditions of her Shona home.

'All about us and within':
Indigenous writing

Since the 1970s, the writing of Indigenous or 'First' peoples in white settler colonies has emerged as an important constituency located at once within and without existing forms of postcolonial self-expression. Aboriginal or 'Koori' writers in Australia, such as Oodgeroo Noonuccal (Kath Walker) and Archie Weller, or Maori New Zealanders like Witi Ihimaera and Patricia Grace, or the native Canadian writer Beatrice Culleton, identify with the vision and objectives of other postcolonial writing: the quest for personal and racial/cultural identity built on the spiritual guardianship of traditional laws; the belief that writing is an integral part of self-definition; the emphasis on historical reconstruction; the ethical imperative of reconciliation with the past.

But at the same time Indigenous writers rightly remain wary of other implications of the postcolonial. For they see themselves as still-colonized, always-invaded, never free of a history of white occupation. As the Aboriginal-identified Mudrooroo once said, they are 'indigenous minorities submerged in a surrounding majority and governed by them' ('White Forms, Aboriginal Content', 1983). Typically, Aboriginality in Australia is defined as a deeply compromised, polysemic state, as an admission of conflicting and hybrid cultural allegiances. In the exposition which follows, Aboriginality will be taken as representative of the Indigenous situation more generally, without, it is hoped, imposing a homogeneous singularity upon otherwise widely differing writers.

Looking back from the vantage point of the new twenty-first century, after a decade aimed at national 'Reconciliation', Indigenous Australians see their history of the last two centuries as painfully if inextricably involved in that of whites—emblematized, for instance, in oral legends which feature both 'good' and 'bad' Captain Cooks.[10] Therefore, even as they underline the importance of their own spiritual traditions and strive to redeem Koori cultural memories, they concede an unavoidable complicity with the occupying culture. Hence their impassioned emphasis on Aboriginality as a *composite part* of contemporary Australia, though under Premier John Howard it has not yet been officially recognized as such in certain key areas. In the words of the eponymous seer-hero of Mudrooroo's 1983 novel *Doctor Wooreddy's Prescription for Enduring the Ending of the World*, a symbolic saga about the embattled Tasmanian Aborigines: 'Now we must become pliable and seek allies and accommodate with fate'. The final revelation scene of the novel confirms that nothing is absolute, truths are never whole, ambivalence must be accepted—as from the 1990s readers have indeed had to accept the ambiguity of Mudrooroo's own claim to Aboriginality. Significantly, Wooreddy comes to realize that Great Ancestor and *Ria Warrawah*, the principles of good and evil which have governed his life, come from a single source, are not diametrically opposed.

As also happened in the Caribbean, to fill those spaces where mother tongues were reduced or lost, Indigenous writers focus on revising the language, narrative styles, and historical representations of the colonialist invader, refracting their experience in and on their own terms, acknowledging the enduring traces of the past. Again, their aim is not to replace white with black. Rather it is to accentuate a painful, always negotiated hybridity which, however, defamiliarizes the established Anglo-Celtic history of Australia, demonstrating that they are 'native Old Australians' not 'aliens' in their own land (Oodgeroo Noonuccal, 'Aboriginal Charter of Rights'). They set out to record traditional legends using so-called 'white forms' like the novel; weave constantly and creatively between what is native, and colonial culture; cross registers and undermine fixed points of view; use what is called *gammon* or bullshitting, a mix of fantasy and humour. Indigenous writers, in other words, try to embrace the inevitability of their impurity at all levels, which includes, as in the writing of Ruby Langford Ginibi (1988), exposing a disturbing legacy of social hardship and domestic violence.

In Aotearoa/New Zealand, somewhat differently, the leading Maori writer Witi Ihimaera has persuasively advocated 'bicultural' co-operation. Distinct from an acceptance of inevitable mixing, biculturism involves a recognition of dual cultural perspectives aimed at withstanding the absorption of the Maori way of life by Pakeha (white) society and safeguarding those areas where native people, unlike in Australia, were not dispossessed of their land or language. As Ihimaera sees it, biculturism, with its stress on the co-existence of the two cultures, is an effective if not always trouble-free way of preserving a sense of Maori cultural difference. As if responding to this perception, in Keri Hulme's somewhat idealizing *The Bone People* (1985), Maori spiritual laws and traditions are woven in with a Pakeha history of invasion to create an allegory of cultural reconciliation in which Indigenous mysteries are preserved. Although with bitter irony, it is within or on the boundaries of another culture that Indigenous writers, as also in Australia, reclaim their own cultural matrices, their sense of the mythic past as alive and present. To take the words of Oodgeroo Noonuccal once again, Indigenous writers attempt to show—at times militantly—that despite long years of depredation, the 'past is all about us and within' ('The Past', 1970). 'Those who remain will always remember', is the title-incantation of an anthology of West Australian/Nyoongah writing (Fremantle, 2000).

In their poetry, too, writers like Kevin Gilbert, Charmaine Papertalk-Green, and Kathy Trimmer have adapted the totemic symbols, cyclical song patterns, and mnemonic codes of oral poetry, as well as features of Aboriginal demotic speech, in this way infiltrating the scribal and poetic conventions of white culture. Alienating or othering non-Aboriginal readers in this manner, using techniques and vocabulary they might find unfamiliar, offers another way of asserting a specifically Aboriginal vision. In Jimmy Chi's 'Acceptable Coon' the rhythmic, slogan-like refrain carries a tough political message: 'Australia's just turning out prototype whites'. In 'Government Paper Talk', which targets ineffectual white bureaucracy, Charmaine Papertalk-Green sardonically puns on her own name. And in Mudrooroo's *The Song Circle of Jacky* (1986), blurred past- and present-tense forms combine with the imagery of Mimi (Dreaming) to resist easy interpretation.

In a different genre again, Sally Morgan's influential *My Place* (1987), a quest for family roots and an Aboriginal aesthetic, while set in an apparently orthodox autobiographical mould, boldly confronts some of Australia's most racist laws and practices, notably, the 1905 Act of Segregation and the subsequent separation of families. The personal investigation of childhood, with which Morgan begins her tale, develops into a tiered narrative, told by different family members, which answers its own appeal to reconstruct Aboriginal history, to give as many different and specifically Aboriginal interpretations of the past as possible. As if picking up this impulse to tell stories, across the 1990s Indigenous writers and activists participated in the powerful 'Australia for Reconciliation' movement of bearing witness which, at times controversially, included white Australians. They sought to tell their own stories in order performatively to come to terms with the past and, in the case of whites, to 'say sorry'. The driving motive was to recognize that *all* Australians lived among the continuing effects of racism, of (post/neo)colonialism.

These Australian approaches, especially the fierce imperative to forge a reckoning with the past, show parallels with the styles and preoccupations of Indigenous expression elsewhere. As in the case of New Zealand once again, Witi Ihimaera's elegiac *Tangi* (1973), the first Maori novel in English, incorporates Maori legend and funeral chants into its extended evocation of a son's bereavement. As do Aboriginal writers, Ihimaera emphasizes that Indigenous customs (*tikanga*) extend back to pre-colonial times in an unbroken line, and that this must be publicly and ceremoniously acknowledged and safeguarded. The liberal inclusion of Maori words, not always explained by context, and certainly not in a glossary, reinforces the sense of a rich and still-independent culture to which the son, following the death of his father, is committed to return. So, too, Patricia Grace's symbolic, self-referential *Potiki* (1986), centred in a Maori cultural world of ceremony, wood-carving, and reverence for trees and the sea, dramatizes the struggle for Maori land rights as reflected in the suffering and survival of a single family. More recently, Alan Duff's *Once Were Warriors* (1990; made into an influential film by Lee Tamahori, 1994) controversially associates the privileging of Maori ways of life with the aggressive assertion of Maori masculinity or 'warriordom'. Whether patriarchal values form an adequate castle-keep for ethnic and cultural survival remains a debate that persists in New Zealand and Australia today.

Where models closer to home have been lacking, Indigenous writers have looked to literatures of liberation in the rest of the decolonizing world for inspiration. They have, for example, borrowed the polemics of anti-colonial indictment and nationalist self-assertion, as well as the belief in reconciliation through self-revelation or the historical talking-cure (as in the South African Truth and Reconciliation Commission, 1996). But a single definitive difference will always separate the work of Indigenous writers in the settler nations from that of other nationalist writers: many believe that full political autonomy is not for them an option outside separate, apartheid-style 'bantustans'.

This once again underscores that seeming contradiction represented by Indigenous cultures. Their distinctiveness lies in their hybrid status: *not* in the way in which cultural authenticity is achieved (if indeed it ever is), but rather in how the non-Indigenous is adapted, translated, transliterated, in order that selfhood and solidarity may be expressed.

Aboriginal writers therefore are self-consciously fringe figures, sensitive to the claims of the past as a source of identification, yet with their feet planted in a postmodern, transcultural world (see Mudrooroo, *Writing from the Fringe*, 1990). Even in an extremely pessimistic Aboriginal story such as Archie Weller's portrait of the 'half-blood' urban underdog in *The Day of the Dog* (1981), a residue of the old spirituality is seen to linger on in the urban wasteland of contemporary Aboriginal life. When the gang of gaolbirds in this novel lose respect for the land they are working, evil fortune and destruction follow. As if speaking to his own emblematically questionable indigenity, Mudrooroo has called his work 'alienated' because it lacks the interconnecting tissues of Aboriginal dialect and oral forms. Yet novels like *Long Live Sandawara* (1979) and *Doctor Wooreddy* do through various means attempt to '[re/enter] Aboriginal history': by retelling the contact story from an Aboriginal perspective; muddling chronology to create 'the unity of the three times'; and, in *Doctor Wooreddy*, incorporating the 'text' of a traditional corroboree, in which Bruny song symbols are not translated for the benefit of non-Aboriginal readers. By asserting their own resistant metaphysic in this way, writers arrive at uneasy yet ultimately productive terms with their ambiguity, their writing for the conquerors of their people.

The writing of 'not quite' and 'in-between'

From national bonding to international wanderings, from rootedness to peregrination. Whereas early post-independence writers tended to identify with a nationalist narrative and to endorse the need for communal solidarity, from the late 1980s and into the twenty-first century many writers' geographic and cultural affiliations became more divided, displaced, and uncertain.

The late twentieth century witnessed demographic shifts on an unprecedented scale, impelled by many different forces: anti-imperialist conflict, the claims of rival nationalisms, economic hardship, famine, state repression, the search for new opportunities. Uprooted masses of people streamed across and away from Sri Lanka, the Sudan, Sierra Leone, Burma—and, more recently, Afghanistan, Zimbabwe, Iraq. According to the United Nations, some 100 million people in the world today qualify as migrants—that is, live as minorities, in states of unbelonging. As Neil Bissoondath has darkly reflected in his short stories (*Digging up the Mountains*, 1985), or Caryl Phillips in work like *A Distant Shore* (2003), the populations of western cities are now formed out of the constant sedimentation of diverse movements of trans-continental drift. In post-independence literature, the result has been that the cosmopolitan rootlessness that developed in urban pockets at the time of early twentieth-century modernism has in a sense become global. Cultural expatriation is now widely regarded as intrinsic to the postcolonial literary experience, impinging on writing and the making of literature world-wide. Novels like *Shame* (1983), *Anthills of the Savannah* (1987), *No Telephone to Heaven* (1988), *Reef* (1994), *Lara* (1997), link the streets of London, sprawling Third World *bustis* and townships, and out-of-the-way mountain, coast, and savannah towns. Narrative dialogue criss-crosses registers high and low, and mixes in variegated pidgins and patois from the various regions of the world. What began in postcolonial writing as the creolization of the English language has become a process of mass literary transplantation, disaggregation, and cross-fertilization, a process that is changing the nature of what was once called English literature—or, more accurately, literature in English—at its very heart.

For different reasons, ranging from professional choice to political exile, writers from a medley of once-colonized nations have participated in the twenty-first-century condition of energized migrancy. These include the St Lucian Derek Walcott, a commuter between Boston and the West Indies; the Bombay-born Salman Rushdie; the Antiguan resident in New York State Jamaica Kincaid; the black British writer of Caribbean descent, now a New Yorker, Caryl Phillips; the Nigerian Londoner Ben Okri; the now Canadian, once-Trinbagonian poet Nourbese Philip; the Canadian-Jamaican Olive Senior; Amitav Ghosh, Indian but based in the United States; Nuruddin Farah, the Somalian Cape Town dweller; Vikram Seth, who

writes about Delhi and San Francisco with equal facility, and trans-
lates medieval Chinese poetry in his spare time. And so on. In the
2000s the generic postcolonial writer is more likely to be a cultural
traveller, or an 'extra-territorial', than a national. Ex-colonial by
birth, 'Third World' in cultural interest, cosmopolitan in almost every
other way, she or he works within the precincts of the Western
metropolis while at the same time retaining thematic and/or political
connections with a national, ethnic, or regional background.

As well as supplying the enabling conditions for migrant postcolonial literature, cultural interaction and metaphysical collision have
also become its standard subjects. Often retracing the biographical
paths of their authors, novels by—for example—Rushdie, Ghosh,
Kincaid, Phillips, Okri, Kamila Shamsie, and Bernardine Evaristo,
ramify across widely separate geographical, historical, and cultural
spaces. They are marked by the pull of conflicting ethics and phil-
osophies—a potential source of tragedy—and often comically contrasting forms of social behaviour. If the postcolonial text generally is,
to borrow from Homi Bhabha's well-tried terminology, a hybrid
object, then the migrant text is that hybridity writ large and in colour.
It is a hybridity, too, which is form-giving and diagnostic, lending
meaning to the bewildering array of cultural translations which the
writers of diasporas both established and emergent must make.

A transnational—and translational—aesthetic will, predictably,
itself produce a hotchpotch, a mosaic, a *bricolage*. Migrant writers
are in this sense like the raggle-taggle group of central characters in
Amitav Ghosh's *The Circle of Reason* (1986), who search for symbols
and patterns with which to explain the world on various planes of
experience—in phrenology and weaving technique and in the theory
of queues. Though 'nothing's whole any more', yet Zindi the old
al-Ghazira prostitute, who speaks a 'welter of languages', can 'bring
together empty air and give it a body just by talking of it'—as, too,
does the polymath Tridib in Ghosh's 1988 novel *The Shadow Lines*.
The infectious speech of the wanderer Alu in *The Circle of Reason*
comes across as 'all stirred together, stamped and boiled', Arabic
mixed with Hindi, 'Hindi swallowing Bengali, English doing a dance;
tongues unravelled and woven together', yet as perfectly meaningful
as a 'mother's lullaby'.

From such evocations it becomes evident that, in migrant writing,
the earth-changing cultural metamorphoses which first began at the

time of colonization have impacted resoundingly on the West. The transplantation of names, the mixing of languages, the diversification of tastes which developed during empire have been further amplified by coming 'home' to the old and now polyglot colonial metropolis. Cultural formations such as the novel, hybridized on the colonial outskirts, are now more intensively hybridized by being returned to the post-imperial western city which, too, is irrevocably transformed.

V. S. Naipaul, one of the more self-conscious and purist among the pioneer migrants, observes in *The Enigma of Arrival* (1987) that the 'great movement of peoples' which characterized the latter part of the twentieth century has fundamentally changed the nature of cities like London. 'They were to cease being more or less national cities', he writes, 'they were to become cities of the world; modern-day Romes'.[11] Another way of looking at it is that London has come to resemble more vibrantly than before colonial cities like Cairo, Kolkata, Hong Kong, Lagos, Mumbai: centres of trade and exchange which were almost from the beginning extravagantly multicultural and polyglot. As Rushdie rightly notes in *The Satanic Verses* (1988), the 'conglomerate nature' of London now mirrors the diversity of the former Empire. The *mélange* which has resulted from immigration—the fragmented and mixed-up histories, the *khichri* or goulash of languages, as Ghosh or Upamanyu Chatterjee might say—has put under extreme pressure the last remnants of old colonialist preconceptions, a vision of the world as divided between white man and other, the West and the rest.

But the mixing goes deeper than this. It is not only the conventional partners in the British colonial relationship who are joined together in migrant writing in English. The ex-colonies of Spain, too, exert a distinct presence. Since Rushdie's first attempts to open up this channel of influence, several others—Ghosh, Okri, B. Kojo Laing, M. G. Vassanji—have on occasion borrowed extensively from Latin American magic realism, again adapting and embellishing its techniques for their own particular needs. Indeed, the proliferation of postcolonial migrant writing in English has become so closely linked to the continuing success of magic realist approaches that the two developments appear almost inextricable. The reasons for the borrowing are easy to see. Postcolonial writers in English share with their South American counterparts like Alejo Carpentier, Gabriel Garcia Márquez, and Isabel Allende a view from the fringe of dominant

European cultures, an interest in the syncretism produced by colonization, and access to local resources of fantasy and story-telling. Drawing on the special effects of magic realism, postcolonial writers in English are able to express their view of a world fissured, distorted, and made incredible by cultural clash and displacement. Like the Latin Americans, they combine the supernatural with legend and imagery derived from colonialist cultures to represent societies which have been repeatedly unsettled by invasion, occupation, and political corruption. Magic effects, therefore, are used at once to convey and indict the follies of both empire and its aftermath. However, others— Okri is here the most obvious example—take the supernatural more seriously, less as device than as actual mystery, a distortion of the real that is a part of lived experience.

In the western academy and liberal literary establishments, polycultural 'translated writing', in Rushdie's phrase, is now widely accepted as one of *the* oppositional, anti-authoritarian literatures or textual strategies of our time.[12] As noted in Chapter 5, it is sometimes described as the fullest expression available of the Bakhtinian dialogic. The multivoiced novel in particular is regarded as essential plurality—noisy, authentic, street-muddied. That this should be so is not too surprising. The minglings of migrant writing accord well with political and critical agendas in western universities. For example, the literature can be read as endorsing an international, democratic vision of multicultural mixing and individual self-expression. Its heterogeneity symbolizes the kind of integration and absence of fusty provinciality that, on a cultural level at least, many critics and opinion-makers seek to promote. It may also be that the notoriety whipped up around Rushdie's work by the 1989 fatwa affair, and also the remarkable publicity generated by Arundhati Roy's 1997 *The God of Small Things*, have contributed to the prominence of migrant writing generally.

But perhaps an even more powerful reason for the agreement between the writing and the criticism is simply the fact of location. As numerous critics have noted in recent years, both postcolonial narrative and narrative criticism are situated in the increasingly more heteroglot yet still hegemonic western (or Northern) metropolis. Critics therefore feel able to identify with migrant writing because they occupy more or less the same cosmopolitan sphere as its authors. Moreover, writing and criticism participate in and are made possible by the global system of transnational information flow which so deeply informs early twenty-first-century culture, especially in the West. Fostered by electronic media networks and the expansion of multinational corporations, as well as by post-1940s immigration patterns, this system encourages the highly marketable juxtaposition of differences—the Benetton idea of 'united colors', the McDonalds concept of local flavour. But, as was nineteenth-century empire, it is also a system dominated by powerful cultural interests and capital centred in and directed from the First World. In this context, migrant literatures tend to win readers because, though bearing all the attractions of the exotic, the magical, and the other, they participate reassuringly in aesthetic and ethical languages privileged within a globalized Anglo-American culture.[13]

It cannot be denied that the West's embrace of migrant writing represents a victory for the transformative contaminations that came with colonialism. However, its enthusiastic reception can raise difficulties for the way in which postcolonial literature is interpreted more generally. The status of 'migrants' like Rushdie, Walcott, Ondaatje, and Okri—and, latterly, those of a *second generation* of more strictly speaking *diasporic* writers (children of migrants) such as Hanif Kureishi, Zadie Smith, or Monica Ali—has produced definitions of the postcolonial as almost invariably cosmopolitan. It is a literature that is *necessarily* transplanted, displaced, multilingual, and, simultaneously, conversant with the cultural codes of the West: it is within Europe/America though not fully *of* Europe/America. This has far-reaching implications for the way in which other kinds of— perhaps more specifically national or regional—postcolonial writing will be read in future.

Here it is important to remember the apparently self-evident, but none the less significant fact that the emergence of migrant literatures in many cases represents a geographic, cultural, and political retreat by writers from the new but ailing nations of the post-colonial world 'back' to the old metropolis. The literatures are a product of that retreat; they are marked by its disillusionment, its turn from the political to the aesthetic as a zone of imaginative transformation. Since the early 1970s, as is widely known, post-independence nations have been increasingly plagued by neo-colonial ills: economic disorders and social malaise, government corruption, state repression, various carry-overs from the prebendal and command structures of the colonial period. In much of the once-colonized world, decolon-ization in fact produced few changes: power hierarchies were main-tained, the values of the former colonizer remained influential. Liberation equated with mere 'flag independence', a change of polit-ical arrangement only. In Arundhati Roy's terms, 'the old order has been consecrated, the rift fortified': far from offering food and free-dom, independence has presented people with a 'wooden loaf' (*The Algebra of Infinite Justice*, 2002; and see Ngugi's *Moving the Centre*, 1993). This shift in nationalist idealism was first registered in the novel of disenchantment which began to emerge from the late 1960s onwards: Achebe's *A Man of the People* (1966) and *Anthills of the Savannah*, Armah's *The Beautyful Ones are not yet Born* (1969), Naipaul's *The Mimic Men* (1967), *Guerrillas* (1975), and *A Bend in the River* (1979), Ngugi's *Devil on the Cross* (1982), Earl Lovelace's *The Wine of Astonishment* (1982), Buchi Emecheta's *Double Yoke* (1982), and *Shame* (1983) by Salman Rushdie.

The practical response by many writers to what Fanon called 'the farce of national independence' has been to seek refuge—if not to be forced to seek refuge—in less repressive and richer places in the world. To speak very generally, in making this move, and in then securing a positive reception, writers have been much advantaged by the class, political, and educational connections with Europe or America that in many cases they enjoyed. They have developed what was anyway a cosmopolitan tendency, often picked up as part of an élite upbringing in their home countries. This fact may not appear important to their writing as such. But it is fundamental in explain-ing their reception and status as privileged migrants in the West, and the imaginative confidence they demonstrate in straddling cultural worlds. Because of their connections or their upbringing, they have tended sooner or later to win acceptance in metropolitan élites. Essentially, they have been able, by migrating, to secure for them-selves a different, more comfortable location in the wider neo-colonial world.

But as the compounded privilege, if nothing else, of many of the writers suggests, their work willy-nilly remains collusive with and an expression of that neo-colonial world. Crudely put, the promotion of postcolonial migrant writing offers a suggestive instance of the appropriation by Europe and America of resources in the Third World. The western powers that retain the economic and military upper hand in relations with ex-colonial territories are also the countries in which migrant literature is given wide support in the form of advances, publicity, and prizes. This is perhaps with the intention of exhibiting greater cultural openness—but it is an openness that is withheld in other respects (such as in restrictions on immigration or economic aid). The promotion or appropriation of the literature effectively keeps in place a cultural map of the world as divided between the richly gifted metropolis and the meagrely endowed margin. A further sign of this is that the writing most often called 'truly' hybrid or 'genuinely' noisy is that which has successfully bridged the gap between Third and First Worlds, and established itself at the centre.

And yet, because of that very success at bridging, the cosmopolitan work can appear far removed from the material and political devastation in many cases associated with its author's nation of origin. True, as Rushdie and Wilson Harris amongst others explain, the hybridity of a migrant's art signifies a freeing of voices, a technique for dismantling authority, a liberating polyphony that shakes off the authoritarian yoke. However, it is a hybridity that remains primarily a symbolic device, or a source of themes. Indeed, in certain lights it may seem that writers' connections with their Third World background have become chiefly metaphorical. They can appear to concern themselves with scenes of national confusion and cultural *brouhaha* primarily to furnish images for their art, or to deconstruct playfully the allegedly bankrupt narrative of the imagined nation. What this means, once again, is that they thus participate in the time-worn processes through which those in the West scrutinize the other, the better to understand themselves. For reasons such as these, although migrant writers are themselves often vociferously opposed to neo-colonial malformations, their work has drawn criticism for being a literature without loyalties, lacking in the regional and local affiliations which are deemed so necessary at a time of mass globalization.[14] To borrow a term used positively by Rushdie, its historical 'weightlessness' is probably one of the main factors explaining migrant writing's popularity in the West. It may be that Western readers find that they are entertained yet at the same time morally absolved by being made to confront, for instance, Okri's surrealist scenes of neo-colonial desuetude.

It remains an open question however whether this kind of writing holds much meaning for the people—even the members of resident élites—who inhabit the scenes of Third World confusion represented. In this context it is significant that postcolonial writers who retain a more national focus, who do not straddle worlds, or translate as well, do not rank as high in the West as do their migrant fellows, or simply remain unknown. In metropolitan circles, the attempt on the part of postcolonial nationalists such as Ngugi or Aijaz Ahmad to preserve cultural integrity or to retain hold of some form of national autonomy exerts relatively little critical or theoretical impact. The dominant view at the centre is that the world is heterogeneous but ultimately one; that cultural difference is transportable through middle-class channels of reception, and if not, is likely to be either uninteresting or intimidating. (As a representative case, consider the 2004 success of Chimamanda Ngozi Adichie's *Purple Hibiscus*, a finely wrought *Bildungsroman* focused on the fortunes of a self-isolated, middle-class mission family in coup-ridden Nigeria.)

In summary, postcolonial migrant literature can be described as a literature written by élites, and defined and canonized by élites. It is writing which foregrounds and celebrates a national or historical rootlessness—what the migrant Czech writer Milan Kundera might call lightness—sometimes accentuated by political cynicism. Yet, viewed from a different angle, weightlessness could also be interpreted as an evacuation of commitment, or as a dilution of those fiery concerns which originally distinguished post-independence writing. To define a literature of migrant floating as the culmination of the postcolonial must inevitably represent a diminution in a long tradition of self-consciously political writing.

The above characterization does, of course, tend to polarize the situation for the sake of drawing out some basic distinctions. It is not necessarily the case, for example, that the cosmopolitan should be apolitical. The phenomenon of Arundhati Roy, author of the international best-seller *The God of Small Things*, and committed campaigner against the building of multinational dams in her homeland India, is an instance in point. In defence of their position, expatriate writers young and old speak passionately of their betwixt-and-between, 'not-quite' position as aesthetic boon and 'net gain', and as offering political and historical insight. Again, it might appear that a cosmopolitan is culturally short-changed, belonging to more than one world, but to no one entirely. However, as Salman Rushdie has often emphasized, the experience of cultural translation not only stimulates invention, but may also give valuable perspective on conditions in a writer's 'home' nation. Diasporic identities, in the influential readings of cultural theorists of Britishness and race like Paul Gilroy and Stuart Hall, effectively demonstrate the contingency and constructedness of all identity. Historically, they submit, definitions of self have been formulated through cultural contact and in motion; in relation more to *routes* of travel than *roots* of belonging. Moreover, being 'borne across' equips 'out-of-country' authors with the materials to give imaginative form to their dislocated worlds. Where the early modernists, therefore, often lamented the fragmentation of trusted traditions, cosmopolitans and migrants enthusiastically embrace it ('Imaginary Homelands', 1982). Theirs is a stance signifying not distance from the world, but connection, a commitment to uniting what colonialism put asunder, linking the Third World and the First, and, above all, emphasizing how the experience of the one has for so long been bound up in that of the other.

In taking up the defence of migrant and diasporic literatures, Rushdie's testimony as writer-advocate is by no means singular. Calcutta-born, once based in Canada, and now a self-identified Immigrant-American writer, the novelist Bharati Mukherjee has strongly endorsed his position. She too has chosen what she sees as the exuberant clash of immigrant cultures as her special theme. To her, the immigrant condition is protean, tirelessly inventive, creatively rooted *at once* in the society of adoption and in recollections of the land of birth ('Immigrant Writing: Give Us Your Maximalists!', *New York Times Book Review*, 1988). Therefore, dislocation as she represents it is not an impoverishment but an expansion of cultural and aesthetic experience. In his more gnomic way, Wilson Harris—a Guyanan long based in Britain—notes that the partial vision or 'complex counterpoint between partial origins' which has developed in a post-imperial world opens up new 'numinous proportions', 'far-flung, regenerative, cross-cultural possibility' ('The Fabric of the Imagination', 1990). Ben Okri, too, takes the view that the suffering associated with colonial occupation and consequent cultural conflict may ultimately be regenerative. The dissemination of cultural influences under empire has had the effect of enriching the spiritual awareness, or 'subtly altering' the psyche, of those who were once conquered ('Redreaming the World', 1990). This is once again a situation of net gain, but it is also, as he emphasizes, one in which the colonized were able to regenerate themselves because they maintained 'the resilience of [their own] spirit, the great dreaming capacities'.[15] Though he does not by any means ignore material realities, we might note that Okri's focus, like that of Harris, is more on the spirit than on politics.

Like its creators, the migrant novel itself draws attention to the regenerative experience of straddling worlds. Grown fat on their different cultural riches, it brings into prominence the translations and migrations of which it is itself a product. Amitav Ghosh's *In an Antique Land* (1992), a witty archaeological travelogue recounting time spent in Egypt as a student anthropologist, gives at once investigative and emblematic shape to this lively narrative travelling, and to the faith in the interpenetrability of cultures on which it rests. Ghosh's autobiographical account tracking his experiences as modern Indian in Egypt, embeds the fragmentary history of a medieval Tunisian-Jewish merchant who spent his days in the Indian port of Mangalore, and of his 'wildly drunk' servant Bomma who eventually travelled with him, the merchant, back to Egypt. Similarly powered by cultural intertwinings and mitosis, Ghosh's earlier *The Circle of Reason*, a loosely structured picaresque, connects the India–Bangladesh border, the Persian Gulf city of al-Ghazira, and the Algerian Sahara. Mingling fantasy and naturalism, joining 'new "modern" worlds' with 'old, legend-haunted civilisations', breaking realist unities of time and space, restlessly crossing borders, *The Circle of Reason* intensively exploits the double perspective or 'stereoscopic vision' that the in-between position allows—as, too, do M. G. Vassanji's stories, or Anita Desai's transnational *Journey to Ithaca* (1995), for example. In place of the 'great gulf' which separated societies in colonialist discourse, as in the Anglo-Indian novel, the translated novel instead creates a constant interaction of styles, voices, anecdotes, geographies, legends. It energetically dramatizes the collision of histories. So Okri in *The Famished Road* (1991) and its sequels, and in his short stories (*Incidents at the Shrine*, 1986; *Stars of the New Curfew*, 1988), upends conventional chronology by introducing cyclical patterns and a seemingly irrational dream logic, derived from Yoruba myth via D. O. Fagunwa and Amos Tutuola. The busy congruence of disparate cultural forces, usually taken as characteristic of cosmopolitan narrative, in his work becomes a conduit into the more bizarre conjunctions of a feverishly visionary Africa.

As was briefly suggested earlier, far from forestalling political commitment, the audacious crossing of different perspectives in post-imperial writing can work as an anti-colonial strategy, indeed one opposed to totalitarian systems of all descriptions. This is, implicitly or explicitly, the view of Desai, Ghosh, Okri, Ondaatje, Rushdie, and also the Latin American writers some have taken as their models. The fantastical or magic realist novel is believed to 'act out' the split perceptions of postcolonial cultures, and so to undermine purist representations of the world which have endured from colonial times. And not only that. The genre itself represents the take-over of a colonial style. By mingling the bizarre and the plausible so that they become indistinguishable, postcolonial writers mimic the colonial explorer's reliance on fantasy and exaggeration to describe new worlds. They now demand the prerogative of 'redreaming' their own lands.[16] Alternatively, writers may expose the extremities of the neo-colonial condition. The phantasmic is used to evoke an Africa or an India that has run out of food, medicine, liberation ideals, and even officially sanctioned identities. The nightmares that jam Okri's stories make a grim point about the Third World city. Lagos is *at once* a cultic zone of supernatural derangement, as Fanon might have described it, *and* the dumping ground of the world's discards, its quack medicines, 'curved syringes', poisoned powdered milk, trashed and defunct beliefs (*Stars of the New Curfew*).

Furthermore, despite all its hybrid phenomena, it may be a zone that is ultimately not fully accessible to the European or American reader. It can happen that, when representing the mystical or the phantasmic, postcolonial writers elect to withdraw their work, in part, from the hermeneutic space of the West. As in Aboriginal literatures, postcolonial writers like Okri, Sia Figiel, or Erna Brodber (in, for example, *Myal*, 1988) at times introduce an *un*translatable strangeness into their work, so emphasizing its borderline situation, positioned both within and without western traditions. To distinguish it, this kind of writing might be named spiritual realism.[17] I shall now look more closely at this important—and perhaps even self-contradictory—question of postcolonial opacity or inaccessibility.

The postmodern and the postcolonial

As I have shown, the title postcolonial literature signifies a multifarious, perhaps even a bewildering array of texts. From the early 1980s it was the polyglot, possibly disruptive aspects of postcolonial writing that attracted the attentions of post-structuralist critics interested in the displacement and de-formation of conventional meaning. Critical theory began to cite the writing for the purposes of illustration or clarification. I have already glanced at this situation of co-operation from the point of view of migrant writing. This last section will explore the effects of the interaction on the criticism and interpretation of the literature. What are the implications for post-imperial writing of the encounter with critical theories based largely in the once- or still-colonizing metropolis?

It will not have failed to strike the readers of the last few chapters that the way in which postcolonial literatures are explicated reiterates key preoccupations in post-structuralist or postmodern theory. There are no real surprises in this convergence. In the area of new writing in English, critical methodologies were until the late 1970s fairly ill-defined. Post-structuralist readings usefully made audible, or organized for discussion, what were arguably the distinctive features of the writing. And the writing of decolonization in turn lent itself to post-structuralism by way of exemplification, as grist to its mill, as an exploration, in a different medium, of its central postulates. Most obviously, as will by now be apparent, the multivoiced migrant novel gave vivid expression to theories of the 'open', indeterminate text, or of transgressive, non-authoritative reading.

Out of the intersection of postmodern and postcolonial discourses, therefore, emerged a postcolonial criticism which champions in particular those aspects of the postcolonial narrative that illustrate and adumbrate the theory: its interest in the provisional and fragmentary aspects of signification; its concern with the constructed nature of identity. Given their transgressive, dispersed energies, the criticism reads postcolonial texts (novels more generatively than poems) as symptomatic of the centrifugal pull of history. They are believed to demonstrate the fragility of 'grand narratives'; the erosion of transcendent authority; the collapse of imperialistic explanations of the world. In short, postcolonial and postmodern critical approaches cross in their concern with marginality, ambiguity, disintegrating binaries, and all things parodied, piebald, dual, mimicked, always-already borrowed, and ironically secondhand.

To quibble about provenance in this area of post-structuralist and postcolonial co-operation is unproductive. Both discourses are products of a process of questioning Enlightenment thought and the institutions that have fostered and embodied it, such as the late eighteenth- or nineteenth-century European nation-state. Both are also clearly spin-offs of a much wider process: the disintegration of western cultural and political authority in its statist, imperial form. In fact, the argument has been made that deconstruction, with Jewish Algerian-origin practitioners like Derrida and Cixous, was itself a transmuted anti-colonial and political response to the apparent turn from history to theory in 1960s France.[18] Decolonization was of course aimed at dismantling (not always successfully) European power structures across the globe. Like post-structuralist theory, therefore, it followed that the writing of decolonization would put in question some of the respected assumptions of earlier imperial times: the faith in the superiority of western rationality, for example, and in the universalizing potential of that rationality.

And yet—to make an important point somewhat simplistically— the writing of decolonization is also *more* than postmodern slippage and disintegration. It exceeds even those conditions of hermeneutic instablity and excess so acclaimed by the criticism. And this in a rather special way. For as well as taking part in the end-of-empire centrifuge, the postcolonial text, it is crucial to remember, also emerges out of the grit and rank specificity of a local culture or cultures, history or histories. That specific culture or history, as we have seen, may not be immediately comprehensible to a foreign reader. Unless metropolitan postcolonial criticism is both highly informed and rigorous in estab-lishing comparative frames, it may not be able to account for all that is contained in literature given the name migrant, postcolonial, inter-national, transnational. Again, those who speak of the migrant novel as the acme of polyglossic cosmopolitan writing often neglect this point. Yet it does require some further attention.

Basically, what is frequently ignored in postcolonial criticism is the difficulty or otherness of the postcolonial text: the implications for us as readers of its possibly untranslatable cultural specificity. For centuries, scholarship and academic disciplines located in Europe and, more recently, in North America, have accepted without question the permeability of other cultures to western understanding. Postcolonial discourse analysis is at times guilty of a similar assumption—and this despite the attention it theoretically pays to cultural difference. It is widely taken for granted that post-imperial cultural diversity is not only comparable across regions, but is all more or less equally transparent and accessible to a European or North American reader, especially given a shared history of colonization by Britain. What we often find is that an ahistorical hybridity is set up as a universal category or structural principle bracketing together writing from very different countries. It is assumed that different historical worlds of meaning can be exposed to one another merely by a leap of imaginative empathy.

It is crucial to perceive, however, that despite the common experience of empire, cultures in relationship will in some measure always experience difficulty in completely understanding one another. If carelessly expressed, a perception such as this can risk resurrecting the old idea that East must remain East, and West West. My claim, I must therefore clarify, is *not* that a society is necessarily enclosed within the scaffolding of its own values and preconceptions. Rather what interests is the *partial* opacity to one another of different conceptual worlds and the importance of trying to clear up that opacity to some degree with diligent research and applied understanding. Moreover, as Kwame Anthony Appiah, Ben Okri, Gayatri Spivak, and others have stressed, indigenous religious, moral, and intellectual traditions in colonized countries were never as fully pervaded by colonialism as the authorities might have desired.[19] The invasion of a people's cultural or 'aesthetic frames', to use Okri's phrase, was never total. The histories of those colonized by Europe extend far back in time, way beyond the moment of colonial invasion. As Nayantara Sahgal expressed it in a powerful essay—a perception since endorsed by, amongst others, Aijaz Ahmad and Harish Trivedi: 'My own awareness as a writer reaches back to x-thousand BC, at the end of which measureless timeless time the British came, and stayed, and left. And now they're gone, and their residue is simply one more layer added to the layer upon layer of Indian consciousness. Just *one* more.'[20] No country is as knowable as a migrant novel, written in English—though seductively alive with local cadences—might lead us to think. To do justice to a text's grounding either in the now, or in the past, it may be necessary to draw on specialized knowledge: to find out about local politics, for example, to read up on ritual practices, or to learn to decipher unfamiliar linguistic codes.

Post-structuralist and/or postcolonial critics, as Aijaz Ahmad and more recently David Scott have argued, tend to address 'Third World literature' as a coherent field of knowledge, defined by the unitary forces of a political history, such as nationalism, secularism, or anti-colonial struggle.[21] This tendency is reinforced because, located in western universities, or the former colonial metropolis, the criticism is set at an objectifying—and also politically comfortable—distance from the once-colonized world. What results, once again, is that situation in which western postcolonial approaches reproduce an uneven discursive geography that dates back to colonial times: a geography characterized by the projection of metropolitan conceptual patterns onto the rest of the globe, based on the knowledge supplied by trusted 'native informants'. The historical drag or time-lag which distinguishes this approach is then further reinforced by the assumption that the critical discourse, by living off the activist energies of an earlier generation of writers and critics, is almost innately political.

As I have already suggested in the section on migrant writing, it is important to guard against a divide emerging where Eurocentric the-ories are split away from cultural artefacts drawn from everywhere other than Europe. It is a situation in which interpretations homogen-izing, depoliticizing and, finally, commodifying those artefacts are almost inevitable; in which writers and texts from different continents, nations, and cultures are indiscriminately blended together as being multicultural, 'Commonwealth', or polyphonic. It has not escaped the attention of some critics that this situation bears uncanny resem-blance to the orientalism of yesteryear. Like orientalist scholarship, post-imperial critical discourse can be presumptuously all-embracing or totalizing in its responses to the various and the mysterious in other cultures. From the point of view of its own assumed cultural centrality, the discourse takes what it needs for its own theoretical purposes, and disregards what is seen as 'incomprehensible'.[22]

To avoid such neo-orientalism, how might the resistant, grainy difference represented by the writing of once-colonized countries be more adequately addressed? A simple but serious recognition of difference, though located within a transnational comparative frame that must to a degree be taken for granted, is probably a good starting-point: some preliminary acknowledgement that post-imperial realities are far more contradictory, agitated, and diverse than any one critical approach could hope to describe. As is apparent, postcolonial critical discourse trusts to the translatability of texts taken from other cultures. The assumption, predicated on the global event of empire, is that some hybridized version of a western language or syncretic cognitive framework will mediate gaps in understanding. The reality is, however, that there are utterances which remain out of reach of postcolonial interpretation. World music, Microsoft, McDonalds, the omnipresence of the Nike swoosh, various aspects of our globalized Coca-Cola culture may camouflage this reality. And yet a certain incommensurability of historical worlds has to be conceded.

Contrary to what the trans-continental embrace of satellite television may encourage us to believe, cultures are not always mutually intelligible. Obscurities and silences will exist no matter how much research is devoted to the task of making lucid what is dim, or of giving voice to what was stilled. We approach the 'truth' of, for instance, the *osu*, untouchables, and outcasts of different societies by way of hybridized and objectifying western representations which by definition cannot give us an accurate reflection. So I am able to comprehend Dreaming as Josie Boyle or Vivienne Sahanna, say, explain it to me in English. But I cannot be, and never really can be, confident of understanding Alcheringa/Mimi fully in its own context as part of a symbolic and mythic system to which I have no access.

Far from postcolonial novels, plays, and poems participating only or mainly in a global framework of understanding, they also represent locally rooted and uniquely distinct perceptions. Therefore, postcolonial readers need to realize, texts from other cultures and regions demand work, the kind of careful attention to local specificity encouraged in area studies, for example. I have alluded to this point several times already, but it is well worth reiterating. The vision or world-view of a story from, say, Barbados or Nigeria, may be inaccessible without textual and extratextual research, the recuperation of oral, ritual, linguistic, popular, and other knowledges. Criticism must address itself to the particularity of different textual situations, to the history of a neighbourhood, or the struggles of a compound. It is crucial to develop what James Clifford calls an 'awareness of discrepant attachments'; to locate texts in their own specific worlds of meaning; to tune into their *verbal recalcitrance* or 'enunciatory disorder': that strangeness which antagonistically yet creatively interrupts western forms of understanding.[23] Alternatively, to build some sense of, say, an Aboriginal cognitive universe, it may be necessary to read several Aboriginal novels, poems, and plays in conjunction, as intertexts and adumbrations of one another.

As well as a respect for partial silences, sensitivity to location also involves giving some attention to the continuing political struggle for self-representation in many parts of the decolonized world. Texts form a part of this politics; but the struggle over meanings is not confined to the texts, nor do the politics transmit unmediated to the reader. Postmodern and even postcolonial notions of meaning as arbitrary, or identity as provisional, are hardly relevant to the lives of those—women, Indigenous peoples, marginalized ethnic, class, caste, and religious groups—for whom self-determination remains a political imperative. For them, the signifiers of home, self, past, far from representing instances of discursive contingency, stand for live and pressing issues.

Does the focus on specificity at the expense of generalization ultimately mean the dissolution of the postcolonial as a unitary object of critical attention? The short answer to this is—not at this point; or, not yet. Postcolonial discourse concentrates its energies on 'mixed', 'in-between' texts because they not only signify but seem to encourage and give support to cultural interaction. The belief in the possibility of that interaction will remain a first premiss, even an article of faith, in postcolonial criticism for some time to come, though—it is hoped—maintained alongside the awareness that a text is a mode of resistance. And the belief need not be undermined by a sense of discrepant attachments. For a critic to look more deeply into the differences and subterfuges of a text from another culture does not necessarily mean abandoning the assumption that discrepant cultures and texts can to some extent interact and mix. It does not imply that the text cannot be translated—more or less, or in some measure—into the terms of that critic's own culture. Decoding a text's resistances without fetishizing them forms part of that process of translation.

Rising from these different points of focus, it is clear, however, that two distinct strains of postcolonial criticism have developed in recent years, which may in the future increasingly diverge the one from the other even while still sharing some basic assumptions. The Afterword will explore the further ramifications of this situation. On the one hand is the cosmopolitan approach, located largely in the West, and focused on literatures written in Englishes, or other European languages, mainly by migrant, and therefore more easily accessible writers. This approach will no doubt continue to make up the bulk of mainstream postcolonial criticism. On the other hand lies a more context-based line of study, still concerned with writing in once-colonial European languages, but more centred on particular verna-cular and cultural regions. A related split may develop in postcolonial literature itself, as, on the one side, migrant writers are absorbed into British, French, or American traditions, and, on the other, literatures in vernacular languages and creolized Englishes flourish and grow increasingly less like each other, and therefore less prone to indiscrim-inate comparison. As memories of empire (finally) recede into the past, both approaches will in time copiously outgrow the name postcolonial.

Especially on the side of the second branch of interest, the con-text-based approach, what we may also find is a more concerted quest for interpretative strategies with which to resist the dominance of western theory. As critics like Carolyn Cooper, Henry Louis Gates, and Juliana Nfah-Abbenyi have argued, the rhetorical and linguistic structures of a text may offer readers their own analytic guidelines. That is to say, a way of reading or a 'theory' is suggested in the form of the story or poem. Interpretative guidelines may inhere, for example, in a mythical framework, or in the symbolic tradition in which a text is embedded. Again, a text may invite an opposi-tional reading by wrenching colonialist conventions, or reworking Europe's defining narratives. Most obviously, where a novel or poem unites godlike personalities from different mythic pantheons, or stirs together, stamps, and boils a *khichri* of languages, it tells us that it is to be read syncretically, impiously. For instance, in the childhood home Jamaica Kincaid describes in *Annie John*, obeah rituals are introduced alongside the medicines offered by the regular house doctor as an ordinary part of healing. A form of exegesis can thus be seen to emerge from within the postcolonial text or context, rather than being intro-duced from outside. This shift in interpretative perspective will, as it develops, signify a move beyond the colonialist-style dependency on metropolitan theory, and a coming-of-age for postcolonial writing.

Further Reading

Ian Adam and Helen Tiffin (eds.), *Past the Last Post: Theorizing Post-Colonialism and Postmodernism* (Hemel Hempstead: Harvester Wheatsheaf, 1991).

Laura Chrisman, *Postcolonial Contraventions: Cultural Readings of Race, Imperialism and Transnationalism* (Manchester UP, 2003).

Carolyn Cooper, *Noises in the Blood* (Macmillan, 1993).

John Docker and Gerhard Fischer (eds.), *Race, Colour and Identity in Australia and New Zealand* (Sydney: UNSW Press, 2000).

Paul Gilroy, *'There Ain't No Black in the Union Jack': The Cultural Politics of Race and Nation* (Hutchinson, 1987).

Inderpal Grewal and Caren Kaplan (eds.), *Scattered Hegemonies: Postmodernity and Transnational Feminist Practices* (Minneapolis: University of Minnesota Press, 1994).

Stuart Hall, *Critical Dialogues in Cultural Studies*, ed. David Morley and Kuan-Hsing Chen (Routledge, 1996).

bell hooks, *Race, Gender and Cultural Politics* (Turnaround Press, 1991).

Graham Huggan, *The Post-Colonial Exotic: Marketing the Margins* (Routledge, 2001).

Linda Hutcheon, *The Politics of Postmodernism*, 2nd edn. (Routledge, 2002).

Jenny Lee et al. (eds.), *Meanjin*, 51/2, Special issue on Aboriginality (winter 1992).

John McLeod, *Postcolonial London: Rewriting the Metropolis* (Routledge, 2004).

Mudrooroo, *Milli Milli Wangka (The Indigenous Literature of Australia)* (South Melbourne: Hyland House, 1995).

Ashis Nandy, *The Intimate Enemy: Loss and Recovery of Self under Colonialism* (New Delhi: Oxford UP, 1983).

Susheila Nasta (ed.), *Motherlands: Black Women's Writing* (Women's Press, 1991).

—— *Home Truths: Fictions of the South Asian Diaspora in Britain* (Basingstoke: Palgrave, 2002).

Juliana Makuchi Nfah-Abbenyi, *Gender in African Women's Writing* (Bloomington: Indiana UP, 1997).

Caryl Phillips, *A New World Order* (Faber, 2001).

R. Radhakrishnan, *Diasporic Mediations: Between Home and Location* (Minneapolis: University of Minnesota Press, 1996).

Peter Read, *Belonging: Australians, Place and Aboriginal Ownership* (Cambridge UP, 2000).

Gayatri Spivak, *In Other Worlds: Essays in Cultural Politics* (Routledge, 1987).

Ismail S. Talib, *The Language of Postcolonial Literatures* (Routledge, 2002).

Afterword:
Belated Reading

The trouble is that colonialism isn't over yet.
Arthur Corunna in Sally Morgan,
My Place, 1987

England has changed.
Caryl Phillips,
A Distant Shore, 2003

Our 'aiga was the first in Malefou to get a TV, even if it was black and white, and most kids said it didn't count and that Mu's 'aiga was actually the first since they had it coloured and clearer, and much, much larger than ours.

We got the TV from New Zealand via my grandmother's brother's son, Misipati, who bought it from an American family who lived there in New Zealand. Our relative there thought it better to send the TV to us in Samoa . . . in Malefou.

That week, before the TV arrived, everyone wanted to be our friends.
Sia Figiel, *Where We Once Belonged*, 1996

The world today has become so intensively interconnected that globalization is seen by many, those of the well-off north in particular, as the definitive condition of twenty-first-century humanity. 'Trans-societal flows', a 'borderless global economy', and electronic communications increasingly undermine the former centrality of national structures and institutions, and demand a re-figuration of the languages of everyday life.[1] Indeed, global interconnection has ramified to such an extent that postcolonial literature itself is now widely perceived as a reflection of that globalized world, or as part of that cross-planet re-figuration.

Looking back on its forty-odd-year institutional history from this new twenty-first-century vantage point, the postcolonial has been established as, ideally, a critical term signifying a theoretical and writerly force field preoccupied with *resistance to empire*, and its post-imperial aftermath, if any. At the same time, however, as the final section of Chapter 6 already suggested, in some contemporary postcolonial and postmodernist critiques, postcolonial writing is often understood as a displaced, 'deregulated' practice in contrast with the writing of decolonization related to the nation. The postcolonial therefore is associated with metropolitan, diasporic, migrant, and minority spaces for which the nation as a horizon of expectation has retreated, to be replaced with the concepts of the anarchic postcolony, the transgressive trans-local, and the infinitely co-optable multi-cultural. For this reason, in certain critical environs, the postcolonial is deemed to be a term synonymous with, though also more (re)tired than, transnational and global, and their various cognates.

This bifurcation of views attaches to a concept of postcolonial*ity*, as opposed to its close verbal analogue, (critical) postcolonialism, as a global arrangement of cultural value that correlates with late-capitalist systems of commodity exchange. In today's globalized world, in other words, cultural movements and perceptions are believed to be more inescapably than before dictated by the market-place: post-coloniality is a knowing acknowledgement of the situation.[2] In the terms of this approach, the multitextured postcolonial artefact is set up as a sign both of the West's preferred hyper-reality, of universal-ized displacement, *and* of its still-persistent exotic interests. The trans-continental journeys described in a Ghosh or Gunesekera novel, for example, even while opening temporary escape-routes from the present-day into, say, 'history' or 'the warm South', simultaneously and profitably connote global operations.

In effect, the postcolonial text, still according to this view, is believed not only to reflect the contemporary world—becoming everywhere standard-issue magic realist, smoothly multivocal—but also, via transnational processes of publishing and marketing, is seen willingly to collude in its market-driven systems. To be truly post-colonial, then, the writer has no other option than to collude. It is because of this emphasis on the reliably unruly, slyly commercial, calculatedly hybrid text that postcolonial literary studies is often accused of helping to create decoys in the realm of culture for the enduring system of empire that governs today's world.[3] Postcolonial criticism is held guilty of the unexamined assumption that post-colonial writers participate equally and knowingly in a transnational circulation of ideas and cultural product, acting as if these were in no way unfairly distributed across the planet.[4]

Despite its coda-esque title, this Afterword cannot speak with any sort of finality about the future of postcolonialism: about such current questions as whether the transnational should replace the postcolonial as a critical term; whether the more creative discussions of self–other have shifted into area studies or anthropology. It does not aim to engage in a contest over explicatory definitions, partly because that contest is at this stage best left productively unresolved between the disciplines dealing with colonial (after-)effects; partly because, as I have suggested throughout, the true burdens of postcolonial study remain concentrated in the still-lingering colonial past, not the future. The 'after' of my Afterword is in this sense as intentionally illusionary as the 'post' in postcolonial, especially in so far as both title and critical approach are pointedly interested in *belatedness*. 'Postcolonialism', as Ali Behdad, and Derek Gregory following him, compellingly suggest, 'reveals the continuing impositions and exactions of colonialism in order to subvert them'.[5] The 'tactical withdrawal' of the British Empire of the 1960s, George Lamming brusquely notes in a 2002 essay, 'made way for a new colonial orchestration': consequently, formerly colonized territories continue to function as imperial frontiers that must be both defended and undermined.[6] Postcolonial writers and readers, in short, must remain interested in the discursive traces of colonial histories in the present, whether these inhere in the text or in the world, in order to work to excavate and dispel them.

Bearing this in mind, in what follows I will review, in most cases in necessarily general terms, those postcolonial trends which to me have distinguished the decade that has elapsed since the first publication of this book. Throughout, my concern as critical practitioner, as already implied, will be to see postcolonial knowledge as *oppositional* to neo-colonial/global discourses and events rather than as collusive, remembering that postcolonialism first emerged as a critical approach involved in movements of cultural opposition to empire, itself an early form of globalization. I say this not by way of providing some palliative 'radical' window-dressing to the display of commercially attractive literary travel that often goes by the name of postcolonial reading. I say it because the postcolonial project of interrogating autocracy, as Joseph Conrad once named imperial power, has by no means yet been satisfactorily wound up.

Transverse currents, sites of struggle

The world of the early 2000s is in several ways markedly different from that of the 1900s. It is a world in which, via communication technologies, via the operation of transnational secret services and 'terrorist' groupings, notably al-Qaeda in or around September 2001, local, context-bound issues have become wrapped in global operations in ever more complicated ways. The invasion of refugee camps in Palestine can visibly have repercussions for the citizens of New York, and an 'attack on America' can within a matter of months produce a 'war on terror' on a global scale. War itself is fought on an increasingly disembodied level. Planes bomb from ever higher, more abstracted altitudes; the casualties of the Western allies are ever more successfully hidden from international view; and so-called terrorist suspects, as at Camp X-Ray, Guantanamo Bay, are rendered non-persons in ways that international law is powerless to redress. At the same time, it is a world that continues to operate according to tried and tested moral absolutes—of 'axes of evil', the good v. the bad, the 'sophistry and fastidious algebra of infinite justice', as Arundhati Roy has termed them. As she notes, they are, however, absolutes enhanced in their brutishness, their simplistic othering, and their tendency unpredictably to reverse their meaning—'peace is war', 'war is peace'—compared to those of the past.[7]

In response to such developments critics, postcolonial, materialist, humanist, post-humanist, have tended to follow one of two main routes. Some have been concerned seemingly to reiterate or rearticulate global relations in their explication of the West's cultural hegemony, as described at the beginning of this Afterword. According to Michael Hardt and Antonio Negri in their influential thesis *Empire* (2000), for instance, societies across the planet are interpenetrated willy-nilly by global forces.[8] Others, however, have looked to extend their postcolonial ethical and activist agendas by continuing to ask searching questions of the global, by refusing to take it at its word—its sensorily stimulating, allegedly post-imperial word. It is in this area, or along this route, that the preoccupations of twenty-first-century postcolonialism may be said to have expanded, diversified, and pro-liferated, as if making common cause with such cross-border activist movements as, say, People's Global Action. It is here that postcolonial writers and critics have concertedly undercut anything resembling a universal or transnational category of postcolonial writing, or global aesthetic; here they have troubled the homogenization of hybridity and migrancy as trans-cultural, universally form-giving conditions.

In this respect, as I will illustrate, the bifurcation into, on the one hand, diasporic writing sited in the metropolis, and, on the other, writing with a national or provincial focus, that was pessimistically outlined in Chapter 6, formerly this book's conclusion, has, if any-thing, split and diversified. Under a banner of decentring the centre, or, in Dipesh Chakrabarty's phrase, provincializing Europe, writers as well as theorists and critics have been concerned to place their representations within situated, grounded co-ordinates; to define, or redefine, home as against world, though they may continue to hold political agendas in common.[9] Whether writers are in fact former migrants, or whether they occupy a self-consciously rooted position in a native land, they question shared languages and common frames of cultural reference, legacies of a colonial history. They work to build local 'structures of feeling' positioned at several removes from the dominant North, drawn from within their own life-worlds, whether located in the Netherlands or Namibia.

Such 'post-migratory', 'post-postcolonial' writing, as 'post-migratory' black British writer Caryl Phillips terms it, explores not only leave-taking and departure, watchwords of the migrant condi-tion, but also the regeneration of communities and selves out of heterogeneous experiences in the new country. To find ways 'to begin again and go on' is today's imperative.[10] The creative landscape that emerges from this impulse can be schematized not only as a *multi-tude* of divergent *margins* (which in terms of the recognition of dif-ferences it of course is), but also as a *collection* of at times connected and overlapping yet distinct *centres* and regions, which would include constituencies of once-migrant writers. My use of spatial metaphors here is intentional. Decentring the centre in many cases involves embodying, materializing, or giving spatial form to what were previously regarded as one-dimensionally temporal and even ahistorical terms: weightlessness, migrancy, in-betweenness, cultural pluralism, postcolonialism.

From the early 1970s the Nobel Prize-winning St Lucian poet Derek Walcott defined a historically mature writing of the Caribbean as one which had moved beyond colonial-period utterances of recrimination and revenge.[11] In similar vein, the Kenyan journalist Parselelo Kantai more recently urged critics to remember that for African literature now 'the narrative of decolonization has collapsed'. In the writer Helon Habila's opinion, too, as African novelists in the 2000s turn increasingly towards local audiences and narrative traditions, and away from the implied European reader, they become ever more independent interpreters of their own internal conflicts and identities. They release themselves from the long-standing fixation on the colonial conflict with Europe.[12] The media-friendly exotic realist prose of the Indian novelist Arundhati Roy may appear to claim a certain statelessness, yet she centres her *The God of Small Things* (1997) in a recognizable late-1960s *region* of south India. Community life in Ayemenem is shaped by the promotional campaigns of the Kerala Tourist Development Corporation on the one hand and the strategizing of Comrade K. N. M. Pillai on the other—local incarnations, in the narrative's own terms, of 'Kurtz and Karl Marx'.[13]

As these various instances suggest, postcolonial writers working at diverse historical conjunctures are energetically, concertedly, confidently, 'grasping' at the particularities of 'the location or the moment'—even while they remain attentive to the 'regeneration of colonialism through other means'.[14] They have been concerned to restore *historicity* and *density* to the communities they describe, to explore forgotten, neglected, and once-peripheral cultural archives.[15] This is not to imply that their 'grasping' and restoration form a radically new departure. As we have seen, postcolonial writers have been exercised to give poetic and narrative form to their own conditions of life for many decades now. They have vigorously interrogated the *post*colonial label from the beginning.[16] The key difference is that they are making fewer excuses to a white, Euro-American audience in doing so, fewer allowances for that audience's assumptions regarding its own cultural centrality.

Of course it may be that this development is enhanced, or in part effected, by shifts within postcolonial theory and criticism. Writers' points of local focus, their insistence on specificities whether migrant or non-migrant, may have become more apparent because postcolonial readings, more openly admitting of their own internal contradictions, are more willing to allow the writers their differences, their poles of contention, as well as their similarities. As Peter Hallward remarks in his idiosyncratic meditation *Absolutely Postcolonial*, the centralizing postcolonial emphasis on interstices, in-betweenness, border-blur, can itself become ironically all-consuming, a totalizing classification in spite of itself.[17] Indeed, as if responding to this critique, postcolonial literary critics are drawing more and more on a diversity of other disciplinary fields and archives for more visibly politicized critical paradigms: their scholarly energies are becoming centrifugal. Postcolonialism in the twenty-first century may be happier to acknowledge that intercultural hybridity is in many contexts no more than a declaration of political good faith, or a convenient rhetoric, which depends on the presumption of an impossibly equal exchange between the different cultural players. To this acknowledgement is linked the changed focus in recent criticism from the concern to translate a history of political resistance into critical practice (as in applying Fanonian paradigms when reading, say, a Kenyan novel), to a critical interrogation of how colonial relations are expressed and resisted *within* cultural texts.[18]

Colonialism was never a smooth, borderless, transhistorical phenomenon, as commentators ranging from Neil Lazarus through Said to Chakrabarty and Caren Kaplan point out. Rather, it represented a particular form of capitalist modernity, which took on different avatars in different places and at different times. One of the prominent ways in which postcolonial writers are noticeably diversifying and deepening their frames of reference is through an engagement with these different concatenations and alloys of the *modern*. Modernity, they suggest, has persistently manifested as a cross-cultural interconnection of violence and idealism, atavism and rationalism, which is nowhere merely an imitation of the European model. Its transmission depended on the transverse and cross-border migration of political and aesthetic ideas, rather than on direct influence or export from a fixed and dominant metropolitan centre.

In his multi-decker novel *A Suitable Boy* (1993), for example,

Vikram Seth explores the mixed, recognizably modern conjunction in early 1950s eastern India of performances of Shakespeare and *ragas*, of traditional expectations surrounding marriage and social mobility, and of the civil service trappings of a modern nation-state. The novel's different interconnected plots dramatize how these different aspects, as it were, call each other into being. Relatedly, a number of southern African novels that have emerged with the new century, like Phaswane Mpe's *Welcome to our Hillbrow* (2002) or Yvonne Vera's *The Stone Virgins* (2002), map the multidimensional contours of the at-once-traditional-and-surreal African city, where geometric road-grids and tangibly sharp street-corners produce unpredictable encounters. Somalian Nuruddin Farah in *Gifts* (1993) probes the dependencies and compromises involved in all acts of gift-giving, even of the most domestic and innocent kind, when giver and receiver are locked into an international context where, more so than in the past, no donation is without its exacting return. Exploring a different trajectory again, the West Australian Tim Winton's *Dirt Music* (2002) considers the bereaved Luther Fox's attempt to break away from sub-urban life into a depthless ur-Australia, into which the contemporary world in the form of planes and fridges none the less repeatedly irrupts. The novel's eponymous 'dirt music', both indigenous 'country' and differently 'western'—'anything you can play on a verandah, you know, without electricity'—emerges as a powerfully felt alternative to Australia's imported, imitative Americanized modernity. For a number of postcolonial artists and some critics, forms of local, popular culture, seemingly collusive with global media, yet also wayward, tricky, gnomic with internal reference, persuasively represent such an alternative.

These writers' notation of *their own* particular dishevelled modernity, of its 'often maddeningly diverse allocation of space, human habitation, and community', as the novelist Amit Chaudhuri comments, is a world away from, for example, V. S. Naipaul's vision of non-European space as doomed to a hopelessly incomplete narrative of 'development'.[19] It is a notation that does, however, pay close attention to what I earlier described as the prevailing situation of colonial belatedness (as does Naipaul), which is often expressed in highly particularized, destructive local forms. Here modernity emerges under a more baleful, far less creative aspect. The theorist Achille Mbembe has illuminatingly described how the 'necropolitics' of the neo-colonial state instrumentalizes destruction; that is to say, it operates using the constant threat of human death, and of displays of state-inflicted death and near-death. The neo-colonial state or post-colony, in other words, repeats in sophisticated, knowing forms the *commandement*, or regime of violence, of the colony.[20] Of this indeed the Kafkaesque J. M. Coetzee and the phantasmagoric writing of Ben Okri and the far-sighted Dambudzo Marechera urge us to take heed.

Sexuality is not a topic that Mbembe specifically raises, yet the confrontation of different manifestations of the modern, of state violence and individual self-expression, has been chillingly demonstrated in those cases where the postcolony polices the sexual expression of its citizens by invoking colonial-period laws, as several novelists record. Edwidge Dandicat's *Breath, Eyes, Memory* (1994), for example, addresses the sexual violence visited upon rural women during Duvalier rule in Haiti at the hands of the 'bogeyman' *tonton macoute*, even as it stages its heroine Sophie Caco's in-other-ways-restorative reconnection with her past. Raising the topic of the postcolonial love which rarely speaks its name, though in order ultimately to mask it, Shani Mootoo in *Cereus Blooms at Night* (1998) observes how in the community on the fictional island of Lantanacamara queer desire and transgender behaviours are cruelly driven underground.[21] In the ironic name of resistance to the colonizer's corrupt ways, sexual rights remain an enduring taboo in many areas of the once-colonized world. Against this background of imposed silence and prohibition it is especially important to recognize how postcolonial writers exploring 'other' loves—Manju Kapur in *A Married Woman* (2002), Dambudzo Marechera in *Mindblast* (1984), Lawrence Scott in *Aelred's Sin* (1998), Shyam Selvadurai in *Funny Boy* (1994)—fiercely confound the self–other binaries that have sustained the hegemony of the West. In their stead, such writers posit a transformative ethics of bodily ecstasy, of being beside oneself, in the space of the other. A comparable *utter* identification with the second, within a duality, is emblematized in the deeply intimate relationship of the two-egg twins in Roy's *The God of Small Things*.

Within the already variegated area of postcolonial women's writing, outlined in Chapter 6, there have been further ramifications, divarications, and digressions related to those which have emerged in the many-centred postcolonial field more generally. For some considerable time women writers in India, the regions of Africa, the

Caribbean, have been concerned to de-romanticize 'strong women' stereotypes, especially when these were used as alienating emblems of the independent nation. Countering these, they have concentrated on giving imaginative shape to their own lived experiences: of domestic space, sexual desire, agency (often covert), guardianship, leadership, and so on. They have been intent, too, on *dismantling 'Woman'*, in particular the subaltern or black woman, as the overarching, universal sign of oppression. At the same time, however, especially more recently, with regard to the *embodying* of histories of displacement and discrimination referred to earlier, they have brought women's physical suffering and pain into language, into story. The writing of Dionne Brand, Deshpande, Figiel, Langford Ginibi, amongst others, articulates women's bodies as sites of protest; expresses their at times unspoken or withheld, always deeply felt, histories of struggle and survival.

Yet women writers, as well as acknowledging transnational agendas in common, have also, importantly, kept alive a discussion of the status of the postcolonial nation and their own position within it, despite the fact that this once-significant entity is frequently dismissed as fatally undermined by globalization. Even though women's life-narratives have conventionally been regarded as subsidiary to defining national myths, women writers including Dandicat, Buchi Emecheta, Nayantara Sahgal, Sindiwe Magona, and also Margaret Atwood and Eavan Boland, and, in French, Assia Djebar, explore the intricate interconnection of personal lives with the nation's official history. They demonstrate how women occupy different, intersecting spaces (class-based, linguistic, religious, rural, institutional, etc.), that at certain points diverge from the apparently gender-neutral, officially masculine, homogeneous space of the nation, yet which may also overlap with it.[22]

Within this area of overlap emerges a potentially important shift in women writers' thinking. Especially in a context where impersonal global forces restrict rather than amplify women's options for exercising agency, the nation, and possibly also the 'world city', come into greater prominence as validated sites of political opposition, where women can organize solidarities and networks that short-circuit the operation of such forces. In this respect it is significant that the women writers listed above, though they may be critical of their home nation's policies, value it as a space for cultural, ethical, and emotional recuperation in the face of the World Bank, deregulation, and tainted international gift-giving of all descriptions. As Saskia Sassen remarks, new geographies of centrality are in formation on the world stage, which will become 'key articulators' with global forces. Amongst these she numbers cities, such as Kolkata and Cairo—but small- and middle-size nations, perhaps backed by regional partnerships, are not necessarily to be excluded.[23]

The creative project of decentring, possibly indeed revising and re-imagining, the centre, is nowhere perhaps more forcefully in operation than amongst *diasporic writers*, self-consciously the descendants of migrants, whose work maps a pathway from displacement to the always qualified decision to belong to their adopted city or nation. Their 'post-migratory' challenge to established perceptions of home, national allegiance, native land, as in 'black' British writers like Fred d'Aguiar, Monica Ali, Moniza Alvi, Jackie Kay, Caryl Phillips, Andrea Levy, Zadie Smith, as well as the work of musicians and film-makers, changes the nature of the 'host'—but often inhospitable—country at its very heart. Such writers and artists break the 'constraints of ethnicity and national particularity', and refigure national traditions of writing in English.[24] They put a foot in the way of those who would slam the door on a more heterogeneously defined nation even while they also acknowledge important cultural and gender fissures in their own understanding of 'black British' as an overarching, all-determining category. There has to be 'a new way of being British after all this time', writes Hanif Kureishi, whose films and novels, like *My Beautiful Launderette* (1985), *The Buddha of Suburbia* (1990), or *My Son the Fanatic* (1998), have contributed significantly to mainstream perceptions of the mixed-race, multicultural British citizen: the white British 'have to learn that being British isn't what it was'.[25] 'Cultural diversity', Stuart Hall elaborates, 'is not [only] something that is coming in from the outside, it is also something that is going on inside, in relation to Britishness itself.'[26]

Perceptions of a reinvented or *other Britain* find a vivid epitome in Bernardine Evaristo's comic verse-epic or novel-in-verse, told in erratically un-rhyming couplets, *The Emperor's Babe* (2001). Paying heed to Britain's long history of cultural mixing and colonization on home ground, Evaristo tells the feisty tale of a third-century African-British woman in Roman London, '*Illa Bella Negreeta*', 'whose parents sailed out of Khartoum on [an un-Shakespearian] barge', making it

to their west, to Londinium, on a very biblical donkey. As this knowing or 'sautéed' *mélange* of iconic motifs suggests, the conjunction of
peoples in a teeming city produces powerfully transformative mixes
and encounters, which for the spirited, punning Zuleika take the
particular shape of her passionate if doomed affair with the Emperor
Septimus Severus, himself of North African descent. Though it is in
several ways a grim tale which does not flinch at acknowledging the
violence of London's streets (past and present), *The Emperor's Babe*
cocks an extremely decisive, if also ribald and cheeky, snook at those
who might doubt that black people have long inhabited Britain's
marshy shores.[27] Significantly, the Nubian 'It girl' Zeeks is herself
trying her hand at poetry because 'what I really want to read I and
hear is stuff about us, about now', 'the jungle that was Britannia'
(sections I and III).

Small texts on a world-wide stage

Throughout, this book has placed emphasis on postcolonial writing
and reading as forms of understanding that can interrogate as well as
uphold power, and in this respect this 2005 Afterword has not changed
the overall focus. If anything, confronted by sweeping, transnational-
izing changes on the world's wide stage, these closing paragraphs are
more fiercely convinced than the foregoing of the disruptive potential
of postcolonial literatures, of their powerful suggestiveness, their invitation to see others as opening new possibilities of self, as challenging
fixed categories of 'us' and 'them'.

If the precise quality of the postcolonial remains a matter for
debate, this, it seems to me, is its definitive activity: to keep a political
and ethical awareness alive *within* a postcolonial reading, not to supply it as a mere adjunct or framework to a text. In Gayatri Spivak's
here directly evocative words: 'Really [let] yourself be imagined
(experience that impossibility) without guarantees, by and in another
culture'.[28] This view may be enhanced by the sense that the language
of a postcolonial text, whether everyday or literary, is never merely
reactive. It seeks to resolve as well as make conflict, to go beyond
retaliation, to act out, not to foreclose, a dilemma. A text, literary,
filmic, or otherwise, can contribute fully, even centrally, to how a

community defines itself and understands its future, especially after situations of trauma and war. Indeed, a number of post/colonial discourse readings, feminist and materialist in particular, have taken account of these at once conflictual and reparative dimensions of postcolonial literature for some time.

To enlarge on this perception I would want to draw more distinct and slightly different lines of definition from those in Chapter 6. The political and ethical contests which postcolonial texts have been waging for many years now have probably significantly gone beyond, in a sense outwitted, what I there called the dependency relationship with western theory. My differing understanding here is sharpened by a focus on ethics as in certain situations exceeding (though not cancelling) politics as a ground for the mobilization of the injured or the oppressed. In the context of the still-continuing colonial project, poems, novels, and theatre have provided space—in the case of theatre and poetry readings, literally—for the historically vanquished to lash out their anger and indignation, but also to produce declarations of restorative, not vengeful, perhaps even transcendent or humanist overcoming. Here I understand 'humanist' (or, more precisely, new humanist) in Fanon's sense of the colonized resuscitating, if not enacting for the first time, the civilizational values nullified by colonialism. Postcolonial literature offers ways of articulating, of putting into play, this justice- and respect-driven struggle. A creolized or polyglot story or poem both recalls the way in which cultures are syncretically interlinked, as they always have been,[29] *and* provides a gateway to *feeling* otherness, experiencing how it might be to be *beside one's self.*

Thinking of postcolonialism's institutional contexts in this ethical light, it is important to avoid the very present danger that this increasingly more recognizable term be viewed merely as the disciplinary marker for a critical approach, like post-structuralism or new historicism, albeit more ecumenically attractive than they. Postcolonialism is already widely regarded as one critical confection amongst a smorgasbord of others which can be pushed to the side and discarded once its sell-by date comes up (no doubt soon). To withstand this tendency, postcolonial criticism needs to remain vigilant about its almost unavoidable complicities with day-to-day, translocalized, mediatized reality; vigilant, too, about those ways in which the 'historical project of invasion, expropriation and domination' continues in globalized forms into the present.[30] This vigilance forms a central part of a postcolonial ethical awareness.

These assertions may, of course, read as deeply pretentious, as the postcolonial giving itself airs in its ivory tower which are unsustainable in the world outside. Maybe this is so. Millions of the world's poor and displaced, the wretched of the earth, are unable to gain access to postcolonial texts let alone to read them. Of what earthly use is a subversive postcolonialism to them? Their struggle—for drinkable water, for food, for land—lies elsewhere. Yet it is because their poverty is real, and must be relentlessly combated, that the postcolonial text and its readers do have a part to play. In the field of culture there is much that postcolonial critical readings can continue to question, tenaciously, militantly, as well as subtly, putting into play that invitation of the text to *think as other*. Such readings are as, if not more, resistant and transformative than the often highly regarded postmodernized appropriations of global culture in Third World contexts, such as, say, wearing a Mickey Mouse t-shirt with a wrappa in Abuja, or incorporating international beer logos in Bali bar décor.[31]

Criticism which acclaims globalization—including such acts of knowing cultural citation—as the new writ explaining the world, pay scant regard to those, whether materialists, or post-humanists, or both, who fiercely oppose its reach. It sidelines those writers and artists whose work moves beyond a sly civility, whose rejection of the world's inequalities is written into the very fabric of their poetic, built into its structures of invoking and involving the reader. For them, culture is still a space of struggle and transformation. In the world today we may well be shot through and through with global capitalism. Who knows, may we not even be able to communicate or even think without the help of its long-embedded transnational networks? Outside of small pockets, as amongst indigenous tree-hugging communities in India or Brazil, or in collectives in Cuba, the postcolonial will appear to many as a mere aspiration, a cruel hope, even a horizon beyond which it is inconceivable to go. Imperialism may have become more obviously differentiated and contingent, but it is imperialism none the less. The more then is it the responsibility of postcolonial readers and writers to derive inspiration from those who continue textually and otherwise to claim agency against colonialist violence, who work ever and anon 'to change the order of the world'.[32]

Chronology of Key Events and Publications

WHILE all chonologies are inevitably selective, every effort has been made to make this one as representative and up-to-date as possible. Writers' first and/or definitive publications are included where the latter category generally comprises those texts thought to be significant within the terms of the book. Many of the texts cited above are listed, as well as names (and their places of origin) that should have appeared were it not for overall considerations of length. Where texts were published over a period of years, they are entered under the final date.

1641	Portuguese cede control of Malacca to the Dutch
1719	Daniel Defoe, *Robinson Crusoe*
1757	Robert Clive defeats the Nawab of Bengal at the Battle of Plassey; the British place Mir Jafar Ali on the Bengal throne
1758	Clive becomes Governor of Bengal
1759	Wolfe defeats Montcalm at Quebec; Britain takes over the plantation island of Guadeloupe from the French
1764	A British force under Major Hector Munro defeats the Mughal allies at Buksar, Bengal
1765	Clive takes over the revenue management of Bengal; British control in Bengal established
1768	Captain James Cook sets out in the *Endeavour* on his first expedition
1772	James Bruce traces the Blue Nile to its confluence with the White Nile
	Ukawsaw Gronniosaw, *A Narrative*
1775	Outbreak of the American War of Independence (–1783)
1779	Mysore and Maratha War (–1783)
1782	Ignatius Sancho, *Letters of the late Ignatius Sancho, An African*
1783	Britain recognizes the independence of the United States
1784	Bengal placed under the dual control of the East India Company and the British Crown
1785	Warren Hastings resigns as Governor-General of India
1788	Arrival of the First Fleet at Botany Bay; beginning of European penal settlement in Australia
1789	Outbreak of the French Revolution

Olaudah Equiano, *The Interesting Narrative of the Life of Olaudah Equiano*

1790   James Bruce, *Travels to Discover the Sources of the Nile, 1768–1773*

1792   William Jones, *Mahomedan Law of Inheritance*

1793   Battle to a draw between Tipu, Sultan of Mysore, and Cornwallis; Permanent Settlement in Bengal

1794   Sake Dean Mahomet, *The Travels of Dean Mahomet, a native of Patna in Bengal*

1795   Mungo Park travels the course of the River Niger

1798   Napoleon invades Egypt; United Irishmen Rebellion, led by Wolfe Tone

Captain George Vancouver, *Voyage of Discovery to the North Pacific Ocean and Round the World in the Years 1790–1795*

1799   Tipu Sultan defeated

Mungo Park, *Travels in the Interior of Africa*

1801   Act of Union with Ireland

John Barrow, *Travels into the Interior of Southern Africa*; Robert Southey, *Thalaba the Destroyer*

1802   France suppresses St Domingo rebellion led by Toussaint L'Ouverture

1806   Britain occupies the Cape of Good Hope

1808   British abolition of the slave trade

1809   *Description de l'Égypte* (–1828)

1814   Jane Austen, *Mansfield Park*

1815   Battle of Waterloo; Congress of Vienna closes

John Campbell, *Travels in South Africa*

1817   James Mill, *The History of British India*

1818   British defeat the Maratha Empire in India, thereby securing the Gangetic plain

Lord Byron, *Childe Harold's Pilgrimage*

1819   British settlement established in Singapore by the East India Company

1821   Thomas De Quincey, *Confessions of an English Opium-Eater*

1822   Sake Dean Mahomet, *Shampooing*

1824   British invasion of Upper Burma (–1826)

Lord Byron, *Don Juan*

1825   John Franklin begins his Arctic explorations to find a north-west passage to Asia and the Pacific

1829   Catholic Emancipation in Ireland

1831   Jamaican slave revolt

      Mary Prince, *The History of Mary Prince, A West Indian Slave*

1832   Robert Southey, *Essays, Moral and Political*

1834   Abolition of slavery in British-occupied territory begins (–1838)

      Thomas Carlyle, *Sartor Resartus*

1835   Thomas Babington Macaulay's 'Minute on Indian Education'

1836   Captain Frederick Marryat, *Mr Midshipman Easy*; Catharine Parr Traill, *The Backwoods of Canada*

1837   Victoria becomes Queen

1839   Philip Meadows Taylor, *Confessions of a Thug*

      Edward John Eyre begins his trans-continental journey from South Australia to Western Australia (–1841)

1840   Transportation of convicts to New South Wales abolished; the Treaty of Waitangi establishes British control over New Zealand

1843   Maori resistance to the British presence in New Zealand

1844   Captain Marryat, *The Settlers in Canada*

1845   Edward John Eyre, *Discoveries in Central Australia*

1846   Convict transportation to Van Diemen's Land (Tasmania) suspended

      Captain Marryat, *The Mission, or Scenes in Africa*

1847   Charlotte Brontë, *Jane Eyre*

1848   Charles Dickens, *Dombey and Son*; William Makepeace Thackeray, *Vanity Fair*

1849   Thomas Carlyle, 'The Nigger Question'

1850   Charles Dickens, *David Copperfield*; Alfred Tennyson, *In Memoriam*

1853   William Arnold, *Oakfield*; Charles Dickens, *Bleak House*; Elizabeth Gaskell, *Cranford*

1854   Richard Burton, *Personal Narrative of a Pilgrimage to Al-Madinah and Meccah*

1855   David Livingstone travels to the Victoria Falls

      Elizabeth Gaskell, *North and South*

1856   Natal established as a Crown Colony; four Australian colonies gain 'responsible government'

      Richard Burton, *First Footsteps in East Africa*

1857   Mutiny (or Rebellion) in the Indian Army

      David Livingstone, *Missionary Travels and Researches in South*

Africa; Mary Seacole (Jamaica), *The Wonderful Adventures of Mary Seacole in Many Lands*

1858   Sovereignty in India is vested in the British monarch through the Government of India Act; Richard Burton and John Speke travel to Lakes Tanganyika and Victoria; John McDouall Stuart begins his south–north journey across Australia (–1862)

R. M. Ballantyne, *The Coral Island*; John Ruskin, *The Two Paths*

1859   Charles Darwin, *The Origin of Species*; George Eliot, *Adam Bede*; Alfred Tennyson, *Idylls of the King*

1860   Maori resistance to British land ownership leads to the Second Maori War (–1863)

Richard Burton, *The Lake Regions of Central Africa*; Multatuli/E. Douwes Dekker (The Netherlands), *Max Havelaar*

1861   Charles Dickens, *Great Expectations*; Anthony Trollope, *Tales of All Countries*

1862   John Ruskin, *Unto this Last*

1863   John Speke, *Journal of the Discovery of the Source of the Nile*

1865   Rebellion in Jamaica

Bankim Chandra Chatterjee, *Durgesnandini*; Charles Dickens, *Our Mutual Friend*; John Ruskin, *Sesame and Lilies*

1867   British North America Act establishes the Dominion of Canada

1869   Emily Eden, *Up the Country*

1870   John Ruskin gives inaugural lectures at Oxford

1871   Edward Tylor, *Primitive Culture*

1872   Benjamin Disraeli gives Crystal Palace Speech

Henry Morton Stanley, *How I Found Livingstone*

1873   Asante Expedition (–1874) leads to the creation of the Gold Coast as a Crown Colony

Anthony Trollope, *Australia and New Zealand*

1874   Marcus Clarke (Australia), *His Natural Life*

1876   Truganini, the last full-blooded Tasmanian Aboriginal, dies; Queen Victoria named Empress of India

1877   Britain annexes the Transvaal

1878   The Second Afghan War breaks out

Henry Morton Stanley, *Through the Dark Continent*; Anthony Trollope, *South Africa*

1879   The British–Zulu War

Boy's Own Paper established; Edwin Arnold, *The Light of Asia*

1882   British occupation of Egypt (–1955)

Bankim Chandra Chatterjee, *Anandamath*; Toru Dutt (India), *Ancient Ballads and Legends of Hindustan*; Robert Louis Stevenson, *New Arabian Nights*

1883 Isabella Bird, *The Golden Chersonese*; Olive Schreiner, *The Story of an African Farm*; Robert Louis Stevenson, *Treasure Island*

1884 G. A. Henty, *By Sheer Pluck: A Tale of the Ashanti* and *With Clive in India*

1885 The Berlin Conference regulating the Partition of Africa among the European powers ends; the Congo recognized as the personal possession of King Leopold II of Belgium; the Mahdi takes Khartoum in the Sudan; General Gordon is killed; the Indian National Congress meets for the first time; the Métis leader, Louis Riel, leads a second rebellion in Canada; Riel is hanged

H. Rider Haggard, *King Solomon's Mines*

1886 Britain annexes Upper Burma, the last major extension of British India

Edwin Arnold, *India Revisited*; Rudyard Kipling, *Departmental Ditties*; Robert Louis Stevenson, *Dr Jekyll and Mr Hyde*

1887 Queen Victoria's Golden Jubilee

H. Rider Haggard, *She: A History of Adventure* and *Allan Quartermain*; G. A. Henty, *With Wolfe in Canada*

1888 Publication of Richard Burton's *Arabian Nights* completed; James Anthony Froude, *The English in the West Indies*; Rudyard Kipling, *Plain Tales from the Hills*; Archibald Lampman (Canada), *Among the Millet*

1889 Cecil John Rhodes launches the British South Africa Company for the development of mining in the region

H. Rider Haggard, *Cleopatra*; W. B. Yeats, *The Wanderings of Oisin*

1890 First publication of J. G. Frazer's *The Golden Bough*; W. E. Henley, 'The Song of the Sword'; Rudyard Kipling; *The Light that Failed*; Henry Morton Stanley, *In Darkest Africa*

1891 Paul Gauguin goes to live and paint in Tahiti; death of Charles Parnell, ending Irish hopes for Home Rule

Rudyard Kipling, *Life's Handicap*; Rabindranath Tagore, 'Khokababur Prayabartan' published in *Sadhana*

1892 R. L. Stevenson, 'The Beach of Falesá'

1893 Gaelic League founded in Ireland

W. E. Henley, *Arabian Nights Entertainments*; Robert Louis Stevenson, 'The Ebb-Tide'

1894   Archibald Lampman, *Lyrics of the Earth*

1895   The Jameson Raid into the Transvaal Republic

       A. B. ('Banjo') Paterson, *The Man from Snowy River*

1896   Henry Lawson, *In Days When the World Was Wide*

1897   Queen Victoria's Diamond Jubilee

       Rudyard Kipling, 'Recessional'; Mary Kingsley, *Travels in West Africa*; Olive Schreiner, *Trooper Peter Halket of Mashonaland*; Flora Annie Steel, *On the Face of the Waters*

1898   Spanish–American War; Kitchener fights Battle of Omdurman against the Mahdists to avenge Gordon; Fashoda Incident on the Nile between the British and the French

       Joseph Conrad, *Tales of Unrest*; Rudyard Kipling, *The Day's Work*

1899   Outbreak of the South African or Second Anglo-Boer War

       Joseph Conrad, 'Heart of Darkness'; Thomas Hardy writes his Boer War poems; Rudyard Kipling, 'The White Man's Burden'

1900   Anti-Western Boxer Rebellion in China; Nigeria becomes a British protectorate; relief of the besieged cities of Ladysmith and Mafeking (in South Africa); First Pan-African Conference, London

       Joseph Conrad, *Lord Jim*; W. E. Henley, *For England's Sake*; Sister Nivedita (Margaret Noble), *Kali, the Mother*

1901   Australian federation (Aboriginals are not counted in the federal census); Queen Victoria dies; in India 1.25 million have died from famine since 1899; Britain annexes the Asante Kingdom as part of the Gold Coast

       Miles Franklin (Australia), *My Brilliant Career*; Rudyard Kipling, *Kim*; Dadabhai Naoroji, *Poverty and Un-British Rule in India*; Alice Perrin, *East of Suez*

1902   Cecil John Rhodes dies; the South African War ends (31 May)

       Joseph Conrad, *Youth*; J. A. Hobson, *Imperialism: A Study*; W. B. Yeats, *Cathleen ni Houlihan*

1903   W. E. B. Du Bois, *The Souls of Black Folk*; Joseph Furphy, *Such is Life*; G. A. Henty, *With Kitchener in the Soudan*; E. D. Morel, *The Congo Slave State*; Alice Perrin, *The Stronger Claim*; Rabindranath Tagore, *Binodini*

1904   Russo-Japanese War (–1905); Herero massacre in German colony of South West Africa (present-day Namibia)

       Joseph Conrad, *Nostromo*; Sara Jeannette Duncan (Canada), *The Imperialist*

1905 Curzon initiates the Partition of Bengal; Swadeshi movement of Indian resistance follows; Magi Magi revolt in Tanganyika (–1907)

   Sarojini Naidu (India), *The Golden Threshold*

1906 Zulu uprising, the Bambata Rebellion, in Natal

1907 Self-governing (white) colonies are declared Dominions

   Aurobindo Ghose, *The Doctrine of Passive Resistance* (publ. in *Bande Mataram*); Pablo Picasso, *Les Demoiselles d'Avignon* (painting); Rabindranath Tagore, *Gora*

1908 Robert Baden-Powell, *Scouting for Boys*

1909 Morley–Minto reforms in India

   Maud Diver, *The Englishwoman in India*

1910 John Buchan, *Prester John*; E. M. Forster, *Howards End*; Mohandas Gandhi, *Hind Swaraj*; Sister Nivedita, *The Master as I Saw Him*

1911 J. E. Casely-Hayford (Gold Coast), *Ethiopia Unbound*; Duse Mohamed, *In the Land of the Pharoahs*

1912 Formation of the South African Native National Congress (later the African National Congress)

   Stephen Leacock (Canada), *Sunshine Sketches of a Little Town*; Claude McKay, *The Dialect Poetry*; Sarojini Naidu, *The Bird of Time*; Rabindranath Tagore, *Gitanjali*

1913 Native Land Act in South Africa; Rabindranath Tagore wins Nobel Prize for Literature

   Sidney and Beatrice Webb, *Indian Diary*; Leonard Woolf, *The Village in the Jungle*

1914 Outbreak of First World War; Northern and Southern Nigeria united

   W. B. Yeats, *Responsibilities*

1916 Easter Rising in Ireland; Battle of the Somme

   James Joyce, *A Portrait of the Artist as a Young Man*; Katherine Mansfield, *The Aloe*; Solomon T. Plaatje, *Native Life in South Africa*

1917 October Revolution in St Petersburg; Balfour Declaration

   V. I. Lenin, *Imperialism: The Highest Stage of Capitalism*; Rabindranath Tagore, *Nationalism*

1918 The Allies and Germany sign Armistice on 11 November; declaration of the Irish Republic

1919 Montagu–Chelmsford reforms (permitting partial self-government in India); Rowlatt Acts and Amritsar massacre in India; Peace Conference at Versailles creates the League of Nations; the Dominions achieve a greater degree of autonomy within the Empire; division of the Austro-Hungarian Empire; outbreak of Anglo-Irish War (–1921)

1920   Britain given mandate control over Iraq, Transjordan, Palestine; Marcus Garvey's 'Back-to-Africa' movement launched; Government of Ireland Act is passed; Indonesian Communist Party formed

Katherine Mansfield, *Bliss, and Other Stories*; Leonard Woolf, *Economic Imperialism*

1921   Non-Co-operation movement in India begins, led by Mohandas Gandhi (–1922); the Anglo-Irish Treaty followed by the outbreak of civil war in Ireland (–1923)

Samuel Johnson, *The History of the Yorubas*; W. B. Yeats, *Michael Robartes and the Dancer*

1922   The Irish Free State is declared

T. S. Eliot, *The Waste Land*; James Joyce, *Ulysses*; D. H. Lawrence, *Aaron's Rod* and *Fantasia of the Unconscious*; M. N. Roy, *India in Transition*; Virginia Woolf, *Jacob's Room*

1923   General strike in Ceylon

D. H. Lawrence, *Kangaroo*; E. J. Pratt (Canada), *Newfoundland Verse*

1924   Communist violence in India

E. M. Forster, *A Passage to India*; Kenneth Slessor (Australia), *Thief of the Moon*

1925   Frederick Philip Grove, *Settlers of the Marsh*; Thomas Mofolo, *Chaka*; Virginia Woolf, *Mrs Dalloway*

1926   D. H. Lawrence, *The Plumed Serpent*

1927   Frederick Philip Grove, *A Search for America*; D. H. Lawrence, *Mornings in Mexico*

1928   John Buchan, *The Dancing Floor*; Morley Callaghan, *Strange Fugitive*; Dorothy Livesay (Canada), *Green Pitcher*; Claude McKay, *Home to Harlem*; Katharine Susannah Prichard (Australia), *Coonardoo: The Well in the Shadow*; Leonard Woolf, *Imperialism and Civilization*; W. B. Yeats, *The Tower*

1929   Women's revolt in Nigeria

Claude McKay, *Banjo*; Virginia Woolf, *A Room of One's Own*

1930   Civil Disobedience movement in India (–1932); launch of Negritude movement in Paris

Una Marson, *Tropic Reveries*; Solomon T. Plaatje, *Mhudi*; Henry Handel Richardson, *The Fortunes of Richard Mahony*

1931   Statute of Westminster creates the British Commonwealth of
        Nations and establishes the constitutional parity of the
        Dominions with Britain

        George Orwell, 'A Hanging'; Una Marson, *Heights and
        Depths*; Edward Thompson, *A Farewell to India*; Virginia Woolf,
        The Waves

1932   J. R. Ackerley, *Hindoo Holiday*; Joyce Cary, *Aïssa Saved*; Kenneth
        Slessor, *Cuckooz Contrey*; Evelyn Waugh, *Black Mischief*

1933   T. S. Eliot, *After Strange Gods*; Frederick Philip Grove, *Fruits of
        the Earth*; Claude McKay, *Banana Bottom*

1934   Morley Callaghan, *Such Is my Beloved*; George Orwell, *Burmese
        Days*; Jean Rhys, *Voyage in the Dark*; Cornelia Sorabji (India),
        India Calling; Christina Stead, *Seven Poor Men of Sydney*;
        Evelyn Waugh, *A Handful of Dust*

1935   Italian invasion of Abyssinia; Government of India Act

        Mulk Raj Anand, *Untouchable*; Rex Ingamells (Australia),
        Gum Tops; R. K. Narayan, *Swami and Friends*

1936   The Spanish Civil War breaks out

        Mulk Raj Anand, *Coolie*; Joyce Cary, *The African Witch*;
        Graham Greene, *Journey without Maps*; C. L. R. James, *Minty
        Alley*; Jawaharlal Nehru, *An Autobiography*; George Orwell,
        'Shooting an Elephant'; Frank Sargeson (New Zealand),
        Conversation with my Uncle

1937   Eire becomes a republic; Congress assumes power in most
        Indian provinces; nationalist riots in Jamaica and Trinidad

        Mulk Raj Anand, *Two Leaves and a Bud*; Karen Blixen, *Out of
        Africa*; Xavier Herbert, *Capricornia*; R. K. Narayan, *The Bachelor
        of Arts*; George Orwell, *The Road to Wigan Pier*

1938   C. L. R. James, *The Black Jacobins*; Jomo Kenyatta, *Facing Mount
        Kenya*; Raja Rao, *Kanthapura*; Evelyn Waugh, *Scoop*; Virginia
        Woolf, *Three Guineas*

1939   German invasion of Poland and outbreak of Second World War;
        provincial governments resign in India

        Leonard Barnes, *Empire or Democracy?*; Joyce Cary, *Mister
        Johnson*; Aimé Césaire, *Cahier d'un retour au pays natal*;
        Graham Greene, *The Lawless Roads*; Kenneth Slessor, 'Five Bells'

1940   Fall of France

        George Orwell, *Inside the Whale*; Christina Stead, *The Man
        Who Loved Children*

1941   Rudyard Kipling, *A Choice of Kipling's Verse*, edited by T. S. Eliot;
        Virginia Woolf, *Between the Acts*

1942   Quit India movement

        Louise Bennett, *Dialect Verse*

1943   Subhas Chandra Bose Launches Indian National Army against the British in Burma

1944   Jamaica achieves self-government

        Louise Bennett, *Anancy Stories and Poems*; Dorothy Livesay, *Day and Night*

1945   End of war in Europe; USA drops atomic bombs on Japan followed by Japanese surrender; Labour government in Britain committed to speeding up Indian independence; Fifth Pan-African Congress in Manchester calls for 'the right of all colonial peoples to control their own destiny'

        R. K. Narayan, *The English Teacher*; Léopold Sédar Senghor, *Chants d'ombre*

1946   First Assembly of the United Nations

        Peter Abrahams, *Mine Boy*; Jawaharlal Nehru, *The Discovery of India*; Evelyn Waugh, *When the Going was Good*; Judith Wright, *The Moving Image*

1947   India wins independence; the Partition of India and the creation of Pakistan

        Birago Diop (Senegal), *Les Contes d'Amadou Koumba*; Malcolm Lowry (Canada), *Under the Volcano*; Kwame Nkrumah, *Towards Colonial Freedom*

1948   Independence of Burma and Ceylon (Sri Lanka); Burma and Eire leave the Commonwealth; Nationalist Party wins elections in South Africa on an apartheid ticket; Britain's Nationality Act allows immigration from colonies and former colonies; arrival of SS *Empire Windrush* at Tilbury, London, bearing 492 West Indian emigrants; UN plan for Partition of Palestine

        G. V. Desani (India), *All About H. Hatterr*; Graham Greene, *The Heart of the Matter*; Alan Paton, *Cry, the Beloved Country*; Jean-Paul Sartre, *Orphée noir*

1949   People's Republic of China proclaimed under Mao Tse-tung after Communist take-over; Indonesia gains independence following four years of fierce conflict with the Dutch

        V. S. Reid, *New Day*

1950   India proclaimed a republic; the Korean War begins (–1953); Mau Mau meetings held in Kenya

        Doris Lessing, *The Grass is Singing*

1951   Nirad C. Chaudhuri, *The Autobiography of an Unknown Indian*; E. M. Forster, *Two Cheers for Democracy*; Rex Ingamells, *The Great South Land*

1952   The African National Congress in South Africa organizes the anti-pass law Defiance Campaign; Mau Mau resistance in Kenya intensifies and a State of Emergency is declared

        Frantz Fanon, *Peau noire, masques blancs*; E. J. Pratt (Canada), *Towards the Last Spike*; Amos Tutuola, *The Palm-Wine Drinkard*

1953   Phyllis Shand Allfrey (Dominica), *The Orchid House*; Alejo Carpentier (Cuba), *The Lost Steps* (in Spanish); Camara Laye (Guinea), *L'Enfant noir*; Bernard Binlin Dadié (Ivory Coast), *Légendes africaines*; E. M. Forster, *The Hill of Devi*; Nadine Gordimer, *The Lying Days*; George Lamming, *In the Castle of my Skin*

1954   Beginning of anti-colonial nationalist uprising in Algeria led by Ahmed Ben Bella (–1962)

        Peter Abrahams, *Tell Freedom*; Camara Laye, *Le Regard du roi*; Nayantara Sahgal, *Prison and Chocolate Cake*; Amos Tutuola, *My Life in the Bush of Ghosts*

1955   Bandung Conference of independent Asian and African countries; final withdrawal of British troops from Egypt; Congress of the People in South Africa and Freedom Charter adopted

        Aimé Césaire, *Discours sur le colonialisme*; Patrick White, *The Tree of Man*

1956   Independence of Sudan; Suez Crisis; Hungarian revolution and Soviet invasion; Castro lands in Cuba and initiates revolution

        Peter Abrahams, *A Wreath for Udomo*; Mongo Beti (Cameroon), *Le Pauvre Christ de Bomba*; Mavis Gallant (Canada), *The Other Paris*; Sembène Ousmane (Senegal), *Le Docker noir*; Ferdinand Oyono (Cameroon), *Une Vie de Boy*; George Padmore, *Pan-Africanism or Communism?*; Sam Selvon, *The Lonely Londoners*

1957   Ghana becomes the first sub-Saharan state to achieve independence from Britain; independence of Malaya

        Mongo Beti, *Mission terminée*; Naguib Mahfouz (Egypt), *Thalathiyya*; Albert Memmi, *Portrait du Colonisé* (*The Coloniser and the Colonised*); Kwame Nkrumah, *Autobiography*; Patrick White, *Voss*

1958   Race riots in Notting Hill, London; the All-African Peoples Conference meets in Accra, Ghana

        Chinua Achebe, *Things Fall Apart*; George Lamming, *Of Age and Innocence*; R. K. Narayan, *The Guide*

1959   Castro gains power in Cuba

        Nirad C. Chaudhuri, *A Passage to England*; Ezekiel Mphahlele, *Down Second Avenue*; Ian Mudie, *The Blue Crane*

1960   British Prime Minister Harold Macmillan's 'winds of change' speech; Sharpeville massacre in South Africa; ANC and PAC banned; Nigeria, Somalia, and Senegal amongst a number of nations win independence

Chinua Achebe, *No Longer at Ease*; Wilson Harris, *Palace of the Peacock*; George Lamming, *The Pleasures of Exile*; Sembène Ousmane, *Les Bouts de bois de Dieu*; Raja Rao, *The Serpent and the Rope*; Wole Soyinka, *A Dance of the Forests* performed for the Nigerian independence celebrations

1961   Berlin Wall goes up; Bay of Pigs invasion attempted, followed by Cuban missile crisis; Albert Luthuli, ANC President, wins Nobel Peace prize; Patrice Lumumba murdered in Congo; Tanzania and Sierra Leone win independence

Frantz Fanon, *Les Damnés de la terre*; Cyprian Ekwensi (Nigeria), *Jagua Nana*; Cheikh Hamidou Kane (Senegal), *L'Aventure ambiguë*; V. S. Naipaul, *A House for Mr Biswas*

1962   Algeria, Jamaica, Trinidad and Tobago, and Uganda win independence; West Indian Federation collapses; Civil Rights movement in the United States grows; Indo-Chinese border dispute

Kenneth Kaunda, *Zambia Shall Be Free*; Christopher Okigbo, *Heavensgate*

1963   Martin Luther King gives his 'I have a dream' speech; Kenya gains independence; treason trials involving Nelson Mandela, Walter Sisulu, and seven others begin in South Africa

Margaret Laurence (Canada), *The Prophet's Camel Bell*; Wole Soyinka, *The Lion and the Jewel*

1964   Malawi, Zambia, and Malaya gain independence; Vietnam War breaks out (–1973)

Chinua Achebe, *Arrow of God*; Margaret Laurence, *The Stone Angel*; Ngugi wa Thiong'o, *Weep Not, Child*; Gabriel Okara, *The Voice*; Christopher Okigbo, *Limits*; Léopold Sédar Senghor, *Poèmes*

1965   Indo-Pakistan War

Ama Ata Aidoo, *Anowa*; Nelson Mandela, *No Easy Walk to Freedom*; Mudrooroo (Colin Johnson), *Wild Cat Falling*; Kwame Nkrumah, *Neo-colonialism: The Last Stage of Imperialism*; Ngugi wa Thiong'o, *The River Between*; Wole Soyinka, *The Interpreters* and *The Road*

1966   Australia sends troops to Vietnam; Nkrumah deposed as president of Ghana; Barbados and Botswana win independence; first Tricontinental Conference, Havana

Chinua Achebe, *A Man of the People*; Elechi Amadi, *The*

Concubine; Margaret Atwood, *The Circle Game*; Louise Bennett, *Jamaica Labrish*; Seamus Heaney, *Death of a Naturalist*; Robert Kroetsch, *The Words of my Roaring*; Flora Nwapa, *Efuru*; Okot p'Bitek, *Song of Lawino*; Jean Rhys, *Wide Sargasso Sea*; Tayeb Salih (Sudan), *Season of Migration to the North* (in Arabic); Paul Scott, *The Jewel in the Crown*; Francis Selormey (Ghana), *The Narrow Path*

1967   Secession of Biafra and outbreak of Nigerian civil war (–1970); Six-day Arab–Israeli War; Aborigines officially 'receive' Australian citizenship; capture and execution of Ernesto 'Che' Guevara in Bolivia

Kamau Brathwaite, *Rights of Passage*; Wilson Harris, *Tradition, the Writer and Society* (essays); Thomas Keneally, *Bring Larks and Heroes*; Alex La Guma (South Africa), *A Walk in the Night*; Gabriel Garcia Marquez (Colombia), *One Hundred Years of Solitude* (in Spanish); V. S. Naipaul, *The Mimic Men*; Ngugi wa Thiong'o, *A Grain of Wheat*; Wole Soyinka, *Idanre, and Other Poems* and *Kongi's Harvest*; Efua Sutherland (Ghana), *The Marriage of Anansewa*

1968   Martin Luther King assassinated; Enoch Powell's 'Rivers of Blood' speech in Birmingham, England; student uprisings in Paris and worldwide; 'Prague Spring' uprising

Kamau Brathwaite, *Masks*; Bessie Head, *When Rain Clouds Gather*; Earl Lovelace (Trinidad), *The Schoolmaster*; Alice Munro (Canada), *Dance of the Happy Shades*; Yambo Ouologuem (Mali), *Le Devoir de violence*

1969   British troops quell riots in Northern Ireland

Elechi Amadi, *The Great Ponds*; Ayi Kwei Armah, *The Beautyful Ones are not yet Born*; Kamau Brathwaite, *Islands*; Robert Kroetsch, *The Studhorse Man*; V. S. Naipaul, *The Loss of El Dorado: A History*

1970   Margaret Atwood, *The Journals of Susanna Moodie*; Nuruddin Farah, *From a Crooked Rib*; Merle Hodge (Trinidad), *Crick Crack, Monkey*; Oodgeroo Noonuccal (Kath Walker), *My People*; Flora Nwapa, *Idu*; Okot p'Bitek, *Song of Ocol*

1971   Civil war erupts in East Pakistan with the declaration by Sheikh Mujibir Rahman of the independent state of Bangladesh; two-week India–Pakistan War ends in defeat for West Pakistan, where Zulfikar Ali Bhutto elected Prime Minister

Kofi Awoonor (Ghana), *This Earth, my Brother*; George Bowering, *Touch*; Northrop Frye, *The Bush Garden*; Bessie Head, *Maru*; George Lamming, *Water with Berries*; Alice Munro, *Lives of Girls and Women*; V. S. Naipaul, *In a Free State*; Wole Soyinka, *Madmen and Specialists*

1972   Aborigines and Torres Strait islanders establish 'Tent Embassy'
        in Canberra to publicize land rights claims; 'Bloody Sunday' in
        Northern Ireland, when British paratroops kill 13 protesters

        Margaret Atwood, *Surfacing* and *Survival*; Steve Biko, *I write
        what I like*; Buchi Emecheta, *In the Ditch*; Thomas Keneally, *The
        Chant of Jimmie Blacksmith*; Walter Rodney, *How Europe
        underdeveloped Africa*; Wole Soyinka, *The Man Died: Prison
        Notes*

1973   Australian Aborigines granted the vote for the first time; Patrick
        White wins Nobel Prize for Literature

        Ayi Kwei Armah, *Two Thousand Seasons*; Amilcar Cabral
        (Guinea–Bissau) *Return to the Source*; Kamala Das, *The Old
        Playhouse and Other Poems*; J. G. Farrell, *The Siege of Krishnapur*;
        Witi Ihimaera, *Tangi*; Robert Kroetsch, *Gone Indian*; Rudy
        Wiebe (Canada), *The Temptations of Big Bear*

1974   Pakistan recognizes Bangladesh; the Labour Prime Minister of
        Australia, Gough Whitlam, is forced to resign

        Buchi Emecheta, *Second-Class Citizen*; Nadine Gordimer, *The
        Conservationist*; Bessie Head, *A Question of Power*; Margaret
        Laurence, *The Diviners*

1975   Indira Gandhi, the Prime Minister of India, is found guilty of
        election fraud and a state of emergency declared (–1977)

        Amilcar Cabral, *Unité et lutte*; Patricia Grace, *Waiariki*;
        Seamus Heaney, *North*; Linton Kwesi Johnson (Jamaica/
        Britain), *Dread Beat an Blood*; Bharati Mukherjee, *Wife*; Charles
        Mungoshi (Zimbabwe), *Waiting for the Rain*; V. S. Naipaul,
        Guerrillas

1976   Students' revolt in Soweto, South Africa

        Les A. Murray, *The Vernacular Republic*; Ngugi wa Thiong'o
        and Micere Mugo, *The Trial of Dedan Kimathi*; Wole Soyinka,
        Death and the King's Horseman and *Myth, Literature and the
        African World* (essays)

1977   Steve Biko dies in South African police custody; General
        Zia-ul-Haq ousts Bhutto in military coup in Pakistan

        Ama Ata Aidoo, *Our Sister Killjoy*; Bessie Head, *The Collector
        of Treasures*; Ngugi wa Thiong'o, *Petals of Blood*

1978   Ayi Kwei Armah, *The Healers*; Patricia Grace, *Mutuwhenua*;
        Dambudzo Marechera (Zimbabwe), *The House of Hunger*;
        Timothy Mo (Britain/Hong Kong), *The Monkey King*; Edward
        Said, *Orientalism*

1979   US embassy hostages seized in Teheran, Iran; Soviet invasion of
        Afghanistan

Mariamma Ba (Senegal), *Une si longue lettre*; Jack Davis (Australia) *Kullark* (play); Buchi Emecheta, *The Joys of Motherhood*; Nuruddin Farah, *Sweet and Sour Milk*; Nadine Gordimer, *Burger's Daughter*; Festus Iyayi, *Violence*; Mazisi Kunene, *Emperor Shaka the Great*; Alex La Guma, *Time of the Butcherbird*; Mudrooroo, *Long Live Sandawara*; V. S. Naipaul, *A Bend in the River*; Paul Scott, *Staying On*; Aminata Sow Fall (Senegal), *La Grève des battus*

1980   Zimbabwe wins independence; Quebec referendum on secession from Canada

George Bowering, *Burning Water*; Anita Desai, *Clear Light of Day*; Linton Kwesi Johnson, *Inglan is a Bitch*; Les Murray, *The Boys who Stole the Funeral*; Stanley Nyamfukudza (Zimbabwe), *The Non-Believer's Journey*; Miriam Tlali (South Africa), *Amandla*; Derek Walcott, *Remembrance and Pantomime*

1981   Women's Peace Camp set up at Greenham Common, England, to protest against siting of Cruise missiles; President Sadat of Egypt assassinated; Israel annexes Golan Heights and bombs Beirut; ten IRA hunger-strike prisoners including Bobby Sands die in the Maze Prison, Northern Ireland

J. M. Coetzee, *Waiting for the Barbarians*; Nadine Gordimer, *July's People*; Robert Kroetsch, *Field Notes*; Ngugi wa Thiong'o, *Detained* and *Writers in Politics* (essays); Salman Rushdie, *Midnight's Children*; Wole Soyinka, *Aké*; Archie Weller, *The Day of the Dog*

1982   Falklands/Malvinas War between Britain and Argentina

Buchi Emecheta, *Double Yoke*; Janet Frame (New Zealand), *To the Is-Land*; Kazuo Ishiguro, *A Pale View of Hills*; Earl Lovelace, *The Wine of Astonishment*; Ngugi wa Thiong'o, *Devil on the Cross*; Medbh McGuckian, *The Flower Master*; Timothy Mo, *Sour Sweet*

1983   USA invades Grenada in the Caribbean and supports Contra rebels against Marxist Sandinista government in Nicaragua

Wilson Harris, *The Womb of Space* (essays); Mudrooroo, *Doctor Wooreddy's Prescription for Enduring the Ending of the World*; Njabulo Ndebele, *Fools*; Ngugi wa Thiong'o, *Barrel of a Pen*; Grace Nichols, *i is a long-memoried woman*; Michael Ondaatje, *Running in the Family*; Sam Selvon, *Moses Migrating*; Salman Rushdie, *Shame*

1984   Anglo-Chinese Hong Kong agreement; toxic leak at Union Carbide factory, Bhopal, India, is largest industrial accident in human history; Indira Gandhi assassinated

Nicole Brossard (Canada), *Double Impression*; David Dabydeen (Guyana/Britain), *Slave Song*; Janet Frame, *An Angel at my Table*; Seamus Heaney, *Station Island*; V. S. Naipaul, *Finding the Centre*

1985 Anglo-Irish agreement

Fred d'Aguiar (Guyana/Britain), *Mama Dot*; Neil Bissoondath, *Digging up the Mountains*; Assia Djebar (Algeria), *L'amour, La Fantasia*; Keri Hulme, *The Bone People*; Jamaica Kincaid, *Annie John*; Ellen Kuzwayo, *Call Me Woman*; Gabriel Garcia Marquez, *Love in the Time of Cholera* (in Spanish); Joan Riley, *The Unbelonging*; Nawal el Saadawi (Egypt), *God Dies by the Nile*; Nayantara Sahgal, *Rich Like Us*; Ken Saro-Wiwa (Nigeria), *Sozaboy*

1986 Wole Soyinka wins Nobel Prize for Literature

Buchi Emecheta, *Head above Water*; Nuruddin Farah, *Maps*; Amitav Ghosh, *The Circle of Reason*; Lorna Goodison, *I am Becoming my Mother*; Patricia Grace, *Potiki*; Festus Iyayi, *Heroes*; Robert Kroetsch, *Excerpts from the Real World*; B. Kojo Laing, *Search Sweet Country*; Mudrooroo, *The Song Circle of Jacky*; Ngugi wa Thiong'o, *Decolonising the Mind*; Ben Okri, *Incidents at the Shrine*; Caryl Phillips, *A State of Independence*; Olive Senior, *Summer Lightning*; Derek Walcott, *Collected Poems*

1987 Outbreak of first Palestinian insurrection or Intifada

Chinua Achebe, *Anthills of the Savannah*; Sally Morgan, *My Place*; V. S. Naipaul, *The Enigma of Arrival*; Michael Ondaatje, *In the Skin of a Lion*; Caryl Phillips, *The European Tribe*

1988 Withdrawal of Soviet troops from Afghanistan followed by civil war

Thea Astley (Australia), *It's Raining in Mango*; Erna Brodber, *Myal*; Peter Carey, *Oscar and Lucinda*; Upamanyu Chatterjee, *English, August*; Michelle Cliff, *No Telephone to Heaven*; J. M. Coetzee, *Foe*; David Dabydeen, *Coolie Odyssey*; Tsitsi Dangarembga, *Nervous Conditions*; Shashi Deshpande, *That Long Silence*; Janet Frame, *The Carpathians*; Amitav Ghosh, *The Shadow Lines*; Lorna Goodison, *Heartsease*; Seamus Heaney, *The Government of the Tongue* (essays); Chenjerai Hove, *Bones*; Jamaica Kincaid, *A Small Place*; Ruby Langford Ginibi, *Don't Take Your Love to Town*; R. K. Narayan, *A Writer's Nightmare* (essays); bp Nichol, *Selected Organs*; Ben Okri, *Stars of the New Curfew*; Salman Rushdie, *The Satanic Verses*; Nayantara Sahgal, *Mistaken Identity*; Bapsi Sidhwa (Pakistan), *Ice-candy Man*

1989 Ayatollah Khomeini pronounces death sentence (fatwa) on Salman Rushdie (rescinded 1998); military repression of student demonstrations in Tiananmen Square, China; the Berlin Wall comes down and Communist regimes collapse in Eastern Europe

Chinua Achebe, *Hopes and Impediments*; Shimmer Chinodya (Zimbabwe), *Harvest of Thorns*; Nadine Gordimer, *The Essential Gesture* (essays); Kazuo Ishiguro, *The Remains of the Day*; Ngugi wa Thiong'o, *Matigari*; M. Nourbese Philip, *She Tries Her Tongue*; Wole Soyinka, *Mandela's Earth and other poems*; Sara Suleri (Pakistan/USA), *Meatless Days*; Shashi Tharoor, *The Great Indian Novel*; M. G. Vassanji, *The Gunny Sack*

1990   Nelson Mandela walks free after 28 years of incarceration

J. M. Coetzee, *Age of Iron*; Alan Duff (Aotearoa/New Zealand), *Once Were Warriors*; Jamaica Kincaid, *Lucy*; Hanif Kureishi, *The Buddha of Suburbia*; Sindiwe Magona, *To my Children's Children*

1991   The First Gulf War; Nadine Gordimer wins Nobel Prize for Literature

Amit Chaudhuri, *A Strange and Sublime Address*; Yasmine Gooneratne (Sri Lanka/Australia), *A Change of Skies*; David Dabydeen, *The Intended*; Jackie Kay, *The Adoption Papers*; Ben Okri, *The Famished Road*; Caryl Phillips, *Cambridge*; Salman Rushdie, *Imaginary Homelands* (essays); Dev Virahsawmy (Mauritius), *Toufann*; Derek Walcott, *Omeros*; Tim Winton, *Cloudstreet*

1992   Australian High Court hands down 'Mabo' decision recognizing Aboriginal land rights for the first time; destruction of Babri Masjid in Ayodya, India by Hindutva militants; Derek Walcott wins Nobel Prize for Literature

Amitav Ghosh, *In an Antique Land*; Michael Ondaatje, *The English Patient*; Ahdaf Soueif (Egypt/Britain), *In the Eye of the Sun*; Marina Warner (Britain), *Indigo*

1993   Eritrea gains independence from Ethiopia; Toni Morrison wins Nobel Prize for Literature

Ben Okri, *Songs of Enchantment*; Nuruddin Farah, *Gifts*; Édouard Glissant, *Tout-Monde*; Ngugi wa Thiong'o, *Moving the Centre* (essays); Vikram Seth, *A Suitable Boy*; Shashi Deshpande, *The Binding Vine*

1994   South Africa holds its first democratic elections and Nelson Mandela is elected President; mass-murder of minority Tutsis by government-supported Hutus in Rwanda begins; controversial Oslo Accords provide for limited Palestinian authority in Gaza and the West Bank

Romesh Gunesekera, *Reef*; Abdulrazak Gurnah (Zanzibar/Britain), *Paradise*; John Muk Muk Burke (Australia), *Bridge of Triangles*; V. S. Naipaul, *A Way in the World*; Shyam Selvadurai (Sri Lanka), *Funny Boy*; Yvonne Vera, *Without a Name*

1995   War in Bosnia; General Abacha's military regime in Nigeria
        sentences Ogoni activist, anti-Shell demonstrator, and popular
        author Ken Saro-Wiwa to death: international protests not
        successful in preventing the sentence from being carried out on
        10 November

        Anita Desai, *Journey to Ithaca*; Hanif Kureishi, *The Black
        Album*; A. K. Ramanujan, *Collected Poems*; Salman Rushdie,
        The Moor's Last Sigh; Olive Senior, *Gardening in the Tropics*
        (poems); M. G. Vassanji, *The Book of Secrets*

1996   Moniza Alvi, *A Bowl of Warm Air*; Sia Figiel, *Where We Once
        Belonged*; Chenjerai Hove, *Ancestors*; Jamaica Kincaid, *The
        Autobiography of my Mother*; Earl Lovelace, *Salt*; Rohinton
        Mistry (India/Canada), *A Fine Balance*; Ben Okri, *Dangerous
        Love* (reworking of 1981 *The Landscapes Within*)

1997   Hong Kong ceases to be a British colony; 'McLibel' trial ends
        with pyrrhic victory for the multinational McDonalds

        Arundhati Roy, *The God of Small Things* becomes one of the
        best-seller postcolonial novels of all time and a Booker Prize
        winner; J. M. Coetzee, *Boyhood: Scenes from Provincial Life*;
        Bernardine Evaristo (Britain), *Lara*; Alexander Kanengoni
        (Zimbabwe), *Echoing Silences*; Pauline Melville (Britain/
        Guyana), *The Ventriloquist's Tale*; Ben Okri, *A Way of Being Free*
        (essays); Caryl Phillips, *The Nature of Blood*; Derek Walcott, *The
        Bounty*

1998   'Good Friday Agreement' initiates power-sharing assembly for
        Northern Ireland; India explodes its first nuclear device;
        Kosovo–Serb conflict breaks out (–1999); first Global Street
        Party, involving People's Global Action and Reclaim the Streets,
        organizes against economic globalization of the World Trade
        Organization and the G8; President Mugabe of Zimbabwe
        orders confiscation of white-owned farms

        Murray Bail (Australia), *Eucalyptus*; Amit Chaudhuri,
        Freedom Song; Romesh Gunesekera, *The Sandglass*; Manju
        Kapur (India), *Difficult Daughters*; Oonya Kempadoo (Guyana),
        Buxton Spice; Jackie Kay, *Trumpet*; Les Murray, *Fredy Neptune*
        (verse novel)

1999   Australian republican referendum fails; Nigeria embarks on
        third period of civilian government since independence, under
        General Obasanjo; Indonesia withdraws from East Timor after
        24-year occupation; J. M. Coetzee's *Disgrace* wins the Booker
        Prize, making Coetzee the first writer to have won the prize
        twice

        David Dabydeen, *A Harlot's Progress*; Sia Figiel, *They Who Do
        Not Grieve*; Yacoob Ghanty (Mauritius), *Clinton and Cleopatra*

(play); Kate Grenville (Australia), *The Idea of Perfection*; Jhumpa Lahiri (India/USA), *The Interpreter of Maladies* (stories); Shani Mootoo, *Cereus Blooms at Night*; Ahdaf Soueif, *The Map of Love*

2000   Outbreak of al-Aqsa (second) Intifada; athlete Cathy Freeman runs lap of honour draped in Australian and Aboriginal flags after symbolic 400 m. victory at Sydney Olympics

Margaret Atwood, *The Blind Assassin*; Fred d'Aguiar, *Bloodlines*; Elleke Boehmer, *Bloodlines*; Rob Nixon, *Dreambirds*; Zadie Smith, *White Teeth*

2001   Robert Mugabe retains hold on power in Zimbabwe after elections accompanied by intimidation and land redistribution promises; Israeli attacks on Rafah refugee camp, in southern Gaza Strip; Islamist '9/11' attack on the World Trade Centre in New York and on the Pentagon, Washington, USA; US-led war on Taliban in Afghanistan in 'retaliation' (14 November– March 2002); V. S. Naipaul wins Nobel Prize for Literature

Peter Carey (2nd twice Booker-winner), *True History of the Kelly Gang*; Amit Chaudhuri, *A New World*; Nadine Gordimer, *The Pickup*

2002   Earth Summit in Johannesburg, South Africa; communal disturbances with serious loss of life in Gujerat, India

J. M. Coetzee, *Youth*; Bernardine Evaristo, *The Emperor's Babe*; Maggie Gee, *The White Family*; Abdulrazak Gurnah, *By the Sea*; Linton Kwesi Johnson, *Mi Revalueshanary Fren*; Paul Muldoon (N. Ireland), *Moy Sand and Gravel* (poems); Kamila Shamsie (Pakistan/Britain), *Salt and Saffron*; Yvonne Vera, *The Stone Virgins*; Tim Winton, *Dirt Music*

2003   US and British invasion of Iraq (March) achieves goal of deposing Saddam Hussein at extremely high cost in terms of lives and civil liberties in all countries involved; Paul Muldoon wins Pulitzer Prize; J. M. Coetzee wins Nobel Prize for Literature

Monica Ali, *Brick Lane*; Caryl Phillips, *A Distant Shore*

2004   Hostilities in Iraq continue; civil war-induced famine in Darfur, Sudan

Chimamanda Ngozi Adichie (Nigeria/USA), *Purple Hibiscus*; Nadeem Aslam (Pakistan/Britain), *Maps for Lost Lovers*; Amitav Ghosh, *The Hungry Tide*; Andrea Levy (Britain), *Small Island*; M. G. Vassanji, *The In-between World of Vikram Lal*

Notes

UNLESS otherwise stated, place of publication for Penguin books is Harmondsworth; that for University Presses is generally implied by the university's name; in other unspecified cases it is London.

Introduction

1. Ben Okri, 'The Marvellous Responsibility of the Unseen', Arthur Ravenscroft Memorial Lecture, University of Leeds, 17 Mar. 1994. Collected (and abridged) as 'Amongst the Silent Stones', in Ben Okri, *A Way of Being Free* (Phoenix House, 1997), 96–108.

2. Chinua Achebe, *Anthills of the Savannah* (London: Heinemann, 1987), 124.

3. Nicholas Thomas, *Colonialism's Culture: Anthropology, Travel and Government* (Cambridge: Polity, 1994), pp. x–xii.

4. Trinh Minh-ha, *Woman, Native, Other* (Bloomington: Indiana UP, 1989), 49–53. See also Gayatri Spivak, *In Other Worlds* (Methuen, 1987).

5. Kwame Nkrumah, *Neo-colonialism: The Last Stage of Imperialism* (London: Nelson, 1965), p. ix.

Chapter 1

1. See Isabel Hofmeyr, *The Portable Bunyan: A Transnational History of* The Pilgrim's Progress (Princeton UP, 2004).

2. On culture-bound interpretation, see e.g. James A. Boon, *Other Tribes, Other Scribes: Symbolic Anthropology in the Comparative Study of Culture* (Cambridge UP, 1982); James Clifford, *The Predicament of Culture: Twentieth-Century Ethnography, Literature and Art* (Harvard UP, 1988); Peter Hulme and Tim Youngs (eds.), *The Cambridge Companion to Travel Writing* (Cambridge: Cambridge UP, 2002); Nicholas Thomas, *Colonialism's Culture: Anthropology, Travel and Government* (Cambridge: Polity, 1994).

3. See Paul Carter, *The Road to Botany Bay: An Essay in Spatial History* (Faber, 1987), and his later collection of essays, *Living in a New Country: History, Travelling and Language* (Faber, 1992).

4. As Brian Friel has forcefully demonstrated in his play about colonial Ireland, *Translations* (Faber, 1981). See also Javed Majeed, *Ungoverned Imaginings: James Mill's* The History of British India *and Orientalism*

(Oxford: Clarendon Press, 1992); Vincent L. Rafael, *Contracting Colonialism: Translation and Conversion in Tagalog Society under early Spanish Rule* (Ithaca, NY, and London: Cornell UP, 1988).

5. The work of Basil Davidson, Lydia Potts, Walter Rodney, Hugh Tinker, and Eric Williams, amongst others, is worth consulting in this regard.

6. Lionel J. Trotter, *The Life of John Nicholson* (John Murray, 1904), 228–30.

7. On the subaltern, see Antonio Gramsci, *Selections from the Prison Notebooks*, ed. and trans. Quintin Hoare and Geoffrey Nowell Smith (London: Lawrence and Wishart, 1971); Gayatri Spivak, 'Can the Subaltern Speak? Speculations on Widow Sacrifice', *Wedge*, 7–8 (winter/spring 1985), and reproduced widely. This usage is to be distinguished from the more conventional military term, as used by Kipling in the story 'Only a Subaltern' (*The Man who would be King*), for example.

8. Homi Bhabha discusses the 'excess' represented by the other in 'Signs Taken for Wonders', in Henry Louis Gates, jun. (ed.), *'Race', Writing and Difference* (University of Chicago Press, 1986); collected in his *The Location of Culture* (Routledge, 1994).

9. Eric Hobsbawm and Terence Ranger (eds.), *The Invention of Tradition* (Cambridge UP, 1983). Bernard S. Cohen's essay 'Representing Authority in Victorian India' also appears in *An Anthropologist among the Historians* (New Delhi: Oxford UP, 1990).

10. For a wide-ranging discussion of empire's energizing myths, see Martin Green, *Dreams of Adventure, Deeds of Empire* (Routledge & Kegan Paul, 1980).

11. Robert Young, *Colonial Desire: Hybridity in Theory, Culture and Race* (Routledge, 1995).

12. Edward Said, *Culture and Imperialism* (Chatto & Windus, 1993), especially 73–229. I am indebted to Said's illuminating discussion of *Mansfield Park*, pp. 69–70 and 100–16; and of *Kim*, pp. 159–96.

13. See You-me Park and Rajeswari Sunder Rajan (eds.), *The Postcolonial Jane Austen* (London: Routledge, 2000); and cf. Caryl Phillips, *Cambridge* (Bloomsbury, 1991); Nancy Henry, *George Eliot and the British Empire* (Cambridge UP, 2002).

14. Eric Williams, *From Columbus to Castro: The History of the Caribbean, 1492–1969* (André Deutsch, 1970), 144–7.

15. Richard Koebner and Helmut Dan Schmidt, *Imperialism: The Story and Significance of a Political Word, 1840–1960* (Cambridge UP, 1964). More recently again, with the rise of American (neo-)imperialism in the late twentieth century, the term Empire has won new currency. See Michael Hardt and Antonio Negri, *Empire* (Cambridge, Mass.: Harvard UP, 2000).

16. E. J. Hobsbawm, *The Age of Empire 1875–1914* (Weidenfeld & Nicolson, 1987).

17. C. A. Bayly, 'Conclusion', *Imperial Meridian: The British Empire and the World 1780–1831* (Harlow: Longman, 1989).

18. Ronald Robinson and John Gallagher, *Africa and the Victorians: The Official Mind of Imperialism* (Macmillan, 1961). See also William Roger Louis (ed.), *Imperialism: The Robinson and Gallagher Controversy* (New York: Franklin Watts, 1976).

19. Social Darwinism involved the evaluative application of Darwin's ideas of biological evolution, and in particular of the survival of the fittest, to the development of societies. A fuller description can be found in the section 'Colonized others' in Ch. 2.

20. See e.g. Robert Baden-Powell, *Scouting for Boys*, Part VI, ed. Elleke Boehmer (1908; Oxford UP, 2004).

21. Jan Morris, *The Spectacle of Empire: Style, Effect and Pax Britannica* (Faber, 1982).

22. Henry Newbolt, 'Vitaë Lampada' (1897), in Elleke Boehmer (ed.), *Empire Writing: An Anthology of Colonial Literature, 1870–1918* (Oxford UP, 1998), 287–8.

23. See Boehmer (ed.), *Empire Writing*, 212–15, 283–6; 16–20; W. E. Henley, *For England's Sake: Verses and Songs in Time of War* (David Nutt, 1900).

24. Samuel Hynes, *The Edwardian Turn of Mind* (1968; Pimlico, 1991).

25. On imperial gothic, see Patrick Brantlinger, *Rule of Darkness: British Literature and Imperialism 1830–1914* (Ithaca, NY, and London: Cornell UP, 1988), 227–53. On degeneration, see Rod Edmond, 'Home and Away', in Howard J. Booth and Nigel Rigby (eds.), *Modernism and Empire* (Manchester UP, 2000), 39–63.

26. Richard Altick, *The Shows of London* (Cambridge, Mass.: Harvard UP, 1978); Paul Greenhalgh, *Ephemeral Vistas: The Expositions Universelles, Great Exhibitions and World's Fairs, 1851–1939* (Manchester UP, 1988); John MacKenzie, *Propaganda and Empire* (Manchester UP, 1984); Rosalyn Poignant, *Professional Savages: Captive Lives and Western Spectacle* (New Haven: Yale UP, 2004).

27. G. A. Henty, *With Clive in India, or the Beginnings of an Empire* (Blackie and Son, 1884), 12.

28. Dadabhai Naoroji, *Poverty and Un-British Rule in India* (Swan Sonnenschein and Co., 1901).

29. Sidney W. Mintz, *Sweetness and Power: The Place of Sugar in Modern History* (Viking, 1985). See such other 'biographies' of colonial commodities and comestibles as: Simon Garfield, *Mauve: How One Man Invented*

a Colour that Changed the World (Faber, 2001); Tim Ecott, *Vanilla: Travels in Search of the Luscious Substance* (Michael Joseph, 2003); or Jack Turner, *Spice: The History of a Temptation* (HarperCollins, 2004).

30. See Robert I. Rotberg, *The Founder: Cecil Rhodes and the Pursuit of Power* (Oxford UP, 1988); Anthony Thomas, *Rhodes* (New York: St Martin's Press, 1996).

31. Imperialist rhetoric of this stripe has proved remarkably durable. Compare US President George W. Bush's scrawled comment to Condoleeza Rice on 30 June 2004, the day of the formal hand-over of power in American-occupied Iraq: 'Let Freedom Reign!'

32. Philip Meadows Taylor, *Confessions of a Thug* (1839; Oxford UP, 1998), 541.

33. See Eric J. Sharpe, *The Universal Gita* (Duckworth, 1985), for a cultural history of the *Bhagavad-gita* as a European construct.

34. Joseph Bristow, *Empire Boys: Adventures in a Man's World* (HarperCollins, 1991).

35. See Martin Green's study of Kipling in *Dreams of Adventure*. See also: Ralph Crane, *Inventing India: A History of India in English Language Fiction* (Macmillan, 1992); John McClure, *Kipling and Conrad: The Colonial Fiction* (Cambridge, Mass.: Harvard UP, 1981); Sara Suleri, *The Rhetoric of English India* (University of Chicago Press, 1992).

36. John Hanning Speke, *Journal of the Discovery of the Source of the Nile* (William Blackwood and Sons, 1863), 467. See also Speke's account in 'Captain J. H. Speke's Discovery of the Victoria Nyanza Lake, The supposed Source of the Nile', Part II, *Blackwood's Edinburgh Magazine*, 86 (Oct. 1859), 412.

37. Thomas Babington Macaulay, 'Minute on Indian Education' and 'Speech in the House of Commons, dated 2 February 1835', *Speeches*, ed. G. W. Young (Oxford UP, 1935); Richard Temple, *Journals* (W. H. Allen, 1887).

38. See J. A. Boone, 'Vacation Cruises; or, The Homoerotics of Orientalism', *PMLA* 110/1 (1995), 89–107; Richard Phillips, 'Writing Travel and Mapping Sexuality: Richard Burton's Sotadic Zone', in James Duncan and Derek Gregory (eds.), *Writes of Passage: Reading Travel Writing* (Routledge, 1999), 70–91; and Richard Burton, *Wanderings in Three Continents*, ed. W. H. Wilkins (Hutchinson and Co., 1901).

39. For an elaboration, see Elleke Boehmer, *Empire, the National and the Postcolonial, 1890–1920: Resistance in Interaction* (Oxford UP, 2002), 12–23; S. P. Cook, *Imperial Affinities* (New Delhi: Sage, 1993); Joseph Lennon, *Irish Orientalism* (Syracuse UP, 2004).

40. Mary Kingsley, *Travels in West Africa*, intro. E. Claridge (1897; Virago, 1986), 356–7.

Chapter 2

1. Thomas R. Metcalf, *An Imperial Vision: Indian Architecture and Britain's Raj* (Faber, 1989).

2. W. D. Arnold, *Oakfield, or Fellowship in the East* (1853; Leicester UP, 1973), 184.

3. For a theoretical exposition of the colonizer's gaze, see Mary Louise Pratt, *Imperial Eyes: Travel Writing and Transculturation* (Routledge, 1992), 15–37.

4. James Macqueen (ed.), *The Nile Basin* (Tinsley Bros., 1864), 98–9.

5. Richard Burton, *Narrative of a Pilgrimage to Mecca and Medinah*, 3rd edn. (1854; William Mullan and Son, 1879), 408–9.

6. Javed Majeed, *Ungoverned Imaginings: James Mill's* The History of British India *and Orientalism* (Oxford: Clarendon Press, 1992), informatively discusses Mill's *History* as a utilitarian document emerging out of an orientalist context.

7. See Thomas Richards, *The Imperial Archive: Knowledge and the Fantasy of Empire* (Verso, 1993).

8. Edward Thompson, *A Farewell to India* (Ernest Benn, 1931), 116.

9. See e.g. Antoinette Burton, *Burdens of History: British Feminists, Indian Women and Imperial Culture 1865–1914* (Bloomington: Indiana UP, 1994); Helen Calloway, *Gender, Culture and Empire: European Women in Colonial Nigeria* (Macmillan, 1987); Nupur Chaudhuri and Margaret Strobel (eds.), *Western Women and Imperialism: Complicity and Resistance* (Bloomington: Indiana UP, 1992); Kumari Jayawardena, *The White Woman's Other Burden: White Women and South Asia during the British Colonial Period* (Routledge, 1995); Clare Midgley (ed.), *Gender and Imperialism* (Manchester UP, 1998); Sara Mills, *Discourses of Difference: An Analysis of Women's Travel Writing and Colonialism* (Routledge, 1992); Evelyn O'Callaghan, *Women Writing the West Indies, 1804–1939* (Routledge, 2004); Pratt, *Imperial Eyes*; Dale Spender, *Writing a New World: Two Centuries of Australian Women Writers* (Pandora, 1988); Vron Ware, *Beyond the Pale: White Women, Racism and History* (Verso, 1992); and Margaret Atwood's poem series *The Journals of Susanna Moodie* (Toronto: Oxford UP, 1970).

10. Joseph Bristow, *Empire Boys: Adventures in a Man's World* (HarperCollins, 1991), and Jeffrey Richards (ed.), *Imperialism and Juvenile Literature* (Manchester UP, 1989), offer extensive coverage of Victorian boys' adventure fiction.

11. Robert Baden-Powell, *Scouting for Boys*, ed. E. Boehmer (1908; Oxford UP, 2004), throughout.

12. Robert Ackerman, *J. G. Frazer: His Life and Work* (Cambridge UP, 1987). See also Robert Young, *Colonial Desire: Hybridity in Theory, Culture and Race* (Routledge, 1995).

13. Gayatri Spivak, *The Post-Colonial Critic: Interviews, Strategies, Dialogues*, ed. Sarah Harasym (Routledge, 1990).

14. Albert Memmi, *The Colonizer and the Colonized* (Boston: Beacon, 1965); Frantz Fanon, *Black Skin, White Masks* (1952; Pluto, 1986).

15. Patrick Brantlinger, *Rule of Darkness: British Literature and Imperialism 1830–1914* (Ithaca, NY, and London: Cornell UP, 1988); Philip D. Curtin, *The Image of Africa: British Ideas and Action, 1780–1850* (Macmillan, 1965); Marcus Wood, *Blind Memory: Visual Representations of Slavery in England and America 1780–1865* (Manchester UP, 2000).

16. See Mrinalini Sinha, *Colonial Masculinity: The 'Manly Englishman' and the 'Effeminate Bengali' in the Late Nineteenth Century* (Manchester UP, 1995).

17. Olive Schreiner, *The Story of an African Farm* (1883; Virago, 1989), 131, 35, 53, 71, 111, 33–4. See also J. M. Coetzee, *White Writing: On the Culture of Letters in South Africa* (New Haven: Yale UP, 1989).

18. O. Douglas [Anna Buchan], *Olivia in India: The Adventures of a Chota Miss Sahib* (Hodder & Stoughton, 1913), 205, 97, 113. Anna Buchan ends her tale, however, with the admission: 'India has thrown gold dust in my eyes' (pp. 315–16).

19. P. J. Marshall, *East Indian Fortunes: The British in Bengal in the Eighteenth Century* (Oxford UP, 1976), and C. A. Bayly, *Imperial Meridian: The British Empire and the World 1780–1831* (Harlow: Longman, 1989). On colonial co-operations, see also Sumit Sarkar, *Modern India 1885–1947* (1983; Macmillan, 1989), and Rajeswari Sunder Rajan, *The Lie of the Land: English Literary Studies in India* (New Delhi: Oxford UP, 1992).

20. Bernard Smith, *European Vision and the South Pacific*, 2nd edn. (New Haven: Yale UP, 1984).

21. See Paul Carter, *The Road to Botany Bay* (Faber, 1987).

22. Maud Diver, *The Englishwoman in India* (William Blackwood and Sons, 1909), 4.

23. Arnold, *Oakfield*, 12–14.

Chapter 3

1. For further discussion of the term nativist, see Edward Said, *Culture and Imperialism* (Chatto and Windus, 1993), and his essay in Terry Eagleton, Fredric Jameson, and Edward W. Said, *Nationalism, Colonialism and*

Literature (Minneapolis: University of Minnesota Press, 1990). See also Kwame Anthony Appiah, *In my Father's House: Africa in the Philosophy of Culture* (Methuen, 1992).

2. Brian Willan, *Sol Plaatje: South African Nationalist 1876–1932* (Heinemann, 1984), 254, 349–61.

3. An illuminating study of reverse discourses is Jonathan Dollimore's *Sexual Dissidence: Augustine to Wilde, Freud to Foucault* (Oxford: Clarendon Press, 1991).

4. See Hannah Arendt, *The Origins of Totalitarianism* (1951; New York: Meridian, 1966), 127.

5. For writers on and of Negritude, see e.g. A. James Arnold, *Modernism and Negritude: The Poetry and Politics of Aimé Césaire* (Cambridge, Mass.: Harvard UP, 1981); Jean-Paul Sartre, *Black Orpheus*, trans. S. W. Allen (Paris: Présence Africaine, 1976); Léopold Sédar Senghor, *Poèmes* (Paris: Éditions du Seuil, 1964). See also Cheikh Anta Diop, *Cultural Unity of Black Africa* (Karnak House, 1989), and ch. 3 in Wole Soyinka, *Myth, Literature and the African World* (Cambridge UP, 1978).

6. A. C. Stephens, 'Introduction', *Bulletin Story Book* (Sydney: Bulletin Newspaper Company, 1901).

7. Joseph Furphy, *Such is Life*, ed. Vance Palmer (1903; Jonathan Cape, 1937), 18–19, 205.

8. See Krishna Dutta and Andrew Robinson, *Rabindranath Tagore: The Myriad-Minded Man* (Bloomsbury, 1995), 49, 349; and Krishna Kripalani's account of Tagore's education in *Rabindranath Tagore: A Biography* (Oxford UP, 1962).

9. To be distinguished from Édouard Glissant's concept of *creolization* as the multiply fluid intermixing of cultures and traditions in the Caribbean. See Édouard Glissant, *Poetics of Relation*, trans. Betsy Wing (1990; Ann Arbor: University of Michigan Press, 1997), and Jean Bernabé, Patrick Chamoiseau, and Raphael Confiant, *Éloge de la Créolité* (1989; Paris: Gallimard, 1993).

10. E. K. Brown, 'The Problem of a Canadian Literature' (1943). Quoted in Margaret Atwood, *Survival: A Thematic Guide to Canadian Literature* (Toronto: Anansi, 1972), 183.

11. These ideas are further developed in Elleke Boehmer, *Empire, the National, and the Postcolonial, 1890–1920: Resistance in Interaction* (Oxford UP, 2002).

12. Jawaharlal Nehru, *An Autobiography*, rev. edn. (London: Bodley Head, 1942), 25.

13. Tim Couzens, *The New African: A Study of the Life and Work of H. I. E. Dhlomo* (Johannesburg: Ravan Press, 1985).

14. See Meenakshi Mukherjee, *Realism and Reality: The Novel and Society in India* (New Delhi: Oxford UP, 1985), and *The Perishable Empire: Essays on Indian Writing in English* (New Delhi: Oxford UP, 2000).

15. Stephanie Newell, *Literary Culture in Colonial Ghana* (Manchester UP, 2002).

16. Claude McKay, *Banjo: A Story without a Plot* (Harper and Brothers, 1929), 57, 323, 105; and *Banana Bottom* (Harper & Row, 1933), 125.

17. For evocations of modernist milieux, see Raymond Williams, *The Politics of Modernism: Against the New Conformists* (Verso, 1989). See also Howard J. Booth and Nigel Rigby (eds.), *Modernism and Empire* (Manchester UP, 2000); Bruce King, *The New English Literatures* (Macmillan, 1980), 162.

18. Paul Gilroy, *The Black Atlantic: Modernity and Double Consciousness* (Verso, 1993).

19. See Angela Smith, 'Fauvism and Cultural Nationalism', *Interventions*, 4/1 (2002), 35–52. See also Paul Gauguin, *Letters from the South Seas*, trans. Ruth Pielkovo (1923; New York: Dover, 1992).

20. Mircea Eliade, *Myths, Dreams and Mysteries*, trans. Philip Mairet (Harvill, 1960), 27–38.

21. See Hugh Stevens and Caroline Howlett (eds.), *Modernist Sexualities* (Manchester UP, 2000).

22. Wole Soyinka, *Art, Dialogue and Outrage: Essays on Literature and Culture*, ed. Biodun Jeyifo (Ibadan: New Horn, 1988).

Chapter 4

1. For an extended discussion of *The Village in the Jungle* and Woolf's anti-colonialism, see Elleke Boehmer, *Empire, the National and the Postcolonial 1890–1920* (Oxford UP, 2002), 201–14.

2. See Kathy J. Phillips, *Virginia Woolf against the Empire* (Knoxville: University of Tennessee Press, 1994).

3. Virginia Woolf, *Mrs Dalloway*, ed. Claire Tomalin (Oxford UP, 1992), 71, 100, 129–30, 197, 233–4; and *Between the Acts*, ed. Frank Kermode (Oxford UP, 1992), 145–6.

4. Homi Bhabha, 'Foreword' to Frantz Fanon, *Black Skin, White Masks* (Pluto, 1986), pp. vii–xv; Gayatri Spivak, *A Critique of Postcolonial Reason: Toward a History of the Vanishing Present* (Cambridge, Mass.: Harvard UP, 1999); Robert Young, *White Mythologies: Writing, History and the West*, 2nd edn. (1990; Routledge, 2004), 1–12, explore at greater length the incorporation of otherness by the colonizer/the West.

5. For a persuasive account of the persistence of the romanticized exotic in twentieth-century cultures, see Nicholas Thomas, *Colonialism's Culture* (Cambridge: Polity, 1994). For the references to Lawrence's 1926 novel which follow, see D. H. Lawrence, *The Plumed Serpent*, ed. Ronald G. Walker (Penguin, 1983), chs. 26 and 27, in particular pp. 452, 457, 464, 466.

6. D. H. Lawrence, *Kangaroo* (Penguin, 1950), 86–7.

7. See Edward Thompson, *A Farewell to India* (Ernest Benn, 1931), 92, 118–19, 144–5.

8. Chantal Zabus, 'Answering Allegations against Alligator Writing', in C. C. Barfoot and Theo D'háen (eds.), *Shades of Empire* (Amsterdam: Rodopi, 1993); and see Chinua Achebe, *Home and Exile* (Oxford UP, 2000).

9. For further discussion of this concept, see Hélène Cixous and Catherine Clément, *The Newly-Born Woman*, trans. Betsy Wing (Manchester UP, 1986).

10. Alan Sandison, *The Wheel of Empire: A Study of the Imperial Idea* (Macmillan, 1967).

11. Valentine Cunningham, *British Writers of the Thirties* (Oxford UP, 1988), especially 384–93.

12. George Orwell, *Burmese Days: A Novel* (Secker & Warburg, 1949), 33, 39–45.

13. Graham Greene, *Journey without Maps* (Penguin, 1980), 19–21, 36.

14. For different arguments concerning colonial nationalisms as borrowed, or internally generated, see Benedict Anderson, *Imagined Communities: Reflections on the Origin and Spread of Nationalism* (1983; Verso, 1991), 47–65; Kwame Anthony Appiah, *In my Father's House: Africa in the Philosophy of Culture* (Methuen, 1992); and Partha Chatterjee, *Nationalist Thought and the Colonial World* (Zed, 1986), and *The Nation and its Fragments: Colonial and Postcolonial Histories* (Princeton UP, 1994).

15. Ashis Nandy, *The Intimate Enemy: Loss and Recovery of Self under Colonialism* (New Delhi: Oxford UP, 1983), p. xii.

16. See Spivak, *A Critique of Postcolonial Reason*, 169–97.

17. See Derek Walcott, 'The Muse of History', *What the Twilight Says* (Faber, 1998), 36–64.

18. R. K. Narayan, *The English Teacher* (Eyre & Spottiswoode, 1945), 178–80.

19. V. S. Naipaul, *A House for Mr Biswas* (Penguin, 1969), 342–6. On the search for a house, see e.g. pp. 13–14, 210–11, 316.

Chapter 5

1. On the nation as imagined construct, see Benedict Anderson, *Imagined Communities: Reflections on the Origin and Spread of Nationalism* (1983; Verso, 1991); Homi Bhabha (ed.), *Nation and Narration* (Routledge, 1990); Joe Cleary, *Literature, Partition and the Nation-State* (Cambridge UP, 2002); Ernest Gellner, *Nations and Nationalism* (Oxford: Blackwell, 1983); Sangeeta Ray, *En-gendering India: Woman and Nation in Colonial and Postcolonial Narratives* (Durham, NC: Duke UP, 2000); and Nira Yuval-Davis and Floya Anthias (eds.), *Woman—Nation—State* (Macmillan, 1989). See also Fredric Jameson's controversial but influential essay 'Third-World Literature in the Era of Multinational Capitalism', *Social Text*, 15 (1986), 65–88.

2. See Peter Abrahams, *Tell Freedom* (Faber, 1954), 197, 161.

3. It is important to note that influence moved in both directions, from the West to the decolonizing world, and vice versa. Martin Luther King, for example, drew on the example of Mohandas Gandhi; left-wing activists in Europe and the United States modelled themselves upon revolutionaries like Ernesto 'Che' Guevara and Amilcar Cabral.

4. V. S. Naipaul, *The Enigma of Arrival* (Viking, 1987), 38, 80, 297.

5. Ngugi wa Thiong'o, *The River Between* (Heinemann, 1965), 51, 78–81.

6. See Elleke Boehmer, *Stories of Women: Gender and Narrative in the Postcolonial Nation* (Manchester UP, 2005), ch. 6; James Olney, *Tell Me Africa: An Approach to African Literature* (Princeton UP, 1973).

7. Frantz Fanon, *The Wretched of the Earth*, trans. Constance Farrington (Penguin, 1986), 30–1.

8. Edward Kamau Brathwaite, *History of the Voice* (New Beacon, 1984), 30–1; Harish Trivedi, *Colonial Transactions: English Literature and India* (1993; Manchester UP, 1995), 68–79, 122–38.

9. See Mikhail Bakhtin, *The Dialogic Imagination*, ed. Michael Holquist, trans. Caryl Emerson and Michael Holquist (Austin: University of Texas Press, 1981), comprising his influential essays on the history and theory of the novel; *Problems of Dostoevsky's Poetics*, ed. and trans. Caryl Emerson (Minneapolis: Minnesota UP, 1984), which describes Dostoevsky's work as a pinnacle of the novel as a genre, due to its 'polyphonic' or many-voiced composition. On subversive rewriting, see e.g. Diana Brydon, 'Re-writing *The Tempest*', *World Literatures Written in English*, 23/1 (1984), 79–88; John Thieme, *Postcolonial Con-Texts: Writing Back to the Canon* (Continuum, 2001).

10. See also Ngugi wa Thiong'o, *Penpoints, Gunpoints, and Dreams* (Oxford UP, 1996).

11. Chinweizu, O. Jemie, and I. Madubuike, *Toward the Decolonization of African Literature* (KPI, 1985).

12. Aijaz Ahmad, *In Theory: Classes, Nations, Literatures* (Verso, 1992).

13. For descriptions of English as a world language, see e.g. S. Gramley and K. M. Patzold, *A Survey of Modern English* (Routledge, 1992); J. Cheshire (ed.), *English around the World* (Cambridge UP, 1991); and the updated David Crystal, *The Cambridge Encyclopedia of the English Language*, 2nd edn. (Cambridge UP, 2003). *The Oxford Companion to the English Language*, ed. Tom McArthur (Oxford UP, 1992), gives a country-by-country overview of the many Englishes spoken around the world today. For more on English in India, see Probal Dasgupta, *The Otherness of English: India's Auntie Tongue Syndrome* (New Delhi: Sage Publications, 1993).

14. See Brian Elliott (ed.), *The Jindyworobaks* (Brisbane: University of Queensland Press, 1979); Thomas Keneally, Robyn Davidson, Patsy Adam-Smith, *Australia: Beyond the Dreamtime* (BBC Books, 1987); and Thomas Keneally, *Memoirs from a Young Republic* (Heinemann, 1993).

15. In 1943 two Australian poets, Harold Stewart and James McAuley, who were united in their opposition to the widespread preoccupation with 'difficult' poetry in avant-garde Australia, wrote mock modernist verse which they tricked the literary world into believing was the work of a dead young poet, Ern Malley. For the full story, see Michael Heyward, *The Ern Malley Affair* (Faber, 1993).

16. Katharine Susannah Prichard, *Coonardoo: The Well in the Shadow* (Jonathan Cape, 1929), 5–6, 42, 45.

Chapter 6

1. Evelyn O'Callaghan, *Women Writing the West Indies 1804–1939* (Routledge, 2004).

2. See e.g. Susheila Nasta (ed.), *Motherlands: Black Women's Writing from Africa, the Caribbean and South Asia* (Women's Press, 1991); Sangeeta Ray, *En-gendering India: Woman and Nation in Colonial and Postcolonial Narratives* (Durham, NC: Duke UP, 2000).

3. Obioma Nnaemeka, 'Urban Spaces, Women's Places', in Nnaemeka (ed.), *The Politics of (M)Othering: Womanhood, Identity and Resistance in African Literature* (Routledge, 1997), 165. See also Shamin Meer, *Women Speak: Reflections on our Struggles 1982–1997* (Cape Town: Kwela, 1998).

4. Yvonne Vera, Preface to her edited *Opening Spaces* (Oxford: Heinemann, 1999), 3.

5. See e.g. Avtah Brah, *Cartographies of Diaspora: Contesting Identities* (Routledge, 1996); Barbara Christian, *Black Feminist Criticism:*

Perspectives on Black Women Writers (Oxford: Pergamon, 1987); Madhu Dubey, *Black Women Novelists and the Nationalist Aesthetic* (Bloomington: Indiana University Press, 1994); bell hooks, *Talking Black: Thinking Feminist Theory, Thinking Black* (London: Sheba Feminist Publishers, 1989); Trinh Minh-ha, *Woman, Native, Other* (Bloomington: Indiana UP, 1989); Chandra Talpade Mohanty *et al* (eds.), *Third World Women and the Politics of Feminism* (Bloomington: Indiana University Press, 1991); Molara Ogundipe, *Re-Creating Ourselves: African Women and Critical Transformations* (Trenton, NJ, Africa World Press, 1994).

6. Gayatri Spivak, 'The Letter as Cutting Edge', *In Other Worlds* (Methuen, 1987).

7. Kwaku Larbi Korang, 'Ama Ata Aidoo's Voyage out', *Kunapipi*, 14/3 (1992), 50–61.

8. See Minh-ha, *Woman, Native, Other*, ch. 2.

9. Sara Suleri, 'Woman Skin Deep: Feminism and the Postcolonial Condition', *Critical Inquiry*, 18 (summer 1992), 758.

10. Chris Healy, *From the Ruins of Colonialism: History as Social Memory* (Cambridge UP, 1997), 16–72. See also Nicholas Thomas, *Discoveries: The Voyages of Captain Cook* (Allen Lane, 2004).

11. V. S. Naipaul, *The Enigma of Arrival* (Penguin, 1987), 130.

12. Rushdie's essay 'Imaginary Homelands' (1982) in *Imaginary Homelands: Essays and Criticism 1981–1991* (Granta, 1991), and also the inset-meditations on the translated condition in *Shame* (1983), have laid down keystone definitions in the debate concerning the strengths of 'out-of-country' as opposed to national writing.

13. Timothy Brennan, *At Home in the World: Cosmopolitanism Now* (Cambridge, Mass.: Harvard UP, 1997), discusses the politics of the Western preference for 'cosmopolitan' over national writing. See also his essay, 'The National Longing for Form', in Homi Bhabha (ed.), *Nation and Narration* (Routledge, 1990); and *Salman Rushdie and the Third World* (Macmillan, 1989).

14. Aijaz Ahmad's now canonical criticism of cosmopolitan postcolonials appears in *In Theory: Classes, Nations, Literatures* (Verso, 1992).

15. Ben Okri, *A Way of Being Free* (Phoenix House, 1997), 100, 128–33

16. Stephen Slemon, 'Magic Realism as Post-colonial Discourse', *Canadian Literature* (spring 1988), 9–24, suggests that definitions of magic realism have been released from their Latin American context to include hybrid-ized postcolonial literatures in English. The essay is collected in Lois Parkinson Semora and Wendy B. Faris (eds.), *Magical Realism: Theory, History, Community* (Durham, NC: Duke UP, 1995), 407–26. See also

Stephen Slemon, ' "Carnival" and the Canon', *Ariel*, 19/3 (July 1988), 59–75; and 'Post-Colonial Allegory and the Transformation of History', *Journal of Commonwealth Literature*, 23/1 (1988), 157–68.

17. See Kwame Anthony Appiah, review of *The Famished Road*, *The Nation* 255/4 (Aug. 1992), 146–8.

18. Robert Young, *Postcolonialism: An Historical Introduction* (Blackwell, 2001), 6; and the new introductory chapter, '*White Mythologies* Revisited', to *White Mythologies: Writing, History and the West*, 2nd edn. (Routledge, 2004), 1–31.

19. See Kwame Anthony Appiah, 'Is the Post- in Postmodernism the Post- in Postcolonial?', *Critical Inquiry*, 17/2 (winter, 1990), 336–97, which reappears as the chapter 'The Postcolonial and the Postmodern', in *In my Father's House: Africa in the Philosophy of Culture* (Methuen, 1992); Ben Okri, 'Redreaming the World: For Chinua Achebe', *A Way of Being Free*, 128–33; Gayatri Spivak, *Death of a Discipline* (New York: Columbia UP, 2003). It is pertinent that in this last-named book, Spivak rousingly calls for a displacement of comparative literary studies through 'careful reading' and an 'engagement with the idiom of the global other(s)' (pp. 10, 66).

20. Nayantara Sahgal, 'The Schizophrenic Imagination', in Shirley Chew and Anna Rutherford (eds.), *Unbecoming Daughters of the Empire* (Aarhus: Dangaroo, 1993); widely reproduced.

21. The debate for and against postcolonial writing as the 'other' of metropolitan critical theory is crystallized (not always self-consciously so) in the Jameson and Ahmad exchange. See Fredric Jameson, 'Third World Literature in the Era of Multinational Capital', *Social Text*, 15 (fall 1986), 65–88, and Ahmad's reply in *In Theory*, 95–122. See also: Aijaz Ahmad, *Lineages of the Present: Ideology and Politics in Contemporary South Asia* (Verso, 2000); David Scott, *Refashioning Futures: Criticism after Postcoloniality* (Princeton UP, 1999), 142; Stephen Slemon and Helen Tiffin, 'Introduction', *After Europe: Critical Theory and Post-Colonial Writing* (Aarhus: Dangaroo, 1989), pp. ix–xxiii.

22. Vijay Mishra and Bob Hodge, 'What is Post(-)colonialism?', *Textual Practice*, 5/3 (winter 1991), 399–414, at 401–4. Also useful are the responses to related questions in *Interventions: International Journal of Postcolonial Studies*, 1/1 (1998).

23. James Clifford, 'Notes on Travel and Theory', *Inscriptions*, 5 (1989), 177–87; Homi Bhabha, *The Location of Culture* (London: Routledge, 1994), 126–7.

Chapter 7: Afterword

1. Mike Featherstone, Scott Lash, and Roland Robertson (eds.), 'Introduction', *Global Modernities* (Sage, 1995), 2–3.

2. See Graham Huggan, *The Postcolonial Exotic* (Routledge, 2001), 5–7.

3. For their comments on postcolonialism's neo-colonial complicities, see also: Ania Loomba, *Colonialism/Postcolonialism* (Routledge, 1998), 245–58; Bart Moore-Gilbert, *Postcolonial Theory: Contexts, Practices, Politics* (Verso, 1997), 3–4, 17–21, 185–203.

4. Padmini Mongia, 'Introduction' to her edited *Contemporary Postcolonial Theory: A Reader* (Arnold, 1996), 7.

5. Ali Behdad, *Belated Travelers: Orientalism in the Age of Colonial Dissolution* (Durham, NC: Duke UP, 1996), 6–8; Derek Gregory, *The Colonial Present: Afghanistan, Palestine, Iraq* (Blackwell, 2004), 9.

6. George Lamming, 'Sea of Stories', *Guardian2* (24 Oct. 2002), 14–15. For obvious geographical reasons, Caribbean writers register acutely this sense of immediate imperial succession.

7. Arundhati Roy, *The Algebra of Infinite Justice* (Viking, 2001), 200.

8. Michael Hardt and Antonio Negri, *Empire* (Cambridge, Mass.: Harvard UP, 2000).

9. Dipesh Chakrabarty, *Provincializing Europe: Postcolonial Thought and Historical Difference* (Princeton UP, 2000). The home v. world opposition is memorably captured in the title of Rabindranath Tagore's novel *Ghare Bhair (The Home and the World)*, trans. Surendranath Tagore (1916/1919), a meditation on the meanings of modernity for 'Renaissance' Bengal in the early twentieth century.

10. Caryl Phillips, *Higher Ground* (Faber, 1989), 79.

11. Derek Walcott, 'The Muse of History' (1974), in *What the Twilight Says* (Faber, 1998), 36–64.

12. Parsilelo Kantai in conversation with Mpalive Msiska, Caine Prize for African Writing Symposium, University of London School of Advanced Studies, Senate House, 21 July 2004; Helon Habila, 'African Renaissance', *Guardian Review* (12 June 2004), 7.

13. Arundhati Roy, *The God of Small Things* (Flamingo, 1997), 126.

14. Ruth Frankenberg and Lata Mani, 'Crosscurrents, Crosstalk: Race, "Postcoloniality", and the Politics of Location', and Ella Shohat, 'Notes on the Post-Colonial', both in Mongia (ed.), *Contemporary Postcolonial Theory*, 322–34, and 347–64. See also Roland Robertson, 'Glocalization: Time–Space and Homogeneity–Heterogeneity', in Featherstone et al. (eds.), *Global Modernities*, 25–44.

15. See Aijaz Ahmad, 'The Politics of Literary Postcoloniality', *Race and Class*, 36/3 (1995).

16. See e.g. Ama Ata Aidoo, 'That Capacious Topic: Gender Politics', in Phil Mariani (ed.), *Critical Fictions* (Seattle: Bay Press, 1991), 152.

17. Peter Hallward, *Absolutely Postcolonial: Writing between the Singular and the Specific* (Manchester UP, 2001). See also Alfred J. Lopez, *Posts and Pasts: A Theory of Postcolonialism* (New York: State University of New York Press, 2001).

18. See e.g. David Scott, *Refashioning Futures: Criticism after Postcoloniality* (Princeton UP, 1999).

19. Amit Chaudhuri, 'In the Waiting Room of History', *London Review of Books*, 26/12 (24 June 2004), 3–8.

20. Achille Mbembe, 'Necropolitics', *Public Culture*, 15 (2003), 11–40; and *On the Postcolony*, trans. A. M. Berrett et al. (Berkeley: University of California Press, 2001).

21. For an in-depth reading of the novel's sexuality, see Alison Donnell, *Twentieth-Century Caribbean Literature* (Routledge, 2005).

22. On women's politics of 'intersectionality', see e.g. Avtar Brah, *Cartographies of Diaspora: Contesting Identities* (Routledge, 1996).

23. Saskia Sassen, *Global Networks, Linked Cities* (Routledge, 2002).

24. See Paul Gilroy, *'There Ain't No Black in the Union Jack'* (Hutchinson, 1987), 19.

25. Hanif Kureishi, *Dreaming and Scheming: Reflections on Writing and Politics* (Faber, 2002), 55.

26. Stuart Hall, 'Reinventing Britain: A Forum', *Wasafiri*, 29 (spring 1999), 38.

27. See Bernardine Evaristo, 'In Conversation' (with Alastair Niven), *Wasafiri*, 34 (autumn 2001), 15–20; Peter Fryer, *Staying Power: The History of Black People in Britain* (Pluto, 1984); John McLeod, *Postcolonial London* (Routledge, 2004), 177–88.

28. Gayatri Spivak, *Death of a Discipline* (New York: Columbia UP, 2003).

29. As a reminder, see Edward Said, *Reflections on Exile* (Granta, 2001), 583.

30. Benita Parry, *Postcolonial Studies: A Materialist Critique* (Routledge, 2004), 9.

31. For a countervailing interpretation of such 're-presencing', see Bill Ashcroft, *Post-Colonial Transformation* (Routledge, 2001), 215–25.

32. Frantz Fanon, *The Wretched of the Earth*, trans. Constance Farrington (1961; Penguin, 1986), 27.

Annotated Bibliography
Compiled with Ranka Primorac

SUBJECTS as broad and ramifying as colonial discourse and postcolonial literature and criticism—which, moreover, remain in a process of formation —are, not surprisingly, served by a growing number of histories, readers, and critical studies. While the following annotated list can make no claim to be exhaustive, it aims to offer a wide, representative range of useful general readings, keynote critical works, and definitive theoretical and thematic studies. The majority of texts cited in the suggested Further Reading sections and in the Notes are included, in particular those which cover topics central to the book's main arguments. Other than where titles are broadly self-explanatory, descriptive tags are used both to offer pointers to readers new to the field, and to assist with and encourage further exploration.

As is the case throughout this book, unless otherwise stated, place of publication for Penguin books is Harmondsworth; that for University Presses is generally implied by the university's name; in other cases where place of publication is unstated it should be taken as London.

1. History and biography

Ackerman, Robert, *J. G. Frazer: His Life and Work* (Cambridge UP, 1987).
  A scholarly biography of the influential armchair anthropologist.
Aldrich, Robert, *Colonialism and Homosexuality* (Routledge, 2003).
  A sometimes derivative narrative which does, however, open new ground in this area.
Anderson, Benedict, *Imagined Communities: Reflections on the Origin and Spread of Nationalism* (1983; Verso, 1991).
  The widely influential theorization of nations as imaginary constructs, rather than entities based on fact or territory.
Angier, Carole, *Jean Rhys* (André Deutsch, 1990).
  Currently the most extensive biography of the Dominican creole writer.
Assad, Thomas, *Three Victorian Travellers: Burton, Blunt, Doughty* (Routledge & Kegan Paul, 1964).
  Concerns itself with the impressions of Arabic culture on three Victorian men of letters who travelled to the Middle or Near East before Lawrence of Arabia.
Barley, Nigel, *White Rajah: A Biography of Sir James Brooke* (Boston: Little, Brown, 2002).

The extraordinary life-story of the Victorian adventurer who became the sole ruler of the small kingdom of Sarawak on the island of Borneo.

Bayly, C. A., *Imperial Meridian: The British Empire and the World 1780–1830* (Harlow: Longman, 1989).

An outline of the expansion of British domination—particularly in Asia and the Middle East—between the loss of America and the subsequent partition of Africa.

—— *Indian Society and the Making of the British Empire* (Cambridge UP, 1988).

A study of the nature and extent of India's transformation under imperial rule.

Beaglehole, J. C., *The Discovery of New Zealand* (Wellington: Department of Internal Affairs, 1939).

A comprehensive early account of settlement in New Zealand, from Maori to European times. Though superseded by later studies, this was a breakthrough in its time.

Berman, Bruce, and John Lonsdale, *Unhappy Valley*, 2 vols. (James Currey, 1993).

Marxist explorations of the violent, contested history of colonial Kenya.

Blackburn, Robin, *The Overthrow of Colonial Slavery 1776–1848* (Verso, 1989).

A monumental study of the interaction between contestations of empire and contestations of slavery in a period of rivalry between empires.

Brown, Judith M., *Gandhi: Prisoner of Hope* (New Haven: Yale UP, 1989).

A humanist treatment of Gandhi's political career.

Brydon, Diana, *Christina Stead* (Macmillan, 1987).

A study of the life and work of the iconoclastic Australian novelist.

Butalia, Urvashi, *The Other Side of Silence: Voices from the Partition of India* (Hurst and Company, 2000).

At the heart of this book lie testimonies of women, men, and children affected by the violent Partition of the Indian subcontinent.

Cain, P. J., and A. G. Hopkins, *British Imperialism: Crisis and Deconstruction 1914–1990* (Harlow: Longman, 1993).

Traces the role of 'Gentlemanly Capitalism'—a set of complex economic, social, and political influences concentrated in the City of London—in the twentieth century, challenging the standard view of the period as one long retreat from empire.

Carrington, C. E., *The British Overseas: Exploits of a Nation of Shopkeepers* (Macmillan, 1955).

An overarching study of the motive force behind the spread of the British Empire, and the behaviour of British pioneers and emigrants 'in the empty lands of the temperate zone'.

Charlesworth, Neil, *British Rule and the Indian Economy 1800–1914* (Macmillan, 1982).
An economic history of India in the nineteenth century, showing the effects of imperial rule on a non-western economy and society.

Cohen, Bernard S., *An Anthropologist among the Historians* (New Delhi: Oxford UP, 1990).
An anthropological 'take' on the history and society of colonial and postcolonial India.

Colley, Linda, *Britons: Forging the Nation 1701–1837* (BCA, 1992).
The prominent historian argues that, during the eighteenth century, war and religion were the main factors in forging a British national consciousness, especially in contradistinction to France.

—— *Captives: Britain, Empire and the World 1600–1850* (Jonathan Cape, 2002).
A study of the fates and writings of Britons who were taken captive in different regions outside Europe during the first quarter-millennium of the British imperial enterprise.

Curtin, Philip D., *The Atlantic Slave Trade: A Census* (Madison: University of Wisconsin Press, 1969).

—— *Death by Migration* (Cambridge UP, 1989).
An empirical study of the human cost of colonization in Africa and its diaspora.

Darwin, John, *Britain and Decolonization: The Retreat from Empire in the Post-war World* (Macmillan, 1988).

—— *The End of the British Empire: The Historical Debate* (Oxford: Blackwell, 1991).
Studies the winding-down of the British imperial system and the deeper motives for decolonization.

Davidson, Basil, *Africa in History* (Paladin, 1984).
In an effort to give Africa its place in history, Davidson offers examples of sophisticated African cultures, including their regional and international transactions.

—— *The Black Man's Burden: Africa and the Curse of the Nation-State* (James Currey, 1992).
A meditation on the nature of the African experience since the beginning of emergence from foreign rule, and the degradation of the hopes and freedoms of postcolonial independence.

Davis, Lance E., and Robert Huttenback, *Mammon and the Pursuit of Empire* (Cambridge UP, 1986).
Focuses on the 'profitability of Empire' in the five decades preceding the First World War, and on the identity of players in the 'imperial game'.

Doyle, Michael W., *Empires* (Ithaca, NY: Cornell UP, 1986).
Combining theoretical analysis and historical description, this study considers empires from the classical and the modern world, beginning with Athens, Sparta, and Rome, and focusing especially on the Scramble for Africa.

Dutta, Krishna, and Andrew Robinson, *Rabindranath Tagore: The Myriad-Minded Man* (Bloomsbury, 1995).
A comprehensive portrait of the great Bengali poet in all his multifariousness.

Dutton, Geoffrey, *The Hero as Murderer: The Life of Edward John Eyre, Australian Explorer and Governor of Jamaica 1815–1901* (Collins, 1967).

—— *Kenneth Slessor: A Biography* (Viking, 1991).
A full-length biography of the early twentieth-century Australian modernist poet.

Eddy, John, and Deryck Schreuder (eds.), *The Rise of Colonial Nationalism 1850–1914* (Sydney: Allen & Unwin, 1988).
A collection of essays exploring the first stirrings of a sense of nationalism in the white settlers of Australia, New Zealand, Canada, and South Africa.

Ellis, David, and James Walvin, *The Abolition of the Atlantic Slave Trade* (Madison: University of Wisconsin Press, 1981).

Esedebe, Olisanwuche, *Pan-Africanism: The Idea and the Movement* (Washington, DC: Howard UP, 1982).
A detailed study of the origins and development of the Pan-Africanist movement.

Fabre, Michel, *From Harlem to Paris: Black American Writers in Paris, 1840–1980* (Urbana: University of Illinois Press, 1991).

Forsdick, Charles, and David Murphy (eds.), *Francophone Postcolonial Studies: A Critical Introduction* (London: Arnold, 2003).
A landmark collection that aims to create a long overdue dialogue between francophone and anglophone postcolonial critics.

Foster, R. F., *Modern Ireland 1600–1972* (Allen Lane, 1988).

Gourevitch, Philip, *We Wish to Inform You that Tomorrow We will be Killed with Our Families: Stories from Rwanda* (Picador, 1998).
A journalistic account of the genocide in Rwanda in the 1990s.

Gellner, Ernest, *Nations and Nationalism* (Oxford: Blackwell, 1983).
A significant study of the historical causes of nationalism, which it sees as rooted in modern/industrial social organization.

Hobsbawm, E. J., *The Age of Capital 1848–1875* (Weidenfeld & Nicolson, 1975).

—— *The Age of Empire 1875–1914* (Weidenfeld & Nicolson, 1987).

—— *The Age of Revolution 1789–1848* (1962; Cardinal, 1988).

This classic series begins with the transformational changes within English and European society at the end of the eighteenth century, and gives a history of western imperialism up to the First World War.

—— *Nations and Nationalism since 1780: Programme, Myth, Reality* (Cambridge UP, 1990).
A history of the advent of nationalism as tied to the concept of the modern state.

Hopkirk, Peter, *The Great Game: On Secret Service in High Asia* (Oxford UP, 1991).
Elaborating Kipling's metaphor in *Kim*, Hopkirk offers a historical narrative of the British and Russian officers and explorers who participated in the clandestine struggle for political ascendency in nineteenth-century central Asia.

Howe, Stephen, *Anti-colonialism in British Politics: The Left and the End of Empire 1928–1964* (Oxford: Clarendon Press, 1993).
Examines anti-colonialist attitudes, activities, and organizations in Britain during the years of decolonization.

Hyam, Ronald, *Britain's Imperial Century 1815–1914: A Study of Empire and Expansion* (Macmillan, 1993).
Incorporates regional examples of British overseas activity into a world-wide imperial pattern, while consciously avoiding 'abstract theorizing'.

James, Lawrence, *The Rise and Fall of the British Empire* (Abacus, 1994).
A sweeping survey of British imperialism and its legacies, spanning four centuries and six continents.

Jeal, Tim, *Baden-Powell* (Hutchinson, 1989).
The authoritative biography of the founder of the world-wide Scout Movement.

Johnson, Gordon (ed.), *The New Cambridge History of India* (Cambridge UP, 1987).
A multi-volume series with an underlying four-part structure, which aims to supersede the original *Cambridge History of India*, published between 1922 and 1937. Concludes with a substantial bibliographical essay.

Joll, James, *Europe since 1870: An International History*, 3rd edn. (Penguin, 1983).
A broad, synthetic work aiming to describe and analyse the great mass movements that evolved between the 1870s and the 1970s: liberalism, imperialism, fascism, socialism, and communism.

Judd, Denis, *Empire: The British Imperial Experience, from 1765 to the Present* (Fontana, 1996).
An authoritative historical treatment of British imperialism, with chapters focusing on individual colonies and key historical episodes.

Judt, Tony, *Past Imperfect: French Intellectuals 1944–1956* (Berkeley: University of California Press, 1993).
A damning study of a 'progressive' cultural élite's 'refusal to listen' during a turbulent period in the world's history.

Kiernan, V. G., *European Empires from Conquest to Collapse* (Leicester UP and Fontana, 1982).
Scrutinizes empire-related wars from the early nineteenth to the mid-twentieth century.

—— *The Lords of Human Kind: Black Man, Yellow Man and White Man in an Age of Empire* (Weidenfeld & Nicolson, 1969).
A survey of European attitudes to 'inferior races', and of their views of Europeans in the age of imperialism.

—— *Marxism and Imperialism* (Edward Arnold, 1974).

Klein, Naomi, *No Logo* (Flamingo, 2001).
An analysis of the rise of the superbrand in a world dominated by transnational corporate power, and of the global forces opposing corporate rule.

Koebner, Richard, and Helmut Dan Schmidt, *Imperialism: The Story and Significance of a Political Word, 1840–1960* (Cambridge UP, 1964).
A historically grounded etymology of the word imperialism.

Louis, William Roger (ed.), *Imperialism: The Robinson and Gallagher Controversy* (New York: Franklin Watts, 1976).
A discussion of the revisionist work of the historians Robinson and Gallagher, which argued that Britain's policy in Africa was not deliberately imperialist, but was precipitated by a persistent crisis in Egypt.

Low, D. A., *Eclipse of Empire* (Cambridge UP, 1991).
Essays dealing with the passing of the British Empire in South Asia and Africa, and the sense of positive achievement that this engendered.

MacKenzie, John, *Propaganda and Empire* (Manchester UP, 1984).

McLynn, Frank, *Burton: Snow upon the Desert* (John Murray, 1990).
A 'psycho-biographical' approach to the life of the Victorian adventurer and translator of the *Arabian Nights*, Richard Burton.

—— *Robert Louis Stevenson* (Hutchinson, 1993).
Both a biography and an attempt to reverse Stevenson's critical reputation as mainly a writer of adventure stories.

Maloba, Wunyabari, *Mau Mau and Kenya: An Analysis of a Peasant Revolt* (Bloomington: Indiana UP, 1994)
A contribution to the debate about the role of the 'Mau Mau' or Land and Freedom peasant revolt in Kenya, within the larger context of the politics of decolonization.

Marshall, P. J., *East Indian Fortunes: The British in Bengal in the Eighteenth Century* (Oxford UP, 1976).
Traces the acquisition of British wealth in Bengal, arguing that territorial empire and commercial hegemony grew out of the pursuit of private fortunes.

Matthews, Brian, *Federation* (Melbourne: Text Publishing, 1999).
A popular account of the coming-into-being of the Australian nation, illustrated with contemporary photographs.

Mills, Sara, *Discourses of Difference: An Analysis of Women's Travel Writing and Colonialism* (Routledge, 1992).
A path-breaking Foucauldian reading of women travel writers.

Moore, R. J., *Escape from Empire: The Attlee Government and the Indian Problem* (Oxford: Clarendon Press, 1983).
Describes the political manoeuvrings involved in British disengagement in India.

Morris, Jan, *Farewell the Trumpets: An Imperial Retreat* (Faber, 1978).
—— *Heaven's Command* (Faber, 1973).
—— *Pax Britannica* (Faber, 1968).
A historical triptych depicting the rise, climax and decline of Queen Victoria's empire, invoking the themes of adventure, duty and burden before final collapse.
—— *The Spectacle of Empire: Style, Effect and Pax Britannica* (Faber, 1982).
A richly illustrated work concerned with the visual impressions that the British Empire sought to imprint on the rest of the world and on its own creators.

Mukasa, Ham, *Uganda's Katikiro in England*, intro. Simon Gikandi (Manchester UP, 1998).
An early twentieth-century narrative representation of England, by a member of the African native élite.

Nixon, Rob, *Homelands, Harlem and Hollywood: South African Culture and the World Beyond* (Routledge, 1994).

Padmore, George (ed.), *History of the Pan-African Congress* (1947; Hammersmith Bookshop, 1963).
The proceedings of the Fifth Pan-Africanist Congress held in Manchester in 1945. The congress 'marked the turning point in pan-Africanism from a passive to an active stage'.

Pakenham, Thomas, *The Scramble for Africa 1876–1912* (Weidenfeld & Nicolson, 1991).
A narrative of the competitive rush of late nineteenth-century European leaders to build empires in Africa.

Pocock, Tom, *Rider Haggard and the Lost Empire* (Weidenfeld and Nicolson, 1993).
A well-grounded biography of Haggard that assesses his achievements as a novelist, soldier, politician, and ideologue of Empire.

Porter, Bernard, *The Lion's Share: A Short History of British Imperialism*, 2nd edn. (Harlow: Longman, 1982).
A synoptic overview of British imperialism from its Victorian heydey to the 1982 Falklands war.

Potts, Lydia, *The World Labour Market: A History of Migration* (Zed, 1990).
A wide-ranging study of the world labour market and the movement of workers across the globe over the past five centuries.

Owen, Roger, *Lord Cromer: Victorian Imperialist, Edwardian Proconsul* (Oxford UP, 2004).
A scholarly biography of Evelyn Baring, Lord Cromer, the uncharismatic and tenacious architect of British primacy in Egypt from 1883.

Robinson, Ronald, and John Gallagher, *Africa and the Victorians: The Official Mind of Imperialism* (Macmillan, 1961).
A controversial study of the motives behind British expansion into Africa, whose argument hinges on the distinction between the 'subjective motives' and 'objective causes' relating to the partition of the continent.

Rodney, Walter, *How Europe Underdeveloped Africa* (Bogle L'Ouverture Publications, 1972).
The classical (and to an extent polemical) account of how the rush to imperialism was a rush for the raw materials of Africa.

Rotberg, Robert I., *The Founder: Cecil Rhodes and the Pursuit of Power* (Oxford UP, 1988).
A detailed biographical account, seeking to be both psychologically and historically convincing.

Sahlins, Marshall, *Historical Metaphors and Mythical Realities: Structure in the Early History of the Sandwich Islands Kingdom* (Ann Arbor: University of Michigan Press, 1982).
A structuralist study of how indigenous Hawaiian culture reacted to the appearance of Captain Cook and later European explorers, traders, and missionaries.

Sarkar, Sumit, *Modern India 1885–1947* (1983; Macmillan, 1989).
A dense, increasingly canonical history which takes on board popular movements from below.

Schneer, Jonathan, *London 1900: The Imperial Metropolis* (New Haven: Yale UP, 1999).
An examination of the relationship between the British Empire and its capital city at the turn of the century.

Shennan, Margaret, *Out in the Midday Sun: The British in Malaya, 1880–1960* (John Murray, 2002).

Sinha, Mrinalini, *Colonial Masculinity: The 'Manly Englishman' and the 'Effeminate Bengali' in the Late Nineteenth Century* (Manchester UP, 1995).

Smith, Angela, *Katherine Mansfield and Virginia Woolf: A Public of Two* (Oxford UP, 1999).

Thompson, Edward, and G. T. Garratt, *Rise and Fulfilment of British Rule in India* (Allahabad: Central Book Depot, 1934).
A colonial history of modern India and its relationship to Britain, which sees the two countries as closely linked by 'fate', yet manages to find, on the eve of decolonization, 'grounds for a guarded optimism about the future of the Indian race'.

Tinker, Hugh, *A New System of Slavery: The Export of Indian Labour Overseas 1830–1920* (Oxford UP, 1974).
A comprehensive study of the process of emigration from rural India across the seas, to more than a dozen countries where cheap labour was needed.

Tomalin, Claire, *Katherine Mansfield: A Secret Life* (Viking, 1987).
Explores the previously under-played aspects of the migrant New Zealand writer's life.

Viswanathan, Gauri, *Outside the Fold: Conversion, Modernity and Belief* (Princeton UP, 1998).
A study of religious conversion as a spiritual, cultural, and political activity which can function as a destabilizing force and therefore as a form of struggle for basic rights. Case studies draw on the histories of Britain and India.

Walvin, James, *Passage to Britain: Immigration in British History and Politics* (Penguin, 1984).
A leading account of the impact of immigration on postcolonial British society.

Willan, Brian, *Sol Plaatje: South African Nationalist 1876–1932* (Heinemann, 1984).
A study of the life and accomplishments of the South African journalist, translator, and political leader.

Williams, Eric, *Capitalism and Slavery* (New York: Russell & Russell, 1961).
A classic account of the contribution of slavery to the development of British capitalism.

—— *From Columbus to Castro: The History of the Caribbean 1492–1969* (André Deutsch, 1970).

A wide-ranging collection of over eighty texts and (mainly) extracts, organized around fourteen thematic headings, amongst others, 'Nationalism', 'The Body and Performance', and 'Place'.

Ashcroft, Bill, Gareth Griffiths, and Helen Tiffin, *Key Concepts in Post-Colonial Studies* (Routledge, 1998).
An easy-to-use glossary of dozens of concepts commonly used in postcolonial studies. Includes a list of terms, a bibliography, and name and subject indexes.

Attridge, Derek, and Rosemary Jolly (eds.), *Writing South Africa: Recent Literature and its Challenges* (Cambridge UP, 1998).

Atwood, Bain, and Andrew Markus (eds.), *The Struggle for Aboriginal Rights: A Documentary History* (Sydney: Allen & Unwin, 1999).
A compilation of historical documents, accompanied by a commentary, that tells the history of the political struggle for Aboriginal rights in Australia.

Barfoot, C. C., and Theo D'háen (eds.), *Shades of Empire* (Amsterdam: Rodopi, 1993).
Diverse articles on a range of postcolonial topics.

Barker, Francis, Peter Hulme, and Margaret Iversen (eds.), *Colonial Discourse/ Postcolonial Theory* (Manchester UP, 1994)
A challenging book of essays dealing critically with some key concepts in postcolonialism, by Simon During, Neil Lazarus, and Anne McClintock amongst others.

—— —— Margaret Iversen, and Diana Loxley (eds.), *Literature, Politics and Theory: Papers from the Essex Conference 1976–84* (Methuen, 1986).
Selected papers from the early Sociology of Literature conferences, some with new introductions. Raymond Williams, Fredric Jameson, Catherine Belsey, and Homi Bhabha, amongst others, are featured.

Bassnett, Susan, and Harish Trivedi (eds.), *Postcolonial Translation: Theory and Practice* (Routledge, 1999).

Baugh, Edward (ed.), *Critics on Caribbean Literature: Readings in Literary Criticism* (Allen and Unwin, 1978).
A frequently cited selection of criticism on the literature of the English-speaking Caribbean.

Bennett, Bruce (ed.), *A Sense of Exile: Essays in the Literature of the Asia Pacific Region* (Perth: Centre for Studies in Australian Literature, 1988).
Explorations of the historical, linguistic, and psychological effects of a sense of 'separation from home' in Australian and other literatures.

—— Susan Cowan, Jacqueline Lo, Satendra Nandan, and Jen Webb (eds.), *Resistance and Reconciliation: Writing in the Commonwealth* (Canberra: ACLALS, 2003).

Twenty-seven essays related to issues concerning the writing, culture, and politics of a variety of late twentieth-century Commonwealth societies.

Benson, Eugene, and L. W. Conolly (eds.), *Encyclopedia of Post-Colonial Literatures in English*, 2 vols. (Routledge, 1994).

A useful, multi-authored reference tool, with entries on a broad range of postcolonial authors, genres, regions, critical categories, and concepts.

Bhabha, Homi (ed.), *Nation and Narration* (Routledge, 1990).

This much-quoted, agenda-setting collection highlights a range of questions and problems concerned with the concepts of nation, national culture, and a national literary canon, strongly influenced by the work of Benedict Anderson.

Boehmer, Elleke (ed.), *Empire Writing: An Anthology of Colonial Literature, 1870–1918* (Oxford UP, 1998).

—— Laura Chrisman, and Kenneth Parker (eds.), *Altered State?: Writing and South Africa* (Sydney: Dangaroo, 1994).

Published to mark the beginning of the post-apartheid era, this collection explores literary and cultural struggles in a changing South Africa.

Booth, Howard J., and Nigel Rigby (eds.), *Modernism and Empire* (Manchester UP, 2000).

Thirteen essays examining various aspects of the mobile interface between modernism and colonialism. The volume includes a theoretical overview and chapters on Yeats, Kipling, Joyce, Lawrence, and Leonard Woolf.

Bove, Paul A. (ed.), *Edward Said and the Work of the Critic: Speaking Truth to Power* (Durham NC: Duke UP, 2000).

A collection of essays enlarging on characteristic aspects of Said's work, including music, aesthetic responsibility, and the role of the intellectual. Includes an interview with Said by Jacqueline Rose.

Breckenridge, Carol A., and Peter van der Veer (eds.), *Orientalism and the Postcolonial Predicament: Perspectives on South Asia* (Philadelphia: University of Philadelphia Press, 1993).

Bruner, Charlotte H. (ed.), *Unwinding Threads: Writing by Women in Africa* (Heinemann, 1983).

A collection of short extracts covering the work of women writers from the three major regions of sub-Saharan Africa and from the Maghreb.

Busby, Margaret (ed.), *Daughters of Africa: An International Anthology of Words and Writings by Women of African Descent from the Ancient Egypt to the Present* (Cape, 1992).

Cantrell, Leon (ed.), *The 1890s: Stories, Verse and Essays* (Brisbane: University of Queensland Press, 1977).

A representative selection of work from the *Bulletin* generation.

Castle, Gregory (ed.), *Postcolonial Discourses: An Anthology* (Oxford: Blackwell, 2001).
Beginning with an overview introduction, this collection of twenty-six essays on postcolonial legacies, mostly by mainstream critics, is organized according to region (for example, 'Indian Nations', 'Caribbean Encounters').

Chambers, Iain, and Lidia Curti (eds.), *The Post-Colonial Question: Common Skies, Divided Horizons* (Routledge, 1996).
Perspectives on a variety of postcolonial topics, ranging from imperial histories to contemporary space–times. The collection includes a creative piece by Hanif Kureishi.

Chaturvedi, Vinayak (ed.), *Mapping Subaltern Studies and the Postcolonial* (Verso: 2000).
A mapping of the intellectual terrain of the Subaltern Studies project and the debates surrounding it. The project set out to revise the elitist approaches to Indian history, and turned into a global academic institution.

Cheshire, J. (ed.), *English around the World* (Cambridge UP, 1991).

Chew, Shirley, and Lynette Hunter (eds.), *Borderblur: Poetry and Poetics in Contemporary Canadian Literature* (Edinburgh: Quadriga, 1996).
Essays on Canadian writers of various ethnic origins.

—— and Anna Rutherford (eds.), *Unbecoming Daughters of the Empire* (Aarhus: Dangaroo, 1993).
Personal reminiscences by women writers and critics brought up in various parts of the Commonwealth.

Childs, Peter, and Patrick Williams, *An Introduction to Post-Colonial Theory* (Hemel Hempstead: Prentice-Hall, 1997).
Summarizes key debates in the work of prominent theorists, in particular, Fanon, Said, Bhabha, and Spivak. Includes a glossary of theoretical terms.

Chrisman, Laura, and Benita Parry (eds.), *Postcolonial Theory and Criticism* (Cambridge: D. S. Brewer, 2000).
Covering the geographical regions of the Americas, India, the Caribbean, the Pacific, Africa, and Britain, literary discussions of colonialist, modern anti-colonial, and contemporary postcolonial writings feature alongside theoretical explorations of imperialism and neo-colonialism.

Cobham, Rhonda, and Merle Collins (eds.), *Watchers and Seekers: Creative Writing by Black Women in Britain* (Women's Press, 1987).

Davies, Carol Boyce, and Anne Adams Graves (eds.), *Ngambika: Studies of Women in African Literature* (Trenton, NJ: Africa World Press, 1986).

—— and Elaine Savory Fido (eds.), *Out of the Kumbla: Caribbean Women and Literature* (Trenton, NJ: Africa World Press, 1990).

Davis, Jack, and Bob Hodge (eds.), *Aboriginal Writing Today: Papers from the*

First National Conference of Aboriginal Writers Held in Perth, Western Australia, in 1983 (Canberra: Australian Institute of Aboriginal Studies, 1985).

Docker, John, and Gerhard Fischer (eds.), *Race, Colour and Identity in Australia and New Zealand* (Sydney: University of New South Water Press, 2000).
An interdisciplinary collection of essays dealing with the multiple inter-sections of identity in the two settler postcolonies.

Donnell, Alison, and Sarah Lawson Welsh (eds.), *The Routledge Reader in Caribbean Literature* (Routledge, 1996).
An authoritative anthology of twentieth-century fiction, poetry, and prose from the anglophone Caribbean, divided according to chronology and genre. Introductory sections precede the chronological segments.

Drayton, Richard, and Andaiye (eds.), *Conversations: George Lamming: Essays, Addresses and Interviews 1953–1990* (Karia Press, 1992).
An assemblage of key essays, talks, and interviews by the eminent Barbadian writer, sympathetic to his radical viewpoints.

Eldridge, C. C., *The Imperial Experience: From Carlyle to Forster* (Macmillan, 1996).
An introductory study tracing the interweaving of history and literature in Britain from the first half of the nineteenth century to the First World War.

Fincham, Gail, and Myrtle Hooper (eds.), *Under Postcolonial Eyes: Joseph Conrad after Empire* (University of Cape Town Press, 1996).
Conrad's fiction is re-assessed within a cultural studies framework, organ-ized under the headings, 'Conrad and Empire', 'Representations of Race, Class and Gender', and 'Intertextuality'.

Fletcher, D. M. (ed.), *Reading Rushdie: Perspectives on the Fiction of Salman Rushdie* (Amsterdam: Rodopi, 1994).
Wide-ranging essays on Rushdie's five novels to date.

Gandhi, Leela, *Postcolonial Theory: A Critical Introduction* (Edinburgh UP, 1998).
A succinct introduction to the intellectual background of postcolonialism, especially concerning India, which places Gandhi as a keynote thinker of anti-colonial resistance alongside Fanon.

Gates, Henry Louis, Jnr. (ed.), *Black Literature and Literary Theory* (Methuen, 1984).
Eminent scholars of African and African American writing examine the consequences of drawing on Western theories to explicate texts by black writers.

—— (ed.), *'Race', Writing and Difference* (University of Chicago Press, 1986).
Distinguished contributors—Jacques Derrida, Sander Gilman, Edward

Said, Tzvetan Todorov, and others—consider the issue of racial difference in various modes of discourse.

Giddings, Robert (ed.), *Literature and Imperialism* (Macmillan, 1991).
Essays on the impact of empire in fiction by Conrad, Forster, Ballantyne, Rushdie, T. E Lawrence, and others.

Goodwin, K. L. (ed.), *National Identity* (Heinemann, 1970).
An important early collection tracing linkages between Commonwealth writing and issues of national identity and cultural exchange.

Graham, Duncan (ed.), *Being Whitefella* (South Freemantle: Freemantle Arts Centre Press, 1994).
Sixteen Australian commentators deal with issues of interracial and inter-cultural relations in the country.

Gramley, S., and K. M. Patzold, *A Survey of Modern English* (Routledge, 1992).

Grewal, Inderpal and Caren Kaplan, (eds.), *Scattered Hegemonies: Post-modernity and Transnational Feminist Practices* (Minneapolis: University of Minnesota Press, 1994).
The collection explores the diverse locations of (post)modernity and marginality, and the possibilities for a transnational feminist politics.

Guha, Ranajit (ed.), *Subaltern Studies: Writing on South Asian History and Society*, 4 vols. (New Delhi: Oxford UP, 1982–6).
The multi-volume collection of the work of the Subaltern Studies group, which interrogates the relationship between nationalist historiography and power in postcolonial India, and searches for the voices and agency of those subordinated on the basis of class, gender, caste or age.

Gurnah, Abdulrazak (ed.), *Essays on African Writing 1: A Re-Evaluation* (Oxford: Heinemann, 1993).

—— *Essays on African Writing 2: Contemporary Literature* (Oxford: Heinemann, 1995).
A two-volume collection of essays, divided chronologically. The first revisits classics of the African literary canon in the light of recent scholar-ship; the second includes criticism of more recent African writing, such as by Ben Okri and Dambudzo Marechera.

Gutmann, Amy (ed.), *Multiculturalism: Examining the Politics of Recognition* (Princeton UP, 1994).

Hall, Stuart, *Critical Dialogues in Cultural Studies*, ed. David Morley and Kuan-Hsing Chen (Routledge, 1996).

Harlow, Barbara, and Mia Carter (eds.), *Imperialism and Orientalism: A Documentary Sourcebook* (Oxford: Blackwell, 1999).
Broadly structured around prominent colonial events, this selection of cultural and historical documents represents the ideological grounds for the British colonial project in the nineteenth century.

Hennessy, Alistair (ed.), *Intellectuals in the Twentieth-Century Caribbean*, 2 vols. (Macmillan, 1992).

Essays on the roles played by intellectuals in developing a sense of distinctiveness within the English-, Spanish- and French-speaking Caribbean.

Hornung, Alfred, and Ernstpeter Ruhe (eds.), *Postcolonialism and Autobiography: Michelle Cliff, David Dabydeen, Opal Palmer Adisa*, intro. Gayatri Spivak (Amsterdam: Rodopi, 1998)

A discussion of autobiographical concepts and constructs focusing on the three named anglophone postcolonial writers.

Howells, Coral Ann, and Lynette Hunter (eds.), *Narrative Strategies in Canadian Literature: Feminism and Postcolonialism* (Milton Keynes: Open UP, 1991).

Essays concerned with the parallel strands of postcolonial and women's writings in Canada in the 1970s and 80s.

James, Adeola (ed.), *In their Own Voices: African Women Writers Talk* (James Currey, 1999).

Interviews with fifteen African women writers accompanied by short biographies.

JanMohamed, Abdul, and David Lloyd (eds.), *The Nature and Context of Minority Discourse* (New York: Telos, 1987).

A relatively early collection on the literary figuration of 'minority'.

Joshi, Svati (ed.), *Rethinking English: Essays in Literature, Language, History* (New Delhi: Trianka, 1991).

Indian academics address the problematic tied to the presence of English language and literature in Indian institutions.

Kiernan, Brian (ed.), *Henry Lawson* (Brisbane: University of Queensland Press, 1976).

A selection from the work of the Australian writer who was among the first to delineate a populist, republican vision of the country.

Killam, Douglas, and Ruth Rowe, *The Companion to African Literatures* (Oxford: James Currey, 2000).

A guide to African literature written in or translated into English, offering information on authors, texts, genres, and key themes.

King, Bruce (ed.), *The Commonwealth Novel since 1960* (Macmillan, 1990).

Essays on national and regional literatures, as well as comparative views of literary movements and directions.

—— (ed.), *New National and Post-Colonial Literatures: An Introduction* (Oxford: Clarendon Press, 1996).

A comprehensive collection of comparative essays by leading practitioners in the field, exploring issues central to colonial and 'new national' literatures, including creolization, exile, diaspora, and the problems of categorizing literature.

King, Bruce (ed.), *West Indian Literature* (Macmillan, 1979).
A survey of the literary history of the West Indies, offering introductions to the socio-historical background and to the major authors.

Kirpal, Viney (ed.), *The New Indian Novel in English: A Study of the 1980s* (New Delhi: Allied Publishers, 1990).
Essays on the innovations that entered the Indian novel in the wake of Rushdie's ground-breaking *Midnight's Children.*

Lazarus, Neil (ed.), *The Cambridge Companion to Postcolonial Literary Studies* (Cambridge UP, 2004).
An astute overview of key postcolonial issues and debates from a closely-knit group of materialist thinkers.

Lewis, Reina, and Sara Mills (eds.), *Feminist Postcolonial Theory: A Reader* (Edinburgh UP, 2003).
A wide selection of texts representing feminist thought about race, power, culture, and empire, suggesting an alternative genealogy to contemporary thinking on (post)colonialism.

Lindfors, Bernth (ed.), *Critical Perspectives on Amos Tutuola* (Three Continents, 1975).
A collection of early reviews and later reappraisals of the Nigerian author's 'magical-realist' writings.

Loomba, Ania, *Colonialism/Postcolonialism* (Routledge, 1998).
A reliable introductory guide. The first part draws terminological distinctions, the second considers the complexities of (post)colonial identities, the third the modes and theories of resistance.

McArthur, Tom (ed.), *The Oxford Companion to the English Language* (Oxford UP, 1992).

McLeod, John, *Beginning Postcolonialism* (Manchester UP, 2000).
A clear, comprehensive and dialogically structured volume, designed for newcomers to the field.

Meyers, Jeffrey (ed.), *Graham Greene: A Re-evaluation* (Macmillan, 1990).
English, American, and Canadian scholars consider the most important aspects of Greene's career and offer a critical analysis of his achievements.

Midgley, Clare (ed.), *Gender and Imperialism* (Manchester UP, 1998).
These essays challenge the traditional British academic separation of gender history and imperial history.

Mohanty, Chandra Talpade, Ann Russo, and Lourdes Torres (eds.), *Third World Women and the Politics of Feminism* (Bloomington: Indiana UP, 1991).

Calls into question the very terms of the definition of feminism, and urges increased specificity in discussing the problems and identities of women in formerly colonized countries.

Mongia, Padmini (ed.), *Contemporary Postcolonial Theory: A Reader* (Arnold, 1996).

Intended as an introduction to the field, this compact volume brackets together vociferous challenges to postcolonialism from critics like Arif Dirlik and Ella Shohat, and 'classic' essays on diaspora and marginality by Homi Bhabha, Benita Parry, Stuart Hall, and Paul Gilroy, amongst others.

Moore, Gerald, *The Chosen Tongue: English Writing in the Tropical World* (Harlow: Longman, 1969).

Moore-Gilbert, Bart, *Postcolonial Theory: Contexts, Practices, Politics* (Verso, 1997).

This careful outline of the institutional and intellectual genesis of post-colonial theory pays valuable attention to the genealogy of Common-wealth literary studies alongside core chapters on the work of Said, Spivak, and Bhabha.

Muponde, Robert, and Mandi Taruvinga (eds.), *Sign and Taboo: Perspectives on the Poetic Fiction of Yvonne Vera* (Harare: Weaver Press, 2002).

The first critical book dedicated to the work of a prolific and courageous contemporary Zimbabwean writer.

Nasta, Susheila (ed.), *Motherlands: Black Women's Writing from Africa, the Caribbean and South Asia* (Women's Press, 1991).

A still-important collection of essays focusing on how the mythologies and meanings of motherhood relate to subjectivity in postcolonial women's writing.

—— (ed.), *Writing Across Worlds: Contemporary Writers Talk* (Routledge, 2004).

Interviews with a range of international writers including Achebe, Chaudhuri, Kincaid, Mistry, Caryl Phillips, Zadie Smith, Soyinka.

Newell, Stephanie (ed.), *Writing African Women: Gender, Popular Culture and Literature in West Africa* (Zed, 1997).

An engaging study of how gender inflects writers' investments in literature and popular culture.

Ngcobo, Lauretta (ed.), *Let it be Told: Essays by Black Women* (Virago, 1988).

Nnaemeka, Obioma (ed.), *The Politics of (M)Othering: Womanhood, Identity and Resistance in African Literature* (Routledge, 1997).

The twelve essays collected in this influential volume foreground the issues surrounding gender, identity, and the nation in African literature. Many are by African and Asian women critics; all show how feminist issues are recast in African contexts.

Nuttall, Sarah, and Carli Coetzee (eds.), *Negotiating the Past: The Making of Memory in South Africa* (Cape Town: Oxford UP, 1998).
    Contributions to the debate on how memory is (re)created and inscribed in the new South Africa, especially in the wake of the 1996 Truth and Reconciliation Commission.

—— and Cheryl-Ann Michael (eds.), *Senses of Culture: South African Culture Studies* (Cape Town: Oxford UP, 2000).
    An ambitious and eclectic collection of essays and interviews, dealing with topics ranging from radio drama and music to soccer and 'hair politics'.

Parker, Andrew, Mary Russo, Doris Sommer, and Patricia Yaeger (eds.), *Nationalisms and Sexualities* (Routledge, 1991).
    Essays on topics related to the interactive discourses of nationalism and sexuality: (neo-)colonialism, the role of dress, citizenship, gender, modes of representation, etc.

Parker, George L. (ed.), *The Evolution of Canadian Literature in English 1914–1945* (Toronto: Holt, Rinehart and Winston, 1973).
    The third of four anthologies tracing the development of Canadian literature in English from the eighteenth century to the 1970s. This volume covers a particularly stormy historical period.

Parker, Michael and Roger Starkey (eds.), *Postcolonial Literatures: Achebe, Ngugi, Desai, Walcott* (Macmillan, 1995).
    The collection offers a range of mainly 1990s critical approaches to these writers from Africa, India, and the Caribbean.

Petersen, Kirsten Holst (ed.), *Criticism and Ideology: Second African Writers' Conference, Stockholm 1986* (Uppsala: Scandinavian Institute of African Studies, 1988).
    A testimony to the mood and preoccupations of African writers in the 1980s. Essays (by Soyinka, Aidoo, and Emecheta, amongst others) engage with the topics of language, South African literature, and women's writing.

—— and Anna Rutherford (eds.), *Chinua Achebe: A Celebration* (Oxford: Heinemann, 1991).
    Texts collected in celebration of Achebe's achievement, on the occasion of his sixtieth birthday, of which several deal with his fifth and to date final novel, *Anthills of the Savannah*.

—— and —— (eds.), *A Double Colonization: Colonial and Post-Colonial Women's Writing* (Aarhus: Dangaroo, 1986).

Porter, A. N. (ed.), *Atlas of British Overseas Expansion* (Routledge, 1991).

Prasad, Hari Mohan (ed.), *Indian Poetry in English* (Aurangabad: Parimal Prakashan, 1983).
    Indian academics map the contours of Indo-English poetry, analyse the

works of significant poets, and explain the process of 'singing native themes on an alien flute, and in the process nativizing it'.

Quartermaine, Peter (ed.), *Diversity Itself: Essays in Australian Art and Culture* (Exeter: University of Exeter Press, 1986).
Essays on Australian literature, cinema, theatre, and visual arts.

Richards, Jeffrey (ed.), *Imperialism and Juvenile Literature* (Manchester UP, 1989).
Taking the view that colonial popular fiction is a form of social control, this collection examines the articulation and diffusion of imperialism in literature for young people.

Rutherford, Anna (ed.), *Aboriginal Culture Today* (Aarhus: Dangaroo, 1988).
A collection of essays, poetry, fiction and interviews, celebrating the survival of Aboriginal peoples despite the atrocities committed against them and their land.

—— (ed.), *From Commonwealth to Postcolonial* (Aarhus: Dangaroo, 1992).
Essays on a wide variety of problems related to Commonwealth literatures and the emergent field of postcolonial studies.

Samuel, Raphael (ed.), *The Making and Unmaking of British National Identity*, 3 vols. (Routledge, 1989).
These volumes explore the changing notions of patriotism and patria in British life.

Sil, Rita (ed.), *Images of India in World Literatures* (New Delhi: National Publishing House, 1987).
Essays on images of India in a wide range of European and Asian as well as Arabic, Mexican, and Kenyan literatures.

Singh, Amritjit, and Peter Schmidt (eds.), *Postcolonial Theory and the United States* (Jackson: University of Mississippi, 2000).
This collection raises questions about the intersections of postcolonial critique with ethnic studies, social history, and cultural developments in the United States since the Second World War.

Singh, Kirpal (ed.), *The Writer's Sense of the Past: Essays on Southeast Asian and Australasian Literature* (Singapore UP, 1987).
How fiction relates and evaluates understandings of the past to the contemporary moment.

Slemon, Stephen, and Helen Tiffin (eds.), *After Europe: Critical Theory and Post-Colonial Writing* (Aarhus: Dangaroo, 1989).
Essays address the relation between Europe-derived reading practices and postcolonial texts, demonstrating some of the ways in which postcolonial writing interrogates European theories.

Spivak, Gayatri Chakravorty, *The Post-Colonial Critic: Interviews, Strategies, Dialogues*, ed. Sarah Harasym (Routledge, 1990).

Twelve 1980s interviews with the prominent postcolonial theorist in which her critical positions are explained in an accessible manner.

Staines, David (ed.), *The Canadian Imagination: Dimensions of a Literary Culture* (Cambridge, Mass.: Harvard UP, 1977).
Margaret Atwood, Northrop Frye, and others explore aspects of both English- and French-language fiction, poetry, and drama, and the much-debated question of the Canadian identity.

Sunder Rajan, Rajeswari (ed.), *The Lie of the Land: English Literary Studies in India* (New Delhi: Oxford UP, 1992).
Engagements with problems related to the pedagogy, ideology, and politics of studying English Literature at Indian universities.

Taylor, Andrew, and Russell McDougall (eds.), *(Un)common Ground: Essays in Literatures in English* (Adelaide: Flinders UP, 1990).

Tharu, Susie, and K. Lalita (eds.), *Women Writing in India: 600 BC to the Present*, 2 vols. (New Delhi: Oxford UP, 1991).
These path-breaking paired anthologies introduce the work of a wide range of Indian women writers and other significant figures, translated into English from thirteen languages, as well as written in English.

Thieme, John (ed.), *The Arnold Anthology of Post-Colonial Literatures in English* (Arnold, 1996).
A broad selection of some 200 extracts from poetic, fictional, and non-fictional texts, divided into eight sections according to the geographical region of origin, giving roughly equal weight to former settler colonies and to 'Third World' countries. Individual texts are briefly contextualized.

Tiffin, Chris, and Lawson, Alan (eds.), *De-Scribing the Empire: Post-Colonialism and Textuality* (Routledge, 1994).
Fifteen essays engaging in colonial discourse analysis relating mainly to the former white settler colonies and the Caribbean.

Trump, Martin (ed.), *Rendering Things Visible: Essays on South African Literary Culture* (Johannesburg: Ravan Press, 1990).
Materialist explorations of the texts and contexts of 1970s and 80s South Africa.

Walder, Dennis, *Post-Colonial Literatures in English: History, Language, Theory* (Oxford: Blackwell, 1998).
An introductory text containing chapters on history, language, and theory in postcolonialism, and case studies dealing with Indian fiction in English, Caribbean and black British poetry, and South African literature.

Wallace-Crabbe, Chris (ed.), *The Australian Nationalists* (Melbourne: Oxford UP, 1971).
Essays on the Australian writers of the 1890, the era that laid the foundations of Australia's national identity.

Walsh, William, *Commonwealth Literature* (Oxford UP, 1973).
A charting of (the then 'new') Commonwealth literatures, discussing English-language writing in India, Africa, the West Indies, Canada, New Zealand, and Australia.

Werbner, Pnina, and Tariq Modood (eds.), *Debating Cultural Hybridity: Multi-cultural Identities and the Politics of Anti-Racism* (London: Zed Books, 1997).

Whalley, George (ed.), *Writing in Canada: Proceedings of the Canadian Writers' Conference July 1955* (Toronto: Macmillan, 1956).

Williams, Patrick, and Laura Chrisman (eds.), *Colonial Discourse and Post-Colonial Criticism: A Reader* (Hemel Hempstead: Harvester Wheatsheaf, 1993).
This pioneering anthology of postcolonial cultural studies is divided into six broadly thematic sections and contains important texts by key theorists as well as a general introduction.

Wisker, Gina, *Post-Colonial and African American Women's Writing: A Critical Introduction* (Macmillan, 2000).
This very broadly conceived introduction to two interrelated areas of women's writing discusses authors from such areas as North America, the Caribbean, India, and Africa.

Young, Robert, *Postcolonialism: A Very Short Introduction* (Oxford UP, 2003)

Yuval-Davis, Nira, and Floya Anthias (eds.), *Woman-Nation-State* (Macmillan, 1989).

3. Critical works

Adas, Michael, *Machines as the Measure of Man: Science, Technology and Ideologies of Western Dominance* (Ithaca, NY: Cornell UP, 1989).
Relates western scientific and technological accomplishments to the nature of European interactions with non-western peoples.

Ahmad, Aijaz, *In Theory: Classes, Nations, Literatures* (Verso, 1992).
A much-debated, polemical critique of mainstream postcolonial theory, directed from a Marxist perspective. The work of Fredric Jameson, Edward Said, Salman Rushdie, and Marx himself is analysed in resonant and now virtually canonical detail, including Jameson's well-known essay 'Third World Literature in the Era of Multinational Capital'.

—— *Lineages of the Present: Ideology and Politics in Contemporary South Asia* (Verso, 2000).
Searching considerations of communalism, secularisim, and other pressing issues in Indian politics and recent history.

Alatas, Syed Hussein, *The Myth of the Lazy Native: A Study of the Image of the*

Malays, Filipinos and Javanese from the 16th to the 20th Century and its Function in the Ideology of Colonial Capitalism (Frank Cass, 1977).

Amadiume, Ifi, *Male Daughters, Female Husbands: Gender and Sex in an African Society* (Zed, 1987).

An anthropological discussion of the marked differences between sex and gender significations, especially with respect to women, in Igbo society in West Africa.

Amuta, Chidi, *The Theory of African Literature* (Zed, 1989).

A functionalist Marxist approach to African literature and its criticism.

Appiah, Kwame Anthony, *In my Father's House: Africa in the Philosophy of Culture* (Methuen, 1992).

Philosophical essays on the highly constructed theories of race and culture that relate to Africa. Includes the well-known 'Is the Post- in Postmodernism the Post- in Postcolonial?'

Arendt, Hannah, *The Origins of Totalitarianism* (1951; New York: Meridian, 1966).

A keynote study by the New York intellectual.

Arnold, A. James, *Modernism and Negritude: The Poetry and Politics of Aimé Césaire* (Cambridge, Mass.: Harvard UP, 1981).

Studies the curve of Césaire's career as both a writer of decolonization and an heir to the poetics of surrealism.

Asad, Talal (ed.), *Anthropology and the Colonial Encounter* (Ithaca, NY: Cornell UP, 1973).

Essays explore the historical connections between the scholarly discipline of anthropology and the spread of colonialism.

Ashcroft, Bill, *Post-Colonial Transformation* (Routledge, 2001).

A study of postcolonialism as internalized subversion rather than external protest, discussed under such headings as: 'Resistance', 'Interpolation', 'Habitation', 'Horizon' and 'Globalization'.

—— Gareth Griffiths, and Helen Tiffin, *The Empire Writes Back: Theory and Practice in Post-Colonial Criticism*, 2nd ed. (1989; Routledge, 2002).

A foundational work within postcolonial studies, which helped establish the contours of the field as embracing subaltern and settler writing. The new edition contains an extra chapter, focusing on recent conceptualizations and debates, especially concerning global impacts.

Atwood, Margaret, *Strange Things: The Malevolent North in Canadian Literature* (Oxford: Clarendon Press, 1995).

This witty, insightful series of lectures discusses images of the wild North in Canadian writing, and how they are manipulated in texts to construct Canadian identities.

—— *Survival: A Thematic Guide to Canadian Literature* (Toronto: Anansi, 1972).
The leading Canadian novelist's definitive study of Canadian writing as shaped by its relation to the Northern environment—a personal manifesto.

Barrell, John, *The Infection of Thomas De Quincey: A Psychopathology of Imperialism* (New Haven: Yale UP, 1991).
Relates the questions of subjectivity raised by De Quincey's writings to the nature and development of the British Empire.

Baucom, Ian, *Out of Place: Englishness, Empire and the Locations of Identity* (Princeton UP, 1999).
Examines the contradictions and ambiguities of an imaginary Englishness, formulated from the vantage point of 'abroad', as in Kipling's writing.

Bernal, Martin, *Black Athena: The Afro-Asiatic Roots of Classical Civilization*, vol. i (New Brunswick, NJ: Rutgers UP, 1988).
The controversial study of ancient African Egypt as the cradle of western culture.

Bhabha, Homi, 'Foreword: Remembering Fanon—Self, Psyche and the Colonial Condition', in Frantz Fanon, *Black Skin, White Masks* (Pluto, 1986), pp. vii–xv.
A reading of Fanon's psychoanalytic works in terms of Bhabha's own articulation of colonial 'doubling and splitting'.

—— *The Location of Culture* (Routledge, 1994).
In this series of influential essays, the leading and controversial post-colonial thinker theorizes (post)colonial identities, relationships and modes of representation, developing such keynote concepts as *mimicry* and *interstitial space*.

Boehmer, Elleke, *Empire, the National and the Postcolonial 1890–1920: Resistance in Interaction* (Oxford UP, 2002).
An investigation of some of the anti-imperial and nationalist movements which came into path-breaking contact with one another at the height of the British Empire.

Bolt, Christine, *Victorian Attitudes to Race* (Routledge & Kegan Paul, 1971).
Relates the question of 'race' to America, Africa, Jamaica and the Indian Empire.

Bongie, Chris, *Exotic Memories: Literature, Colonialism and the Fin de Siecle* (Stanford UP, 1991).
A thorough study of nineteenth-century exoticism as a discursive practice intent on recovering 'elsewhere' values deemed lost with the modernization of European society.

Boon, James A., *Other Tribes, Other Scribes: Symbolic Anthropology in the Comparative Study of Culture* (Cambridge UP, 1982).

Introduces semiotic concepts to the comparative study of other, non-Western cultures.

Booth, James, *Writers and Politics in Nigeria* (Hodder & Stoughton, 1987).
Studies the work of Tutuola, Okara, Achebe, Soyinka, and others in the light of Nigerian political processes.

Bourke, Lawrence, *A Vivid Steady State: Les Murray and Australian Poetry* (Sydney: University of New South Wales Press, 1992).
An analysis of the foremost Australian poet's work, exploring how it interacts with its social and literary contexts.

Bowering, George, *The Mask in Place: Essays on Fiction in North America* (Winnipeg: Turnstone, 1982).
Essays on pre-realist, realist, and post-realist Canadian and American fiction.

Brantlinger, Patrick, *Rule of Darkness: British Literature and Imperialism 1830–1914* (Ithaca, NY: Cornell UP, 1988).
An influential study of the literary representation of the second British Empire in formation.

Brathwaite, Edward Kamau, *History of the Voice: The Development of Nation Language in Anglophone Caribbean Poetry* (New Beacon, 1984).
An essay on the process of using English in non-standard ways, closer to the vernacular, following slavery and colonization in the Caribbean.

Brennan, Timothy, *At Home in the World: Cosmopolitanism Now* (Cambridge, Mass.: Harvard UP, 1997).
A testing discussion of the political collusions involved in the assertion of First World brands of seemingly rebellious cosmopolitanism.

—— *Salman Rushdie and the Third World* (Macmillan, 1989).
Brennan places Rushdie among other Third World literary cosmopolitans and charts the role they play both in politicizing fiction and diluting the combativeness of anti-colonization movements.

Bristow, Joseph, *Empire Boys: Adventures in a Man's World* (HarperCollins, 1991).
An accessible study of adventure fiction written at the height of the British Empire, and the historical and political processes it embodies.

Brown, Lloyd, *West Indian Poetry* (Heinemann, 1984).
A survey of the history of West Indian poetry as it moved away from the derivativeness and 'colonial conversions' of earlier decades to the more complex 'transformations' of the contemporary period.

—— *Women Writers in Black Africa* (Westport, Conn.: Greenwood, 1981).
A relatively early study of the writings of Buchi Emecheta, Efua Southerland, Ama Ata Aidoo, Flora Nwapa, and Bessie Head.

Brydon, Diana, and Helen Tiffin, *Decolonizing Fictions* (Sydney: Dangaroo, 1993).
A comparative look at English-language writing from Australia, Canada, and the West Indies, containing readings of fiction by Patrick White, V. S. Naipaul, Margaret Atwood, and others.

Buhle, Paul, (ed.), *C. L. R James: His Life and Work* (Allison & Busby, 1986).
Intellectual and cultural portraits of the important Caribbean writer, critic, historian, and spokesman.

—— *C. L. R. James: The Artist as Revolutionary* (Verso, 1988).

Buruma, Ian, and Avishai Margalit, *Occidentalism* (Atlantic, 2004).
Investigates contradictory politico-religious aversions to the West—its secularism, liberalism, and industrialism.

Cairns, David, and Shaun Richards, *Writing Ireland: Colonialism, Nationalism and Culture* (Manchester UP, 1988).
An examination of the imbrications of culture, literature, and identity in nineteenth- and twentieth-century nationalist Ireland.

Carroll, David, *Chinua Achebe: Novelist, Poet, Critic*, 2nd edn. (Macmillan, 1990).
The focus of this close study is on Achebe's novels, although other writings are also taken into account.

Carter, Paul, *Living in a New Country: History, Travelling and Language* (Faber, 1992).
Explores Australian writing, arguing that 'the new country is never simply a geographical location and [is] always a historical and poetic destiny'.

—— *The Road to Botany Bay: An Essay in Spatial History* (Faber, 1987).
An influential, contentious re-reading of the source documents of Australian history, charting the spatio-social processes that accompanied the eighteenth- and nineteenth-century founding of the country.

Césaire, Aimé, *Discours sur le colonialisme* (Paris: Présence Africaine, 1955).
The classic work by one of the key founders of the Negritude movement is a moral and cultural critique of the double standards of western culture in respect of racism and humanism. It functions as an underlying complement to the work of Frantz Fanon.

Chakrabarty, Dipesh, *Provincializing Europe: Postcolonial Thought and Historical Difference* (Princeton UP, 2000).
Influential reflections on the limitations of western definitions of modernity.

Chakravarty, Suhash, *The Raj Syndrome: A Study in Imperial Perceptions* (New Delhi: Penguin, 1989).
An assessment of imperial perceptions of India and its institutions,

especially since the 'over-confident days of the adolescent Raj' in the late nineteenth century.

Chatterjee, Partha, *Nationalist Thought and the Colonial World* (Zed, 1986).
An analysis of Indian nationalism exploring the thesis that, when non-Western nationalists set out to declare their freedom from European domination, they nevertheless remained imprisoned within European modes of thought.

Chaudhuri, Amit, *D. H. Lawrence and 'Difference'* (Oxford: Clarendon Press, 2003).
A thought-provoking post-structuralist engagement with the explorations of otherness in Lawrence's poetry, by the prize-winning novelist.

Chaudhuri, Rosinka, *Poets in Colonial Bengal: Emergent Nationalism and the Orientalist Project* (Calcutta: Seagull Books, 2002).
An illuminating poetic history of nineteenth-century Calcutta.

Chinweizu, Onwuchekwa Jemie, and Ihechukwu Madubuike, *Toward the Decolonization of African Literature: African Fiction and Poetry and their Critics* (KPI, 1985).
A combative, impassioned outcry against (neo-)colonial mentalities in African writing. The authors call for a return to pre-colonial oral traditions as the source of literary inspiration.

Chrisman, Laura, *Postcolonial Contraventions: Cultural Readings of Race, Imperialism and Transnationalism* (Manchester UP, 2003).
United by a materialist approach, this collection of combative review essays combines literary, cultural, and theoretical discussion.

—— *Rereading the Imperial Romance: British Imperialism and South African Resistance in Haggard, Schreiner, and Plaatje* (Oxford UP, 2000).

Christian, Barbara, *Black Feminist Criticism: Perspectives on Black Women Writers* (Oxford: Pergamon, 1987).
Essays on fiction by (mainly) African-American women.

Cleary, Joe, *Literature, Partition and the Nation-State: Culture and Conflict in Ireland, Israel and Palestine* (Cambridge UP, 2002).
A powerful study of minority and sub-nationalist movements.

Clifford, James, *The Predicament of Culture: Twentieth-Century Ethnography, Literature and Art* (Cambridge, Mass.: Harvard UP, 1988).
An examination of the ways in which western ethnographic practices respond to forces that challenge their authority and identity.

Clingman, Stephen, *The Novels of Nadine Gordimer: History from the Inside* (1986; Bloomsbury, 1993).
A study of how Gordimer's fiction refracts the historical, social, cultural, and ideological currents of apartheid and contemporary South Africa.

Coetzee, J. M., *White Writing: On the Culture of Letters in South Africa* (New Haven: Yale UP, 1989).
Essays dealing with early white colonial writing in South Africa, in particular with respect to how the land was constructed as empty of indigenes.

Cook, David, and Michael Okenimkpe, *Ngugi wa Thiong'o: An Exploration of his Writings* (Heinemann, 1983).

Cooper, Brenda, *Magical Realism in West African Fiction: Seeing with a Third Eye* (Routledge, 1998).
Cooper argues that the work of three West African writers (Sly Cheney-Coker, Ben Okri and B. Kojo Laing) mixes the elements of magic, myth, and historical reality.

Cooper, Carolyn, *Noises in the Blood* (Macmillan, 1993).
A gendered perspective on Jamaican written and oral popular culture.

Couzens, Tim, *The New African: A Study of the Life and Work of H. I. E. Dhlomo* (Johannesburg: Ravan Press, 1985).
Cultural history as autobiography, tracking the iconic career of this remarkable 1930s Zulu playwright.

Crane, Ralph J., *Inventing India: A History of India in English Language Fiction* (Macmillan, 1992).
A study of representations of India's past in novels by British and Indian writers.

Cronin, Richard, *Imagining India* (Macmillan, 1989).
Essays on how India is imagined in the novels of Kipling, Forster, Narayan, Desai, Prawer Jhabvala, and others.

Cullingford, Elizabeth, *Yeats, Ireland and Fascism* (Macmillan, 1984).
Explores the interrelation between W. B. Yeats's poetry, his Irish nationalism, and his later passing interest in fascism.

Curtin, Philip D., *The Image of Africa: British Ideas and Action, 1780–1850* (Macmillan, 1965).
Examines British constructions of Africa that emerged as a result of travels, explorations, and conquest.

Darby, Philip, *The Fiction of Imperialism: Reading Between International Relations and Postcolonialism* (Cassell, 1998).
Bridging the academic fields of International Relations and Postcolonial Studies, this book traces the ways in which fiction has depicted the interaction between the West and its others.

Dasgupta, Probal, *The Otherness of English: India's Auntie Tongue Syndrome* (New Delhi: Sage Publications, 1993).
A socio-linguistic analysis of the role and function of English in modern India, especially as compared to classical Sanskrit.

Dawson, Graham, *Soldier Heroes: British Empire, Adventure and the Imagining of Masculinities* (Routledge, 1994).

Dollimore, Jonathan, *Sexual Dissidence: Augustine to Wilde, Freud to Foucault* (Oxford: Clarendon Press, 1991).
An incisive study of the western concept of 'perversion' where the perverse is that which subverts 'normality' by undercutting the dominant from within.

Drew, John, *India and the Romantic Imagination* (New Delhi: Oxford UP, 1987).
Traces the origin and development of the tendency to idealize India in European writing.

Eagleton, Terry, *Exiles and Emigrés* (Chatto and Windus, 1970).
Critical explorations of the 'émigré' theme in the works of Conrad, Waugh, Orwell, Greene, Eliot, Auden, and Lawrence.

—— Fredric Jameson, and Edward W. Said, *Nationalism, Colonialism and Literature* (Minneapolis: University of Minnesota Press, 1990).
Essays on the political, especially nationalist, implications of work by Joyce, Forster, and Yeats, concentrating on the traces of imperialism in Western modernism.

Echeruo, Michael, *Joyce Cary and the Novel of Africa* (Harlow: Longman, 1973).
An account of the representations of Africa in Joyce Cary's 1930s fictions.

Edmond, Rod, *Representing the South Pacific: Colonial Discourse from Cook to Gauguin* (Cambridge UP, 1997).
Edmond illuminatingly investigates the complexities of colonial representation in the South Pacific, emphasizing how postcolonial theory tends not to account for the anomalies of the local, especially where it views indigenous cultures as passive.

Etherton, Michael, *The Development of African Drama* (Hutchinson, 1982).
An analysis of the development of African drama within the context of contemporary African societies.

Fanon, Frantz, *Black Skin, White Masks* (Fr. 1952), trans. Charles Lam Markmann (1967; Pluto, 1986).
A pioneering study of the array of psychological conditions created in the native by the colonial system.

—— *Studies in a Dying Colonialism*, trans. Haakon Chevalier (Earthscan Press, 1989).
The celebrated theorist of African revolution examines aspects of the Algerian struggle for independence, such as the role of veiled women, the dynamics of the family, and the position of white settlers.

—— *The Wretched of the Earth*, trans. Constance Farrington (1961; Penguin, 1986).

A revolutionary call for a radical restructuring of colonial societies through the unavoidable medium of violence.

First, Ruth, and Ann Scott, *Olive Schreiner* (Women's Press, 1989).
An examination of Schreiner's life from the combined perspectives of a leading South African political activist and a British feminist.

Fraser, Robert, *Lifting the Sentence: A Poetics of Postmodern Fiction* (Manchester UP, 2000).

—— *Victorian Quest Romance: Stevenson, Haggard, Kipling and Conan Doyle* (Plymbridge: Northcote House, 1988).
An eccentric, anti-theoretical study which examines the stylistic traits of a selection of postcolonial narratives.

Freire, Paolo, *Pedagogy of the Oppressed*, trans. M. B. Ramos (Penguin, 1972).
A cry against the 'culture of silence' and an eloquent plea for an understanding of the world so that the oppressed might change it, which later had significant implications for the revolutionary struggle in Guinea.

Frye, Northrop, *The Bush Garden: Essays on the Canadian Imagination* (Toronto: Anansi, 1971).
Critical essays, written between 1943 and 1969, on Canadian literature and painting.

Fullbrook, Kate, *Katherine Mansfield: Reception and Reputation* (Hemel Hempstead: Harvester Wheatsheaf, 1986).
A feminist reading of the New Zealand modernist writer's life and fiction.

Gates, Henry Louis, Jr., *The Signifying Monkey: A Theory of African-American Literary Criticism* (Oxford UP, 1989).
An attempt to lift the discursive traditions of 'peculiarly black texts of being' from the realm of vernacular speech to that of literary theory.

Geertz, Clifford, *Local Knowledge* (1983; Fontana, 1993).
The influential exegesis of anthropology from within.

George, Rosemary Marangoly, *The Politics of Home: Postcolonial Relocations and Twentieth-Century Fiction* (Berkeley: University of California Press, 1999).
Starting from the premiss that 'home is a way of establishing difference', George discusses the work of transnational intellectuals—Conrad, Naipaul, Ishiguro, Said—in order to plot the changing relationship between 'home' and 'nation' in modern and postcolonial fiction and theory.

Gibbs, James, *Wole Soyinka* (Macmillan, 1986).
A study of Soyinka the dramatist that includes a biography and a survey of the plays, combined with detailed analyses of texts and contexts.

Gikandi, Simon, *Maps of Englishness: Writing Identity in the Culture of Colonialism* (New York: Columbia UP, 1996).

A study of the extent to which colonialism shaped not only overseas identities, but also English domestic social spaces.

—— *Reading Chinua Achebe* (James Currey, 1991).
Gikandi reads Achebe's novels as 'formal instruments in the invention and reinvention of African cultures' and of new national realities.

—— *Reading the African Novel* (James Currey, 1987).
Rejecting the view of literature propagated by critics like Chinweizu, this study puts forward a typology of the African novel based on key clusters of structural elements.

Gilbert, Helen, and Joanne Tompkins, *Post-Colonial Drama: Theory, Practice, Politics* (Routledge, 1996).
An inquiry into how performance has been instrumental in resisting imperialism. The book establishes a theoretical framework for studying postcolonial drama and considers plays from Australia, Canada, India, Ireland, Africa, and the Caribbean.

Gilbert, Sandra M., and Susan Gubar, *No Man's Land: The Place of the Woman Writer in the Twentieth Century*, 2 vols. (New Haven: Yale UP, 1988).
Impact-making studies of women's writing as resistance from the authors of *The Madwoman in the Attic*, which, however, curiously pay no attention to the foremost twentieth-century issue of empire.

Gilman, Sander, *Difference and Pathology: Stereotypes of Sexuality, Race and Madness* (Ithaca, NY: Cornell UP, 1985).
Essays examining stereotypes of the other in western European texts ranging from the medieval period to the twentieth century.

—— *'There Ain't No Black in the Union Jack': The Cultural Politics of Race and Nation* (Hutchinson, 1987).
A cultural and political analysis of the relationship between race, class, and nation in modern Britain, which refuses to define 'race' in purely ethnic terms and argues that culture develops along syncretic rather than ethnically absolute lines.

Gilroy, Paul, *The Black Atlantic: Modernity and Double Consciousness* (Verso, 1993).
A ground-breaking and influential text, which introduces the concept of a black diasporic cultural (or 'outernational') formation connecting three continents, initially via the slave trade, and acting as a counter-culture to Western modernity.

Glissant, Édouard, *Poetics of Relation*, trans. Betsy Wing (1990; Ann Arbor: University of Michigan Press, 1997).
A theoretical exploration of Glissant's concept of cultural interrelation in the francophone Caribbean.

Gooneratne, Yasmine, *Diverse Inheritance* (Adelaide: Centre for Research in the New Literatures in English, 1980).
Essays on aspects of Commonwealth literature, written as the field was emerging in the 1960s and 1970s.

Goonetilleke, D. C. R. A., *Developing Countries in British Fiction* (Macmillan, 1977).
An exploration of how post-1880 British fiction set in 'developing countries' embodies and represents British attitudes towards those countries. The primary focus is on the works of Joseph Conrad.

—— *Images of the Raj: South Asia in the Literature of Empire* (Macmillan, 1988).
Examines the British fiction of South Asia by Rudyard Kipling, Leonard Woolf, E. M. Forster, George Orwell, and Paul Scott.

Gorra, Michael, *After Empire: Scott, Naipaul, Rushdie* (University of Chicago Press, 1997).
Analyses the work of the three novelists of empire and its aftermath in relation to the phases of the decolonization of India.

Green, Martin, *Dreams of Adventure, Deeds of Empire* (Routledge & Kegan Paul, 1980).
Based on the premiss that adventure forms the energizing myth of empire, Green looks at British, American, and Russian adventure novels of the nineteenth century against the backdrop of the imperial history of that time.

—— *The English Novel in the Twentieth Century* (Routledge & Kegan Paul, 1984).
A discussion of six British authors whose careers and work span the high-point and decline of the British Empire: Kipling, Lawrence, Joyce, Waugh, Kingsley Amis, and Lessing.

Greenberger, Allen J., *The British Image of India: A Study in the Literature of Imperialism 1880–1960* (Oxford UP, 1969).
Explores images of India in British literature written during 'The Era of Confidence' (1880–1910), 'The Era of Doubt' (1910–35), and 'The Era of Melancholy' (1935–60).

Greenblatt, Stephen, *Marvelous Possessions: The Wonder of the New World* (Oxford: Clarendon Press, 1988).
This study of the medieval and early modern representations of the New World argues that perceptions of 'the wondrous' became instrumental in the process of colonization.

Gregory, Derek, *The Colonial Present: Afghanistan, Palestine, Iraq* (Blackwell, 2004).
A daring analysis of the perpetuation of imperial geographies within contemporary world politics.

Grewal, Inderpal, *Home and Harem: Nation, Gender, Empire and the Cultures of Travel* (London: Leicester University Press, 1996).
  In this investigation of transnational interaction across the colonial divide, Grewal looks at gendered discourses of travel and nation, taking into account Indian women's travels to the West alongside English women's tours of the East.

Griffiths, Gareth, *A Double Exile: African and West Indian Writing between Two Cultures* (Marion Boyars, 1978).
  Essays on the problems and concerns faced by anglophone authors of Africa and the Caribbean.

Gualtieri, Claudia, *Representations of West Africa as Exotic in British Colonial Travel Writing* (Lampeter: Edwin Mellen, 2002).
  A densely documented account of the construction of West Africa as exotic space.

Gurr, Andrew, *Writers in Exile: The Identity of Home in Modern Literature* (Brighton: Harvester, 1981).
  Studies the prose fiction of 'creative exiles': Katherine Mansfield, V. S. Naipaul, Ngugi wa Thiong'o, amongst others.

Hallward, Peter, *Absolutely Postcolonial: Writing Between the Singular and the Specific* (Manchester UP, 2001).
  Departing from the 'consensuality' of postcolonial criticism, especially with regard to its emphasis on specificity, Hallward argues that its overcontextualization breaks down into an infinitely reductive particularity.

Hammond, Dorothy, and Alta Jablow, *The Africa that Never Was: Four Centuries of British Writing about Africa* (New York: Twayne, 1970).
  Demonstrates the relationship between the perceptions of Africa and Africans by British writers, and the British economic interests during the eras of slavery and Empire.

Hampson, Robert, *Cultural Encounters in Joseph Conrad's Malay Fiction* (Palgrave, 2000).

Hannerz, Ulf, *Transnational Connections: Culture, People, Places* (Routledge, 1996).

Hardt, Michael, and Antonio Negri, *Empire* (Cambridge, Mass.: Harvard UP, 2000).
  The authors of this ambitious work define Empire, in contrast to imperialism, as a decentred and deterritorializing apparatus of rule emerging in the era of globalization.

Harlow, Barbara, *Resistance Literature* (Methuen, 1987).
  Still an important survey of non-western literature which seeks to contribute as political activity, in particular by supporting organized liberation struggle.

Hassam, Andrew, *Sailing to Australia: Shipboard Diaries by Nineteenth-Century British Emigrants* (Manchester UP, 1994).

An exploration of how personal narrative constructs the experience of emigration by ship to an unknown continent.

Healy, Chris, *From the Ruins of Colonialism: History as Social Memory* (Cambridge UP, 1997).

In three sections examining, respectively, the figure of James Cook, the role of museums and schools, and two archetypal nineteenth-century historical events, Healy addresses the ways in which social memory in Australia is a product of colonialism.

Henry, Nancy, *George Eliot and the British Empire* (Cambridge UP, 2002).

Heyward, Michael, *The Ern Malley Affair* (Faber, 1993).

A biography of the 'marvellous boy' of Australian poetry—a complicated 'classless genius coming from nowhere and cut off in his prime' in 1943—who was in fact the fictitious creation of two anti-modernist Australian poets concerned to make a point about cultural cringe.

Hobsbawm, Eric, and Terence Ranger (eds.), *The Invention of Tradition* (Cambridge UP, 1983).

A seminal work of socio-anthropology, in which the authors argue that much 'tradition' is a recent invention, produced out of a complex inter-action between the old and the new.

Hogan, Patrick Colm, *Colonialism and Cultural Identity: Crises of Tradition in the Anglophone Literatures of India, Africa and the Caribbean* (Albany: State University of New York Press, 2000).

A culturalist analysis of identity issues in a body of anglophone postcolo-nial texts, which includes a glossary of theoretical concepts.

hooks, bell, *Ain't I a Woman: Black Women and Feminism* (Pluto, 1982).

The prominent critic's landmark work on sexism, feminism, and black women's historical experience.

—— *Race, Gender and Cultural Politics* (Turnaround Press, 1991).

Horner, Avril, and Sue Zlosnik, *Landscapes of Desire: Metaphors in Modern Women's Fiction* (Hemel Hempstead: Harvester Wheatsheaf, 1990).

Feminist readings of writing by Edith Wharton, Charlotte Perkins Gilman, Kate Chopin, Virginia Woolf, Jean Rhys, and Margaret Atwood.

Howe, Stephen, *Ireland and Empire: Colonial Legacies in Irish History and Culture* (Oxford UP, 2000).

A comprehensive analytical discussion of the application of colonial models in contemporary thinking about Ireland.

Huggan, Graham, *The Post-Colonial Exotic: Marketing the Margins* (Routledge, 2001).

An energetic, refreshingly polemical study of the global commodification of cultural difference.

Hulme, Peter, *Colonial Encounters: Europe and the Native Caribbean 1492–1797* (Methuen, 1986).

An influential study structured around five versions of the encounter between Europe and the Caribbean, including those between Prospero and Caliban, John Smith and Pocahontas, Robinson Crusoe and Friday.

Hutcheon, Linda, *A Poetics of Postmodernism: History, Theory, Fiction* (Routledge, 1988).

—— *Splitting Images: Contemporary Canadian Ironies* (Oxford UP, 1991).

Looks at the various forms of irony and their cultural/political implications and applications in Canadian writing and visual arts.

—— *The Politics of Postmodernism*, 2nd edn. (Routledge, 2002).

An overview of postmodernism and its politics that investigates the challenges presented to the notion of artistic representation. The volume builds on the core notions developed in the author's earlier work on the poetics of postmodernism (above).

Innes, C. L., *Chinua Achebe* (Cambridge UP, 1990).

Innovative close readings of Achebe's novelistic cycle.

—— *A History of Black and Asian Writing in Britain, 1700–2000* (Cambridge UP, 2002).

A historical and cultural mapping of writing by black and Asian writers who made their home in Britain from 1750 onwards. The main body of the study concludes with 1948.

—— *Woman and Nation in Irish Literature and Society, 1880–1935* (Harvester Wheatsheaf, 1993).

A study of the complex interplay of gender and nation in Irish nationalist writing by both men and women.

Irele, Abiola, *The African Experience in Art and Literature* (Heinemann, 1981).

Essays on the ideologies and meanings of African writing.

JanMohamed, Abdul, *Manichean Aesthetics: The Politics of Literature in Colonial Africa* (Amherst: University of Massachusetts Press, 1983).

A study of six authors whose fiction was markedly influenced by colonial social structures: Joyce Cary, Karen Blixen, Nadine Gordimer, Chinua Achebe, Ngugi wa Thiong'o, and Alex La Guma.

Johnston, Anna, *Missionary Writing and Empire* (Cambridge UP, 2003).

Ambiguous positions in missionary writing.

Jones, Eldred Durosimi, *The Writing of Wole Soyinka*, 3rd edn. (Heinemann, 1988).

Recounts Soyinka's life and analyses his autobiography, plays, poetry, and fiction.

Joshi, A. N., *The West Looks at India: Studies on the Impact of Indian Thought on Shelley, Emerson, Thoreau, Whitman, Ruskin, Tennyson, D. H. Lawrence and James Joyce* (New Delhi: Prakash Book Depot, 1969).

Kabbani, Rana, *Europe's Myths of the Orient* (Macmillan, 1986).

A diligent application of Said's ideas to a number of orientalist texts.

Kanneh, Kadiatu, *African Identities: Race, Nation and Culture in Ethnography, Pan-Africanism and Black Literatures* (Routledge, 1998).

This monograph explores a range of constructions and significations historically associated with Africa and blackness.

Kaplan, Caren, *Questions of Travel: Postmodern Discourses of Displacement* (Durham, NC: Duke UP, 1996).

Suggests that postmodernity is that which troubles and resists normative assumptions of Euro-American modernity.

Kaplan, Cora, *Sea Changes: Essays on Culture and Feminism* (Verso, 1990).

Drawing on psychoanalytical and Marxist critical frameworks, this collection of essays poses questions about the place of women's writing in the construction of race, class, and gender hierarchies. Three sections relate feminism to cultural politics, literature, and autobiography, respectively.

Kaul, Suvir, *Poems of Nation, Anthems of Empire: English Verse in the Long Eighteenth Century* (Charlottesville: University of Virginia Press, 2000).

Khair, Tabish, *Babu Fictions: Alienation in Contemporary Indian English Novels* (New Delhi: Oxford UP, 2001).

Reading work by Raja Rao, Anita Desai, Salman Rushdie, Amitav Ghosh, and others, Khair offers a Marxist analysis of contemporary Indian fiction in English as élitist, occluding the class relations of broader Indian society.

King, Bruce, *Modern Indian Poetry in English* (New Delhi: Oxford UP, 1987).

An introduction to the English-language poetry of India since independence, focusing on aesthetics, sociology, and the process of canon-making.

—— *The New English Literatures: Cultural Nationalism in a Changing World* (Macmillan, 1980).

Kirpal, Viney, *The Third World Novel of Expatriation: A Study of Émigré Fiction by Indian, West African and Caribbean Writers* (New Delhi: Sterling, 1989).

Kumar, Radha, *The History of Doing* (Verso, 1994).

Illuminates the social history of day-to-day work, mainly by women.

Lane, Christopher, *The Ruling Passion: British Colonial Allegory and the Paradox of Homosexual Desire* (Durham, NC: Duke UP, 1995).

An involved study of the conflicted relationship between masculinity, homosexual desire, and empire in the British fictions of high imperialism, which suggests that it may be to an extent 'unamenable' to contemporary representation.

Lazarus, Neil, *Nationalism and Cultural Practice in the Postcolonial World* (Cambridge UP, 1999).

Challenging idealist and transnationalist tendencies in the postcolonial field, this volume rejects the conviction that the nation as an entity and a concept has been rendered obsolete by the forces of globalization.

Lennon, Joseph, *Irish Orientalism* (Syracuse UP, 2004).

Maps to date unacknowledged parallels between the constructions of Ireland and Asia as 'Orient', and Irish nationalist responses to these perceptions of kinship.

Lévi-Strauss, Claude, *Tristes Tropiques* (Paris: Librairie Plon, 1955).

The path-breaking work on the construction of myth in cultures in the process of being rapidly marginalized.

Liddle, Joanna, and Rama Joshi, *Daughters of Independence: Gender, Caste and Class in India* (Zed, 1986).

A study of the shift from caste-orientated to class-orientated strategies for maintaining status amongst educated women in India.

Lloyd, David, *Anomalous States: Irish Writing and the Post-Colonial Moment* (Dublin: Lilliput Press, 1993)

Five linked essays which explore modern Irish literature (Heaney, Beckett, Yeats, Joyce) in relation to its political, specifically postcolonial contexts by drawing on Fanon and Gramsci.

Low, Gail Ching-Liang, *White Skins, Black Masks: Representation and Colonialism* (Routledge, 1996).

A reading of Henry Rider Haggard's African romances and Rudyard Kipling's short fiction and travelogues on India which analyses constructs of fantasy and body image in relation to colonial networks of power.

McClintock, Anne, *Imperial Leather: Race, Gender and Sexuality in the Colonial Contest* (Routledge, 1995).

An influential, vividly illustrated critique of the knotted and ramifying inter-linkages of gender, race, and class that shaped British imperial relations and representations.

McClure, John A., *Kipling and Conrad: The Colonial Fiction* (Cambridge, Mass.: Harvard UP, 1981).

Focuses on the colonial struggle as represented by Kipling and Conrad, especially their social and psychological portrayals of colonial officials.

McCullock, A. M., *A Tragic Vision: The Novels of Patrick White* (Brisbane: University of Queensland Press, 1988).

McLeod, John, *Postcolonial London: Rewriting the Metropolis* (Routledge, 2004).

A lively analysis of the imaginative transformation of the city by African, Asian, Caribbean, and South Pacific writers since the 1950s.

Majeed, Javed, *Ungoverned Imaginings: James Mill's* The History of British India *and Orientalism* (Oxford: Clarendon Press, 1992).
An investigation of the relationship between the emergence of utilitarianism as a political language in Britain, and British imperial exploits in India, that sees Mill's *History* as an exercise in both philistinism and disenchantment.

Mbembe, Achille, *On the Postcolony* (Berkeley: University of California Press, 2001).
A series of theorizations of issues to do with power and subjectivity in postcolonial Africa—a context characterized by twin, often destructive, processes of 'displacement' and 'entanglement'.

Medalie, David, *E. M. Forster's Modernism* (Basingstoke: Macmillan, 2002).

Memmi, Albert, *The Colonizer and the Colonized* (Boston: Beacon, 1965).
The lucid classic analysis of the social dynamic of a colony, based on 'profit, privilege, and usurpation'.

Metcalf, Thomas R., *An Imperial Vision: Indian Architecture and Britain's Raj* (Faber, 1989).
Examines the relationship between culture and power as expressed in the architecture of the British Raj during the heyday of European colonialism.

Milbury-Steen, Sarah, *European and African Stereotypes in Twentieth-Century Fiction* (Macmillan, 1980).
A study of contrasting and reciprocal views of Africans and Europeans in British, French, and West African novels.

Miller, Christopher L., *Blank Darkness: Africanist Discourse in French* (University of Chicago Press, 1985).
Writing in the wake of Said's *Orientalism*, Miller usefully analyses the ways in which francophone texts about Africa construct the continent as the utter negation of Europe, a blank third term in the orientalist equation.

Minh-ha, Trinh, T., *Woman, Native, Other* (Bloomington: Indiana UP, 1989).
Poetic feminist explorations of ethnicity, femininity, difference, and women's writing.

Mintz, Sidney W., *Sweetness and Power: The Place of Sugar in Modern History* (Viking, 1985).
This study inaugurated a spate of 'biographies' of the favourite commodities and comestibles of empire, including tobacco and spices. See Ch. 1 n. 29.

Misra, Udayon, *The Raj in Fiction: A Study of Nineteenth-Century British Attitudes towards India* (New Delhi: BR Publishing, 1987).
Misra explores British attitudes towards India as reflected in Anglo-Indian fiction published 1820–70, especially the works of W. B. Hockley, P. M. Taylor, W. D. Arnold, and I. Pritchard.

Moore-Gilbert, B. J., *Kipling and 'Orientalism'* (Croom Helm, 1986).
    Moore-Gilbert analyses Kipling's complex relationship to the character-
    istic discourses of nineteenth-century Anglo-Indian culture in order to
    offer a nuancing critique of Said's main thesis in *Orientalism.*

Morey, Peter, *Fictions of India: Narrative and Power* (Edinburgh UP, 2000).
    A critical study relating fictional narrative techniques to issues of power in
    the work of British writers dealing with India: Kipling, Forster, Farrell, Paul
    Scott, and others.

Mudimbe, V. Y., *The Invention of Africa: Gnosis, Philosophy and the Order of
    Knowledge* (James Currey, 1988).
    An outline of the Western discursive construction of Africa as a paradigm
    of difference is accompanied by a subtle archaeology of African systems of
    knowledge.

Mudrooroo, *Milli Milli Wangka (The Indigenous Literature of Australia)*
    (South Melbourne: Hyland House, 1995).
    In this sister-study to *Writing from the Fringe: A Study of Modern
    Aboriginal Literature* (Melbourne: Hyland House, 1990), the Aboriginal-
    identified writer surveys the history of oral and written literature by
    dispossessed Indigenous peoples of Australia.

Mukherjee, Arun, *Postcolonialism: My Living* (Toronto: TSAR, 1998).
    The Indian-born Canadian-resident literary scholar struggles against
    some of the theoretical attitudes dominating the academic field in which
    she makes a living.

Mukherjee, Meenakshi, *Realism and Reality: The Novel and Society in India*
    (New Delhi: Oxford UP, 1985).
    This now-canonical study develops a view of the novel in India as a multi-
    language genre born out of colonial tensions and modified by indigenous
    pressures. A precursor and companion to Mukherjee's 2000 volume:

—— *The Perishable Empire: Essays on Indian Writing in English* (New Delhi:
    Oxford UP, 2000).

Murray, Stuart, *Not on Any Map: Postcoloniality and Cultural Nationalism*
    (University of Exeter Press, 1997).

Naik, M. K., *A History of Indian English Literature* (New Delhi: Sahitya
    Akademi, 1982).
    A historical survey of Indian writing in English, from the nineteenth
    century onwards.

—— *Studies in Indian English Literature* (New Delhi: Sterling, 1987).
    Essays on Indian fiction, poetry, and drama in English, attempting to
    formulate an aesthetic of Indian English literature.

Nairn, Tom, *The Break-up of Britain: Crisis and Neo-nationalism* (New Left
    Books, 1977).

Deals with the controversial 1970s assertions of separate national identities for Northern Ireland, Wales, and Scotland by exploring the suggestive concept of nationalism as Janus-faced.

Nandy, Ashis, *The Intimate Enemy: Loss and Recovery of Self, under Colonialism* (New Delhi: Oxford UP, 1983).

Keynote essays on the emasculating psychology of colonial India, and psychological resistances to it.

Nasta, Susheila, *Home Truths: Fictions of the South Asian Diaspora in Britain* (Basingstoke: Palgrave, 2002).

In a series of informed close readings Nasta explores the diverse textures of South Asian im/migrant writing in Britain, placing these within an evolving tradition of negotiating 'home' and 'abroad' which extends back to the pre-war period.

Needham, Anuradha Dingwaney, *Using the Master's Tools: Resistance and the Literature of the African and South Asian Diasporas* (Macmillan, 2000).

Newell, Stephanie, *Literary Culture in Colonial Ghana: 'How to Play the Game of Life'* (Manchester UP, 2002).

A critical examination of the activities of African readers in colonial Ghana, the cultural and political networks that existed in West Africa in the colonial era, and specifically West African interpretative practices.

Newman, Judie, *The Ballistic Bard: Postcolonial Fictions* (Arnold, 1995).

A study of intertextual strategies in works by Jean Rhys, Ruth Prawer Jhabvala, Anita Desai, J. M. Coetzee, Buchi Emecheta, V. S. Naipaul, Bharati Mukherjee, and Nadine Gordimer.

Nfah-Abbenyi, Juliana Makuchi, *Gender in African Women's Writing: Identity, Sexuality and Difference* (Bloomington: Indiana UP, 1997).

Contending that a proto-feminist or at least woman-centred analysis has been developed by African women and women writers within their own cultural and literary practice, Nfah-Abbenyi reads the work of nine anglophone and francophone sub-Saharan women writers from within a feminist framework.

Ngugi wa Thiong'o, *Decolonising the Mind* (Heinemann, 1986).

—— *Moving the Centre* (James Currey, 1993).

—— *Penpoints, Gunpoints, and Dreams: Towards a Critical Theory of the Arts and the State in Africa* (Oxford: Clarendon Press, 1998).

Across three volumes the noted Kenyan fiction writer and critic explores the continuing relationship between language, art, and political power in Africa.

Nixon, Rob, *London Calling: V. S. Naipaul, Postcolonial Mandarin* (Oxford UP, 1992).

In this ironically titled study focused on his travel writing, Nixon argues

that the supposedly unconventional Naipaul in fact holds received notions
about 'backward' and 'static' non-Western societies.

Nkosi, Lewis, *Home and Exile* (Harlow: Longman, 1983).
Essays by the peripatetic African intellectual on South Africa, African
literature, and the 'complex fate' of exile.

—— *Tasks and Masks: Themes and Styles of African Literature* (Harlow:
Longman, 1981).
Searching if also at times polemical meditations on the ideologies of
African writing.

Nzegwu, Femi, *Love, Motherhood and the African Heritage: The Legacy of
Flora Nwapa* (Dakar: African Renaissance, 2001).
This study rejects the western critical trope of 'subordinated African
woman', and calls instead for a return to the pre-colonial 'dual-sex
complementarity' of relations, as epitomized in the work of the Nigerian
Flora Nwapa.

Obiechina, Emmanuel, *Culture, Tradition and Society in the West African
Novel* (Cambridge UP, 1975).
An influential study of the background factors that influenced the themes
and content of West African novels in the 1950s and 1960s.

Ogundipe, Molara, *Re-Creating Ourselves: African Women and Critical Transformations* (Trenton, NJ, Africa World Press, 1994).
Essays on women in African, particularly Nigerian, texts and society,
divided into two parts and linked by a poetic interlude.

Ojinmah, Umelo, *Witi Ihimaera: A Changing Vision* (Dunedin: University of
Otago Press, 1993).
A Nigerian perspective on the fiction of the New Zealand Maori writer
Ihimaera, and his preoccupation with Maori cultural identities.

Olney, James, *Tell Me Africa: An Approach to African Literature* (Princeton,
1973).
Proposes to read as intertexts autobiography and fiction emerging from
the same social matrix.

Parry, Benita, *Conrad and Imperialism: Ideological Boundaries and Visionary
Frontiers* (Macmillan, 1983).
A probing critical analysis of Conrad's imperial contradictions.

—— *Delusions and Discoveries: Studies on India in the British Imagination
1880–1930*, rev. edn. (Allen Lane, 1998).
Beginning with a survey of Anglo-Indian colonial attitudes, this path-
breaking work looks at representations of India in writers such as Kipling,
Forster, and Flora Annie Steel.

—— *Postcolonial Studies: A Materialist Critique* (Routledge, 2004).

Brings together Parry's important materialist essays challenging colonial discourse theory and postcolonialism.

Phillips, Caryl, *New World Order* (Faber, 2001).

Pratt, Mary Louise, *Imperial Eyes: Travel Writing and Transculturation* (Routledge, 1992).

An influential study of European travellers' accounts of their experiences in the 'contact zones' of Africa and South Asia, between 1750 and 1980.

Puri, Shalini, *The Caribbean Postcolonial: Social Equality, Post-nationalism, Cultural Hybridity* (Basingstoke: Palgrave Macmillan, 2004).

Questions the ways in which hybridity is interpreted in the Caribbean theoretical industry and in cultural practice.

Quayson, Ato, *Postcolonialism: Theory, Practice or Process?* (Cambridge: Polity, 2000).

A critical introduction to postcolonial studies which develops a 'postcolonizing' methodology, namely, an interdisciplinary mode of reading cultural and political realities, informed by the work of the anthropologist Arjun Appadurai.

—— *Strategic Transformations in Nigerian Writing: Orality and History in the Work of Rev. Samuel Johnson, Amos Tutuola, Wole Soyinka and Ben Okri* (Oxford: James Currey, 1997).

Quayson studies the named Nigerian writers' appropriations of indigenous, oral resources as a special form of intertextuality, termed interdiscursivity.

Radhakrishnan, R., *Diasporic Meditations: Between Home and Location* (Minneapolis: University of Minnesota Press, 1996).

Raj, G. V., *Tagore the Novelist* (Sterling, 1983).

An appraisal of Tagore's novels in English translation, focusing on thematic concerns and novelistic technique.

Ramchand, Kenneth, *An Introduction to the Study of West Indian Literature* (Sunbury: Thomas Nelson, 1976).

An important, early postcolonial survey of Caribbean writing.

Ray, Sangeeta, *En-gendering India: Woman and Nation in Colonial and Post-colonial Narratives* (Durham, NC: Duke UP, 2000).

An interpretation of the figure of the Hindu woman as a symbolic nexus interlinking the discourses of imperialism, nationalism, postcolonialism, and feminism in a selection of India-related writings.

Read, Peter, *Belonging: Australians, Place and Aboriginal Ownership* (Cambridge UP, 2000).

Grapples with questions of emotional attachment to place, ownership, and belonging in relation to Australia. How can non-indigenous Australians justify their presence in and love of the country, while Indigenous people remain dispossessed?

Richards, David, *Masks of Difference: Cultural Representations in Literature, Anthropology and Art* (Cambridge UP, 1995).

Ridley, Hugh, *Images of Imperial Rule* (Croom Helm; 1983).
Studies French, British, and German fiction portraying European colonial activity during the period of 'New Imperialism', 1870–1914.

Rushdie, Salman, *Imaginary Homelands: Essays and Criticism 1981–1991* (Granta, 1991).
Often-cited essays written during the decade that ended the Cold War and saw the emergence of a new, unipolar world order. Rushdie discusses, amongst other topics, the culture and politics of India, the nature of memory, the experience of migrants in Britain, and the crisis occasioned by the publication of *The Satanic Verses.*

Saakana, Amon Saba, *The Colonial Legacy in Caribbean Literature* (Karnak, 1987).
Interpretations of Afro-Caribbean literature as an expression of anti-colonial struggle, from the nineteenth century onwards.

Said, Edward W., *Covering Islam*, rev. edn. (1981; Vintage, 1997).

—— *Culture and Imperialism* (Chatto & Windus, 1993).
Said's influential study unpicking the tangled involvements of European cultures with the figuration and justification of imperial expansion.

—— *Orientalism* (1978; Penguin, 1987).
The discussion of Western representations of the orient which is generally taken to be the foundational statement of the discipline of postcolonialism.

—— *Reflections on Exile and Other Literary and Cultural Essays* (Granta Books, 2001).
Written over the course of three decades, these essays are on a wide variety of literary, cultural, and political topics, covering Said's trademark themes: marginality and exile, culture and politics, the West and the Middle East.

—— *The World, the Text and the Critic* (Faber, 1984).
Essays on questions of literary theory and appreciation, based on the assumption that texts participate in the historical social world, even when they appear to deny it.

Sanders, Mark, *Complicities: The Intellectual and Apartheid* (Durham, NC: Duke UP, 2002).
An exploration of the role played by intellectuals during the apartheid years in South Africa.

Sandison, Alan, *The Wheel of Empire: A Study of the Imperial Idea in Some Late Nineteenth- and Early Twentieth-Century Fiction* (Macmillan, 1967).
Considers the writings of Rider Haggard, Rudyard Kipling, Joseph Conrad, and John Buchan.

Sangari, Kumkum, and Sudesh Vaid (eds.), *Recasting Women: Essays in Colonial History* (New Delhi: Kali for Women, 1989).
A keynote collection which looks at the historical processes that regulated and reproduced patriarchy within different caste and class formations in colonial India.

Sartre, Jean-Paul, *Black Orpheus*, trans. S. W. Allen (Paris: Présence Africaine, 1976).
The 1948 introduction to Leopold Senghor's anthology of new Black poetry, this essay helped underpin Senghor's views on Negritude.

—— *Colonialism and Neocolonialism*, trans. Azzedine Haddour, Steve Brewer, and Terry McWilliams (Routledge, 2001)
Prefaced by Robert Young, these anti-colonial essays, first published in 1964, include Sartre's preface to Fanon's *The Wretched of the Earth*.

Sarvepalli, Gopal, *Anatomy of a Confrontation: The Rise of Communal Politics in India* (Zed Press, 1993).

Schaffer, Kay, *Women and the Bush: Forces of Desire in the Australian Cultural Tradition* (Cambridge UP, 1989).
Explores constructions of masculinity and femininity, and how they circulate in Australian culture, from the narratives of early exploration and settlement to contemporary writing, film, and popular culture.

Scott, David, *Refashioning Futures: Criticism after Postcoloniality* (Princeton UP, 1999).
Objecting to the tendency to import the historical struggles of the past into contemporary postcolonial frameworks, Scott is interested in discovering where colonialism continues to alter the terrain of contemporary (Caribbean) culture.

Senior, Olive, *Working Miracles: Women's Lives in the English-Speaking Caribbean* (James Currey, 1991).
Challenges both the stereotype of Caribbean women as strong and assertive matriarchs, and the view that reliance on economic solutions is sufficient to promote gender equality.

Sethi, Rumina, *Myths of the Nation: National Identity and Literary Representation* (Oxford UP, 1999).
Focuses on the imaginative construction of the nation in Indian writers in English, including Raja Rao.

Sharrad, Paul, *Raja Rao and the Cultural Tradition* (New Delhi: Sterling Publishers, 1987).
A study of literary form and cultural meanings in Rao's 1960 novel *The Serpent and the Rope*.

Shoemaker, Adam, *Black Words, White Page: Aboriginal Literature 1929–1988* (Brisbane: University of Queensland Press, 1989).

The first comprehensive study of Aboriginal Australian writing in English.

Singh, Bhupal, *A Survey of Anglo-Indian Fiction* (1934; Curzon, 1975).
This colonial-era survey of fiction describing the life of Englishmen in India points out that, when it comes to representing Indians, 'Anglo-Indian art is not always a faithful copy of life'.

Smith, Bernard, *European Vision and the South Pacific*, 2nd edn. (New Haven: Yale UP, 1984).
The path-breaking and now canonical account of how Europeans represented the South Pacific in terms of the familiar and the typical.

Spender, Dale, *Writing a New World: Two Centuries of Australian Women Writers* (Pandora, 1988).
A history of Australian women's writing, covering the two hundred years of white settlement.

Spivak, Gayatri Chakravorty, *A Critique of Postcolonial Reason: Toward a History of the Vanishing Present* (Cambridge, Mass.: Harvard UP, 1999).
Seeking to 'chart a practitioner's progress from colonial discourse studies to transnational cultural studies', four wide-ranging chapters cover philosophy, literature, history, and postmodern culture.

—— *Death of a Discipline* (New York: Columbia UP, 2003).
A compelling defence of cultural translation, under the rubric of comparative literature, in which Spivak urges an encounter with the linguistic competences and close knowledges offered by area studies.

—— *In Other Worlds: Essays in Cultural Politics* (Routledge, 1987).
These combative, at times rebarbative essays bracingly combine theoretical approaches drawn from deconstruction, psychoanalysis, Marxism, and feminism in dealing with a variety of subjects related to literature, culture, and politics.

Spurr, David, *The Rhetoric of Empire: Colonial Discourse in Journalism, Travel Writing and Imperial Administration* (Durham, NC: Duke UP, 1993).
Examines the rhetorical features and tactics shared by a variety of discourses across several historically distinct versions of colonialism.

Stoler, Ann Laura, *Carnal Knowledge and Imperial Power* (Berkeley: University of California Press, 2002).
Focused on the Netherlands Indies, this important study offers comparative observations on variability and disjuncture in the colonial order of things, especially in relation to sexuality and the domestic.

Strachan, Lynne, *Just City and the Mirrors: Meanjin Quarterly and the Intellectual Front 1940–1965* (Melbourne: Oxford UP, 1984).
An analysis of Australia's intellectual history as refracted through the history of the influential literary journal.

Stratton, Florence, *Contemporary African Literature and the Politics of Gender* (Routledge, 1994).

Stratton contrastively examines male and female African literary traditions, analysing work by Grace Ogot, Flora Nwapa, Buchi Emecheta, and Mariama Bâ.

Street, Brian V., *The Savage in Literature: Representations of Primitive Society in English Fiction 1858–1920* (Routledge & Kegan Paul, 1975).

A study of the relationship between literary, evolutionary, and anthropological discourses.

Suleri, Sara, *The Rhetoric of English India* (University of Chicago Press, 1992).

An acute if stylistically demanding study of (post)colonial writing related to India: there are chapters on Edmund Burke, Kipling, Forster, Naipaul, and Rushdie.

Sunder Rajan, Rajeswari, *Real and Imagined Women: Gender, Culture and Postcolonialism* (Routledge, 1993).

Strong-minded feminist essays on a variety of cultural representations of women in India, including those involving rape, wife-murder, and ritual suicide (*sati*).

—— *The Scandal of the State* (Durham, NC: Duke UP, 2003).

In a series of case studies Sunder Rajan explores the relationship between the postcolonial Indian nation-state and women's day-to-day experience.

Talib, Ismail S., *The Language of Postcolonial Literatures* (Routledge, 2002).

A wide-ranging survey of a central postcolonial concern: the deconstruction and survival of English in the literatures of former British colonies.

Taylor, D. J., *Orwell: The Life* (Chatto & Windus, 2003).

Thieme, John, *Postcolonial Con-Texts: Writing Back to the Canon* (Continuum, 2001).

Focuses on postcolonial literary texts that take as their departure points the classics of the English literary canon such as *The Tempest*, *Robinson Crusoe*, and 'Heart of Darkness'.

—— *The Web of Tradition: The Use of Allusion in V. S. Naipaul's Fiction* (Aarhus: Dangaroo, 1987).

A general introduction to Naipaul's fiction that examines his use of literary and cultural allusion, and considers the relation of textual detail to broader themes and problems.

Thomas, Nicholas, *Colonialism's Culture: Anthropology, Travel and Government* (Cambridge: Polity, 1994).

Focusing on Australia and the South Pacific, Thomas argues powerfully that colonialism can only be mapped through its 'plural and particularized' expressions.

Thompson, Elizabeth, *The Pioneer Woman: A Canadian Character Type* (Montreal: McGill–Queens UP, 1991).
Examines this uniquely Canadian character type in English-Canadian fiction from its beginnings up to the present day.

Trivedi, Harish, *Colonial Transactions: English Literature and India* (Calcutta: Sangam, 1993; Manchester UP, 1995).
Investigates colonialism as an interactive, two-way transaction, concentrating in particular on literary exchanges between England and India.

Viswanathan, Gauri, *Masks of Conquest: Literary Study and British Rule in India* (Faber, 1990).
The important study of the institution, practice and ideology of English studies in India during colonial rule.

Walker, Alice, *In Search of our Mother's Gardens* (San Diego: Harcourt Brace Jovanovich, 1983).
A collection of essays, articles, reviews, and statements written between 1966 and 1982 on the subjects of literature, gender, culture, and race.

Watts, Jane, *Black Writers from South Africa: Towards a Discourse of Liberation* (Macmillan, 1989).
Studies the forging of the black South African literary tradition during the era of apartheid.

Waugh, Patricia, *Feminine Fictions: Revisiting the Postmodern* (Routledge, 1989).
A study of the relationship between postmodernism and feminism and the fiction of contemporary women writers such as Sylvia Plath, Margaret Drabble, Margaret Atwood, Fay Weldon, and others.

White, Hayden, *Metahistory: The Historical Imagination in Nineteenth Century Europe* (Baltimore: Johns Hopkins UP, 1973).
The agenda-shifting analysis and classification of the narrative structures and devices that go into the writing of history, widely adapted in postcolonial criticism.

White, Richard, *Inventing Australia: Images and Identity 1688–1980* (Sydney: Allen and Unwin, 1981).
Traces some of the ideas and images that have moulded perceptions of Australia and Australian identities, from the Renaissance to the 1980s.

Whitlock, Gillian, *The Intimate Empire: Reading Women's Autobiography* (Cassell, 2000).
Situated readings of autobiographical writings by women from Australia, Africa, Britain, Canada, and the Caribbean that seek to disperse assumptions of a transhistorical female experience and further demonstrate that self-definition is intimately informed by colonial relations of power.

Williams, Raymond, *The Country and the City* (Oxford UP, 1973).

Explores the transformation of views of England from the pastoral populist to the metropolitan. As Edward Said pointed out, Williams gives space to the colonial dimension of this process only towards the very end of the book.

—— *The Politics of Modernism: Against the New Conformists* (Verso, 1989).
A posthumously published critique of modernism as deeply informed by national and international commodity exchange, which further affirms Williams's socialist vision.

Wood, Marcus, *Blind Memory: Visual Representation of Slavery in England and America 1780–1865* (Manchester UP, 2000).
Assembling visual art and artefacts created across England and the Americas at the time of the slave trade and of abolition, this volume poses an unsettling question: what do we see when we look at western art devoted to the memory of slavery?

Woodcock, George, *The World of Canadian Writing: Critiques and Recollections* (Vancouver: Douglas & McIntyre, 1980).

Wurgaft, L. D., *The Imperial Imagination: Magic and Myth in Kipling's India* (Middletown, Conn.: Wesleyan UP, 1983).
A psychoanalytically informed historical study of the imaginative dimensions of British involvement in India.

Yelin, Louise, *From the Margins of Empire: Christina Stead, Doris Lessing, Nadine Gordimer* (Ithaca, NY: Cornell UP, 1998).
A nuanced discussion of the striated construction of national identity in the writing of three white women novelists associated with (post)colonial societies.

Young, Robert J. C., *Colonial Desire: Hybridity in Theory, Culture and Race* (Routledge, 1995).
This book traces the emergence of desire for the colonial other and its disavowal in the history of western thought. Young critiques the postcolonial concept of 'hybridity', arguing that it originates in the vocabulary of Victorian racism.

—— *Postcolonialism: An Historical Introduction* (Oxford: Blackwell, 2001).
A compendious account of the emergence of postcolonial theory from anti-colonial movements and freedom struggles both European and 'tricontinental' (that is, of Africa, Asia, and Latin America).

—— *White Mythologies: Writing, History and the West*, 2nd edn. (1990; Routledge, 2004).
A paradigm-shifting, teleologically structured investigation of how Western history and social theory have been implicated in European colonialism, culminating in an analysis of postcolonial theories which break away from that tradition.

Zaman, Niaz, *A Divided Legacy: the Partition in Selected novels of India, Pakistan and Bangladesh* (Karachi: Oxford UP, 2000).
An analysis of Partition novels written in three major languages of the Indian subcontinent (English, Bengali, and Urdu), as well as Punjabi novels available in English translation.

4. Journals

ARIEL: A Review of International English Literature
Interventions: International Journal of Postcolonial Studies
Journal of Commonwealth and Postcolonial Studies
Journal of Commonwealth Literature
Kunapipi: Journal of Post-Colonial Writing
Moving Worlds
SPAN: Journal of the South Pacific Association for Commonwealth Literature and Language Studies
Wasafiri: Caribbean, African, Asian and Associated Literatures in English
World Literature Written in English

5. Websites

Like organisms, websites grow, divide, and change; hence this list is intended to be suggestive only.

http://www.alternet.org
http://www.emory.edu/ENGLISH/Bahri
http://www.postcolonial web.org
http://www.warincontext.org

Index

A comprehensive history of the 'discovery', colonization and liberation of the Caribbean, which sees the islands as united by history and culture.

Winder, Robert, *Bloody Foreigners: The Story of Immigration to Britain* (Boston: Little, Brown, 2004).

A history of post-war migration to Britain set in the context of longer British traditions of imperial and pre-imperial migration, and refracted from the perspectives of the migrants themselves.

Wolf, Eric, *Europe and the People without History* (Berkeley: University of California Press, 1982).

Based on the premiss that the history of humankind forms a totality of interconnected processes, this study examines how the advent of capitalism and European expansion penetrated, subordinated, destroyed or absorbed many global 'peripheries'.

2. Edited criticism, introductions, and reference works

(For edited collections, the titles in a number of cases are self-explanatory.)

Adam, Ian, and Helen Tiffin (eds.), *Past the Last Post: Theorizing Post-Colonialism and Postmodernism* (Hemel Hempstead: Harvester Wheatsheaf, 1991).

Essays seeking to characterize postmodernist and postcolonial discourses in relation to each other and to chart their intersecting trajectories.

Afzal-Khan, Fawzia, and Kalpana Seshadri-Crooks (eds.), *The Pre-Occupation of Postcolonial Studies* (Durham, NC: Duke UP, 2000).

A collection of viewpoints (including an interview with Homi Bhabha) interrogating the configuration of the postcolonial field at the close of the twentieth century.

Ahmed, Durre S. (ed.), *Gendering the Spirit: Women, Religion and the Post-Colonial Response* (Zed, 2002).

A collection of essays on the subcultures of defiance created by women within various religious traditions, of Asia in particular. Case studies illustrate how women have always challenged religious establishments by demanding equal rights within them.

Ahsan, M., and R. Kidwai (eds.), *Sacrilege versus Civility: Muslim Perspectives on the Satanic Verses Affair* (Markfield: Islamic Foundation, 1993).

Ashcroft, Bill, and Pal Ahluwalia, *Edward Said* (Routledge, 1999).

An introduction to the US-Palestinian intellectual's work, one of the Routledge Critical Thinkers series, which includes volumes on other postcolonial thinkers, including *Gayatri Spivak* by Stephen Morton (2002) and *Stuart Hall* by James Procter (2004).

—— Gareth Griffiths, and Helen Tiffin (eds.), *The Post-Colonial Studies Reader* (Routledge, 1995).